SHOPPING FOR A BETTER ENVIRONMENT

A brand name guide to environmentally
responsible shopping

Laurence Tasaday

with Katherine Stevenson

Meadowbrook Press
Distributed by Simon & Schuster
New York

Library of Congress Cataloging-in-Publication Data

Tasaday, Laurence.
  Shopping for a better environment: a brand name guide to environmentally responsible
shopping/Laurence Tasaday.
      p.   cm.
  Includes bibliographical references and index.
  ISBN: 0-88166-143-0.
  1. Brand name products—Environmental aspects—United States—Handbooks, manuals, etc.
2. Shopping—United States—Handbooks, manuals, etc. 3. Consumer education—United States—
Handbooks, manuals, etc. 4. Environmental protection—United States—Handbooks, manuals, etc.
I. Title.
HF1040.8.T37 1991   91-18716
670'.29'473—dc20   CIP

Simon & Schuster Ordering #: 0-671-72560-2

Editor: Katherine Stevenson
Managing Editor: Kerstin Gorham
Copy Editor: Bonnie Gruen
Production Manager: JoAnn Krueger
Production Assistant: Matthew Thurber
Cover Design: Kevin Bowen
Text Design: Nancy McLean
Typography: Monica Schoenbauer

Publisher's note: The author has made a good faith effort to be as complete and accurate as
possible. The publisher is not responsible for any inaccuracies or omissions that may have
inadvertently occurred. The author would be happy to consider any information that would make
the book more accurate and complete in future editions.

BOOK TRADE DISTRIBUTION by Simon & Schuster, a division of Simon and Schuster, Inc.,
1230 Avenue of the Americas, New York, NY 10020.

96 95 94 93 92 91 6 5 4 3 2 1

Printed in the United States of America

To Julia Vesta Byrd,

1929-1990.

I loved her a lot.

ACKNOWLEDGMENTS

The range and depth of this book would not have been possible without the long, hard work of Kathy Stevenson. She enlarged the concept of the original manuscript, reshaped its format, and added valuable new material and perspectives, in addition to the more routine tasks of making the book consistent and easy to read. For doing it all, I thank her deeply.

I also thank managing editor Kerstin Gorham for her patience, thoughtfulness, and intelligence; copy editor Bonnie Gruen; researchers Clare Corcoran in Colorado and Clara Jeffery in Minnesota, and all the staff at Meadowbrook Press; readers/advisers Christina Nealson and Maureen Kirchhoff; friends Jeffrey Duvall, Mary McHenry, and David Lillie for many kindnesses; Mike Jones, Dave Martini, and Gregg Marland for technical assistance; John MacNeil for inspiration from afar; my mother, Ellen Dudley; and especially Bruce Lansky, publisher and magician.

Of the many organizations across the United States whose actions, research, and publications bring us closer to environmental well-being, I would like to especially acknowledge a few, to whom a portion of this book's proceeds are donated: American Council for an Energy-Efficient Economy; Citizens Clearinghouse for Hazardous Wastes; Environmental Action Foundation; Earth Island Institute; Greenpeace; Natural Resources Defense Council; People for the Ethical Treatment of Animals; Rainforest Action Network; Rocky Mountain Institute; Sierra Club; World Resources Institute; and Worldwatch Institute.

CONTENTS

TABLES

HOW TO USE THIS BOOK

This reference book is for the environmental shopper in all of us. In it are 102 categories of consumer products, with sections on each product's environmental problems, including any health risks, and on how to choose and use the product wisely.

Within each entry different products are described and given recommendations—ranging from highly recommended to never recommended—based on the total impact of the product's environmental life cycle: its production, its use, and its disposal (see Consumers and the Environment and The Life Cycle of Consumer Products). Throughout the book I have listed brand names of the many environmentally superior products that are widely distributed in the United States.

Also included in the entries are alternatives, do-it-yourself options, and tips on wise use and disposal. For readers interested in the sources of my information on environmental problems, I have added references for important facts and figures; these appear at the end of each entry.

Some terms that appear frequently in this book should be explained here:

Natural-ingredient is a term I have used to describe products made primarily from naturally occurring, renewable raw materials, rather than petrochemicals or other nonrenewable synthetic materials. Some of these products contain *only* natural ingredients. Others are made with predominantly natural substances, but rely on chemicals and petroleum derivatives for secondary purposes.

Toxic is a technical term that refers to the ability of a substance, when relatively concentrated, to harm people. Not surprisingly, many substances that are toxic to people also damage the environment.[1]

Cruelty-free is a term trademarked over 15 years ago by Golden Lotus to describe its personal-care products, which contain ingredients neither derived from nor tested on animals. Today the term is often used by companies and consumers to mean "free of animal testing" only; that is how I have used it here, though many of the brand-name tables also identify products made without any animal ingredients. The cruelty-free designations for products in this book are based on lists from two excellent organizations, People for the Ethical Treatment of Animals and the National Anti-Vivisection Society, and on extensive independent research.

All the brand names listed in this book are widely available in the United States. Some products, however, might not be carried in your local stores, so I have included companies' addresses and phone numbers in the Directory of Manufacturers in the Resources section. Call them (it's a better environmental choice than writing) and ask for information on their products and how to get them in your area. Other good sources of products are mail-order catalogs, whose names and phone numbers are often included with brand-name listings; see the Resources section for a comprehensive list of environmentally sound mail-order companies.

To provide more information on our planet's daunting ecological problems—and on solutions we can all be a part of—I have included extensive lists of environmental agencies and organizations in the Resources section. For brief descriptions of major issues and terms, see the Environmental Glossary.

A NOTE

This book is the result of nearly three years of independent research, conducted by several people around the United States. As author, I take full responsibility for the book's factual content and have worked in good faith to ensure its accuracy. If a typographical error has been made, or if a product has changed over time, upon receipt of authoritative material showing new or corrected information I will make the changes in the next edition.

Though I have made many product recommendations here and listed many brand names, I cannot be personally responsible for their performance, effectiveness, or safety, nor can their inclusion here be construed as an endorsement.

Finally, no agreements of any kind have been made with any company, manufacturer, or seller regarding any product's inclusion in this work.

AN INVITATION

As environmental awareness continues to grow among consumers, new products will continue to appear in the marketplace, making up-to-date information about them essential. I invite readers everywhere to send me any appropriate material—clippings, catalogs, fact sheets, journal articles, your comments and ideas—for the next edition of this book. This is information we'll all need to be environmentally wise consumers in an ever-changing world.

With warmest regards—

Laurence Tasaday
Eldora Star Route
Nederland, CO 80466

1. Unless otherwise noted, the reference used throughout this book for toxicity ratings is *Hawley's Condensed Chemical Dictionary*, 11th ed., N. Irving Sax and Richard J. Lewis, Sr., eds. (Van Nostrand Reinhold, 1987).

CONSUMERS AND
THE ENVIRONMENT

Every day we hear more about our planet's environmental problems—from smog and water pollution to the greenhouse effect, the list goes on and on. Yet we may find it difficult to relate these global problems to our own lives—to see how the everyday things we do affect the vast world around us. Perhaps the simplest way to make this connection is to learn more about the effects of the products we buy and use—to learn how we are altering our environment whenever we plan a meal, clean the house, or commute to work.

Each product we buy has a past, a present, and a future: its past is its manufacture, its present is the time in which we use it, and its future begins the moment we throw it away. We're most familiar with the environmental effects of *using* a product, the middle stage of its life cycle, but often the other two stages have even greater impacts that we never see.

The total impact of each consumer product—its manufacture, use, and disposal—multiplied by the hundreds of billions of products used each year—adds up to an environmental crisis of epic proportions.

WHAT CAN ONE PERSON DO?

So what can each of us, as a consumer, do? For a start, it's essential that we make careful choices about the products we buy—for two reasons. First, choosing and using products wisely can make a real difference in our personal impact on the environment. When we buy a fuel-efficient car, for example, each gallon of gasoline we save keeps us from spewing 20 pounds of carbon dioxide into the air.[1] That might not seem like much on a global scale, but if you multiply that figure by the number of gallons saved over the car's lifetime, it's clear that this simple consumer choice can make a very real difference.

Second, being an environmentally aware consumer can help change the marketplace itself. We can use the tremendous power of our consumer dollars to tell companies what we want—to encourage those that act responsibly and make environmentally sound products, and to discourage those that create waste and pollution.

Inevitably, our lives will change in the future as we accept responsibility for the environmental consequences of our lifestyle. Some of those changes will mean sacrifices. For example:

- Not only will we have to buy fuel-efficient cars, we'll have to drive less.

- We'll have to replace toxic chemicals in our homes with safer, natural products—some of which will mean a bit more work for us.

- Ultraconvenient but environmentally destructive packaging, such as aerosol cans and other mixed-material containers, will have to go.

- Recycling, which takes a bit more time than simply putting out the trash, will have to become standard practice.

Rather than waiting for the government, hamstrung as it is by budget deficits and an already impossible workload, to force change on us through regulation, we can take the initiative and make some less painful, voluntary changes now. As consumers we can foster innovation and change by spending our dollars wisely.

Fortunately, American consumers have been showing increasing interest in environmental issues. We still want the best deal for our money, but we're also considering each product's cost to the environment.

HOW CAN I CHOOSE ENVIRONMENTALLY SOUND PRODUCTS?

Is it really possible to know which products are better for the environment? In most cases, yes. First we consider the product's life cycle—its manufacture, use, and disposal—to determine its total impact on the environment. Then we weigh its benefit to humans against its environmental costs. Third, we ask whether any less harmful alternatives are available. And finally we ask the most important question, Is it worth it? That is, does the value of the product outweigh its environmental costs?

We're still a long way from having enough data to make close calculations on environmental effects. Undoubtedly debates on such topics as paper versus plastic will rage for years as new research results emerge and as industries seek to defend old products and promote new ones. But we already know enough about most products and our planet's limited resources to make some good, common-sense choices right now.

HOW MUCH WILL IT COST ME?

Do environmentally sound products cost more? Sometimes. Personal care items, such as soap and toothpaste, that use high-quality natural ingredients usually do cost more than their synthetic-chemical counterparts; natural foods, especially those grown organically, cost more than chemically fertilized, pesticide-laced foods.

But many other environmentally sound products actually cost *less*. A new push-reel lawn mower might cost only one-third as much as a power mower, and it costs nothing to run; fuel-efficient gas heating is much cheaper than electric; water-soluble latex paint is cheaper than more toxic alkyd paint; fuel-efficient cars, being smaller, often have smaller price tags; a do-it-yourself glass cleaner might cost only one-fiftieth as much as a commercial cleaner; ventilating a house with a well-designed fan system costs much less than installing and operating an air conditioner.

Still other products cost more to purchase initially but have a longer usable life, or lower operating costs, or both. Some examples: compact fluorescent light bulbs, solar water heaters, long-life auto batteries, high-quality radial tires, gas cooking stoves, energy-efficient refrigerators, rechargeable household batteries and flashlights, low-flow showerheads and faucets, and front-loading washing machines.

Undoubtedly, environmentally sound products will become even better bargains in the future as consumer demand, new technology, and competition change these products from novelties to the norm.

THREE RULES TO REMEMBER

By remembering three simple rules, we can make a real difference in the struggle for a habitable, healthy environment:

- *Shop wisely.* "Precycle" by choosing environmentally sound products. Just think about the product and what you'll use it for, and ask the basic question, Is it worth it? Buy only those products for which you can answer, Yes.

- *Use wisely.* Use each product carefully and safely, and make it last as long as possible.

- *Dispose wisely.* Recycle whenever possible; make sure you dispose of nonrecyclables properly.

Your actions *do* make a difference.

1. "Nucleus" (Union of Concerned Scientists, 26 Church St., Cambridge, MA 02138), p. 1.

THE LIFE CYCLE OF CONSUMER PRODUCTS

As mentioned in the previous chapter, deciding whether a product is environmentally sound requires looking at its whole life cycle—its past, present, and future. An item might seem harmless, even beneficial, when we use it, yet cause hidden environmental effects when it is manufactured or discarded.

PRODUCTION: A PRODUCT'S PAST

Where does a product come from? We might use a household item every day without having any inkling of where its raw materials come from, how it's manufactured, or how much energy is required to produce it. Yet the impact of a product's past can be terribly important.

RAW MATERIALS

Ideal raw materials are renewable, reusable, and degradable: they are either obtained carefully from abundant natural sources or grown or raised in a sustainable, humane way, and once used they can be used again for something else. The worst raw materials are those that come from scarce, nonrenewable sources; that are obtained in a destructive or inhumane way; that can be used only once; and that create problems when thrown away.

Coals, ores, and other minerals. Obtained by mining and quarrying, these materials are nonrenewable—what we have right now must last us forever. Some are more abundant or more accessible than others, but extracting them is always a dirty job. Quarrying and surface ("strip") mining destroy huge areas of land and either require careful and expensive landscape reconstruction or render the land useless for most other purposes. Shaft mining is costly and dangerous. Both types generate mountains of useless waste called tailings.

Oil and natural gas. Pumped from underground reservoirs, these petrochemicals are used as fuels and also form the raw materials for an almost infinite array of plastics, fibers, pharmaceuticals, lubricants, solvents, and other manufactured chemicals. Oil and gas are nonrenewable fossil fuels—compounds produced by buried plants and animals over 10 million to 20 million years. Extracting this oil and gas is a big business—one that leads to every imaginable form of pollution.

Farm products. Farming is the source of most of the world's food. In theory it's environmentally sound (though it places a low value on animal life): generations of domesticated plants and animals can be grown and harvested as completely renewable resources. In practice, however, it's full of flaws, most of them resulting from the desire to increase short-term yields even at the expense of long-term productivity. Heavy reliance on chemical fertilizers and pesticides destroys the natural productivity of the soil, pollutes soil and water, and exposes farm workers and consumers to harmful chemicals. The factory approach to raising livestock leads to extreme cruelty as animals are raised in cramped, unhealthy conditions. Conversion of even poor-quality land to farmland destroys natural plant and animal communities such as wetlands, woodlands, and rainforests, and leads to erosion of fragile, fertile topsoil.

Other plant and animal resources. From natural communities we harvest wood for paper and building, furs and other animal products, a few foods such as fish, and wild plants for myriad products from drugs to perfumes. Like farming, it's a sound concept in theory—certain products can be extracted or plants and animals can be culled without destroying the whole community. But in practice it's fraught with dangers. Cutting timber, for example, leads to destructive logging practices such as clear-cutting and the replacement of complex forest communities, which support many plants and animals, with convenient but largely sterile tree farms. Hunting and trapping become cruel industries. Overharvesting of fairly abundant creatures such as ocean fish can imperil the ecosystems of which they are a part. And overharvesting of scarcer resources can lead to extinctions—a real possibility even for such well-known animals as the elephant.

PROCESSING AND MANUFACTURING

After their raw materials are obtained, most products go through an incredibly complex series of manufacturing processes before they become the items we recognize. Ideal manufacturing processes are energy-efficient, nonpolluting, safe for their workers, and make use of recycled materials. Most are far removed from the ideal. In some cases the environmental effects are obvious; one need only drive through a heavily industrialized area to see—or smell—them. But others are less visible—trees dying from acid rain hundreds of miles away, or workers dying from cancer decades after their exposure to toxic substances.

Energy consumption. American manufacturers use a lot of energy—about a third of our country's total.[1] Almost all of this energy (84 percent) is produced by burning nonrenewable fossil fuels (coal, petroleum, and natural gas), which greatly depletes the world's remaining supplies. These fuels also cause serious air pollution problems—power plants are a prime source of the pollutants that cause acid rain, smog, and the carbon dioxide that heightens the greenhouse effect. Another 7.5 percent of the energy is produced by nuclear power plants, which cause less pollution but create the danger of radioactive leaks and waste disposal. A scant 4 percent is produced by hydroelectric dams, which are fairly pollution-free but cause drastic, destructive changes to riverine environments.

Air, water, and soil pollution. During the manufacturing process, industrial smokestacks and vents spew out a vast array of air pollutants ranging from toxic chemicals and ash to the greenhouse gas, carbon dioxide. Their wastewater includes a similar array of pollutants that either find their way into rivers, lakes, and groundwater reservoirs, or must be removed at considerable expense by wastewater treatment plants. Soil is polluted by leaks, spills, and dumped wastes.

Worker health and safety hazards. Manufacturing-plant workers are exposed to many situations that endanger their safety and their short- and long-term health. Industrial machines cause injuries; the assembly-line atmosphere leads to stress and fatigue; and chemical toxins and irritants cause respiratory problems, cancer and other long-term dangers, and an increased risk of birth defects.

Animal cruelty. Many products manufactured for human use are tested on animals first, often under extremely cruel conditions. Much of this testing is not even for important products, such as breakthroughs in medical research; instead it's just routine testing of household or personal care products. Alternative tests and computer models are now available, and an increasing number of companies are avoiding animal testing altogether, but many continue the practice.

PACKAGING

Really the last stage of manufacturing, packaging is the process that puts the product in the form you see in the store and is one of the few manufacturing issues we *can* weigh just by looking at a product in the store. Perfect packaging is no bulkier than necessary, easy and clean to produce, and made of materials that can be reused or recycled many times (glass bottles are a good example). Most packaging is far from perfect and can turn even simple, harmless products into environmental nuisances.

Manufacturing impacts. Manufacturing a product's packaging can be even more costly, energy-consuming, and polluting than manufacturing the product itself. Nonrenewable fossil fuels are used to supply both the energy for manufacture and the raw materials for all forms of plastic packaging; valuable timber resources are harvested for paper packaging; and all manner of chemicals are used to mix, stamp, coat, and print packages into their final form.

Transportation costs. Unnecessarily bulky or inefficient packaging adds substantially to transportation costs, in both dollars and fuel. A truck loaded with efficiently packaged material carries a lot of the product and very little packaging; a truck loaded with inefficiently packaged material carries just the reverse, so it takes more truckloads to get the same amount of product to you.

Disposal problems. About half of our household trash, by volume, is product packaging. Some packaging materials, such as corrugated cardboard, are easy to recycle and, even if discarded, will eventually break down. Others, however, are difficult or impractical to recycle and nearly indestructible when discarded, which makes them a problem for our rapidly filling landfills. The most difficult packages to recycle are those made from mixed materials—for example, coated paperboard that is encased in plastic. Even though some of the layers of mixed-materials packaging might be recyclable in theory, they must be separated first, making recycling highly impractical.

TRANSPORTATION

Also hidden in a product's past is the cost of transporting it from its manufacturing plant to your local store.

Fuel consumption. Carting products around the country and the world, whether by truck, train, ship, or plane, takes a tremendous amount of fuel—further depleting the world's dwindling supplies of nonrenewable fossil fuels.

Air pollution. Most freight carriers burn diesel fuel, which is less expensive but even more polluting than gasoline. When burned, diesel fuel emits high levels of particulates, nitrogen oxides, and other serious air pollutants. Freight carriers are a major contributor to air pollution problems such as urban smog and the greenhouse effect. In cold weather diesel fuel thickens, making the engines hard to start, so they are often allowed to run for hours even when they're not in use—creating the odor and haze common to freight yards and all-night truck stops.

USE: A PRODUCT'S PRESENT

This is the stage of a product's life with which we are most familiar—the time from when we take it off the store shelf to when we throw it away. In some cases it's an alarmingly short stage, considering all the money, energy, and resources that went into creating the item. And even though we might see the product every day, we still might not be aware of the environ-mental effects of using it. A product should be safe, clean, and energy-efficient to use, and should have a long useful life. Many products fall far short of these standards.

ENERGY AND FUEL CONSUMPTION

From automobiles to electric toothbrushes, the products we use in our everyday lives consume a vast amount of energy. In fact, each year American homes use over 84 billion gallons of gasoline, 850 billion kilowatt-hours of electricity, and 4.3 trillion cubic feet of natural gas[2]—numbers so huge they're difficult to comprehend. The results? Depletion of dwindling fossil-fuel supplies; increased air and water pollution; heightening of the greenhouse effect; short-term and long-term risks to human health; and damage to wildlife and wildlife habitat.

WATER CONSUMPTION AND POLLUTION

The average American household uses nearly 300 gallons of water every day for everything from brushing teeth to watering the lawn.[3] Unless we're faced with an immediate and severe shortage, we don't often stop to think about the effects of our heavy use of water.

Water shortages. Some areas of the country, most notably the Southwest, use far more water than naturally occurs there. Such areas gradually deplete their own water resources and become dependent on borrowing water from wetter regions—a fragile arrangement that hinges on the other regions consistently having enough to spare. And as the past few years have demonstrated, even regions that normally have more water than they can use sometimes experience costly, even crippling, droughts.

Water treatment costs. If your home is connected to a municipal water supply, every drop of water you use must go through an expensive process to bring it up to drinking quality—even if you're just going to use it to wash your car. Typically it's tested, filtered, and treated with chemicals such as chlorine to kill microorganisms and fluoride to prevent tooth cavities, then stored and pumped to each household.

Wastewater treatment costs. Once wastewater leaves your home, it must be treated once more to remove all the pollutants added to it during use—an even more complex and expensive process than its initial treatment. The pollutants include everything from disease-carrying human wastes to improperly discarded hazardous chemicals. The task is daunting at best, and treatment facility costs and adequacy are common sources of wrangling between local officials, government monitoring agencies, and taxpayers. The stakes are high, since inadequate facilities pass on pollutants to their downstream neighbors, and every gallon of wasted water adds to their task.

Surface and groundwater pollution. Pollutants run into surface water when we spill fuel or other chemicals in ditches or waterways, or pour chemicals down storm sewers, which often bypass treatment plants. Even detergent from washing a car in your driveway, or oil spilled in the middle of the street, makes its way through storm sewers into waterways. Groundwater is polluted by seepage from landfills, improperly discarded chemicals, lawn and garden chemicals, and drainage into abandoned wells.

AIR POLLUTION

Besides burning valuable fuels, many of the consumer products we use contribute to air pollution, which has both immediate health risks and long-term environmental effects.

Indoor air pollution. Many of the chemicals we use remain trapped inside our homes and offices. Tightly sealed, newly constructed buildings often contain dangerous levels of formaldehyde and other chemicals emitted by particleboard, new carpet, vinyl, and other plastics. Even older, less tightly sealed buildings can contain harmful vapors from common items such as cleaners, aerosol propellants, waxes and polishes, paints, and solvents. Indoor air quality is being increasingly implicated in a wide range of short-term and long-term illnesses.

Outdoor air pollution. Automobile exhaust is one of the most noticeable forms of outdoor air pollution that individual consumers generate.

Yet the other volatile compounds we use—paints and strippers, aerosol propellants, even nail polish remover—can find their way into the outdoor air. They contribute significantly to urban smog and the overall deterioration of the air we breathe. Some of the everyday products we use contribute to two especially sinister environmental problems: the greenhouse effect, a probable cause of global warming; and destruction of the fragile ozone layer that protects us from deadly solar radiation.

RISKS TO PEOPLE, PETS, AND WILDLIFE

Some products we use are just plain hazardous—even when used properly they are dangerous, and when used carelessly they can maim or kill.

Accidental injuries. Countless people and animals are injured every year by common, yet dangerous, household items, from lawn mowers to stoves to insecticides. When you consider rising health-care costs and how many people are living without the safety net of adequate health insurance, the costs become high in both human and economic terms.

Long-term health risks. Even more frightening—and probably far more costly—are health effects we can't see. The link between a stove and a burned hand is obvious, but what about the link between a little-known chemical and an increased cancer risk or an increased risk of birth defects? It's useful to remember the lesson of asbestos, which was considered a safe "wonder mineral" until the horrors of a lung disease and increased cancer rates became known. The vast array of chemicals to which we are now exposed every day, many of which have been invented in our own lifetimes, means we are living among health risks we can't even begin to assess.

DISPOSAL: A PRODUCT'S FUTURE

What happens to a product after we're done using it? In most cases we simply throw it away and think no more about it. It usually ends up in a landfill where, depending on what it's made from, it might sit intact for decades or even centuries. Americans throw away a tremendous amount of trash—far more than people of any other country—and it all adds up to an environmental crisis of staggering proportions.

LANDFILLS

About 80 percent of our household wastes are carted to sanitary landfills.[4] In the not-so-distant past landfills were created wherever and whenever somebody felt like starting one. But hard, costly lessons in just how polluting haphazard landfills can be have led to much-needed regulation.

Landfill space. We're using up existing landfill sites at an alarming rate, especially in metropolitan areas. According to the Environmental Protection Agency, one-third of the landfills operating in 1987 will have been closed by 1993.[5] Only certain settings are suitable for landfills, and people who live near proposed sites are bound to protest construction of new ones—two factors that make the outlook for new sites grim, particularly in urban areas. Some cities are already forced to ship their trash elsewhere, sometimes over long distances, and the disposal process is bound to get more costly and complex as time goes on.

Pollution from landfills. Sanitary landfills are, despite their name, filthy places full of rotting food, human and animal wastes, and toxic chemicals. Liquids percolating through the waste create a toxic ooze that, especially in a poorly constructed landfill, can leak through and around the site, polluting soil and surface water, and even seeping down to pollute the groundwater below it. Landfills also generate odors and methane gas, which contributes to the greenhouse effect.

Nondecomposing garbage. The traditional assumption behind landfills has been that the organic garbage would break down over time, leaving only such nondecomposing garbage as plastics. Recent research, however, has shown that modern landfills create dry, tomblike environments that can preserve newspapers and even food for decades.

INCINERATION

As landfill space becomes more scarce, many communities are turning to incineration as an alternative—nationwide, about 10 percent of our household trash now ends up incinerated.[6] Incineration sounds like a good idea—the volume of trash is greatly reduced, and the heat can be used to generate electricity. Unfortunately, there are some major problems:

Air pollution. Even well-designed incinerators can't burn things completely; instead they emit smoke that contains particulates, heavy metals, and other toxic compounds. Unless new technology leads to major improvements, construction and use of incinerators will continue to be hotly debated between local officials struggling with a burgeoning wastestream and local residents rightly concerned about air quality.

Toxic residues. The ash or sludge left over from incineration contains most of the garbage's toxic pollutants, in highly concentrated form, and presents a disposal problem in itself; it must be treated as a hazardous waste, and a suitable disposal site found.

HAZARDOUS WASTE DISPOSAL

Certain household wastes—pesticides and chemical solvents, for example, or heavy metals such as lead or mercury—are classified as hazardous. These toxic substances are dangerous if discarded with other trash; however, very few are currently disposed of properly. Even well-constructed modern landfills are not designed to accommodate hazardous wastes, which should go to specially designed hazardous waste disposal sites that use incineration, chemical, or biological treatments. These special sites are locally unpopular, expensive to build, and costly to use. Yet they still present dangers of soil, air, and water contamination, and the disposal costs are high enough that many people and companies end up discarding their wastes illegally instead.

LITTERING

More than a nuisance, littering is a serious environmental problem—the most irresponsible way of disposing of trash. Most of us get annoyed when we see a sidewalk strewn with paper wrappers or a roadside littered with cans, but the problems go deeper than that.

Hazards to wildlife. Everyday trash tossed in the water or on land kills untold thousands of animals every year, often in particularly gruesome ways. Such mundane objects as plastic bags, nets, fishing line, and six-pack yokes become death traps for animals that become entangled in them; often a growing animal will get its head caught in a loop of plastic and slowly strangle or starve to death as it grows. Other animals are killed by litter that is poisonous, sharp-edged, or can be mistaken for food.

Pollution. Some litter contains toxic chemicals—heavy metals in the dyes and colors of packaging, for example—that pollute the soil and water where they are discarded. Empty containers can also contain hazardous residues of the chemicals with which they were filled.

RECYCLING: EXTENDING A PRODUCT'S LIFE CYCLE

Recycling is the most sensible form of waste disposal because the wastes are reused rather than discarded. The beauty of recycling is that it not only reduces the amount of trash that must be landfilled or burned, it also saves raw materials and energy needed for product manufacturing. In effect it extends a product's useful life.

Recycling, though becoming more popular, still accounts for only a small portion of the trash we discard. The reason? Straight-ahead economics have ruled the recycling industry—with few of the enormous public costs of developing new landfills finding their way back to manufacturers—so the true cost-effectiveness of recycling has remained hidden. As American cities face upcoming landfill shortages, recycling will become increasingly common.

TYPES OF RECYCLING

In the home all recycling seems pretty much the same: we sort our recyclables and cart them to the curb or a recycling center. From an environmental perspective, however, there are three distinct kinds:

- In *primary* recycling the product is simply reused. For example, returnable beer bottles are washed and refilled; old motor oil is filtered and processed for reuse; glass jars are reused in the home as storage containers. It is by far the most resource- and energy-efficient form of recycling.

- In *secondary* recycling, the most common type, certain types of waste are used as raw materials to make new products. Aluminum cans, for example, are melted to make new ones; waste paper is reduced to pulp to make new paper; glass bottles are melted to make new glass. Ideally such materials can be reused many times.

- *Dead-end* recycling is a form of secondary recycling with one important difference: the waste is reused for another product only once, after which it must be landfilled or incinerated. Most plastics recycling is dead-end, with plastic bottles and jugs being turned into nonrecyclable carpeting, lawn furniture, and other products.

RECYCLABLE MATERIALS

In theory most of our household trash could be recycled; the technology exists, but the logistics and economics are limiting. Household recycling programs in this country usually stress the following packaging materials, which make up about half of our total household trash:[7]

Packaging	Produced Yearly	Percent Recycled
Aluminum cans	76 billion cans	50.5
Paper	87 billion pounds	32
Glass bottles	40 billion bottles	27
Plastics	13 billion pounds	< 2
Steel cans	33 billion cans	0.5

- *Aluminum cans* are the single most popular recycling item, because the price of new aluminum is high enough to make their recycling profitable.

- *Paper*—especially newspaper and office paper—is another commonly recycled item. Paper is heavier and less valuable than aluminum, so it's not as profitable to recycle, but the paper industry is moving to expand its recycling capability.

- *Glass bottles* are easy to melt down and mix with new glass, but they're also heavy, not terribly valuable, and somewhat difficult to sort and transport. Like paper, glass recycling should increase in the near future.

- *Plastics* are difficult and not very profitable to recycle. They must be sorted into several different types; they're bulky to transport; and they are usually recycled only once, into a completely different product.

- *Steel ("tin") cans* are made of steel and tin, and the two metals must be separated chemically during recycling. That complication, plus their relatively low value and high transportation costs, have kept the recycling rate low.

- *Organic matter* can be recycled through composting—a unique form of recycling that has been gaining favor as a remedy for the vast amounts of yard and food wastes that otherwise sit intact in bone-dry landfills. Composting is simply putting organic waste in a place where it will decay, and then using it as fertilizer. Some municipal landfills have banned certain types of yard waste altogether. Many cities have started municipal composting programs during the warm months.

CONSIDERING A PRODUCT'S LIFE CYCLE

Despite the grimness of our current environmental situation, it *is* possible to buy environmentally sound products. If we as consumers learn as much as possible about each product's total life cycle, we can make informed choices

and shop for products that meet the following guidelines:

- don't cause serious environmental damage when they're produced

- have a long, safe, useful life

- can be reused or recycled to extend their useful life

- do not present disposal problems

The following chapters discuss many consumer products in detail, weighing their usefulness against the environmental damage they cause throughout their life cycles, to help you make those informed choices that are so vital to our future.

1. Energy Information Administration, "Energy Facts 1987" (Department of Energy, Forrestal Bldg., EI-231, Washington, DC 20585), pp. 3–4.
2. Ibid., pp. 4, 10, 24, 38.
3. John Elkington et al., *The Green Consumer* (Viking Penguin, 1990), p. 205.
4. "Household Waste: Issues and Opportunities" (Concern, Inc., 1794 Columbia Road NW, Washington, DC 20009), p. 2.
5. *Environmental Quality 1987–1988* (Council on Environmental Quality, 1987), p. 3.
6. "Household Waste," op. cit., p. 2.
7. Lewis Erwin and L. Hall Healy, Jr., *Packaging and Solid Waste* (American Management Association, New York, 1990), pp. 55, 58, 65, 80; American Paper Institute, "Paper Recycling and Its Role in Solid Waste Management" (260 Madison Ave., New York, NY 10016), p. 6-14.

PRODUCT MATERIALS
AND PACKAGING

AEROSOL CANS

An aerosol can uses highly pressurized gases to expel its contents as a mist, foam, or cream. Though popular—about 2.5 billion are made each year in the United States alone[1]—aerosol cans are the single most environmentally destructive form of packaging in use.

ENVIRONMENTAL PROBLEMS

Manufacturing impacts. Aerosol cans are made through a complex, multistage process that uses energy and resources and creates pollution at every step. The body of the can consists of thin sheets of steel that are rolled, cut, and welded with a lead seam, after which steel disks are placed in the bottom. These metals are obtained through mining, smelting, and energy-intensive processing; their impacts include resource depletion, soil erosion, wildlife habitat destruction, and air and water pollution. After the ingredients are added to the can, its plastic valves and stems are fitted under high pressure, and the propellant gas—often flammable and toxic—is forced in.

Safety hazards. Aerosol cans are hazardous to use. Many spray their active ingredients in a fine mist that is easily inhaled deep into the lungs, then absorbed directly into the bloodstream.[2] (Some particles are fine enough to remain suspended in your household air for days.) In addition, many of the gases used as propellants are hydrocarbons, which are highly flammable—or even explosive—if heated or exposed to sparks or flame.

Air pollution. The hydrocarbon propellants, once expelled, pollute outdoor as well as indoor air. Outdoors they react with sunlight and other chemicals to form ozone, which near the earth's surface is a pollutant and health hazard.

Ozone depletion. Though a pollutant near the ground, ozone is vital in the stratosphere, where a thin, fragile layer protects the earth from solar radiation. This ozone shield has been badly damaged by pollutants, particularly chlorofluorocarbons (CFCs), once popular as aerosol propellants. CFC propellants were banned in most American aerosol products in 1978 but are still used in a few products; their use contributes directly to ongoing ozone layer destruction.

Disposal problems. Aerosol cans present special disposal problems because of both the materials from which they are made and their volatile, pressurized contents. They are nonrecyclable, nondegrading in landfills, dangerous to incinerate, and potentially explosive.

CHOOSING A PRODUCT

GENERAL GUIDELINES

Nonaerosol alternatives. Aerosol cans are such a serious environmental problem that they should be used only when there is no alternative—a rare situation.

COMMERCIAL PRODUCTS

Reusable aerosol sprayers *(highly recommended).* Two companies make reusable air-powered sprayers:

♦ Abbeon, Cal, Inc., (805) 966-0810, makes a spray can you can recharge with a bicycle pump or air hose. It can be used with paints, cleaners, and other liquids.

♦ Biomatik USA Corp., (303) 938-8999 makes a plastic spray bottle that comes with its own air pump. It can be used with household cleaners and other water-based liquids.

Aerosols without CFCs *(never recommended).* Even if they use non-CFC propellants, products packaged in aerosol cans are not an environmentally sound choice. Virtually all aerosol-packaged products also come in nonaerosol versions (see Alternatives). Look for the nonaerosol products on the same shelves as their aerosol counterparts.

Aerosols with CFCs *(never recommended).* Exempted from the 1978 ban on CFC propellants were such products as pressurized drain openers, emergency tire inflaters, cleaning sprays for electronic equipment, and boat emergency horns. Depletion of the ozone layer is such a serious problem that CFC-propelled products should *never* be used. Check labels carefully; most CFC-propelled products carry an ozone-depletion warning on their labels.

DO-IT-YOURSELF

Refillable pump sprayers. For many products, such as household cleaners, refillable plastic bottles with manual pump sprays provide a simple, inexpensive option to aerosol cans.

ALTERNATIVES

Pump-spray products. Most products work just as well in a manual pump sprayer as they do in an aerosol can. Even products that require a very fine mist—hair spray, for example—are now available in pump form.

Nonspray products. Many products are available as solids or creams; often, they're more concentrated and less expensive than their spray counterparts. Examples are tube or bar shaving cream, stick deodorants, cream furniture polish, and hairstyling gel.

WISE USE

Safe use. If you must use a product in an aerosol can, keep the can away from heat or flames and use it only in ventilated areas.

Proper disposal. Aerosol cans pose an explosion hazard, so empty them of all pressure before putting them in the trash. *Never* puncture or incinerate them, or put them in trash compactors.

1. *Can Shipments Report, 1987* (Can Manufacturers Institute, 1625 Massachusetts Ave. NW, Washington, DC 20036), p. 5.
2. Stephen Brobeck and Anne Averyt, *The Product Safety Book* (E.P. Dutton, 1983), p. 8.

CANS

There are two kinds of cans—aluminum and steel. Many steel cans, especially those used for foods, have a thin coating of tin on the outside; hence their name, "tin" can. Can manufacturing is a big business: Americans use a total of 109 billion a year, or about 435 per person.[1] Such heavy use adds up to significant manufacturing, disposal, and health problems.

ENVIRONMENTAL PROBLEMS

Consumption of raw materials. The metals used to make aluminum and steel cans come from nonrenewable supplies of bauxite and iron ore. Mining these ores often causes great environmental damage, including wildlife habitat destruction, soil erosion, and water pollution. The United States does not produce as much of these ores as it uses in manufacturing, so it must import more, adding long-distance transportation to the environmental costs.

Manufacturing impacts. Processing ores into aluminum and steel uses tremendous amounts of energy and water, pollutes both water and air, and creates monumental heaps of unusable slag—in fact, it is one of the nation's most polluting manufacturing processes.[2] Transforming the metals into finished cans adds another energy-consuming step to this complicated process.

Health hazards. Some steel cans are sealed with a lead seam running up the side. Lead is a toxic metal that accumulates in the body's tissues and causes nerve and other damage to humans, particularly children.

Disposal problems. The vast number of cans used makes them a major disposal problem. They do not break down in landfills, nor do they burn in incinerators (instead they create waste slag). Unless they contain nonfood items such as paints and solvents, both steel and aluminum cans are recyclable, and recycling them takes only a fraction of the energy and resources needed to make new ones. Unfortunately, too few cans are currently recycled. Though aluminum cans are our most commonly recycled item, about 50 percent—38 billion per year—are still discarded instead. Less than 1 percent of steel cans are currently recycled, leaving 33 billion dumped in the trash each year.[3]

CHOOSING A PRODUCT

GENERAL GUIDELINES

Recyclability. Choose containers you can recycle easily in your area. Most communities now recycle aluminum cans; some also recycle steel cans.

Sensible packaging. Choose large sizes whenever practical. Manufacturing a single large can uses fewer materials and less energy than making two smaller ones.

COMMERCIAL PRODUCTS

Aluminum cans *(recommended)*. Superlight, nontoxic, and easy to crush for recycling, aluminum cans are a sound form of packaging *if recycled.* They are most often used for beverages. Aluminum cans, however, are still less desirable than glass bottles, which can be refilled—the best form of recycling.

Steel cans, lead-free *(sometimes recommended)*. Many foods now come in lead-free cans, the best choice for canned foods. Look for cans with a rounded edge on the bottom instead of the usual protruding edge, or check the seam itself. Many lead-free cans are welded and have a distinctive dark line running down the seam.

Steel cans, lead-sealed *(not generally recommended)*. These cans have a visible lead seam down the side and are often coated with plastic on the inside. The lead seam can contaminate the contents, and the mixture of materials makes the cans difficult to recycle. Use these cans as a last resort—particularly if you can't recycle them.

Composite cans *(not generally recommended)*. These cans are made with a combination of different materials, such as steel and aluminum, steel and paper, or steel and plastic; they are used for fruit juices and other beverages, foods, motor oils, and general packaging. These cans are totally nonrecyclable, so avoid them whenever possible.

DO-IT-YOURSELF

Home preserving. Preserve foods such as fruits, vegetables, and meats in reusable glass jars with vacuum lids.

ALTERNATIVES

Fresh or bulk products. Choose unprocessed, unpackaged foods instead of canned foods whenever possible.

Glass containers. Buy foods and beverages in glass containers. Glass is as recyclable as aluminum (though not as commercially valuable), completely nontoxic, and reusable; its manufacturing process is also less damaging (see Glass, p. 27).

WISE USE

Safe use. Never leave food in opened cans, even if they're covered or resealed. Oxygen in the air causes lead and other metals or contaminants to leach from the can into the food.

Proper disposal. You can reduce the impact of can manufacturing and disposal by making sure every can you use is recycled. Aluminum can recycling is common nationwide, and often pays well. Unless used for paint or other toxic substances, steel cans are also recyclable, although steel recycling programs are not yet common. If your local recycling programs don't accept steel cans, urge them to start.

1. *Can Shipments Report, 1987* (Can Manufacturers Institute, 1625 Massachusetts Ave. NW, Washington, DC 20036), p. 5.

2. *Toxics Release Inventory, A National Perspective, 1987* (Environmental Protection Agency, 1987), p. 15.
3. *Environmental Quality 1987–88* (Council on Environmental Quality, 1987), pp. 19–21; *Can Shipments Report, 1987*, op. cit.

EXOTIC PLANT AND ANIMAL PRODUCTS

Colorful, interesting, and beautiful, exotic plant and animal products are usually imported— legally or illegally—by professional traders and returning tourists. The environmental impacts on the countries of origin are profound.

ENVIRONMENTAL PROBLEMS

Wildlife and habitat destruction. Trade in exotic materials causes worldwide damage, sometimes irreparable, as land is stripped of plants and animals, and coral reefs are blown up with dynamite:[1]

- *Orchids.* About half of the 822,000 whole orchid plants our nation imports annually are from the wild, many from India. Thousands of wild orchids also leave the United States illegally, threatening species viability and damaging habitat.

- *Reptiles.* Each year 1.5 million skins and 30 million other products from reptiles enter the United States, often illegally. Among the species killed are some facing extinction: the black caiman alligator, the Asian saltwater crocodile, the Hawksbill turtle, the green sea turtle, and the Kemp's and olive ridley turtles.

- *Corals.* Each year our nation imports 90 percent of all the corals traded worldwide: 1,000 to 1,500 tons of raw coral and 2 million to 3 million manufactured products. Many coral reefs, which protect beaches from erosion and shelter countless marine species, are being destroyed solely for this purpose.

- *Ivory.* An estimated 5 million to 6 million carved ivory products and 5,000 raw tusks enter this country each year, hastening the destruction of both the Asian elephant, an endangered species now found only in the most isolated areas of India and Asia, and the African elephant, a threatened species. Since the late 1970s, the African elephant population has declined nearly 60 percent, from 1.5 million to about 625,000.

CHOOSING A PRODUCT

GENERAL GUIDELINES

Careful shopping. The safest course of action is to avoid buying *any* exotic products obtained from the wild. If a product looks exotic, assume that it is, and ask about its origin before you buy. When shopping either in this country or abroad, take precautions; ask to see invoices or shipping receipts, if necessary, to determine an item's source. If a store manager cannot answer your questions or show proof of origin, don't buy the article.

COMMERCIAL PRODUCTS

Flower bulbs *(sometimes recommended)*. Most imported flower bulbs specifically for consumers are cultivated in the Netherlands and other countries. Tens of millions of wild-harvested bulbs, however, find their way into the world trade from Turkey, Portugal, and Spain, threatening those countries' local flower populations. Avoid any bulbs labeled as "wild" or "botanical"; if you are uncertain about a bulb's origin, don't buy it. The following popular bulbs are often taken from the wild:

- Crown imperial (*Fritillaria imperialis*)
- Snowdrops (*Galanthus* species)
- Winter aconite (*Eranthis hymenalis*)
- Narcissus, angel's tears (*N. triandus albus*)
- Summer snowflake (*Leucojum aestivum*)
- Sea daffodil (*Pancratium maritimum*)
- Madonna lily (*Lilium candidum*)
- Sternbergia (various species)
- *Tulipa pulchella humilis*

- Cyclamen (all species except *C. persicum*)
- Crocus (various species)

Orchids *(sometimes recommended)*. About half of our imported orchid plants come from the wild, so verify the origin of any plant before you buy.

Corals *(not generally recommended)*. Many countries now prohibit sale and export of their corals, and some coral species are restricted altogether from international trade. Still, huge amounts of coral are on the world market, mostly in the form of jewelry and ornaments. Given the important ecological role of coral reefs, it is best to avoid this product altogether.

Ivory *(never recommended)*. Importing ivory from the endangered Asian elephant is illegal; importing ivory from the threatened African elephant is still legal, with certain restrictions on its origin. Because of the ongoing destruction of both species, however, *all* ivory should be avoided.

Reptile products *(never recommended)*. Because the wild populations are so threatened, importing of many reptile products is illegal, including most crocodile and lizard-skin products, many snakeskin products from Latin America and Asia, and all sea turtle products. This category of products should be avoided altogether.

ALTERNATIVES

Cultivated products. Instead of wild-harvested flowers, bulbs, or plants, look for those cultivated commercially, preferably in this country (to cut back on transportation-caused pollution). Ask for information at greenhouses, nurseries, and garden clubs.

Native plants. Look for seeds from hardy native plants in your area. Check with your local parks and wildlife office before gathering any wild seeds or plants. For information on cultivating native plants contact

- Abundant Life Seed Foundation, (206) 385-5660

◆ National Wildflower Research Center, (512) 929-3600

Leather and jewelry substitutes. Fine leather goods, though not the perfect choice environmentally, are far preferable to reptile-skin products. Instead of coral jewelry, look for items made with precious and semiprecious stones or metalwork.

FOR FURTHER INFORMATION: Brochures and fact sheets on many exotic plants and animals traded worldwide are available from the World Wildlife Fund, 1250 24th St., NW, Washington, DC 20037.

SEE ALSO Exotic Wood Products, p. 19; Furs, p. 26; Jewelry, p. 243; Pets, p. 273.

1. "Flower Bulb Trade," "Elephant Ivory Trade," "Psittacine Trade," "U.S. Imports of Wildlife," "World Trade in Wildlife," "Watch Out for Wildlife Products—The Caribbean" (Traffic [USA], World Wildlife Fund, 1250 24th St. NW, Washington, DC 20037).

EXOTIC WOOD PRODUCTS

Of all the hardwood used in the United States—most of it for furniture, paneling, cabinets, and tableware—about 12 percent is imported, and one-third of that comes from tropical rainforests.[1]

ENVIRONMENTAL PROBLEMS

Deforestation. Destruction of tropical rainforests has accelerated worldwide, despite massive publicity about potential effects on global warming (the trees store carbon dioxide and supply oxygen) and loss of biodiversity (roughly 30 species of rainforest plants and animals become extinct every day). Today, an area of rainforest the size of San Francisco is cleared every three-and-a-half hours; an area the size of Arizona is cleared every year.[2] The activities causing most deforestation are cattle ranching, agriculture, and construction of human settlements. Logging, however, plays a major role in opening up rainforests to these destructive activities; it also severely damages forest ecology itself.

Disruption of indigenous tribes. Logging and deforestation harm not only the environment but also the native peoples who inhabit rainforests. These cultures have occupied the rainforests for hundreds (or even thousands) of years without damaging their environment's delicate ecology, but they are now being driven from their homelands—or murdered—as the forests are opened for development.

CHOOSING A PRODUCT

GENERAL GUIDELINES

Careful shopping. Learn to recognize tropical exotic woods. Tropical hardwoods often have a

TABLE 1

TROPICAL HARDWOODS TO AVOID

Used in:	Building Materials	Cabinets	Carved Wood	Doors, Trim	Furniture	Kitchenware, Housewares	Veneer, Plywood
Made with these species:							
Afrormosia (West Africa)		✔			✔	✔	
Almaciga[a] (Philippines, Malaysia)							✔
Apitong-Keruing (Philippines, Malaysia)	✔						
Bocote (Central, South America)			✔		✔		
Bubinga (West Africa)		✔	✔			✔	
Canarywood (South America)					✔		✔
Cedar, Spanish[a] (South America)	✔				✔		
Cocobolo (Central America)			✔		✔		
Ebony, African (West Africa)			✔			✔	
Ebony, Black (Malaysia)			✔			✔	
Jatoba (Mexico, Central, South America)					✔		
Mahogany, African (West Africa)			✔				✔
Mahogany, Genuine (Mexico, Central, South America)		✔		✔	✔		
Mahogany, Lauan (Philippines)		✔		✔	✔		✔
Meranti-Seraya (Malaysia)		✔		✔			
Primavera (Mexico, Central America)		✔					
Purpleheart (Central, South America)		✔			✔		
Ramin (Malaysia)					✔		
Rosewood (Brazilian)		✔					✔
Rosewood (Honduran)							✔
Teak (Southeast Asia)	✔		✔		✔		
Vermillion-Padauk (West Africa, Southeast Asia)			✔			✔	
Wenge (West Africa)		✔	✔			✔	

Source: Rainforest Action Network, *"Tropical Hardwoods"* (draft, 1989); Boulder Rainforest Action Group, *"Tropical Rainforests and the Timber Trade."*

[a] Classified as a softwood.

dark, rich color, with red hues. Lauan mahogany is distinguished by its lighter brown color (before staining) and uniform grain. Before you purchase any wood product, verify its country of origin. If you can't get adequate, reliable information, don't buy the item.

COMMERCIAL PRODUCTS

Tropical woods *(never recommended)*. Tropical hardwoods are used for many common consumer products, including furniture; doors; plywood paneling and veneer; kitchenware such as bowls, spoons, serving utensils and chopsticks; tool handles; picture frames; art work; and ornamental objects. Table 1 lists the most common tropical woods to avoid and their typical uses. Although it's possible in theory to harvest tropical woods using ecological, sustainable methods, in practice it is virtually unknown.[3] However, the Rainforest Alliance, (212) 941-1900, has instituted the Smart Wood Program to certify those companies selling consumer products made of tropical woods harvested with sustainable forestry practices. (Thus far it has certified Plow & Hearth, [800] 627-1712, which sells teak outdoor furniture.) Until this program is developed and more information is made available, no products made from tropical woods should be purchased.

- Ask lumberyard managers or contractors about the types and origins of any exotic wood building materials you may be considering for remodeling or new construction.

- With store-bought consumer products, all goods manufactured entirely outside the United States must be labelled as such, with the country of origin listed; look for these labels on kitchen and housewares, indoor and outoor furniture, carved wood objects, etc. However, furniture is sometimes imported unassembled and, if then assembled in the United States before sale, it need not carry an identifying label. Ask salespeople about the species and origin of any exotic woods before purchase.

Redwood *(not generally recommended)*. Redwood, which grows only in the damp coastal areas of northern California and southern Oregon, is the domestic equivalent of an exotic wood. It is much valued for its beauty and water resistance. But because its habitat is so tiny—less than 0.0003 percent of the total forested area of North America[4]—and because stands are often logged by clear-cutting, its use can be environmentally unsound. Avoid purchasing redwood lumber or finished products whenever practical.

ALTERNATIVES

Domestic woods. Instead of buying tropical exotics, look for high-quality domestic wood products:

- For *plywood paneling* and *veneer* use birch, cherry, cottonwood, red gum, white oak, Ponderosa pine, yellow poplar, or black walnut.

- For *lumber* and *millwork* use basswood, beech, birch, butternut, cherry, cypress, elm, Douglas fir, black gum, red gum, hackberry, sugar maple, red oak, white oak, Ponderosa pine, southern yellow pine, yellow poplar, Sitka spruce, sycamore, or black walnut.

- For *furniture*, see Furniture, p. 226.

- For *roofing*, use alternative roofing products such as asphalt shingles, metal, or clay tile. Avoid shingles made of redwood, cedar, or cypress; they are often cut from old-growth timber that is important both to present forest ecology and to future generations as a biological preserve.

FOR FURTHER INFORMATION: Rainforest Alliance, Smart Wood Program, 270 Lafayette St., Suite 512, New York, NY 10012; (212) 941-1900.

1. Mike Roselle and Tracy Katelman, *Tropical Hardwoods* (draft) (Rainforest Action Network, 301 Broadway, Suite A, San Francisco, CA 94133; 1989), p. 9.
2. Ibid., introduction.
3. Ibid., p. 1.
4. Based on calculations from figures in World Resources Institute, *World Resources 1988–89* (Basic Books, 1988), p. 70; "Redwood," *Encyclopedia Americana* (Grolier, 1988), p. 311.

FIBERS AND FABRICS, NATURAL

Unlike synthetic fibers, natural fibers are non-toxic, biodegradable, and made from renewable resources. Producing them, however, does have some harmful environmental effects.

ENVIRONMENTAL PROBLEMS

Farming impacts. Chemicals are used heavily on fiber-producing crops, especially cotton. Cotton crops are usually treated with fungicides, weed killers, insecticides, and defoliants. These agricultural chemicals deplete the soil, pollute the groundwater, and create health hazards for farm workers.

Animal cruelty. Wool-producing sheep are treated better than most domesticated animals, but some cruelty is still involved:

- High-speed shearing can cut and abrade the animals' skin, leading to infections.

- Keeping sheep in large flocks makes them more susceptible to diseases and parasites.

- Commercial sheep herds have only one ram (male) for about 35 ewes (females), so most male lambs are separated from their mothers early, fattened, and killed for food.

Chemical treatments. Virtually all natural fabrics are dyed with petrochemical derivatives, some of which—aniline dyes, for example—are both allergenic and toxic if absorbed through the skin. Many finished fabrics are treated with formaldehyde resins to reduce wrinkling; these resins are polluting to manufacture and cause allergic reactions in sensitive individuals.

Cleaning requirements. Some natural fabrics require dry cleaning, which uses toxic and polluting chemicals as cleaning solvents (see Dry Cleaners, p. 207).

CHOOSING A PRODUCT

GENERAL GUIDELINES

All-natural materials. Despite their problems, natural fibers and fabrics are far superior environmentally to synthetics (see Fibers and Fabrics, Synthetic, p. 24). Look for fabrics made of all-natural fibers instead of synthetics or natural-synthetic blends.

Chemical-free finishes. Avoid chemically treated, permanent press, or "wrinkle-free" products; instead, look for weaves such as cotton knits that resist wrinkling naturally.

Washable fabrics. Choose products that are hand or machine washable instead of those that require dry cleaning.

Used fabrics. To save resources and money, look for used fabrics and clothing at second-hand stores, garage sales, estate sales, vintage clothing shops, and through want ads.

COMMERCIAL PRODUCTS

Cotton *(highly recommended).* Cotton, which is woven from the cotton plant's long fibers, is an environmentally sound choice despite its chemical treatments and other problems. Naturally strong, cotton fabric absorbs moisture and "breathes," making it especially suitable for heat or humidity. It can be machine or hand washed, with mild soap, and machine dried. Unbleached, untreated, and undyed or naturally dyed cotton is the best choice; avoid cotton treated with chemical wrinkle-resistant finishes. The following two companies sell organically grown (chemical-free) cotton products:

- Dona Designs, (214) 235-0485, makes futons, comforters, and pillows from organic cotton.

- The Cotton Place, (214) 243-4149, supplies a wide range of cotton clothing, bedding, fabrics, and household linens, most of which are free of chemical finishes.

Linen *(highly recommended)*. An excellent alternative to synthetic fabrics, linen comes from the flax (or linseed) plant, which is grown all over the world. Linen fibers are stiffer than cotton but have a smooth, lustrous texture that makes them well suited for tailored or delicate clothes and household items such as tablecloths. Most linen fabric is machine washable but should be air dried, not machine dried; avoid linen items that require dry cleaning.

Ramie *(highly recommended)*. Ramie is made from the shrubby ramie plant (also called China grass), grown in Asia, the United States, and Brazil. It is harder to spin than other natural fibers, but is becoming more widely available as production methods improve. Ramie fibers are durable, nonshrinking, flexible, and lustrous; they are well suited to many types of clothing and household items such as napkins, tablecloths, and towels. Like cotton, ramie can be machine washed and dried. The best products are machine washable, naturally dyed ramie fabrics or ramie/cotton blends; avoid dry-clean-only or chemically treated items.

Wool *(recommended)*. Wool's advantages outweigh its environmental problems; nevertheless, the animal cruelty involved in its production—and the fact that producing fibers from animal fur uses natural resources inefficiently—makes it a less sound choice than cotton. Wool strands, which are actually a form of fur, can be either spun and woven or used as batting or felt. Wool's extraordinary ability to absorb moisture and to insulate even when wet make it ideal for cold-weather clothing; its toughness makes it ideal for carpets and rugs. Look for wool products that are machine or hand washable; avoid chemically treated wools and those that must be dry cleaned.

Silk *(recommended)*. Like wool, silk is a better choice than synthetics. It is, however, made through an ancient, complicated process that is lethal for the insects that produce it. Silkworms produce continuous strands of silk fibers inside a cocoon. The worm is killed, and the unbroken strands are carefully drawn out and processed into fabric. Strong but soft and very comfortable, silk is used to make delicate shirts, blouses, undergarments, and lightweight tailored clothing. Silk fabrics cannot be machine washed or dried but can be hand washed, with mild soap, and air dried. Avoid silk clothes that require dry cleaning.

WISE USE

Proper care. Natural fibers look and feel better and last longer if you treat them properly:

- Always wash new clothes, preferably several times, before wearing them, to remove any chemical finishes and other residues.

- Avoid dry cleaning; hand or machine wash whenever possible. If you have your laundry done professionally, use top-quality laundries that hand wash and steam press (see Dry Cleaners, p. 207).

- Try nontoxic stain removers before resorting to chemical treatments (see Stain Removers, p. 210).

- To foil moths, clean clothing and household linens before sealing them tightly for storage (see Mothproofing, p. 96).

Reuse. Instead of discarding old clothing or fabrics, look for ways to prolong their life: sell them to secondhand stores, give them to churches or charities, or use them as rags or stuffing.

FIBERS AND FABRICS, SYNTHETIC

Durable, cheap, and versatile, synthetic fibers have many practical advantages. But their popularity—the United States produces 7 billion pounds a year, 22 percent of the world's output[1]—causes significant environmental impact.

ENVIRONMENTAL PROBLEMS

Fossil-fuel consumption. True synthetic fibers (acetate and rayon are semisynthetic) are derived entirely from fossil fuels such as petroleum, natural gas, and coal, depleting these nonrenewable resources.

Manufacturing impacts. Processing petrochemicals into fibers uses energy, consumes fossil fuels, creates toxic chemicals, endangers workers' health, and pollutes the air and water. Making nylon, for example, involves at least a dozen steps and uses two carcinogens (benzene and butadiene), a poisonous gas (chlorine), caustic lye (sodium hydroxide), a toxic acid (hydrogen cyanide), and a toxic alkaline (sodium cyanide).[2] Each step, and each chemical, requires special equipment and handling and creates the risk of spills and other accidental releases.

Chemical treatments. Formaldehyde-based resins are commonly used as antiwrinkle or antistain finishes on synthetic fabrics; their production also consumes petrochemicals, and their presence on new fabrics can pollute indoor air and cause allergic reactions in sensitive people. In addition, virtually all synthetic fabrics are dyed with petrochemicals; the widely used aniline dyes are both allergenic and toxic if absorbed through the skin.

Cleaning requirements. Synthetic fabrics are popular because they are machine washable and need little or no ironing; many synthetics,

however, require dry cleaning, which uses toxic, polluting chemicals as cleaning solvents (see Dry Cleaners, p. 207). And machine-washable synthetics often need chemical fabric softeners to reduce static electricity.

Disposal problems. Synthetic fibers are nonrecyclable and, except for acetate and rayon, nonbiodegradable. Some synthetics release toxic fumes when burned in incinerators.

CHOOSING A PRODUCT

GENERAL GUIDELINES

Weighing your needs. Buy synthetics only for special applications—such as outdoor wear, sporting gear, or camping equipment—where strength or durability is especially important.

All-natural materials. Whenever possible choose natural fabrics and fibers, or at least natural/synthetic blends, instead of all-synthetic materials.

Chemical-free finishes. Avoid clothing and household goods with chemical finishes, such as permanent-press or stainproofing treatments.

Washable fabrics. Choose products that are hand or machine washable, rather than dry-clean-only, and those that are naturally wrinkle-free and need less ironing.

Used fabrics. To save resources and money, look for used fabrics and clothing at second-hand stores, garage sales, estate sales, vintage clothing shops, and through want ads.

COMMERCIAL PRODUCTS

Acetate, rayon *(sometimes recommended).* Acetate and rayon are semisynthetics, made from wood cellulose rather than petrochemicals; they are superior to true synthetics because they come from a renewable resource and are biodegradable. Their manufacture, however, is far more polluting than the manufacture of all-natural fibers, with which they are often blended. Acetate and rayon fabrics have a soft, pliable texture that makes them popular for such items as better clothing and drapes. Many people routinely dry clean acetate and rayon items, but most can be hand washed and air dried safely.

Nylon *(sometimes recommended)*. Nylon is very strong and rugged, but stiff and somewhat rough to the touch, making it best for high-stress, long-wearing items such as outdoor apparel and equipment. Nylon can be machine washed and dried, using low heat.

Polyester *(not generally recommended)*. Strong but softer than nylon, polyester is often used for clothing and household fabrics, and is often blended with cotton and wool fibers to add strength and reduce wrinkling. Its low moisture absorption can make pure polyester uncomfortable next to the skin, especially in warm weather. Except for some tailored clothing, polyester is machine washable and can be machine dried using low heat.

Acrylic *(not generally recommended)*. Acrylics are not as strong or as long-lasting as nylon or polyester, but they are somewhat more comfortable than pure polyester in clothing because they absorb more moisture. Most acrylics are machine washable, and all can be easily hand washed and air dried.

ALTERNATIVES

Natural fibers and fabrics. Natural fibers—especially cotton or wool—can successfully replace synthetics for most clothing and household linens; they cause far less harm to the environment.

WISE USE

Proper care. Keeping synthetic fabrics clean and well maintained makes them last longer:

- Always wash new clothing, preferably several times, before wearing it, to remove chemical finishes and other residues.

- Avoid dry cleaning; hand or machine wash whenever possible. If you have your laundry done professionally, use top-quality laundries that hand wash and steam press (see Dry Cleaners, p. 207).

- Try nontoxic stain removers before resorting to chemical treatments (see Stain Removers, p. 210).

Reuse. Instead of discarding old clothing and fabrics, look for ways to prolong their life: sell them to secondhand stores, give them to churches or charities, or use them as rags or stuffing.

1. *U.S. Industrial Outlook 1990* (Department of Commerce, 1990), p. 9-2.
2. N. Irving Sax and Richard J. Lewis, Sr., eds., *Hawley's Condensed Chemical Dictionary,* 11th ed. (Van Nostrand Reinhold, 1987), pp. 255, 600, 845, 1057.

FURS

Furs, our distant ancestors' first clothing, are now luxury items that support a lucrative industry: in the last decade American fur sales have tripled to nearly $2 billion a year.[1] The biggest price is paid by fur-bearing animals, dozens of which might be killed to make a single coat.

ENVIRONMENTAL PROBLEMS

Wildlife destruction. An estimated 17 million wild animals, including beaver, fox, mink, muskrat, nutria, raccoon, bobcat, lynx, and coyote, are trapped for fur each year in the United States alone.[2] Furs from an additional 3 million animals are imported.[3] Though not endangered, these species play critical roles in maintaining the delicate ecology of their natural habitats, and killing them disrupts that natural balance. Other species (referred to by trappers as "trash animals") die by accident in the traps—dogs, cats, deer, birds—at a rate of two for every one commercially usable animal.

Animal cruelty. Inhumane treatment causes suffering for both ranch-raised animals and those trapped in the wild:

- Many commonly used traps are designed to preserve the fur, not prevent or minimize pain. Steel-jaw traps, for example, hold the animal by the leg, in excruciating pain, until it is clubbed to death by the trapper or dies of its wounds.

- Most American furs come from ranch-bred animals—about 30.5 million ranch-bred beavers, silver and blue foxes, mink, fitches, ocelots, and chinchillas are killed every year.[4] Ranch-bred animals usually spend their entire lives in tiny cages, which causes abnormal behavior such as continuous pacing, self-mutilation, tail-biting, and cannibalism. When their coats are ready for harvesting, the animals are killed with gas, by lethal injection, or by anal electrocution.

Cleaning requirements. Furs require dry cleaning, a process that uses toxic, polluting chemicals as cleaning solvents (see Dry Cleaners, p. 207).

CHOOSING A PRODUCT

GENERAL GUIDELINES

Non-fur alternatives. Skip not only the expensive, all-fur coats and stoles, but also fur lining or trim on apparel such as gloves and coats. Instead, choose garments made from natural fibers; they can be just as attractive, warm, and practical as furs, without the environmental damage.

COMMERCIAL PRODUCTS

Fur products *(never recommended)*. Environmentally, neither trapped nor ranch-bred furs have a single point in their favor. Most of the animals used for furs are killed solely for their skins—an unnecessarily cruel and wasteful treatment of living creatures and the natural resources that support them.

ALTERNATIVES

Natural-fiber garments. All fur or fur-trimmed garments can be easily replaced by ones made from natural fibers. A tailored wool coat, for example, can be just as fashionable as a fur one—and far more versatile and practical.

Fake furs. Also called *faux* furs, fake furs are made from synthetic fibers such as acrylics and rayon. One modacrylic (modified acrylic) from Japan, Kanecaron, looks very real, even to details such as varying fiber lengths and colors and imperfections. Faux fur is less expensive than animal fur but much more expensive than natural-fiber textiles. No animals are killed to produce faux fur, but it is made from nonrenewable fossil fuels and can look real enough to fool people, thereby indirectly supporting the fur industry.

FOR FURTHER INFORMATION: *The Animal Rights Handbook*; Living Planet Press, 1990.

1. Katherine Bishop, "From Shop to Lab to Farm, Animal Rights Battle Is Felt," *New York Times* (January 14, 1989).
2. *The Animal Rights Handbook* (Living Planet Press, 1990), p. 9.
3. "Fur Trade" (Traffic [USA], World Wildlife Fund, 1250 24th St. NW, Washington, DC 20037).
4. *Humane Quarterly* (Humane Society of Ramsey County, 1115 Beulah Lane, St. Paul, MN 55108; 4th quarter, 1990), p. 2.

GLASS

Glass is one of the most environmentally sound materials used in consumer products. Made from an abundant natural material—sand—glass is nontoxic, simple to manufacture, and easy to reuse or recycle.

ENVIRONMENTAL BENEFITS

Reusability. Glass is the only beverage container that can be reused—the most efficient way to recycle—by washing, sterilizing, and refilling. Refilling bottles was once very common, but today only 15 percent of our nation's soft drink bottles and 6 percent of its beer bottles are refillable.[1] This shift was caused by changing economics: bottlers have opted for fewer but larger bottling plants, increasing transportation distances and, therefore, refilling costs.

Recyclability. Recyclers break glass into small pieces, called cullet, that are added to new glass during manufacture, lowering its melting temperature and saving energy. Currently only 27 percent of glass bottles and jars are recycled, but 90 percent *could* be recycled.[2]

ENVIRONMENTAL PROBLEMS

Fossil-fuel consumption. Glass is made by mixing three simple raw materials—sand (75 percent), soda ash (20 percent), and lime (5 percent). Unfortunately, melting these raw materials requires a lot of energy—the equivalent of burning 38 gallons of oil for every ton of glass.[3]

Disposal problems. Over 20 billion pounds of glass enters our nation's municipal wastestream each year, 90 percent of it from bottles and jars.[4] If bottles and jars are discarded instead of recycled, they become a nuisance: they are indestructible in a landfill and they won't burn in an incinerator (instead, they form a dense slag that must be painstakingly removed). Most other types of glass—windows, plate glass, mirrors, light bulbs—are not recycled because of coatings or processing problems, so they must be sent to landfills instead.

CHOOSING A PRODUCT

GENERAL GUIDELINES

Reusability. Buy bottles and jars that you can either reuse at home or return to a store that will send them to a bottler for washing and refilling. Look for soft drinks, beer, and other beverages in bottles labeled "returnable."

Sensible packaging. To reduce resource and energy consumption, always choose the largest practical sizes of products in bottles and jars.

Longevity. When buying nonrecyclable glass products, select those that will last for a long time, postponing their inevitable trip to a landfill.

COMMERCIAL PRODUCTS

Glass bottles and jars *(highly recommended).* As a packaging material, glass has many advantages: it's waterproof, nontoxic, nonreactive, transparent, impervious to air or oxygen, and cheap. For consumers the one drawback of glass is that it's breakable, making it unsuitable for shampoos, dish detergents, and other products where breakage is a major safety concern. But for most beverages, foods, and household goods, glass presents little danger. Glass bottles and jars are recycled nationwide, making them an environmentally sound choice.

Other glass products *(highly recommended).* Most other glass products, such as kitchenware, windows, light bulbs, and mirrors, are not recyclable as cullet, either because the glass is coated or mixed with other materials or because the products are too dangerous to transport and process at a recycling plant. Most such products are made from partially recycled glass, however, and are environmentally superior to fossil-fuel-based plastics unless breakage is an overriding issue.

WISE USE

Reuse. The strength and durability of glass makes it ideal for reuse:

- Always buy returnable, refillable soft drink and beer bottles if you can find them.

- Wash and reuse glass jars as storage containers.

- Look for salvage businesses, stained-glass shops, or artisans who accept old windows, mirrors, and other nonrecyclable glass products.

Proper disposal. Always recycle bottles and jars; ask your local recycler what types they accept. Most take all three colors of glass—clear, green, and brown. Be sure to remove all caps or other plastic or metal attachments, and rinse food containers before recycling. *Never* recycle any other types of glass with bottles and jars; ceramics or coated glass can ruin an entire batch of cullet, which then must be landfilled.

1. Lewis Erwin and L. Hall Healy, Jr., *Packaging and Solid Waste* (American Management Association, New York, 1990), pp. 54–55.
2. Ibid.
3. John Seymour and Herbert Girardet, *Blueprint for a Green Planet* (Prentice Hall, 1987), p. 81.
4. *Environmental Quality 1987–88* (Council on Environmental Quality, 1987), pp. 13–15.

PAPER AND PAPER PRODUCTS

At first glance, paper looks environmentally sound: it's recyclable, biodegradable, and made from a renewable resource. But paper production is one of the most polluting industries in the United States, in part because we use so much paper—154 billion pounds in 1988 alone.[1]

ENVIRONMENTAL PROBLEMS

Destruction of forests. Every year nearly 900 million trees are cut down to provide raw material for American paper and pulp mills.[2] Even careful logging disrupts forest ecology by cutting roads and taking out large, mature trees. Clear-cutting, which removes *all* the trees, both large and small, devastates the entire ecosystem. Large paper companies often replant clearcut areas with genetically selected or cloned trees, then apply chemical herbicides to discourage any competing growth. Although this process speeds the production of raw materials for the industry, it provides almost no food or habitat for wildlife.

Manufacturing impacts. Turning trees into paper is a complex, polluting process:

- Mechanically grinding trees into pulp consumes enormous amounts of electricity.

- Making better grades of paper requires breaking down the wood fibers; large amounts of harsh chemicals (caustic soda or sulfuric acid) are needed.

- White paper owes its color to a chlorine bleaching process; the chlorine reacts with wood compounds to form highly toxic organochlorines and dioxins, which are then discharged into surface waters.

- The aluminum salts used to purify water for pulp processing are highly toxic to fish and other aquatic life when released.

- Wood fibers are discharged in wastewater; as these fibers decompose, they consume oxygen needed by aquatic life.

- A wide range of organic and inorganic chemicals and fillers (currently over 800) are used to produce smoothness, opacity, water repellence, strength, color, and finish, adding more potential pollutants.

- Papermaking on such a gigantic scale seriously affects air and water quality. For every ton of wood pulp processed, for example, 2 to 10 pounds of sulfur dioxide (a cause of acid rain) is released into the air.[3] In 1987 alone the 214 major American paper facilities released a total of 2.18 billion pounds of chemicals into rivers, lakes, and streams.[4]

Health hazards. The highly toxic dioxins created by chlorine bleaching show up not only in nearby waters, but also in the paper products themselves.[5] The amounts are minuscule, but no amount of dioxin, a carcinogen, is considered "safe" by the Food and Drug Administration.[6] Dioxins can leach from bleached paper, so products such as bleached paper coffee filters and superabsorbent disposable diapers can cause exposure during use (see Coffee Filters, p. 174; Diapers, p. 238).

Disposal problems. Paper products make up over 40 percent by weight—slightly higher by volume—of this country's municipal solid waste, by far the largest single contributor. Unfortunately, only about 32 percent of all paper is recycled today, 3 percent less than the rate in 1944.[7]

CHOOSING A PRODUCT
GENERAL GUIDELINES

Weighing your needs. Before buying paper goods or using them as packaging, consider whether you really need them; if you do, look for products that are either made from recycled paper or are recyclable themselves.

TABLE 2

RECYCLED PAPER PRODUCTS

Mail-Order Suppliers:	What They Carry:
Atlantic Recycled Paper Co. (800) 323-2811	Computer paper, envelopes, napkins, office paper, paper towels, stationery, toilet tissue
Brush Dance (415) 389-6228	Greeting cards, stationery, wrapping paper
Conservatree (800) 522-9200	Coated stock, lined tablets, office paper
Earth Care (608) 256-5522	Computer paper, desk pads, greeting cards, stationery, wrapping paper
Ecco Bella (201) 226-5799	Desk pads, envelopes, greeting cards, lined tablets, office paper, stationery, wrapping paper
Eco Design (505) 438-3048	Envelopes, notebooks, sketch paper, stationery
Recycled Paper (617) 277-9901	Brochure and flyer stock, computer paper, envelopes, stationery
Seventh Generation (800) 456-1177	Desk pads, facial tissue, greeting cards, lined tablets, napkins, paper towels, stationery, toilet tissue, wrapping paper

Recycled paper. There are two main types of recycled paper. Paper made from *post-consumer waste* incorporates paper that was used by consumers and then returned to mills for reprocessing. Paper made from *pre-consumer waste* incorporates leftover scraps from printers and paper mills. Both types of recycling are environmentally and economically sound; products made of post-consumer waste also encourage the development of full-cycle recycling. Since the term "recycled paper" is used for both types, determining a paper's source of raw materials is difficult unless the package is labeled with a phrase such as "100% post-consumer waste recycled." Few products are made from all-recycled materials, because new pulp is often added for strength or other characteristics. Always choose 100-percent-recycled paper if it's available; if it's not, simply look for "recycled" (for a list of recycled paper products available through mail order, see Table 2).

Unbleached or lightly bleached paper. Look for paper that is either unbleached or lightly bleached rather than pure white; it is equally clean and hygienic, but is processed without chlorine. Lightly bleached paper is treated with less toxic bleaching agents.

Recyclable paper. Choose paper products you can recycle locally; different recyclers handle different types of paper. Most communities now recycle office paper, newspaper, and cardboard; call your local recycling office for information.

Simple processing. Use undyed and unprinted paper whenever possible, to cut back on the use of chemical inks and dyes.

COMMERCIAL PRODUCTS

Bags and sacks. These products vary in their environmental soundness, depending on the type and treatment of the paper used (bags made with recycled paper are often labeled to that effect):

- **Brown grocery bags** *(highly recommended).* These strong paper bags are made from unbleached wood pulp, sometimes with recycled paper. You can reuse them many times as grocery sacks or for other purposes, and they are easy to recycle.

■ **Shopping bags and colored paper sacks** *(not generally recommended)*. These sacks are usually made from chlorine-bleached paper, heavily inked, coated, or otherwise treated. They are difficult or impossible to recycle.

Boxes. Boxes vary in both their recyclability and their recycled-fiber content:

■ **Cardboard boxes** *(highly recommended)*. Lightweight and very strong, corrugated cardboard is made from unbleached wood pulp, often with recycled materials included; it is a sound choice *if* recycled or reused.

■ **Paperboard boxes** *(sometimes recommended)*. Paperboard packaging (noncorrugated cardboard such as that used for cereal boxes) is made with many different combinations of papers, coatings, and special treatments, making it hard to recycle. Much paperboard is made from either recycled or unbleached material. Look for a label stating that the material is recycled, or tear the paperboard slightly to look under the coating: if it's gray, it's made from recycled material; if brown, from unbleached wood pulp; if white, from chlorine-bleached wood pulp.

Cartons for milk and juices *(never recommended)*. Milk and juice cartons are made from nonrecycled, chlorine-bleached paper coated with wax or plastic to act as a moisture barrier. These cartons are contaminated with dioxins, which evidently can migrate through the coating, causing potential health hazards.[8] They are not recyclable.

Cellophane *(never recommended)*. Basically a packaging material for other products, cellophane is a semisynthetic substance made from wood pulp through an intense, chemical-laden process that uses chlorine bleach. Cellophane is brittle, hard to reuse and reseal, and nonrecyclable (see Food Wraps and Bags, p. 181).

Coffee filters. See Coffee Filters, p. 174.

Copier, computer, and writing paper. This paper can be divided into three types, which differ in their environmental soundness:

■ **Unbleached or lightly bleached, recycled paper** *(highly recommended)*. Although usually made from a mixture of post-consumer waste, industrial waste (scraps from mills and misprints from printers), and virgin pulp, some unbleached or lightly bleached paper is made from all-recycled material. It is either completely unbleached or bleached with hydrogen peroxide or oxygen, which are much less harmful than chlorine. This paper is not bright white but is usually quite suitable for reading and writing. For bulk orders (ten reams or more) of copier, computer, or office paper, call Conservatree, (800) 522-9200, or write for a list of nationwide distributors from E.H. Pechan & Assoc., 5537 Hempstead Way, Springfield, VA 22151.

■ **Chlorine-bleached, recycled paper** *(sometimes recommended)*. Bright white recycled office paper (either 100 percent recycled or mixed with virgin pulp) has been chlorine bleached. If you must use ultrawhite paper, make sure it is all-recycled. You can find distributors through the listing above.

■ **Chlorine-bleached, nonrecycled paper** *(never recommended)*. This paper, the most common type, is available in white and an almost infinite array of colors, in either bond or specialty grades. Most of it is made from virgin wood pulp. If you must use this paper, choose white: it's easy to recycle, while colors are not.

Diapers. See Diapers, p. 238.

Fax paper *(not generally recommended)*. Most fax machines use temperature-sensitive paper coated with a layer of pigments that render it completely nonrecyclable. Keep an eye out for plain-paper fax machines; like plain-paper copiers, they should become increasingly common.

Magazines. Printed on a wide variety of papers, magazines can be divided into two general categories:

■ **Plain-paper (nonglossy) magazines** *(recommended)*. Nonglossy magazines are made from simpler materials than are glossy magazines and are therefore less polluting to produce. The paper recycling industry, however, still has trouble accommodating the variety of products that are used in nonglossy magazines, so they are not widely recycled, though they could be.

- **Glossy-paper magazines** *(not generally recommended)*. Glossy, or slick, paper is coated with clays that are polluting to produce and that complicate recycling; some of the clays also contain heavy metals, creating a separate disposal hazard when they are thrown away. The paper can be recycled if the clays are removed, but the process is complex and uncommon.

Newspapers *(sometimes recommended)*. Newsprint, one of the cheapest, lowest-quality papers, is made mostly from mechanically ground wood pulp, with some chemically processed, chlorine-bleached wood pulp added. Often recycled materials are added—sometimes 50 percent or more—but because the fibers break down each time they are recycled, new pulp must be added for strength. Unfortunately, many newspapers do not yet use recycled newsprint, citing higher prices or supply problems (recycled-paper mills cannot always compete with giant mills using all-new wood pulp).

Tampons and sanitary napkins. See Tampons and Sanitary Napkins, p. 263.

Towels, napkins, tissue. Though difficult to recycle, these products can easily be made from recycled paper. Some bleaching is required to remove resin acids that prevent water absorption, but the chlorine bleaching that produces the bright white color of typical products is unnecessary.

- **Recycled, unbleached, or lightly bleached towels, napkins, and tissue** *(highly recommended)*. Made with predominantly or all-recycled materials, these products are completely unbleached, are bleached with chemicals less toxic than chlorine, or contain relatively small amounts of chlorine-bleached material. Look for (or ask for) these brands

in better grocery stores, co-ops, and natural foods stores:

Brand	Products
C.A.R.E.	Napkins, facial and toilet tissue, towels
Envision	Napkins, facial and toilet tissue, towels
Marcal	Napkins, facial and toilet tissue, towels
Mardi Gras	Napkins, towels
117	Towels
Page	Towels
Park Avenue	Toilet tissue
Project Green	Facial tissue
Tree-Free	Towels
Soft 'n Gentle	Tissue

- **Nonrecycled, chlorine-bleached towels, napkins, and tissue** *(never recommended)*. The standard products found in most grocery stores are made from virgin pulp (often with small amounts of recycled paper), are bleached with chlorine, and usually have added dyes, inks, and fragrances.

ALTERNATIVES

Substitutes for paper. Avoid unnecessary paper products by using these environmentally sound substitutes:

- Reusable cloth bags, string bags, or backpacks instead of grocery bags

- Cloth napkins instead of paper napkins (they can often be used more than once before washing)

- Cloth handkerchiefs instead of facial tissues (though disposable tissues might be a better choice if you are ill)

- Ceramic, glass, or thermos containers instead of paper cups, plates, and bowls

- Cloth towels or rags instead of paper towels

WISE USE

Conservative use. There are some easy ways to cut back on paper:

- For small purchases skip the paper sacks.

- Use writing and printing paper on both sides.

- Make notepads from waste sheets of paper with blank sides: just fold them evenly, cut, and staple them together.

- Postcards waste less paper and energy than sheets of paper with envelopes.

- Paying with cash instead of checks and credit cards saves paper.

- Phone calls are more environmentally sound than letters.

- Reduce junk mail: write (on a postcard) the Direct Marketing Association (6 E. 43rd St., New York, NY 10017) and tell them to eliminate you from mailing lists that pass through their office. Be sure to include any variants of your name or address.

Proper disposal. Call your local recycler or waste-disposal office for information; ask about recycling high-grade office and writing paper, newspaper, mixed paper, cardboard and paperboard, brown grocery sacks, and magazines.

FOR FURTHER INFORMATION: The Greenpeace Guide to Paper, by Renate Kroesa (Greenpeace, 1436 U St. NW, Washington, DC 20009), 1990.

1. *1989 U. S. Industrial Outlook* (Department of Commerce, 1989), p. 6-4.
2. Based on calculations from figures in *Business Statistics 1986* (Department of Commerce, 1987), p. 129; *Environmental Quality 1987–88* (Council on Environmental Quality, 1987), p. 8; *Recycled Paper Catalog* (Earth Care Paper, Inc., P.O. Box 3335, Madison, WI 53704), p. 16.
3. Renate Kroesa, *The Greenpeace Guide to Paper* (Greenpeace USA, 1436 U St. NW, Washington, DC 20009; 1990), pp. 5–6.
4. *The Toxics Release Inventory: A National Perspective, 1987* (Environmental Protection Agency, 1987), p. 99.
5. Peter von Stackleberg, "White Wash: The Dioxin," *Greenpeace Magazine* (March/April 1989), p. 8.
6. Janet Raloff, "Dioxin: Paper's Trace," *Science News* (February 18, 1989), p. 106.
7. *Paper Recycling and Its Role in Solid Waste Management* (American Paper Institute, 260 Madison Ave., New York, NY 10016), p. 6.
8. Janet Raloff, op. cit.

PLASTICS

Plastics are cheap, durable, strong, lightweight, and extremely versatile, but their immense popularity has led to some major environmental problems.

ENVIRONMENTAL PROBLEMS

Fossil-fuel consumption. Plastics (except for natural rubber, a plant-based plastic) are made from nonrenewable fossil fuels—petroleum, natural gas, and coal—which supply the complex hydrocarbons that are processed into polymer resins. Americans use over 50 billion pounds of these plastic resins every year.[1]

Manufacturing impacts. The major resins used for plastics are (in order of volume used) polyethylene, polyvinyl chloride, polypropylene, polystyrene, and phenolic resins. The resins are manufactured at large chemical plants, then sent to thousands of smaller plants that use chemical plasticizers, fillers, and colorants to transform the resins into finished products. The environmental impacts include the following:

- *Air pollution.* In 1987 alone the plastics industry released 143 million pounds of toxic chemicals into the air.[2] Some of the worst pollutants are halocarbons—such as 1,1,1-trichloroethane, dichloromethane, and trichloroethylene—and volatile organic compounds such as toluene, methanol, and xylene. These compounds contribute to smog and ozone formation and are serious health hazards in themselves.

- *Water pollution.* In 1987 plastics manufacturers also discharged over 54 million pounds of chemical pollutants—especially acids, salts, and alkaline compounds—directly into rivers, lakes, and streams and another 48 million pounds into public sewage systems, adding to wastewater treatment burdens.[3]

- *Ozone depletion.* Despite the fact that certain chlorofluorocarbons (CFCs) are known to be destroying the stratospheric ozone layer that protects the earth from solar radiation, many plastic foams are still made using CFC-11 and CFC-12 as blowing agents.

- *Worker health risks.* Plastics plants can be unhealthy for their workers, because about 25 percent of the plants' chemical air emissions are from uncontrolled evaporation and leaks.[4] Workers in vinyl chloride plants, for example, have increased rates of rare liver cancers and other cancers, with their cancer rates directly correlated to length of time on the job.[5]

Disposal problems. By volume plastics make up 25 to 30 percent of the nation's municipal solid waste.[6] Plastics disposal problems include the following:

- If buried, plastics last hundreds of years, and even degradable plastics don't readily decompose in modern, oxygen-starved landfills, despite manufacturers' claims.

- If incinerated, plastics can emit toxic chemicals, such as hydrogen chloride from polyvinyl chloride, and heavy metals such as lead, cadmium, and nickel. Any pollutants trapped by incinerator filters become highly toxic hazardous wastes, which present another disposal problem.

- Because they do not degrade, carelessly discarded plastics pose serious dangers to wildlife. In oceans, for example, an estimated 100,000 marine mammals worldwide—plus many more fish, turtles, and sea birds—die every year from ingesting plastic or becoming entangled in plastic fishing lines or strangled by the plastic yokes that hold aluminum soft drink and beer cans together.[7]

- Only about 2 percent of all plastics are recycled.[8] This low rate is due primarily to two factors: the many different types of plastics in use, which must be carefully separated before recycling; and the fact that plastics are bulky and lightweight, making transportation for reprocessing costly.

CHOOSING A PRODUCT

GENERAL GUIDELINES

Nonplastic alternatives. Look first for alternatives to plastics—for example, glass, paper, and aluminum—that can be recycled or reused.

Durability. If you must buy a plastic product, choose a practical, high-quality item with a long usable life.

Recyclability. Find out what types of plastics local recyclers will accept, and separate the plastics by type. Look for triangular recycling symbols on bottles, bags, and containers, each with a number that indicates the type of plastic:

Recycling Number	Type of Plastic
1	Polyethylene terephthalate (PET)
2	High-density polyethylene (HDPE)
3	Polyvinyl chloride (PVC)
4	Low-density polyethylene (LDPE)
5	Polypropylene
6	Polystyrene (Styrofoam)

COMMERCIAL PRODUCTS

Plastic household goods *(sometimes recommended)*. Because plastic is light, strong, and waterproof, it is well suited for many household items such as storage crates and containers, buckets, tools and utensils, toys and outdoor equipment, and personal care items. Many such items, however, are far from indestructible: in cold weather some plastics break; in direct heat some soften and lose their shape; simple wear and tear takes a toll on all types. When considering any plastic item, think about its usable life and whether you can substitute another material (metal, glass, wood) with better results. Plastic can be a sound choice *if* well matched to a specific use.

Polyethylene bottles *(sometimes recommended)*. Made of high-density polyethylene (HDPE), and used at a rate of 1.8 billion pounds per year, these bottles are often used for house-hold cleaners and detergents, personal care products, milk, water, and other products. Only 2 percent are currently recycled. Some HDPE bottles, such as shampoo and lotion containers, are safer to use than glass and have a fairly long usable life as packaging; others, such as milk jugs, have extremely short life spans and should be avoided unless they are recyclable or reusable. (Recycling number for sorting: 2.)

Polyethylene grocery, food, and trash bags *(not generally recommended)*. These bags, made of low-density polyethylene (LDPE), are strong, water resistant, light, and extremely popular: Americans use 9 billion per year. Less than 1 percent, however, are currently recycled. (Recycling number for sorting: 4.) *Note:* biodegradable bags, sold to bag trash or lawn clippings and used as packaging, have no environmental value, decompose slowly in landfills, and are weaker than regular plastic bags, requiring more material to achieve similar strength.

Polyethylene terephthalate soft-drink bottles *(not generally recommended)*. Besides being unbreakable and light, polyethylene terephthalate (PET) retains carbonation, making it popular for soft drinks. Americans now use 750 million pounds per year; only 20 to 25 percent of the bottles are recycled. (Recycling number for sorting: 1.)

Styrofoam containers *(never recommended)*. Styrofoam is a trademark for polystyrene, which is used in about 11 percent of all plastic packaging and containers. Polystyrene is a good, light, and cheap insulator. Unfortunately, some polystyrene is still made using ozone-destroying CFCs, though many manufacturers have switched to other chemicals. Because it is so bulky and difficult to recycle (less than 1 percent is currently recycled), polystyrene should be avoided whenever practical. (Recycling number for sorting: 6.)

Polyvinyl chloride bottles and containers *(never recommended)*. Polyvinyl chloride (PVC) is impermeable to oxygen, so it keeps oily substances fresher than other plastics do; that makes it popular for cooking-oil containers. Americans use 560 million pounds of PVC per year; less than 1 percent is recycled. Toxic vinyl chloride can leach from the packaging into oils and foods,[9] so avoid this type of packaging whenever practical. (Recycling number for sorting: 3.)

ALTERNATIVES

Substitutes for plastic. Reduce plastic use by choosing these environmentally sound substitutes:

- Reusable cloth or string bags, backpacks, or paper sacks instead of polyethylene shopping bags

- Glass or aluminum containers instead of PET soft-drink bottles

- Glass containers instead of polyethylene plastic bottles, when practical

- Glass, paper, or hard reusable plastics instead of Styrofoam containers or packaging

- Glass bottles instead of PVC bottles

WISE USE

Conservative use. To keep your household use of plastics at a minimum, take the following steps:

- Buy products either in bulk or in the largest containers available.

- Buy high-quality plastic utensils and household goods that will last a long time.

- Refill and reuse containers: produce bags can be washed (if necessary) and reused many times; shampoo and lotion bottles can be refilled from bulk supplies at co-ops and natural foods stores.

Proper disposal. *Never* burn plastics or discard them as litter. Call your local recycler or waste disposal office for information on plastics recycling in your area.

FOR FURTHER INFORMATION: *Wrapped in Plastics: The Environmental Case for Reducing Plastics Packaging,* by Jeanne Wirka (Environmental Action Foundation, 1525 New Hampshire Ave. NW, Washington, DC 20036), 1990.

1. Pat Wittig, "Persistent Peril," *Organic Gardening* (February 1989), p. 66.
2. *The Toxics Release Inventory, A National Perspective, 1987* (Environmental Protection Agency, 1987), p. 115.
3. Ibid., pp. 137, 157.
4. Ibid., p. 115.
5. Mike Samuels and Hal Bennett, *Well Body, Well Earth* (Sierra Club Books, 1983), p. 157.
6. "Re:Sources," (Environmental Action, 1525 New Hampshire Ave. NW, Washington, DC 20036; July/August 1988), p. 20.
7. Pat Wittig, op. cit., p. 67.
8. *Environmental Quality 1987–88* (Council on Environmental Quality, 1987), p. 25.
9. N. Irving Sax and Richard J. Lewis, Sr., eds. *Hawley's Condensed Chemical Dictionary,* 11th ed. (Van Nostrand Reinhold, 1987), p. 946.

AUTOMOTIVE
PRODUCTS

AIR CONDITIONERS, AUTO

Auto air conditioning improves the comfort of hot-weather travel, but considering that there are 100 million air-conditioned cars in the United States alone,[1] it also has some serious environmental consequences.

ENVIRONMENTAL PROBLEMS

Ozone depletion. The refrigerant used in all auto air conditioners, CFC-12, is one of the worst of all the ozone-depleting chlorofluorocarbons. CFC-12 is harmless while sealed within the air conditioner. When it leaks into the air, however, its molecules travel up to the stratosphere, where sunlight breaks them down and liberates ozone-destroying chlorine. With every air-conditioned car leaking on average a pound of CFCs per year, car air conditioners account for about 4.5 percent of all the CFCs released worldwide into the atmosphere every year.[2]

Fossil-fuel depletion. Operating an air conditioner reduces your gas mileage by up to 3 miles per gallon in city driving, contributing to excess consumption of fossil fuels and increased air pollution.[3]

CHOOSING A PRODUCT

GENERAL GUIDELINES

Weighing your needs. In terms of efficiency, air conditioners differ very little from one make of car to another, so currently your only real choice lies in deciding whether to get air conditioning in a new car. Consider skipping the air conditioner in favor of the following alternatives.

ALTERNATIVES

Light color. When you buy your next car, think light. Light-colored cars reflect heat rays rather than absorb them.

Tinted windows and shades. Choose tinted windows, which keep you cooler by blocking sunlight. Use cardboard window shades when you're parked in the sun and see-through shades to keep direct sunlight off passengers when you're traveling.

Cloth upholstery. Choose cloth upholstery or seat covers rather than plastic, which heats up easily.

WISE USE

Conservative use. To help stop coolant leaks and conserve gasoline, use your air conditioner as little as possible.

Regular maintenance. Check regularly for leaks by looking for oil on the bottom of the seals around the air-conditioning unit when the engine is off. A mechanic can do this easily when changing or adding oil to the engine.

Professional repair. If you find a leak, do *not* attempt to recharge or repair the system yourself. Instead, take the car to a reputable repair shop that can trap and recycle the coolant. (Coolant recycling is becoming more common, but be sure to ask first.)

Proper disposal. Before you junk a car with air conditioning, try to find an auto repair shop that can remove and recycle the coolant.

1. Matthew Wald, "Coping with Leaking Auto Air Conditioners," *New York Times* (April 29, 1989).
2. Ibid.
3. Jack Gillis, *The Car Book 1989* (Harper & Row, 1988), p. 62.

ANTIFREEZE

Antifreeze, the yellow or greenish liquid added to the water coolant in your radiator, has two important tasks: it prevents the coolant from freezing in cold weather (when it could crack the engine block) and prevents it from boiling over in very hot weather. Unfortunately, antifreeze is poisonous, and no alternatives are currently available.

ENVIRONMENTAL PROBLEMS

Toxic ingredients. The main ingredient of antifreeze, ethylene glycol, is toxic to humans, pets, and wildlife. Animals are attracted by its sweet smell and taste, but drinking just a few ounces or inhaling its fumes can be lethal. It is one of the most common causes of poisoning among cats and dogs.

WISE USE

Careful maintenance. When changing or adding antifreeze to your car's coolant system, always follow the manufacturer's instructions. The safest method is to use a device often called an "antifreeze thermometer" to determine accurately the level of protection you need. You can buy antifreeze thermometers at automotive-product stores.

Reuse. Although manufacturers neglect to mention this fact, antifreeze can last two years instead of one. After the first year, when it is time to drain and clean the cooling system, collect the antifreeze in a clean pan. Strain it through a clean cloth to remove impurities, pour it back into the radiator or reservoir, and add new coolant if necessary. Be sure to clean up any spills.

Proper disposal. If you must dispose of antifreeze, *never* pour it on the ground or in the street. Before pouring it down a drain or storm sewer, contact your city water department. Because certain bacteria are needed to break down antifreeze, some wastewater treatment systems are not able to remove it. Furthermore, some storm sewers bypass water treatment facilities and empty directly into rivers or lakes.

AUTOMOBILES

Automobiles have become an integral part of the American lifestyle, offering us a kind of mobility earlier generations could never have imagined. According to the Motor Vehicle Manufacturers Association, nearly 123 million cars are on the road in the United States today, traveling 1.3 trillion miles each year.[1] Unfortunately, we're paying a steep environmental price for our mobility.

ENVIRONMENTAL PROBLEMS

Fossil-fuel depletion. Automobile gasoline consumption accounts for over one-fourth of our nation's total petroleum use. Gas mileage ratings for new cars continue to improve, but increases in both the number of cars and the number of miles traveled have actually raised our overall gas consumption—Americans used 1.5 billion gallons more gasoline in 1987 than in 1985.[2] Burning our nonrenewable oil supply at the current rate is robbing future generations of a precious resource, while seriously damaging the present-day environment.

Air pollution. Cars are a primary source of many dangerous air pollutants:

- *carbon monoxide*, a colorless, odorless, poisonous gas

- *lead*, a highly toxic metal

- *particulates*, bits of material that remain floating in the air

- *nitrogen oxides*, gases created by any high-temperature burning

- *hydrocarbons*, the unburnt leftovers from combustion

Nitrogen oxides and hydrocarbons mix with sunlight and other chemicals to create the infamous smog that shrouds many cities. Ozone, a major component of smog, is a serious pollution problem in many areas, impairing the lung

capacity of people sensitive to it and reducing crop yields by up to 30 percent.[3] Currently, more than 60 American cities do not meet federal clean-air standards for ozone and carbon monoxide.[4]

Greenhouse effect. Our heavy use of fossil fuels produces so much carbon dioxide that we might well be compounding the greenhouse effect (the trapping of heat by carbon dioxide and other gases), which could lead to global warming and severe climate changes. Automobiles play a major role in this carbon dioxide buildup: the Union of Concerned Scientists estimates that the average car pumps out over 20 pounds of carbon dioxide for each gallon of gasoline burned—over 10,000 pounds every year.[5]

Manufacturing impacts. Making cars at a rate of over 10 million per year causes serious environmental damage worldwide. The United States alone has 335 vehicle-manufacturing plants that consume huge amounts of resources: 74 percent of all the natural rubber consumed; 46 percent of all the synthetic rubber; 43 percent of all the malleable iron; 15 percent of all the steel; 54 percent of all the lead; and 16 percent of all the aluminum.[6] Turning these raw materials into automobiles uses vast amounts of energy and produces significant air, water, and soil pollution at the factory sites.

CHOOSING A PRODUCT
GENERAL GUIDELINES

Weighing your needs. If a small, fuel-efficient car will satisfy *most* of your needs, buy one, and find other alternatives for unusual tasks (for example, borrow a friend's light truck to move furniture, or rent a larger car for a long family trip).

Fuel efficiency. Make fuel efficiency a top priority. If you already own a fuel-efficient car, keep it, and save the environmental damage of building a new one to achieve only minor gas savings. If your car is a gas hog, however, trade it

TABLE 3

FUEL-EFFICIENT AUTOMOBILES

Manufacturer	Model	Fuel Economy (MPG)[a]	Repair Cost	Warranty Rating[b]
Subcompacts				
Daihatsu	Charade	38/42	High	Poor
Dodge	Colt	31/36	High	Good
	Colt Wagon	28/34	Medium	Average
	Omni	25/34	Low	Poor
Eagle	Summit	28/34	Low	Good
Ford	Escort	32/42	Low	Poor
	Festiva	35/41	Low	Poor
Geo	Metro	46/50	High	Average
	Prizm	25/31	High	Average
Honda	Civic	33/37	High	Poor
	CRX	29/36	High	Poor
Hyundai	Excel	29/33	Medium	Poor
Mazda	323	26/33	Medium	Average
Mitsubishi	Mirage Wagon	28/34	High	Good
Nissan	Pulsar	26/34	High	Poor
	Sentra	29/36	High	Poor
Plymouth	Colt	31/36	Medium	Good
	Colt Wagon	28/34	Medium	Good
	Horizon	25/34	Low	Poor
Pontiac	LeMans	29/38	High	Average
Subaru	Justy	33/37	High	Poor
	Loyale	25/32	High	Poor
Toyota	Corolla	28/33	High	Good
	Tercel	31/36	High	Good
Volkswagen	Fox	25/30	Low	Average
	Golf	25/32	Low	Average
	Jetta	37/43	Medium	Average
Yugo		28/31	Low	Poor
Compacts				
Acura	Integra	24/28	High	Poor
Buick	Skylark	23/31	Low	Average
Chevrolet	Cavalier	25/36	Medium	Average
Chrysler	LeBaron	20/28	Low	Poor
Dodge	Shadow	24/31	Low	Poor
Ford	Tempo	21/28	Low	Poor
Mazda	626	24/31	Medium	Average
Mercury	Topaz	21/28	Low	Poor
Nissan	Stanza	22/29	High	Poor
Oldsmobile	Cutlass Calais	22/31	Low	Average
Plymouth	Sundance	24/31	Low	Poor
Pontiac	Grand Am	22/31	Low	Average
	Sunbird	21/30	Medium	Average
Toyota	Celica	28/33	High	Good

(continued on next page)

TABLE
3

FUEL-EFFICIENT AUTOMOBILES *(continued)*

Manufacturer	Model	Fuel Economy (MPG)[a]	Repair Cost	Warranty Rating[b]
Intermediates				
Buick	Century	23/31	Low	Average
	Regal	19/30	Low	Average
Chevrolet	Beretta	24/34	Medium	Average
	Corsica	24/34	Medium	Average
Dodge	Dynasty	22/27	Low	Poor
	Spirit	24/32	Low	Poor
Ford	Probe	24/30	Medium	Poor
	Taurus	18/27	Low	Poor
Honda	Accord	24/30	High	Poor
Mercury	Sable	20/29	Low	Poor
Mitsubishi	Galant	21/27	High	Good
Oldsmobile	Cutlass Supreme	22/29	Low	Average
	Cutlass Ciera	23/31	Low	Average
Pontiac	6000	23/31	Low	Average
	Grand Prix	22/29	Low	Average
Toyota	Camry	26/34	High	Good

Sources: Table from **THE CAR BOOK** by Jack Gillis. Copyright ©1990 by Jack Gillis. Reprinted by permission of HarperCollins Publishers. Fuel-economy figures from the Environmental Protection Agency's *1990 Gas Mileage Guide.*

[a] Figures shown are for miles per gallon of gasoline, city/highway, for 1990 models with standard manual transmissions (unless manual transmission unavailable).

[b] Based on averages of basic, powertrain, and corrosion warranties; transfer fees; and deductibles.

in as soon as you can. The average car on the road gets under 20 miles per gallon, but some newer cars get at least 40, and many models get around 30.

COMMERCIAL PRODUCTS

Fuel-efficient models *(recommended).* Table 3 lists the most fuel-efficient cars now sold in the United States, as determined by the Environmental Protection Agency. Also included in the table are ratings for repair costs and warranties.

Alternative-fuel vehicles *(sometimes recommended).* Although alternative fuels are becoming more widely discussed, none has a serious chance of lessening the automobile's overall environmental damage (see Fuels, Auto, p. 45). Alternative fuels might, however, be advantageous for certain vehicles—such as buses in polluted urban areas.

Trucks and vans *(not generally recommended).* Most trucks and vans are much less fuel-efficient than cars. If you need one for hauling people or freight, check gas-mileage figures carefully before you buy.

ALTERNATIVES

Carpooling. Sharing rides, not only for work but also for shopping and recreation, can help break this country's one-car/one-person mentality.

Other transportation. Bicycling, walking, and taking the bus or train are all environmentally sound alternatives to driving. Learning and using local public-transportation systems and safe biking and walking routes might take a little effort and patience, but you'll save money and decrease your contribution to global pollution.

WISE USE

Regular maintenance. If you maintain your car properly, it will run more efficiently and last longer:

- Get your engine tuned up and adjusted every 10,000 miles; out-of-tune autos use much more gas. Newer cars do not need an annual tune-up but should be checked every year.

- Change the air, fuel, and oil filters as recommended by the manufacturer.

- Use a top-quality, multiviscosity motor oil to protect the engine (see Motor Oils, p. 48). Be sure to change the oil as recommended in your service manual.

- Have the brakes adjusted regularly, for both safety and gas economy.

- Choose high-mileage radial tires and check their pressure regularly (see Tires, p. 50).

Fuel-efficient driving. Driving habits can make a real difference to fuel economy:

- Drive smoothly and conservatively, accelerating gradually to moderate speeds.

- Never leave your car idling; restarting it uses less gas and produces less pollution.

- In cold weather warm the car engine for only a few minutes, as recommended in your service manual; that's enough to warm the engine and oil, if not the car's interior.

- Remove all heavy items from the car to increase your gas mileage.

FOR FURTHER INFORMATION: *The Car Book 1991,* by Jack Gillis; Harper & Row, 1990 (updated annually).

1. "Facts & Figures '90" (Motor Vehicle Manufacturers Association, P.O. Box 11170, Detroit, MI 48211), pp. 28, 52.
2. Ibid., p. 52.
3. Jon Luoma, "Crop Study Finds Severe Ozone Damage," *New York Times* (February 21, 1989).
4. Michael Renner, "Rethinking Transportation," *State of the World, 1989* (Norton, 1989), p. 108.
5. "Nucleus" (Union of Concerned Scientists, 26 Church St., Cambridge, MA 02138), p. 1.
6. "Facts and Figures '89," op. cit., p. 71.

BATTERIES, AUTO

An auto battery converts chemical energy into the electrical energy needed to start your car. Unfortunately, the 80 million batteries that need replacement each year in the United States are a major environmental hazard.

ENVIRONMENTAL PROBLEMS

Hazardous wastes. A typical auto battery holds about one gallon of extremely corrosive sulfuric acid and about 19 pounds of lead. Lead, a toxic metal, can accumulate in the body and cause nervous disorders, reduced production of red blood cells, and impaired mental development in children.[1] Only 80 percent of auto batteries are recycled, leaving another 16 million toxic cubes in the environment each year.[2] Burying them in landfills causes lead and acid to leach into the groundwater. Burning them in incinerators either spews lead into the air or condenses it into toxic ash.

Safety hazards. The advent of sealed car batteries, which keep the sulfuric acid from spilling out easily, has made batteries much safer. Still, burns and explosions can occur when batteries are dropped, opened improperly, or jump-started incorrectly.

CHOOSING A PRODUCT

GENERAL GUIDELINES

Long life. Look for a battery with a long warranty and, therefore, the likelihood of a longer life span.

Recent manufacture. Batteries often sit on store shelves for months or even years, losing performance power the whole time. Look for a battery manufactured no more than six months before you buy; ask the salesperson to decipher the production code stamped on each one.

COMMERCIAL PRODUCTS

Long-life batteries *(recommended)*. These batteries have warranties for 72 to 75 months (the standard is 30 to 60 months) and high cold-cranking power, which gives cars an extra boost on cold days. Although longer-life batteries are bigger and contain more lead and sulfuric acid, fewer must be manufactured and disposed. (Five 72-month batteries, for example, can replace six 60-month batteries.)

- Here are some widely available long-life batteries, with their warranty lengths and cold-cranking amps:

Brand	Warranty (months)	Cold-Cranking Amps
Exide 1000	84	1000
Exide Megatorque 75	75	675
Mastercraft Magnum 875	75	875
Mastercraft Ultra-tech 700	75	700
Ward's Auto Express 700/75	75	700
Ward's Auto Express 850/75	75	850
Delco Freedom Dura Power 72	72	650
GNB Champion CCA675	72	675
Napa The Power 9460	72	510
Sears DieHard Gold	72	690-900

Standard-life batteries *(not generally recommended)*. Because the average 30- to 60-month battery uses large amounts of resources and has a shorter usable life, it is not the best environmental choice.

WISE USE

Regular maintenance. You can prolong your battery's life by taking the following precautions.

- Check low-maintenance batteries (those that are not permanently sealed) periodically for fluid level; add distilled water when necessary.

- Keep terminals corrosion-free with a metal brush; if continued corrosion occurs, coat them with grease (heavy bearing grease, special terminal coatings, or petroleum jelly).

Safe jump-starting. If you use one car to start another car with a dead battery, avoid sparks or an explosion by following these steps:

1. Connect one red handle of the jumper cables to the positive terminal on the live battery.

2. Connect the other red handle to the positive terminal on the dead battery.

3. Connect one black handle to the *engine block* of the car with the live battery.

4. Connect the other black handle to the negative terminal on the dead battery.

5. Start the car with the dead battery.

6. Remove the cables in reverse order.

Never attempt to jump-start a battery that's frozen or very low on fluid.

Recycling. *Never* throw batteries away; recycle them instead:

- Before you buy a new battery, ask if the dealer will accept your old one in trade.

- If you cannot trade the battery in, ask your city or county waste disposal office about recycling it.

- If you must wait for a recycling pickup, store the battery safely in a cool, dry, protected place.

1. Mike Samuels and Hal Bennett, *Well Body, Well Earth* (Sierra Club Books, 1983), p. 153.
2. "Household Waste: Issues and Opportunities" (Concern, Inc., 1794 Columbia Rd. NW, Washington, DC 20009), p. 11.

FUELS, AUTO

Gasoline, once cheap and plentiful, has been the predominant fuel since cars were first mass-produced. Worsening pollution and rising petroleum costs, however, have prompted interest in alternative fuels. Unfortunately, no alternative fuel can solve the array of problems caused by our heavy use of automobiles.

ENVIRONMENTAL PROBLEMS

Fossil-fuel depletion. Except for ethanol, all auto fuels are made from petroleum, natural gas, or coal; using them depletes these valuable, nonrenewable resources.

Production impacts. Producing any automotive fuel causes environmental damage:

- *Petroleum*, the raw material for gasoline, diesel fuel, and some electricity, badly pollutes the air, water, and soil with hydrocarbons and other toxic substances (including radioactivity) as it's extracted, processed, transported, and used.

- Most *electricity* comes from plants that burn fossil fuels, which deplete nonrenewable resources and cause pollution; from hydroelectric dams, which destroy natural riverine ecosystems; and from nuclear reactors, which produce radioactive wastes and create contamination risks.

- *Methanol*, made from natural gas or coal, gives off huge amounts of carbon dioxide (CO_2), the greenhouse gas, during its production.

Air pollution. As they burn, gasoline and diesel fuel contaminate the air with pollutants such as carbon monoxide, lead, particulates, nitrogen oxides, and hydrocarbons. Carbon dioxide is produced in even greater quantities: burning one gallon of gasoline in a car releases about 20 pounds of CO_2.[1] Burning methanol releases fewer particulates and less CO_2 than gasoline, but does emit formaldehyde, a toxic and carcinogenic gas.

Groundwater pollution. Leaking petrochemical storage tanks pose a serious threat to groundwater; the federal government estimates that there are up to 100,000 leaking gasoline storage tanks across the United States.[2]

Safety hazards. Except for electricity, all automotive fuels are flammable and explosive, and release harmful vapors, creating serious risks to safety.

CHOOSING A PRODUCT

GENERAL GUIDELINES

Weighing your needs. Alternative fuels are being used experimentally around the United States; in most cases, however, they are unavailable or impractical for the average consumer.

Fuel efficiency. Far more important than your choice of fuel is the fuel efficiency of your auto and the amount of driving that you do. Before considering alternative fuels for your car, think about trading it in on a highly efficient gasoline model—and then driving it less.

COMMERCIAL PRODUCTS

(*Note:* No alternative fuels are widely available in the United States at this time, so rating them environmentally is impractical. Instead, each fuel is described, along with its advantages and disadvantages.)

Gasoline. Our nation's cars use gasoline at the rate of 70 billion gallons per year—over 500 gallons per vehicle.[3] Most of this gas is unleaded, because American cars are now equipped with catalytic converters to reduce pollution, and leaded gas ruins them. Gasoline has a very high capacity for storing energy, which allows you to travel long distances between refuelings. Even without lead, however, gasoline is one of our most harmful and polluting consumer products.

Diesel fuel. Diesel fuel is refined from crude oil after the lighter hydrocarbons used to make gasoline are removed. Though used mostly for very large engines, such as power generators, trucks, and locomotives, diesel fuel is also used in some autos. Diesel engines achieve high compression ratios, making fairly efficient use of the fuel's energy. Since diesel fuel consists of heavy hydrocarbons, however, high temperatures are required to evaporate it. This high-temperature burning emits large amounts of air pollutants, especially particulates and nitrogen oxides, and foul odors, dooming the future of diesel fuel.

Methanol. An experimental fuel made from natural gas or coal, methanol might become widely used in California as the state struggles with its air-pollution crisis. Methanol's raw materials are either cleaner (in the case of natural gas) or far more plentiful (in the case of coal) than petroleum. Methanol burns well in standard gasoline engines and has both a high octane level and low particulate emissions. It does, however, require special fuel lines and tanks because it eats through standard ones. It also takes up twice as much space in the fuel tank as gasoline, necessitating either a larger tank or more frequent fill-ups. When burned it emits formaldehyde, a pollutant that is toxic but odorless. Worst of all, methanol gives off significant carbon dioxide, the greenhouse gas, during its manufacture and use—double that of gasoline.[4]

Electricity. Powering cars with electricity produces no local pollution and could cut overall carbon dioxide emissions. Electric-car technology, however, is still primitive; the batteries are bulky and heavy, last for only short trips, and need frequent recharging. But even if better batteries are invented, electricity is neither efficient enough nor plentiful enough to replace gasoline on any significant scale; to do so would require greatly expanding our nation's electric-generating capacity. However, if you make primarily short daily trips in a dense urban area, electricity might work for you. GM and BMW are both producing electric cars; check with local dealers for information.

Natural gas. Natural gas is the most popular and widely available alternative fuel, is somewhat competitive in price with gasoline, and burns relatively cleanly. It can be used in gasoline engines (with some modifications) and cuts carbon dioxide emissions by up to 50 percent.[5] Although natural gas is low in most pollutants, it is thought to emit significant amounts of nitrogen oxide, a component of smog. Fuel tanks for natural gas also have some safety problems and provide less traveling distance per tank than gasoline. The major drawback to natural gas, however, is its impracticality: it is unavailable in some parts of the country and must be transported via pipelines, which are both expensive and environmentally destructive. Using natural gas widely as an automotive fuel would require major efforts to discover, drill, and pipe new sources. Natural gas can also be made synthetically, either from biomass (organic material) or from coal. Limited supplies, however, make using biomass impractical, while carbon dioxide emissions make using coal environmentally unsound.

Ethanol. The only fuel based on renewable resources, ethanol is made from corn, wheat, sugar beets, and other crops. It is typically added to gasoline without causing any engine damage or operating problems; it greatly reduces poisonous carbon monoxide emissions by adding oxygen to the gasoline, resulting in more complete combustion. Currently Americans use about 880 million gallons per year. Ethanol produces less carbon dioxide than gasoline, since the crops, while growing, absorb from the atmosphere the same amount of CO_2 that they later emit during combustion. Because it is a strong solvent, however, ethanol can damage parts in cars, especially older models. And huge amounts of plant material are needed to manufacture it: if just corn were used as a raw material, for example, we would need nearly 40 percent of our country's annual harvest to meet only 10 percent of our automotive-fuel needs.[6]

ALTERNATIVES

Alternative transportation. Riding mass-transit systems, bicycling, walking, and carpooling are more efficient ways of reducing pollution and using energy than are individual cars and trucks, regardless of fuel choice.

WISE USE

Fuel efficiency. Take every opportunity to reduce your fuel consumption: buy a fuel-efficient car, keep it well maintained, and drive wisely and less often (see Automobiles, p. 40).

Avoiding leaded gasoline. If you still run your car or other machinery with leaded gas, which produces poisonous lead, switch to unleaded. Most older cars run just as well on standard or high-octane unleaded gas.

Safe handling and storage. Automotive fuels are volatile and must be handled carefully:

- When pumping gasoline into your car, never keep pumping after the pump initially shuts off; the gasoline releases vapors which pollute the air and rags or other combustibles.

- Keep fuels away from any flames or heat sources and rags or other combustibles.

- Never let fuels come in contact with your skin, eyes, mouth, or mucous membranes.

- Store fuels properly, in tightly sealed, well-marked containers.

- *Never* pour any fuel down a drain or a sewer or onto the ground.

- Keep a fire extinguisher handy near any fuel, including in your automobile.

1. "Nucleus" (Union of Concerned Scientists, 26 Church St., Cambridge, MA 02138), p. 1.
2. John Elkington et al., *The Green Consumer* (Viking Penguin, 1990), p. 29.
3. "Facts & Figures '89" (Motor Vehicle Manufacturers Association, P.O. Box 11170, Detroit, MI 48211), pp. 52, 55.
4. Mark A. Deluchi et al., "Transportation Fuels and the Greenhouse Effect," *Transportation Research Record 1175* (1988), p. 41.
5. Ibid.
6. Lester Brown et al., *State of the World, 1989* (Norton, 1989), p. 102.

MOTOR OILS

Each year Americans cycle over 200 million gallons of motor oil through their vehicles; only about 10 percent of this product is recycled.[1]

ENVIRONMENTAL PROBLEMS

Soil and water pollution. Motor oil absorbs large amounts of hydrocarbons and other combustion byproducts from the engine, making used oil highly toxic. If this oil is dumped on the ground, in a landfill, or down a drain or sewer, it causes serious pollution. On the ground, oil first poisons any nearby plants, then slowly seeps down to the underlying groundwater. If dumped in water, 1 quart of motor oil can create an oil slick over two acres of water, or pollute 250,000 gallons of drinking water.[2]

Safety hazards. Used motor oil, which is a suspected carcinogen because of its combustion byproducts, can easily come into contact with skin during do-it-yourself oil changes.

Fossil-fuel depletion. Motor oil is a highly refined product made from petroleum. The hundreds of millions of gallons of oil used each year help deplete our limited supplies of this nonrenewable fossil fuel and add to the environmental costs of extracting, processing, and transporting it.

Wasteful packaging. Packaging oil in single-quart containers—either the older paper-and-metal cans or the newer plastic bottles—requires considerably more energy and resources than packaging it in gallon jugs.

CHOOSING A PRODUCT

GENERAL GUIDELINES

Weighing your needs. To save wear on your car, choose the right type and weight of motor oil for your car and climate or season.

Fuel efficiency. Make fuel efficiency a top priority. Look for brands that carry an energy-conservation "EC" code.

Sensible packaging. If you change your own oil, look for gallon containers instead of quarts to save on packaging materials.

COMMERCIAL PRODUCTS

Oil-change service centers *(highly recommended).* In environmental terms, having your oil changed at a service center is better than doing it yourself because the shops drain old oil efficiently, with no spills; recycle the old oil; and use large drums of new oil, saving vast amounts of packaging.

Re-refined motor oil *(highly recommended).* With special processing, old motor oil can be made usable again, meeting American Petroleum Institute quality standards for automobile engines. Look for API-approved re-refined oil at auto supply stores; Penn-Pride Recycled Motor Oil, SAE 10W30, is also available in one-gallon jugs from Seventh Generation, (800) 456-1177.

Reusable oil filters *(highly recommended).* Disposable oil filters made of aluminum, plastic, and paper are nearly impossible to recycle. One company, however, makes a reusable oil filter that adapts to fit virtually any car or light truck. The stainless-steel-mesh filter can be washed with soapy water and reused indefinitely. Order from System 1 Filter Systems, (800) 554-3533 or, in California, (800) 231-9137.

Oil-change tubs *(highly recommended).* You can buy special containers that collect the oil as it drains from your car and then seal tightly for transport to a recycler. Look for these containers in auto supply stores, or ask the manager to order the Pac-Lube Oil Changer, (503) 222-2343, or the Scott Oil Change Recycling Tub, (800) 321-2250.

Standard-brand motor oil *(recommended)*. Unless your car requires a special formula oil, look for energy-conserving motor oils with "EC" or "ECII" in the API codes on their labels. These oils slightly increase your car's fuel efficiency.

Long-life motor oil *(sometimes recommended)*. Mobil makes an oil with a longer life-span rating based on the oil's ability to resist breakdown. Even the most durable oil, however, has a life span limited by the metals, unburnt hydrocarbons, and other particles that accumulate in it, making it dirty and contributing to engine wear and pollution.

DO-IT-YOURSELF

Changing your own oil. Changing motor oil can be easy, economical, and safe for the environment *provided* you follow all safety and cleanup rules, buy your oil in large containers, and recycle the used oil.

WISE USE

Regular oil changes. Most auto manufacturers suggest changing your oil every 6,000 miles or so to minimize wear on engine parts. Some professionals, however, suggest changing it every 3,000 miles if you take many long, high-engine-temperature trips.

Safe oil changes. If you change your own oil, do it properly:

- Carefully drain the oil from the crankcase and oil filter into a pan or special container.

- If you inadvertently spill some oil, soak it up with an absorbent material such as cat litter. Dispose of this material at a hazardous waste collection center.

- Remember, used oil is toxic because of the contaminants it contains. Try not to get it on your skin; if you do, wash it off thoroughly.

Recycling. *Never* dispose of old oil by throwing it in the trash or by pouring it on the ground, in the street, or down the drain or sewer. Old motor oil is a valuable product; it can be reprocessed back into motor oil or into other lubricants, fuel, coatings, or preservatives. Recycling also prevents the soil and water pollution caused by careless disposal.

- Collect used oil in a closable container, such as an empty gallon jug, and call your local recycling center or waste disposal agency for collection points.

- If there is no community collection program, call service stations, oil-change centers, or the place you bought your oil. (Some places charge a small fee for accepting used oil.)

1. "Household Waste: Issues and Opportunities" (Concern, Inc., 1794 Columbia Rd. NW, Washington, DC 20009), p. 9.
2. Ibid.

TIRES

Tires are an indispensable part of an automobile, but they're also an environmental headache.

ENVIRONMENTAL PROBLEMS

Manufacturing impacts. Tires are complicated, high-technology products made from natural and synthetic rubber and other compounds, reinforced with layers of steel and synthetic fibers. Manufacturing tires requires large amounts of energy and raw materials and generates significant air and water pollution.

Air pollution. As tires wear, tiny bits of rubber fly into the air and remain suspended, creating particulates that contribute significantly to air pollution in areas with heavy traffic. Older bias-ply tires are the worst offenders.

Disposal problems. Americans throw out tires at the rate of one per person every year, and recycling possibilities (such as burning to generate electricity or shredding for reuse) are only starting to evolve.[1] When buried in landfills tires often work their way back to the surface, and when stored above ground they fill with water and create an ideal breeding ground for mosquitoes. Tire dumps are also a serious fire hazard; once alight tires can burn for months.

CHOOSING A PRODUCT

GENERAL GUIDELINES

Quality. The highest-quality radial tires you can find are the best choice for both the environment and your family's safety. Longer-wearing tires mean less air pollution and fewer tires to be manufactured and discarded. And over the long term, they might even save you money.

COMMERCIAL PRODUCTS

Radials *(highly recommended).* Radial tires last longest and cause the least pollution. Table 4 lists the longest-wearing radial tires for cars and light trucks sold in the United States.

Retreads *(sometimes recommended).* If you rarely drive your car, consider outfitting it with high-quality retreads. Retreads reuse the cores of old tires, saving important energy and raw materials. The National Tire Dealers and Retreaders Association, an industry group, rates retreads from A to F. Be sure to ask the dealer for a rating before buying retreads; purchase only those with an A or B rating.

Bias-ply tires *(never recommended).* These tires wear much more quickly than radials and pollute the air badly during their short life.

WISE USE

Regular maintenance. Take good care of your tires for longer tire life and better gas mileage:

- Check the air pressure frequently.

- Rotate the tires regularly.

- Have the wheel alignment checked at the first sign of uneven wear.

FOR FURTHER INFORMATION: Auto Safety Hotline, (800) 424-9393.

---

1. "Household Waste: Issues and Opportunities" (Concern, Inc., 1794 Columbia Rd. NW, Washington, DC 20009), p. 10.

TABLE
4

THE LONGEST-WEARING RADIAL TIRES

Brand	Model	Size	Trac.	Heat	Tread	Estimated Mileage[b]
				Ratings[a]		
General	Ameri Classic	15	A	B	400	60,000–120,000
Armstrong	Five Star	15	A	B	370	55,500–111,000
Dunlop	Elite	All	A	B	370	55,500–111,000
Kelly	Voyager 1000	All	A	B	370	55,500–111,000
Arizonian	Silver Edition	14 & 15	A	B	360	54,000–108,000
Centennial	Constitution	All	A	B	360	54,000–108,000
Cordovan	Grand Prix SE	All	A	B	360	54,000–108,000
Cornell	1000	14 & 15	B	B	360	54,000–108,000
Hallmark	Ultimate PSR	14 & 15	A	C	360	54,000–108,000
Kumho	Centurion	14 & 15	A	C	360	54,000–108,000
Lee	GT V Trak	14 & 15	A	B	360	54,000–108,000
Monarch	Ultra STL Trac	14 & 15	A	B	360	54,000–108,000
Remington	Society	All	A	B	360	54,000–108,000
Star	Centurion PSR	14 & 15	A	C	360	54,000–108,000
Armstrong	Five Star	14	A	B	350	52,500–104,000
Atlas	Pinnacle 70	All	A	B	350	52,500–104,000
Cooper	Lifeliner	14 & 15	B	C	350	52,500–104,000
	Lifeliner SR	All	A	B	350	52,500–104,000
Dean	AST Steel	14 & 15	B	C	350	52,500–104,000
	Quasar	All	A	B	350	52,500–104,000
Duralon	IV Plus	All	A	B	350	52,500–104,000
El Dorado	Crusader	All	A	B	350	52,500–104,000
	Odyssey	14 & 15	B	C	350	52,500–104,000
Falls	Mastercraft	14 & 15	B	C	350	52,500–104,000
	Mastercraft SR	All	A	B	350	52,500–104,000
General	Ameri Classic	14	A	B	350	52,500–104,000
Gillette	Peerless/ Kodiak +4	70 Series	A	B	350	52,500–104,000
Hercules	Ultrapreme	14 & 15	B	C	350	52,500–104,000
	Ultra Plus	All	A	B	350	52,500–104,000
Kleber	CP70S	All	A	B	350	52,500–104,000
Mohawk	Millenium	14 & 15	A	B	350	52,500–104,000
Sigma	Supreme 70SE	All	A	B	350	52,500–104,000
	Supreme 80SE, 75SE	14 & 15	B	C	350	52,500–104,000
Starfire	Spectrum SRW	All	A	B	350	52,500–104,000
	Spectrum	14&15	B	C	350	52,500–104,000
Dayton	S/R	13	A	B	340	51,000–102,000
Gillette	Sprint G/T	13	A	B	340	51,000–102,000
Road King	Widetrack S/R	13	A	B	340	51,000–102,000
Armstrong	Five Star	13	A	B	330	49,500–99,000
Firestone	FR480	All	A	B	330	49,500–99,000
General	Ameri Classic	13	A	B	330	49,500–99,000
Michelin	XH	All	A	B	330	49,500–99,000
Mohawk	Millenium	13	A	B	330	49,500–99,000
Sumitomo	SC660	All	A	B	330	49,500–99,000
Arizonian	Silver Edition	13	A	B	320	48,000–96,000
	Silver Edition	14 & 15	A	B	320	48,000–96,000

(continued on next page)

TABLE

4

THE LONGEST-WEARING RADIAL TIRES (continued)

| Brand | Model | Size | Ratings[a] | | | Estimated Mileage[b] |
			Trac.	Heat	Tread	
Aurora	R838	All	B	C	320	48,000–96,000
CBI	Pacemaker	All	A	C	320	48,000–96,000
	Redline H/T	All	A	C	320	48,000–96,000
Co-op	Pacemaker SR60, 70	All	A	C	320	48,000–96,000
Cordovan	Grand Prix G/T 60, 70	All	A	C	320	48,000–96,000
Cornell	1000	13	A	B	320	48,000–96,000
	SS G/T	All	A	C	320	48,000–96,000
Dayton	S/R	15	A	B	320	48,000–96,000
Doral	Revenger HP	All	A	C	320	48,000–96,000
Douglas	Premium	13	A	B	320	48,000–96,000
	Grand Trac	All	A	C	320	48,000–96,000
Gillette	Sprint G/T	15	A	B	320	48,000–96,000
Hallmark	Centurion	All	A	C	320	48,000–96,000
	Super GT Sport	All	A	C	320	48,000–96,000
	Ultimate PSR	13	A	C	320	48,000–96,000
Jetzon	Import Metric	13	B	C	320	48,000–96,000
	S-Revenger 60, 65, 70	All	A	C	320	48,000–96,000
Kelly	Charger SR	All	A	C	320	48,000–96,000
Lee	GT V Trak	13	A	B	320	48,000–96,000
	Turbo Action	All	A	C	320	48,000–96,000
Monarch	Road Hugger	All	A	C	320	48,000–96,000
	Ultra STL Trac	13	A	B	320	48,000–96,000
Montgomery Ward	Gas Miser 70	All	A	C	320	48,000–96,000
NTP	Pacemark SR	All	A	C	320	48,000–96,000
Patriot	Performance 60-70	13, 14 & 15	A	C	320	48,000–96,000
Peerless	Sprint	All	A	C	320	48,000–96,000
Pos-A-Traction	Twister	All	A	C	320	48,000–96,000
Ram	Invader	All	A	C	320	48,000–96,000
Road King	Widetrack S/R	15	A	B	320	48,000–96,000
Shell	60, 65, 70	All	A	C	320	48,000–96,000
Sigma	Grand Sport G/T 60-70	All	A	C	320	48,000–96,000
Star	Centurion HP	All	A	C	320	48,000–96,000
	Centurion PSR	13	A	C	320	48,000–96,000
	Super Star SR	All	A	C	320	48,000–96,000
Vanderbilt	Turbo Tech SR 60-70	All	A	C	320	48,000–96,000
Vogue	Custom	14 & 15	B	C	320	48,000–96,000
Winston	Signature SR	All	A	C	320	48,000–96,000
	RWL 60,70	All	A	C	320	48,000–96,000
Firestone	Triumph 4000	All	A	C	310	46,500–93,000
Goodrich	T/A 60, 65,	14 & 15	A	C	310	46,500–93,000
Michelin	XA4, XZ4	All	A	B	310	46,500–93,000
Sears	RD Handler 70S	All	A	B	310	46,500–93,000

TABLE 4

THE LONGEST-WEARING RADIAL TIRES *(continued)*

| Brand | Model | Size | Ratings[a] | | | Estimated Mileage[b] |
			Trac.	Heat	Tread	
Uniroyal	Tiger Paw XTM Gold	All	B	C	310	46,500–93,000
	Tiger Paw XTM	14 & 15	B	C	310	46,500–93,000
Atlas	Pinnacle 75/80	14 & 15	A	B	300	45,000–90,000
	Radial A/W	All	B	B	300	45,000–90,000
	Roadhawk GT	P215/ 65R15	B	B	300	45,000–90,000
Big-O	Legacy II	14 & 15	B	C	300	45,000–90,000
CBI	Classic	All	A	B	300	45,000–90,000
Co-op	Co-operator	15	B	C	300	45,000–90,000
Cooper	Cobra 65 SR	15	B	B	300	45,000–90,000
	Discoverer	All	B	B	300	45,000–90,000
	Monogram	14 & 15	A	B	300	45,000–90,000
Cordovan	Wild Trac RTV	All	A	B	300	45,000–90,000
	Grand Prix SE70	14 & 15	A	C	300	45,000–90,000
Cornell	900	14 & 15	A	B	300	45,000–90,000
Dayton	Triple Crown	All	A	C	300	45,000–90,000
	S/R	14	A	B	300	45,000–90,000
Dean	Stinger 65 SR	15	B	B	300	45,000–90,000
	Starstream SR	14 & 15	A	B	300	45,000–90,000
Dunlop	Axiom	15	A	B	300	45,000–90,000
Duralon	IV	All	A	C	300	45,000–90,000
El Dorado	Wide Boss	All	B	B	300	45,000–90,000
	GT 65	15	B	B	300	45,000–90,000
	Marquis	14 & 15	A	B	300	45,000–90,000
Empco	Supreme	14 & 15	B	C	300	45,000–90,000
	Techna	14 & 15	B	C	300	45,000–90,000
Escort	Premium 5000	14 & 15	B	C	300	45,000–90,000
	SLX 5000	14 & 15	B	C	300	45,000–90,000
Falls	Mastercraft Custom	14 & 15	A	B	300	45,000–90,000
Falls	Courser	All	B	B	300	45,000–90,000
	Starfire 65	15	B	B	300	45,000–90,000
Firestone	Regency L	All	A	C	300	45,000–90,000
	FR721	All	A	C	300	45,000–90,000
Frontier	Performance	14 & 15	A	B	300	45,000–90,000
	SR-1000 185/195	14	A	B	300	45,000–90,000
General	Ameri Tech 4	All	B	B	300	45,000–90,000
	Ameri Way SE	All	B	B	300	45,000–90,000
	XP 2000	14 & 15	B	C	300	45,000–90,000
Gillette	Peerless/ Kodiak +4	75 Series	A	C	300	45,000–90,000
	Sprint G/T	14	A	B	300	45,000–90,000
Goodrich	Advantage	14 & 15	A	C	300	45,000–90,000
	T/A 50S	14 & 15	A	C	300	45,000–90,000
	T/A HR60, 65, 70H	14 & 15	A	A	300	45,000–90,000
	Euro T/A 60, 65H	14 & 15	A	A	300	45,000–90,000

(continued on next page)

TABLE
4

THE LONGEST-WEARING RADIAL TIRES (continued)

Brand	Model	Size	Ratings[a] Trac.	Heat	Tread	Estimated Mileage[b]
Hallmark	Trail Buster	All	A	B	300	45,000–90,000
Hercules	Superior Mega IV	All	A	B	300	45,000–90,000
	MR1	14 & 15	A	B	300	45,000–90,000
	Terra Trac	All	B	B	300	45,000–90,000
	HP 4000 SR 65	All	B	B	300	45,000–90,000
Kelly	Safari AWR	All	A	B	300	45,000–90,000
Kleber	CP75S	14 & 15	A	B	300	45,000–90,000
Kumho	79H, 788	All	A	B	300	45,000–90,000
Medalist	Modifier	14 & 15	A	C	300	45,000–90,000
Mohawk	Performance SR1000	14 & 15	A	B	300	45,000–90,000
	Premium	15	A	B	300	45,000–90,000
Montgomery Ward	Spectra	14 & 15	B	C	300	45,000–90,000
Multi-Mile	Grand Am SE70	14 & 15	A	C	300	45,000–90,000
	Wild Ctry RVT	All	A	B	300	45,000–90,000
Ohtsu	Hi-Steel 301, PAS 610	14 & 15	B	B	300	45,000–90,000
Phillips	66XPR	14 & 15	B	C	300	45,000–90,000
Pos-A-Traction	Miramas SPR-60	All	A	B	300	45,000–90,000
Road King	Widetrack S/R	14	A	B	300	45,000–90,000
Shell	2000	All	A	C	300	45,000–90,000
Sigma	Grand Sport SE70	14 & 15	A	C	300	45,000–90,000
Sonic	Golden	14 & 15	B	C	300	45,000–90,000
	Maxima GTS	13	B	C	300	45,000–90,000
Sumitomo	SC870	All	B	B	300	45,000–90,000
	HTR 70	14 & 15	A	A	300	45,000–90,000
Star	Trail Buster APR	All	A	B	300	45,000–90,000
Starfire	Vantage	14 & 15	A	B	300	45,000–90,000
Tire Brands	Golden	14 & 15	B	C	300	45,000–90,000
Toyo	800	13 & 14	B	B	300	45,000–90,000
	800 P-70	15	A	B	300	45,000–90,000
Ultrax	GTS	14 & 15	B	C	300	45,000–90,000
Winston	Classic	All	A	B	300	45,000–90,000

Source: *Uniform Tire Quality Grading* (National Highway Traffic Safety Administration, U.S. Department of Transportation, revised ed., 1989).

[a] *Traction* (Trac.) represents the tire's ability to stop on wet pavement when brakes are applied; a rating of A indicates best traction. *Heat resistance* (Heat) is the tire's ability to dissipate heat, avoiding high temperature buildups that can shorten tire life or lead to sudden tire failure; a rating of A indicates the best heat resistance. *Treadwear* (Tread) grade is a comparative rating based on the wear rate of specific tires tested under controlled conditions: a rating of 100 is set as the comparison standard; a rating of 300 indicates a tire will last about three times longer than the standard. Ratings do not apply to deep-tread snow tires.

[b] Estimated mileage is based on the tire's treadwear rating and can vary widely, depending on climate, terrain, driving habits, service practices, and other conditions.

FOODS AND
BEVERAGES

BEEF

Beef, the all-American food, conjures up pictures of the family backyard, grilling, and a wholesome, healthy life. But the production and consumption of this satisfying, high-protein staple does significant damage to the environment and can contribute to serious health problems.

ENVIRONMENTAL PROBLEMS

Grazing and overgrazing. Even well-controlled cattle grazing causes massive changes in the landscape: complex natural communities of trees, grasses, wildflowers, and wildlife are replaced by very limited communities of grasses, weeds, and cattle. And in areas where overgrazing occurs—such as in many impoverished parts of the world—soil erosion quickly follows. Soil erosion is devastating in areas where the soil is poor to begin with; once the fertile topsoil is gone, these areas can no longer be used for either grazing or farming.

Rainforest destruction. Foreign demand for beef has triggered the burning of huge areas of tropical rainforest to make room for short-term grazing land. This change takes place at the expense of native people's livelihoods and uncounted and even unknown species of plants and animals. Because the rainforests are storehouses for carbon dioxide and producers of oxygen, burning them increases the threat of global warming.

Inefficient use of resources. Beef might be a great source of protein, but raising a steer is not an efficient way to produce it. Most American beef cattle are fed grain and grass until they are about a year old. Then they go to a feedlot, where each one eats about 2,500 pounds of grain and 350 pounds of soybeans—about 16 pounds for every pound of beef it produces.[1] The grain needed to produce a single pound of meat requires up to 2,500 gallons of water.[2]

Water pollution. Some of the chemicals used in raising cattle (in their feed and to keep them healthy) pollute surface water and groundwater, as do the huge volumes of animal wastes generated at feedlots.

Animal cruelty. The beef industry's main concern is production, not the humane treatment of animals. Calves are confined in tiny pens to make veal. All commercial beef cattle are kept for months in crowded feedlots, after which they make a journey in cramped trucks or boxcars to slaughterhouses, where they are slaughtered while still conscious.

Chemical use. Forty percent of our country's output of antibiotics is used to try to keep animals healthy under distinctly unhealthy conditions.[3] Overuse of antibiotics can lead to the development of antibiotic-resistant strains of bacteria. Food poisoning in people caused by antibiotic-resistant bacteria can be difficult to treat. For a person with an infection who is already taking antibiotics, eating meat containing antibiotic-resistant bacteria can be especially dangerous. Antimicrobial sulfa drugs are also used to keep animals healthy; meat contaminated with these drugs can cause severe allergic reactions in some individuals.[4]

Hormone use. Most beef cattle are given hormones; in their final three months, steers have hormone pellets implanted in their ears to make them gain weight faster. American researchers have not found these hormones to be carcinogenic, but European nations, citing earlier hormones that did prove carcinogenic, have banned imports of American beef containing hormones. No such bans are in effect in the United States.[5]

Health risks. Beef contains high levels of saturated fat and cholesterol, making it a major contributor to heart disease.

Processing and additives. Highly processed products, such as lunch meat and hot dogs, require energy to manufacture and contain unhealthy added fat, sodium, and chemicals.

Wasteful packaging. Beef is usually wrapped in plastic and placed on Styrofoam trays, both of which are environmentally costly to manufacture and impractical to recycle.

CHOOSING A PRODUCT

GENERAL GUIDELINES

Natural, humane beef-raising practices. Look for beef raised in a humane, healthy, and chemical-free environment.

Moderation. For your health's sake and the planet's, consider alternative sources of protein. Buy beef only in moderation.

Minimal processing. Instead of wasteful and unhealthy lunch meats, hot dogs, and other processed beef products, buy unprocessed cuts of meat.

Lean cuts. To avoid unhealthy fat, choose lean cuts.

Sensible packaging. Instead of buying beef wrapped in wasteful plastic and placed on Styrofoam trays, shop at markets where butchers will wrap your meat in paper. If paper is not an option, choose products vacuum-packed in plastic over those on Styrofoam trays.

COMMERCIAL PRODUCTS

Small-scale producers *(sometimes recommended)*. Look for local suppliers that offer organically raised or chemical-free beef; co-ops and natural foods stores are good sources of information. Ask how the animals are raised; cattle raised on a small farm might be treated more humanely than those in a large commercial feedlot. Look for the following labels:

- *Natural* usually means raised without drugs.

- *Organically raised* implies that the feed has no chemical additives (but not necessarily that the feed itself is organically grown) and that the cattle received no antibiotics, growth regulators, or other drugs.

Large-scale producers *(not generally recommended)*. All large-scale, commercial beef producers use chemicals and many inhumane practices; avoid them whenever possible.

ALTERNATIVES

Vegetarian cuisine. Many vegetarian foods—including tofu and tempeh, both made from soybeans—combine high protein, nutrition, and excellent flavor and involve no animal cruelty. Eating them is good for the environment because they are low on the planet's food chain. (See Fruits and Vegetables, p. 60; Grains and Grain Products, p. 64.)

Poultry, fish, and shellfish. These foods are lower than beef on the earth's food chain and are much more efficient sources of protein. (See Poultry and Eggs, p. 74; Fish and Shellfish, p. 58.)

WISE USE

Conservative use. Eat small portions of beef and don't let any go to waste. Use bones from a roast, for example, to make soup. Such efficient use will help your grocery budget, too.

FOR FURTHER INFORMATION: Diet for a Small Planet, by Frances Moore Lappé; Ballantine, 1985. *Diet for a New America*, by John Robbins; Stillpoint, 1987.

1. Jacques Yves Cousteau, *The Cousteau Almanac* (Doubleday, 1981), p. 210.
2. John Robbins, *Diet for a New America* (Stillpoint, 1987), p. 367.
3. Cousteau, op. cit., p. 210.
4. Patrick G. Marshall, "How Safe Is Your Food?" *Editorial Research Reports* (November 18, 1988), p. 588.
5. Gina Kolata, "Many Fear Widening of Beef Dispute," *New York Times* (January 1, 1989).

FISH AND SHELLFISH

Americans currently eat less than 20 pounds of fish per person annually, while they eat over 150 pounds of meat.[1] Health concerns, however, have been increasing our consumption of fish; unlike beef, fish is a low-fat, low-cholesterol source of protein, and some researchers believe that the natural oils in fish have a beneficial effect on the heart.[2] Eating fish, however, can cause other health problems, and harvesting them can do environmental damage.

ENVIRONMENTAL PROBLEMS

Chemical contamination. Many fish and shellfish consumed in the United States come from polluted waters and carry traces—or sometimes dangerous amounts—of pesticides, industrial and agricultural chemicals, heavy metals, and other contaminants. Some states warn residents to follow strict guidelines on the amounts or types of local fish they eat. Pollutants build up to especially dangerous levels in large fish that swim in highly polluted waters, and in shellfish, which are unable to swim away from pollutants.

Bacteria and parasites. Fish and shellfish are far more likely to be contaminated with bacteria and parasites than are beef, poultry, and pork, according to the Centers for Disease Control.[3] Fish and shellfish harbor natural parasites and spoil easily; most food-poisoning cases are caused by improper storage or inadequate cooking.

Fishing impacts. Some large-scale fishing practices cause serious environmental damage:

- For years thousands of dolphins were killed in nets used for yellowfin tuna. In response to continued public pressure, the three major tuna producers announced in 1990 that they would buy only tuna caught in dolphin-safe nets and that the Earth Island Institute would monitor fleets for compliance.

- Shrimp fishing in the southeast United States kills vast numbers of sea turtles that get caught in the nets and drown. The National Marine Fisheries Service reports that of 48,000 turtles caught in nets each year, 11,000 die. All six species of these turtles are endangered or threatened. A 1988 federal law requiring turtle excluders in shrimp nets is bitterly opposed by shrimpers and weakly enforced.[4]

- Miles-long drift nets used in ocean fishing snare everything in their path and feed their catch to factory processing ships. The long-term effects of this fishing technique—the equivalent of clear-cutting a forest—have not been determined.

Processing and additives. Highly processed products such as fish sticks require energy to process and contain unhealthy added fat, sodium, and chemicals.

Wasteful packaging. Fish is usually wrapped in plastic and placed on Styrofoam trays, both of which are environmentally costly to manufacture and impractical to recycle. Processed fish products come in similarly costly and nonrecyclable packaging, such as coated boxes.

CHOOSING A PRODUCT

GENERAL GUIDELINES

Known sources. Know the source of the fish or shellfish you buy:

- Shop at a reliable market where you can ask about the source of particular fish.

- For local and regional fish, inquire at your state health department about health or environmental concerns.

Minimal processing. Instead of wasteful and unhealthy processed fish products such as fish sticks, buy plain fillets or whole fish.

Sensible packaging. Instead of buying fish wrapped in wasteful plastic and placed on Styrofoam trays, shop at markets where butchers will wrap your fish in paper. If paper is not an option, choose products vacuum-packed in plastic over those on Styrofoam trays.

COMMERCIAL PRODUCTS

Saltwater fish *(recommended)*. These fish are caught mostly in deep, cold ocean waters and are considered to be the least contaminated from industrial pollution:

anchovies	pompano
butterfish	red snapper
cod	sablefish
flounder	salmon
haddock	sardines
hake	scrod
halibut	sole
herring	squid
mackerel	tilefish
ocean perch	tuna
pollack	yellowtail snapper

Freshwater fish *(sometimes recommended)*. Freshwater fish are more likely to be contaminated with industrial toxins than ocean fish.[5] Determine the sources of freshwater species before buying them (including saltwater fish that live near shore or spend time in fresh water):

- High-quality markets will know the sources of all fish they sell and which species are liable to be contaminated.

- Some states issue guidelines about types and amounts of fish that are safe to eat; check with your state health department.

- Farm-raised fish are generally free from industrial pollutants.

Look for small, young fish; they have had less time to absorb contaminants. Fish species with low fat levels are considered safer because many chemicals tend to accumulate in fat. Among the more popular freshwater fish with a low fat content are the following:

bass	rainbow trout
brook trout	white perch
lake trout	yellow perch
lake whitefish	

Shellfish *(sometimes recommended)*. Saltwater and freshwater shellfish such as lobster, crabs, clams, scallops, oysters, and mussels are filter feeders that absorb the chemical contaminants in the water they process. Unless you know the exact source of these species, limit consumption of them to an occasional meal.

Shrimp *(currently not recommended)*. Until the sea turtle issue has been resolved, you should either avoid shrimp altogether or verify that turtle-excluder nets were used to catch them.

DO-IT-YOURSELF

Catching your own. An easy way to know the source of fish is to catch them yourself, but check first with your state's wildlife and fisheries agency if you are unsure of the water's purity. A general rule regarding sport fish and possible contamination: throw back the larger fish and eat only the smaller ones.

ALTERNATIVES

Fish-oil supplements. These supplements have gained in popularity since researchers reported that eating fish helps fight heart disease. Their effectiveness compared with eating fish has not yet been confirmed.

Vegetarian cuisine. Many vegetarian foods—including tofu and tempeh, both made from soybeans—combine high protein, nutrition, and excellent flavor and involve no animal cruelty. Eating them is good for the environment because they are low on the planet's food chain. (See Fruits and Vegetables, p. 60; Grains and Grain Products, p. 64.)

WISE USE

Moderate use. High in protein and other nutrients, fish should be eaten in small portions. Three or four ounces as a course for a meal provides ample protein, and poses less risk of contamination.

Thorough cooking. To avoid food poisoning be sure to cook fresh or frozen fish thoroughly. Pay special attention to the following, which are most likely to carry bacteria or viruses:

amber jack	red snapper
barracuda	sea bass
bonita	shellfish
grouper	swordfish
mackerel	

Fat removal. If you are preparing a whole fish for cooking (or for eating after it has been cooked whole), carefully cut away the skin and fat deposits, where many toxic chemicals accumulate. Fat deposits, which tend to be brown-colored, run in streaks along the top, bottom, and sides of the body of the fish. Avoid also the green-colored tomalley, or liver, in lobster.

Proper storage. Be sure not to refreeze thawed fish; cook it as soon as possible after thawing.

FOR FURTHER INFORMATION: Safe Food, by Michaelson Jacobson et al.; Center for Science in the Public Interest/Living Planet Press, 1991.

1. Sarah Glazer, "How America Eats," *Editorial Research Reports* (April 29, 1988), pp. 220–221.
2. Jane E. Brody, "Fish Diet Fights Heart Disease, Study Confirms," *New York Times* (November 9, 1989).
3. Patrick G. Marshall, "How Safe Is Your Food?" *Editorial Research Reports* (November 18, 1988), p. 588.
4. Jack and Anne Rudloe, "Shrimpers and Lawmakers Collide over a Move to Save the Sea Turtles," *Smithsonian* (December 1989), p. 47.
5. Jane E. Brody, "Personal Health," *New York Times* (June 12, 1991).

FRUITS AND VEGETABLES

In general the more fruits and vegetables we eat, the better; they are excellent sources of essential vitamins, minerals, fiber, and water. Unfortunately, most commercial produce contains added substances we don't need.

ENVIRONMENTAL PROBLEMS

Chemical use. Every year our nation's farmers use more than 1.5 billion pounds of pesticides to kill fungi, bugs, and weeds; control rodents; or simply make the end product look better.[1] These chemicals pollute both soil and groundwater and make soil and crops dependent on them. They can also end up in our food. The Environmental Protection Agency has identified 55 cancer-causing pesticides that sometimes leave residues in food, calling pesticide use one of the country's worst health and environmental problems.[2] Besides cancer, pesticide-related health risks include birth defects, miscarriages, genetic mutations, and sterility. Consumers are not the only ones threatened; farm workers who handle and apply these chemicals are at far greater risk.

Long-distance shipping. Long-distance transport consumes fossil fuels and causes air pollution. Areas with cold climates depend on long-distance shipping to supply their winter produce; there is really no feasible alternative for most items. But long-distance shipping makes little sense during the warm season, when most fruits and vegetables can be produced locally.

Processing and additives. The natural wholesomeness of fruits and vegetables—to say nothing of their delicate flavor—can be adulterated when processed into the products we see in the store:

- Some fresh produce is covered with a synthetic, waxlike coating to enhance its cosmetic appeal and prolong its freshness. This coating makes the product's vitamin- and mineral-rich skin unpleasant or even unhealthy to eat.

■ Canned or frozen fruits and vegetables often have added sodium, sugar, artificial colors or flavors, and other substances that add nothing to—and in some cases detract from—the food's nutritional value.

Wasteful packaging. Fruits and vegetables are often packaged in Styrofoam trays with plastic wraps, plastic bags, and plastic nets—materials that are petroleum-derived and virtually nonrecyclable. Processed fruits and vegetables are usually canned or frozen and are sometimes overpackaged in nonrecyclable materials, such as plastic single-serving containers or small waxed-paper boxes.

CHOOSING A PRODUCT

GENERAL GUIDELINES

Fresh, organic produce. Buy organic produce whenever possible and insist on fresh, crisp food.

Local sources. Look for locally grown produce at farmers' markets, co-ops, stores, and pick-your-own farms. You'll get fresh produce from known sources, and you'll save the environmental costs of packaging and long-distance transport.

Sensible packaging. Avoid prepackaged fresh produce; if it is not available without packaging, change stores or talk to the produce manager. Use cloth or mesh bags or reuse plastic carrying bags. For processed fruits and vegetables (canned or frozen), choose brands with sensible, recyclable packaging; glass jars are good choices.

COMMERCIAL PRODUCTS

Organically grown produce *(highly recommended).* Organically grown produce is raised without chemical fertilizers or pesticides. It often costs more than commercially grown produce but is usually fresh and flavorful and carries the lowest threat of chemical residues. Check co-ops and farmers' markets for sources, and look for the "organic" label (see Organic Foods, p. 68).

Nonorganically grown produce *(sometimes recommended).* This produce is grown with chemical fertilizers and pesticides, so look for fruits and vegetables that are less likely to contain residues or that have residues you can wash off (see Table 5). Try to pick domestically grown produce, which has both a much lower incidence of chemical-residue problems (38 percent of Food and Drug Administration samples) than does imported produce (64 percent)[3] and lower transportation costs.

Canned and frozen produce *(sometimes recommended).* Look for products with no added sodium, sugar, coloring, preservatives, or other chemicals. Buy organic canned or frozen produce whenever possible. And check for recyclable packaging materials.

California grapes *(currently not recommended).* California's United Farm Workers union has called another long-term grape boycott to push for safer working conditions, including abandonment of highly toxic agricultural chemicals still in use.

DO-IT-YOURSELF

Gardening. Organically grown fruit trees, berry bushes, and vegetable gardens are an economical source of healthy, chemical-free food.

Home preserving. Home canning, freezing, and drying allow you to enjoy warm-weather fruits and vegetables throughout the year; they also let you make the most of locally or home-grown produce.

TABLE
5

PESTICIDES ON FRUITS AND VEGETABLES

Food	Percent of Food Samples with Pesticide Residues[a]		Hazardous Pesticides	Can Residues Be Reduced by Washing?
	Imported	Domestic		
Apples	53%	48%	Captan	Yes
			Phosmet	Yes
Bananas	2%	0%	Carbaryl	Yes
			Diazinon	Unknown
Bell peppers	81%	30%	Acephate	No
			Dimethoate	Unknown
Broccoli	33%	14%	Parathion	Unknown
			Dimethoate	Unknown
Cabbage	53%	20%	Permethrin	Yes
			BHC	Unknown
			Dimethoate	Unknown
Cantaloupes	78%	11%	Chlorothalonil	Yes
			Methyl-Parathion	Unknown
			Dimethoate	Unknown
Carrots	58%	46%	DDT[b]	Yes
			Trifluralin	No
			Parathion	Unknown
			Dieldrin[b]	Unknown
			Diazinon	Unknown
Cauliflower	16%	2%	Chlorothalonil	Yes
			Diazinon	Unknown
			Dimethoate	Unknown
Celery	75%	72%	Chlorothalonil	Yes
			Acephate	No
Cherries	65%	62%	Parathion	Unknown
			Captan	Yes
			Diazinon	Unknown
Corn	5%	1%	Sulfallate	Unknown
			Dieldrin[b]	Unknown
			Lindane	Unknown
			Carbaryl	Yes
Cucumbers	80%	30%	Dieldrin[b]	Unknown
			Dimethoate	Unknown
Grapefruit	52%	63%	Carbaryl	Yes
Grapes	44%	28%	Captan	Yes
			Carbaryl	Yes
			Dimethoate	Unknown
Green Beans	46%	27%	Acephate	No
			Chlorothalonil	Yes
			Dimethoate	Unknown
Lettuce	57%	52%	Permethrin	Yes
			Dimethoate	Unknown

TABLE 5

PESTICIDES ON FRUITS AND VEGETABLES *(continued)*

Food	Percent of Food Samples with Pesticide Residues[a]		Hazardous Pesticides	Can Residues Be Reduced by Washing?
	Imported	Domestic		
Onions	18%	28%	DDT[b]	Yes
			Diazinon	Unknown
Oranges	49%	36%	Parathion	Unknown
			Carbaryl	Yes
Peaches	58%	53%	Captan	Yes
			Parathion	Unknown
			Carbaryl	Yes
Pears	35%	45%	Cyhexatin	Unknown
			Phosmet	Yes
Potatoes	24%	39%	DDT[b]	Yes
			Dieldrin[b]	Unknown
			Aldicarb	No
			Chlordane	Unknown
Spinach	23%	42%	DDT[b]	Yes
			Dimethoate	Unknown
Strawberries	86%	70%	Captan	Yes
			Methyl-Parathion	Unknown
Sweet Potatoes	11%	30%	Phosmet	Yes
			DDT[b]	Yes
			Dieldrin[b]	Unknown
			BHC	Unknown
Tomatoes	70%	23%	Chlorothalonil	Yes
			Permethrin	Yes
			Dimethoate	Unknown
Watermelon	25%	2%	Carbaryl	Yes
			Captan	Yes
			Chlorothalonil	Yes
			Dimethoate	Unknown

Source: Lawrie Mott and Karen Snyder/Natural Resources Defense Council, *Pesticide Alert: A Guide to Pesticides in Fruits and Vegetables* (Sierra Club Books, 1987).

[a] Percentages of food samples tested by the Food and Drug Administration include all types of pesticide residues, both hazardous and nonhazardous.

[b] DDT and Dieldrin are carcinogens banned from use in the United States; however, residues can occur in imported foods from countries still using the chemicals.

WISE USE

Washing and peeling. *Always* wash produce carefully. Foods with chemical residues that can't be washed off (see Table 5) should be peeled despite the fact that many peels are vitamin- and mineral-rich.

FOR FURTHER INFORMATION: Pesticide Alert, by Lawrie Mott and Karen Snyder; Natural Resources Defense Council/Sierra Club Books, 1987.

1. Keith Schneider, "Biological Pesticides Win Converts as Fear of Chemicals Grows," *New York Times* (June 11, 1989).
2. "Unfinished Business" (Environmental Protection Agency, 401 M St. SW, Washington, DC 20460; 1987).
3. Lawrie Mott and Karen Snyder, *Pesticide Alert* (Sierra Club Books, 1987), p. 22.

GRAINS AND GRAIN PRODUCTS

Grains are healthy foods that contain complex carbohydrates, protein, and lots of fiber, vitamins, and minerals. They are also low on the food chain, using natural resources efficiently to provide human sustenance. Still, commercial agriculture takes a heavy toll on the environment.

ENVIRONMENTAL PROBLEMS

Farming impacts. Both monoculture—growing the same crops on the same land year after year—and the use of marginal land for crops lead to soil erosion and depletion.

Chemical use. Every year our nation's farmers use more than 1.5 billion pounds of pesticides to kill fungi, bugs, and weeds; control rodents; or simply make the end product look better.[1] These chemicals pollute both soil and groundwater and make soil and crops dependent on them. They can also end up in our food. The Environmental Protection Agency has identified 55 cancer-causing pesticides that sometimes leave residues in food; the agency called pesticide use one of the country's worst health and environmental problems.[2] Ethylene dibromide (EDB), for example, was banned in 1984 as a grain pesticide—after 35 years of use—when the carcinogen was found in foods at alarmingly high levels.[3] Besides cancer, pesticide-related health risks include birth defects, miscarriages, genetic mutations, and sterility. Consumers are not the only ones threatened; farm workers who handle and apply these chemicals are at far greater risk.

Processing and additives. Many grain products have their nutrients and fiber milled out, while sugar, fats, salt, nonnutritive conditioners and fillers, and artificial flavors and colors are added.

Wasteful packaging. Processed wheat and grain foods are often packaged in unnecessary layers of paper and plastic that have manufacturing and disposal impacts of their own.

CHOOSING A PRODUCT

GENERAL GUIDELINES

Simple, natural ingredients. Read labels carefully to find products that contain whole grains and few or no additives, and require minimal processing. Beware of misleading or exaggerated claims.

Organically grown grains. Look for products made with organically grown grains and ingredients.

Sensible packaging. Avoid excess packaging:

- Look for bulk foods—such as rice, flour, dried pasta, and popcorn—available in bins at many grocery and natural foods stores (and bring your own sack).

- Choose the largest-sized packages practical, preferably recycled or recyclable paper or paperboard boxes.

- Avoid plastic packaging, foods in single-serving containers, and individually wrapped or overpackaged foods (those with two or three packaging layers when one would do).

COMMERCIAL PRODUCTS

Whole grains *(highly recommended)*. In their basic, least-processed form, grains are among the cheapest and healthiest foods available. You can buy them in bulk at better grocery and natural foods stores; organically grown grains are easy to find. Common whole-grain foods include rolled oats, whole wheat flour, cornmeal, popcorn, brown rice, and whole rye flour.

Bread *(sometimes recommended)*. Bread can be either a wholesome, nutritious food, rich in natural fiber, or an overprocessed "filler":

- Whole-grain breads are nutritionally the best choice. Bread made from whole wheat flour, for example, contains 5 percent more protein, 18 percent less fat, 650 percent more fiber, and 10 percent fewer calories than white bread.[4]

- Check the ingredients carefully—many commercial breads use misleading terms on their labels. A bread labeled "whole wheat" might actually have only a small proportion of whole wheat flour, with the bulk being white flour (also called "wheat flour," "enriched flour," or just "flour").

- Local bakeries often offer whole-grain breads, sometimes made from organically grown grains, without the long storage periods and transportation costs of national brands.

Pasta *(sometimes recommended)*. Like bread, pasta can be both nutritious and filling, provided you choose wisely:

- Whole wheat pasta is higher in fiber than standard white-flour pasta, and is sometimes available made from organically grown ingredients. It can taste grainier or heavier than white-flour pasta but is still delicious.

- Dried pasta is often available in bulk at grocery and natural foods stores, saving on packaging.

- Fresh pasta is tasty but requires refrigeration, is more expensive than dried, and often comes heavily packaged in plastic.

- Prepackaged pasta mixes often contain large amounts of sodium and other additives, and come in wasteful packaging.

Cereal *(sometimes recommended)*. The nutritional value and environmental soundness of cereal products vary widely:

- Commercial breakfast cereals often contain refined flour, sugar, fat, and sodium with little fiber and few vitamins and minerals (except those synthetically added). Whole-grain cereals without these unnecessary and unwholesome additives are now widely available in grocery as well as natural foods stores. Check ingredients lists carefully.

- Cereal is often available in bulk at co-ops and natural foods stores and sometimes at grocery stores (especially oat-based cereals such as granola).

Desserts and snacks *(sometimes recommended).* Few foods have more potential for nutritional abuse than desserts and snacks, many of which contain refined flour, fats, sugars, conditioners, fillers, and artificial flavors and colors. However, high-quality snacks and desserts are available: look for those made with whole wheat rather than white flour; vegetable oils rather than butter or lard; fruit juices and grain sweeteners instead of sugar and honey; and natural flavors instead of artificial.

WISE USE

Healthy use. Eat lots of grain products every day, but be sure they are whole grains that are high in fiber and low in fat, sugar, and salt. Eat organically grown grains whenever possible.

Combining grains and beans. To enhance your protein intake, combine grain-based foods with beans at the same meals.

FOR FURTHER INFORMATION: Diet for a Small Planet, by Frances Moore Lappé; Ballantine, 1985.

1. Keith Schneider, "Biological Pesticides Win Converts as Fear of Chemicals Grows," *New York Times* (June 11, 1989).
2. "Unfinished Business" (Environmental Protection Agency, 401 M St. SW, Washington, DC 20460; 1987).
3. "Dealing with EDB, a Dangerous Pesticide," *EPA Journal* (January/February 1984), p. 17.
4. CIBA-GEIGY Limited, "Documenta Geigy, Nutrition" (Basel, Switzerland), p. 507.

MILK AND DAIRY PRODUCTS

Since the 1960s, reports linking fat and cholesterol to serious disease have prompted Americans to greatly reduce their consumption of milk and butter (as well as red meat). Cheese, however, has more than doubled in popularity; the average American now consumes about 22 pounds each year.[1] Environmentally, cheese is a good substitute for meat, but milk is much healthier.

ENVIRONMENTAL PROBLEMS

Animal cruelty. The modern dairy farm—which may or may not allow cows to graze outdoors—uses concrete stalls, artificial lighting, and milking machines to enhance production. The cow is kept pregnant throughout her adult life so that she continues to give milk, but spends little time with her calves. If she becomes stressed and hyperactive by her environment, she is given tranquilizers; often hormones are implanted to increase her yield. Though able to live 20 to 25 years, most dairy cows are slaughtered at age three or four, when the volume of milk they produce falls off.[2]

Farming impacts. Like farms that raise cattle for meat, dairy farms have serious environmental effects that can include wildlife and habitat destruction, overgrazing, surface water consumption, and pollution of surface and groundwater with animal wastes (see Beef, p. 56). Overall, dairy farming is an inefficient use of the earth's resources.

Dioxin contamination. Dioxins, which are carcinogenic and highly toxic, are found in milk packaged in wax-coated containers. Though the amounts of dioxin in milk are extremely small, the Food and Drug Administration has estimated that young children drinking all their milk from contaminated paper cartons double their daily dioxin intake.[3]

Health risks. Heart disease and other health problems are linked to milk and dairy products that have a high fat and cholesterol content. Lactose intolerance, a condition characterized by stomach cramps, gas, and diarrhea, occurs in many people after the age of four, when they no longer produce the enzyme needed to digest lactose, the carbohydrate in milk.

Processing and additives. The producers of dairy products often add sugar, sodium, fillers and conditioners, and artificial flavors and colors to the milk base.

Wasteful packaging. Nonreturnable plastic milk jugs, made of hard-to-recycle high-density polyethylene, have replaced the returnable glass bottle. Other wasteful packaging includes waxed paper cartons, which are dioxin-contaminated and nonrecyclable, and plastic containers holding small portions.

CHOOSING A PRODUCT

GENERAL GUIDELINES

Simple, natural, and fresh ingredients. Read labels carefully to find products that contain few or no additives and require minimal processing. Always look for the freshest products available.

Humane dairy-farming practices. Co-ops and natural foods stores sometimes carry products from dairies that employ humane, healthful methods or organic farming techniques.

Lowfat, low-cholesterol dairy products. You can find lowfat, low-cholesterol varieties of most dairy products—they are much better for your health.

Sensible packaging. Always choose large, recyclable containers, preferably glass, and avoid overpackaged and small-serving products. Because waxed paper cartons and containers are dioxin-contaminated and nonrecyclable, plastic containers are better choices at present; recycle them whenever possible.

COMMERCIAL PRODUCTS

Milk *(recommended)*. Extracted from dairy cows via milking machines and then pasteurized to kill bacteria, milk is important both as a beverage and as an ingredient for all dairy products. It's available whole (with all its natural butterfat), lowfat, or skimmed and with added flavors, such as chocolate. Adults should drink lowfat or skim milk when possible to avoid extra fat and should avoid chocolate milk and other sweetened milk drinks.

Yogurt *(recommended)*. Made from milk and milk solids with added cultures of bacteria, particularly *L. acidophilus,* which aids digestion, yogurt is available in plain, flavored, and frozen varieties. (When frozen, the beneficial bacteria in yogurt die.) Similar to milk nutritionally, yogurt is a healthful dairy treat. Look for lowfat or nonfat products without numerous added ingredients (especially sugars, gelatin, and artificial flavors). Buy it plain and add a little fruit or juice.

Cheeses *(sometimes recommended)*. Made from milk, usually with rennet (derived from the stomach linings of calves), cheese is protein-rich and more environmentally sound than meat (since the producing animal continues to live). Yet the high fat and cholesterol content of most cheeses makes them unhealthy to eat in large amounts.

- Look for lowfat cheeses such as cottage cheese, Camembert, and Parmesan, and others specifically labeled as lowfat.

- Rennetless cheeses, which don't involve the killing of calves, are available in natural foods stores.

- Avoid processed cheese products, which often contain unhealthy added ingredients and are wastefully packaged.

Ice cream *(sometimes recommended)*. Usually made with milk, cream or butterfat, flavorings, sweeteners, and eggs, ice cream can also contain numerous other ingredients. Some ice creams are healthier than some cheeses in terms of fat and cholesterol but may be loaded with sugar or honey to add carbohydrate-based calories. Look for premium brands, often labeled *natural,* to avoid chemical ingredients, but eat them in moderation.

Butter *(never recommended).* Made from milk fat, butter should be avoided due to its extremely high fat and cholesterol content.

ALTERNATIVES

Soy products. For an all-purpose dairy substitute, use soybean products, which include soy milk, soy cheese (tofu), tempeh, and soy-based frozen desserts.

Vegetables. Green leafy vegetables are much more efficient sources of calcium than most dairy products because their calcium/phosphorus ratio (essential to calcium absorption) is better. (Very large amounts of vegetables must be eaten, however, to receive the megadoses of calcium sometimes advised by physicians.)

Calcium supplements. Dolomite or other calcium-rich diet supplements are available at natural foods stores.

Vegetable oils. To replace butter, cook with vegetable oils or margarine, which are both healthier and more environmentally sound.

Fruit-based frozen desserts. Sorbets, ices, all-fruit popsicles, and milk-free sherbets are healthy alternatives to ice cream and frozen yogurt.

WISE USE

Healthy use. Try using lowfat or nonfat milk and dairy products as supplements to meals of fruits, vegetables, grains, and beans, rather than as main courses themselves. If you suffer from lactose-intolerance symptoms, look in natural foods stores or pharmacies for lactase enzyme supplements to aid digestion.

1. Sarah Glazer, "How America Eats," *Editorial Research Reports* (November 18, 1988), p. 220.
2. John Robbins, *Diet for a New America* (Stillpoint, 1987), pp. 109–111.
3. Janet Raloff, "Dioxin: Paper's Trace," *Science News* (February 18, 1989), p. 105.

ORGANIC FOODS

Organic foods are raised and processed entirely without synthetic chemicals—without the chemical fertilizers, pesticides, antibiotics, hormones, preservatives, and other compounds so prevalent in modern American factory farming. Organic farming methods often require more work, but take far less of a toll on the environment and on human health; in fact, they often *improve* the environment through soil building, crop rotation, and careful harvesting.

ENVIRONMENTAL BENEFITS

Chemical-free food. Many chemical residues find their way into our foods (see Table 5), some with health hazards that are discovered only after years of widespread use, so organic foods are important for what they do *not* contain.

Natural, sustainable agriculture. The goal of organic agriculture is to establish a self-sustaining system, much like a natural biological community. Soil is seen as a working ecosystem—with microbes, worms, insects, and decaying organic matter all playing essential roles. Crops grown in this soil with naturally acquired fertilizers become healthy, living communities themselves; beneficial insects and wildlife help ward off opportunistic weeds, pests, and diseases.

Farm worker safety. The people who apply agriculture chemicals are the most at risk from them. The United Farm Workers union in California, for example, has renewed its grape boycott to protest continued use of hazardous substances in the fields. Organic methods, by avoiding the use of chemicals, greatly improve worker safety.

Humane treatment of animals. Animal husbandry practices vary greatly among farmers, but organically raised animals tend to be treated more humanely. They are given healthy feed and no drugs, and are usually kept in open pastures instead of stalls. If they are in stalls, they

TABLE
6

ORGANIC FOODS SAMPLER[a]

Type of Food	Brands
Baby Food	Earth's Best; Summa
Beans	Eden; Health Valley; Little Bear
Cereals	Amaranth; American Prairie; Erewhon; Health Valley; Lundberg's; Nature's Path Manna
Chips and Crackers	Cascadian Farms; Garden of Eatin'; Little Bear; Lundberg's; Mexi-Snax; Ohwawa
Cookies and Sweets	Bee Pollen Sunrise; Farm Barley Wafers; Health Rice Snack Bars; Health Valley; Nanak's; Westbrae
Cooking Oils	Arrowhead Mills; Spectrum Naturals
Jams and Sweeteners	Cascadian Farms; Eden; Lundberg's; Santa Cruz; Shady Maple Farms; Sweet Cloud
Juices and Drinks	After the Fall; Edensoy; R.W. Knudsen; Santa Cruz; Westbrae; Westsoy
Nut Butters	Arrowhead Mills; Walnut Acres; Westbrae
Pancake Mix	David's Goodbatter
Sauces, Garnishes, and Condiments	Cascadian Farms; Cold Mountain; Duggan's; Eden; Emperor's Kitchen; JB; Lima; Señor Filipe; Tree of Life; Walnut Acres
Soups	Health Valley; Walnut Acres
Spaghetti and Pasta	Arrowhead Mills; Tree of Life; Udon; Westbrae

[a] These foods are listed by their manufacturers as containing all or some organic ingredients.

usually have natural lighting, cleaner conditions, and less crowding.

Reduced pollution. By avoiding chemicals, organic farming does not contribute to the air, water, and soil pollution caused by the manufacture and use of fertilizers, pesticides, and processing compounds used in factory farming.

CHOOSING A PRODUCT

GENERAL GUIDELINES

Weighing costs and quality. Be prepared to pay more for some organic foods. Organic agriculture takes more labor and attention—sometimes much more—to produce the same

amount of food as nonorganic methods. For consumers, the benefits are environmental and health-related rather than financial.

Careful selection. As more food labeled "organic" becomes available, you need to know who decided the food was organic, and using what criteria. Labels on prepared foods often specify what the company's certification is, or what practices were used to produce the food. If you have any doubts—particularly regarding produce—ask the store or produce manager whether either the food or the grower is certified.

Locally grown foods. The freshest—and probably cheapest—organic foods are those grown or processed near you. Co-ops, natural foods stores, and farmers' markets are good places to look.

Tolerating imperfections. Organically grown foods (especially fruits and vegetables), although just as tasty, do not always look as perfect as their chemically treated counterparts. They might have spots, for example, or be misshapen because that's the way they grow naturally; they haven't been grown with appearance as the main goal.

COMMERCIAL PRODUCTS

Certified organic foods *(highly recommended)*. Organically grown foods can be certified through state programs, producers' organizations, and soon, the federal government. Table 6 lists some nationally distributed brands of certified organic foods.

- In stores look both for display signs pointing out organic foods and for small labels that verify their certification (such as "Certified Organically Grown" stickers). Certified produce or bulk items might not be individually labeled; just ask the store manager whether they're certified.

- Farmers' markets and cooperatives are good sources of certified organic foods; for a list of organic growers, processors, and distributors in your area, call the Organic Foods Production Association of North America, (413) 323-6821.

- For a list of American mail-order sources of organic foods, call Americans for Safe Food, part of the Center for Science in the Public Interest, (202) 332-9110. Not all mail-order companies are certified, but the list shows which ones are and which others self-certify their foods. Table 7 lists some certified and self-certified organic growers who offer a wide range of products.

Noncertified organic foods *(sometimes recommended)*. Not all growers and producers can afford to have their foods certified—which usually involves testing and auditing—even though they meet certification standards. Other growers aren't certified because their methods aren't completely organic, or because of a problem beyond their control (such as pesticides occasionally drifting over from a neighbor's farm).

But be careful: organic foods generally command higher prices than commercially grown foods, so there is incentive for misusing the term. If you see foods marked as organic but without certification labels, or foods labeled "Claimed Organically Grown," ask for further information before you buy.

Pesticide-free/Integrated Pest Management foods *(sometimes recommended)*. Some produce growers manage to avoid chemical pesticides but not ammonia-based fertilizers—which are fairly cheap and sometimes hard to replace—or other chemical compounds. Other growers use Integrated Pest Management (IPM) methods, which permit some use of chemicals but hold it to a minimum. Although both types of foods are better choices than commercially grown products, they are not on a par with organically grown products.

DO-IT-YOURSELF

Gardening. Growing your own food organically is not only possible, it's also cheap and usually very easy. See the Resources section for publications on organic gardening methods.

TABLE 7

ORGANIC FOODS SUPPLIERS (MAIL ORDER)

Company	Address and Phone No.	Products
Certified Organic Growers		
Diamond K Enterprises	R.R. 1, P.O. Box 30 A St. Charles, MN 55972 (507) 932-4308	Dried fruits, grains, nuts
Ecology Sound Farms	42126 Road 168 Orosi, CA 93647 (209) 528-3816	Variety of fruits
Gravelly Ridge Farms	Star Route 16 Elk Creek, CA 95939 (916) 963-3216	Grains, produce
Lundberg Family Farm	P.O. Box 369 Richvale, CA 95974 (916) 882-4551	Rice, rice products
Macrobiotic Mall	18779-C N. Frederick Ave. Gaithersburg, MD 20879 (800) 533-1270	Beans, grains, other foods
Natural Beef Farms	4399-A Henninger Ct. Chantilly, VA 22021 (703) 631-0881	Breads, meats, produce, other foods
Natural Way Mills, Inc.	Route 2, P.O. Box 37 Middle River, MN 56737 (218) 222-3677	Cereals, flours, grains, other foods
Nu-World Amaranth	P.O. Box 2202 Naperville, IL 60565 (312) 369-6819	Cereals, flour, grains
Self-Certified Organic Growers		
Deer Valley Farm	R.D. 1 Guilford, NY 13780 (607) 764-8556	Baked goods, grains, meats, produce, other foods
Fiddler's Green Farm	R.R. 1, Box 656 Belfast, ME 04915 (207) 338-3568	Coffee, grains, jams, and syrups
Gold Mine Natural Food Co.	1947 30th St. San Diego, CA 92102 (800) 647-2929	Variety of foods
Jaffe Brothers	P.O. Box 636 Valley Center, CA 92082 (619) 749-1133	Beans, fruits, grains, nuts, other foods
Krystal Wharf Farms	R.D. 2, Box 191A Mansfield, PA 16933 (717) 549-8194	Beans, dried fruits, grains, produce, nuts, other foods
Mountain Ark Trading Co.	120 S. East Ave. Fayetteville, AR 72701 (800) 643-8909	Beans, grains, seeds, other foods
Paul's Grains	2475-B 340 St. Laurel, IA 50141 (515) 476-3373	Beef, chicken, grains, other meats
Walnut Acres	Penns Creek Rd. Penns Creek, PA 17862 (800) 433-3998	Baked goods, cereals, grains, soups, meats, other foods

PORK

Raising pigs is far less damaging to the environment than raising cattle; pigs do not need much space and will eat almost anything. For these reasons pigs are raised on small farms throughout much of the world. In the United States, however, pork has become a large-scale industry, with unhealthy consequences.

ENVIRONMENTAL PROBLEMS

Animal cruelty. Whether raised indoors in a tiny stall or raised outdoors on a tiny lot with hundreds of others, the typical pig has a miserable existence:[1]

- Sows (females) are forced to give birth to many more piglets than is natural.

- The concrete and metal slatted floors of indoor pens severely damage the pigs' feet.

- Overcrowding drives many pigs crazy, leading them to attack one another.

Chemical use. Commercially raised pigs are treated routinely with antibiotics and other drugs in an effort to keep them healthy under unhealthy conditions. Overuse of antibiotics can lead to the development of antibiotic-resistant strains of bacteria. Food poisoning in people caused by antibiotic-resistant bacteria can be difficult to treat. For a person with an infection who is already taking antibiotics, eating meat containing antibiotic-resistant bacteria can be especially dangerous. Antimicrobial drugs, which can cause adverse reactions in human beings, are often found in pork. Sulfa drugs, for example, which can cause severe allergic reactions in some individuals, were found above violation levels in 4 percent of market hogs in 1986 tests.[2]

Bacteria and parasites. Among meats and fish, pork products are ranked second only to beef in causing food disease outbreaks from bacteria, and are the leading cause of parasitic illnesses.[3]

Health hazards. Pork products are among the unhealthiest foods in the American diet, because of their high content of fat, cholesterol, and sodium.

Processing and additives. Highly processed products, such as bacon, sausage, and hot dogs, require energy to process and contain unhealthy added fat, sodium, and chemicals.

Wasteful packaging. Pork is usually wrapped in plastic and placed on Styrofoam trays, both of which are environmentally costly to manufacture and impractical to recycle.

CHOOSING A PRODUCT

GENERAL GUIDELINES

Natural, humane pork-raising practices. Look for pork raised in a humane, healthy, and chemical-free environment.

Moderation. For your health's sake, consider alternative sources of protein. Buy pork only in moderation.

Minimal processing. Instead of wasteful and unhealthy processed pork products, such as bacon, sausage, and hot dogs, buy unprocessed cuts of meat.

Lean cuts. Choose lean cuts of pork, especially loin, which is much lower in fat than cutlets, chops, ribs, or processed pork.

Sensible packaging. Instead of buying pork packaged in wasteful Styrofoam trays or oversized plastic packages, buy lean cuts directly from a butcher who will wrap them in paper. If paper is not an option, choose products vacuum-packed in plastic over those on Styrofoam trays.

COMMERCIAL PRODUCTS

Small-scale producers (*sometimes recommended*). Only at smaller, often family-run operations will you find pigs raised under more humane and healthful conditions. Check for sources at co-ops or natural foods stores. Look for the following labels:

- *Natural* usually means raised without drugs.

- *Organically raised* implies that the feed has no chemical additives (but not necessarily that the feed itself is organically grown) and that the pigs receive no antibiotics, growth regulators, or other drugs.

- *Free-ranging* indicates that the animals are not kept permanently in tiny stalls indoors but are allowed outdoors to dig for roots and wallow, as is natural for them.

Large-scale producers *(not generally recommended)*. All large-scale hog producers use chemicals and many inhumane practices; avoid them whenever possible.

ALTERNATIVES

Vegetarian cuisine. Many vegetarian foods—including tofu and tempeh, both made from soybeans—combine high protein, nutrition, and excellent flavor and involve no animal cruelty. Eating them is good for the environment because they are low on the planet's food chain. (See Fruits and Vegetables, p. 60; Grains and Grain Products, p. 64.)

Poultry, fish, and shellfish. These foods are lower than pork on the earth's food chain and are much more efficient sources of protein. (See Fish and Shellfish, p. 58; Poultry and Eggs, p. 74.)

WISE USE

Conservative use. Eat pork lightly, as a supplement to meals rather than as a main dish. Don't let any go to waste; use bones, for example, to make soup.

Careful preparation. Make sure pork is prepared in a healthy way:

- Trim and cook the fat out. With a fine, sharp knife, cut away all visible portions of fat; do not fry but instead grill, broil, or microwave.

- Cook all pork well to kill any trichinae or other parasites and microbes that might be present; an internal meat temperature of at least 160°F is recommended by the Food and Drug Administration.

FOR FURTHER INFORMATION: *Diet for a Small Planet,* by Frances Moore Lappé; Ballantine, 1985. *Diet for a New America,* by John Robbins; Stillpoint, 1987.

1. John Robbins, *Diet for a New America* (Stillpoint, 1987), pp. 80–96.
2. Patrick G. Marshall, "How Safe Is Your Food?" *Editorial Research Reports* (November 18, 1988), p. 588.
3. Ibid., p. 583.

POULTRY AND EGGS

Americans' concern over heart disease has triggered both a rise in the consumption of poultry, which is lower in fat and cholesterol than beef, and a decline in the consumption of eggs, which are high in cholesterol. Environmentally, poultry is a better choice than beef in one respect: raising one pound of chicken requires only 3 pounds of grain, whereas raising a pound of beef requires 16.[1] Both poultry and eggs, however, have some disadvantages.

ENVIRONMENTAL PROBLEMS

Animal cruelty. Unlike the old days on the family farm, today's factory-farmed chickens live short lives under inhumane, unhealthy conditions:[2]

- Most live crammed into cages too tiny to allow any movement.

- The cages are stacked in banks inside huge, windowless, almost constantly lit warehouses.

- Egg-producing hens live in slant-bottomed cages, where they are packed together by gravity.

- Because such conditions lead to neurotic, incessant fighting, chickens are "debeaked" (their beaks are sliced off).

Bacterial contamination. Chickens and turkeys are slaughtered in fast-moving production lines where their intestines are removed, allowing the bacteria in their feces—including salmonella—to contaminate many carcasses on the line. According to one government estimate, one of every three store-bought chickens is contaminated with salmonella or other harmful bacteria.[3] Many eggs also contain salmonella bacteria. Because of the birds' close quarters, even heavy doses of antibiotics cannot prevent infection.

Health risks. Egg yolks contain extraordinarily high amounts of cholesterol, the consumption of which is linked to heart disease.

Processing and additives. Highly processed products such as chicken nuggets require energy to process and contain unhealthy added fat, sodium, and chemicals.

Wasteful packaging. Poultry is often wrapped in plastic and placed on Styrofoam trays, both of which are environmentally costly to manufacture and impractical to recycle. Styrofoam egg cartons have replaced paper cartons in many stores.

CHOOSING A PRODUCT

GENERAL GUIDELINES

Natural, humane poultry-raising practices. Look for poultry raised in a humane, healthy, and chemical-free environment.

Minimal processing. Instead of wasteful and unhealthy chicken nuggets and other processed products, buy unprocessed poultry.

Sensible packaging. Instead of buying poultry wrapped in wasteful packaging materials such as Styrofoam trays and plastic, shop at markets where butchers will wrap your poultry in paper. If paper is not an option, choose products vacuum-packed in plastic over those on Styrofoam trays. Buy eggs in paper cartons (which are usually made from recycled paper) rather than Styrofoam cartons, or bring your own carton to the store if eggs are sold in bulk.

COMMERCIAL PRODUCTS

Small-scale producers *(sometimes recommended).* Some small-scale poultry farms use healthier, more humane production methods. Check for sources at co-ops or natural foods stores, then call to ask for information on their production methods or look for the following terms on their packages:

- *Free-ranging* might or might not refer to outdoor pens for the animals; it does imply that they are not tightly caged.

- *Organically raised* implies that the feed has no chemical additives (but not necessarily that the feed itself is organically grown) and that the birds receive no antibiotics or other drugs.

- *Fertile,* used with eggs, means that a rooster inseminated the hens who produced the eggs. Most commercial eggs are not fertile, because roosters are aggressive and a nuisance. There's no nutritional or health difference, but fertile eggs often come from hens raised in a more natural setting.

Large-scale producers *(not generally recommended).* All large-scale poultry producers use many inhumane practices; avoid them whenever possible.

ALTERNATIVES

Vegetarian cuisine. Many vegetarian foods—including tofu and tempeh, both made from soybeans—combine high protein, nutrition, and excellent flavor and involve no animal cruelty. Eating them is good for the environment because they are low on the planet's food chain. (See Fruits and Vegetables, p. 60; Grains and Grain Products, p. 64.)

WISE USE

Conservative use. Try not to serve large amounts of poultry and eggs as main courses; instead use small portions to enliven a dish or a meal. Don't let any go to waste; use a chicken or turkey carcass, for example, to make soup.

Safe preparation. Minimize your risk of exposure to salmonella poisoning by taking the following precautions:

- Use good hygiene. Rinse raw poultry thoroughly; scrub your hands, countertops, and

any utensils that come in contact with raw poultry with soap and hot water.

- Cook your eggs, chicken, or turkey *well*—heat is your last defense. The Food and Drug Administration recommends cooking eggs three minutes *on each side* and avoiding raw eggs altogether. Poultry should be cooked to an internal temperature of at least 160° F.

FOR FURTHER INFORMATION: *Diet for a Small Planet,* by Frances Moore Lappé; Ballantine, 1985. *Diet for a New America*, by John Robbins; Stillpoint, 1987.

1. Jacques Yves Cousteau, *The Cousteau Almanac* (Doubleday, 1981), p. 591.
2. John Robbins, *Diet for a New America* (Stillpoint, 1987), pp. 48–72.
3. Patrick G. Marshall, "How Safe Is Your Food?" *Editorial Research Reports* (November 18, 1988), p. 584.

SOFT DRINKS

Set against the backdrop of global environmental problems, a can of soda pop looks fairly harmless. But since the average American drinks nearly 45 gallons of soft drinks every year, far more than any other commercial beverage, the ingredients and packaging of this product *do* have an impact on the environment.[1]

ENVIRONMENTAL PROBLEMS

Unhealthy ingredients. The older brands of soft drinks, such as Coke Classic and Pepsi, are basically highly processed, expensively packaged forms of sweetened water. Their ingredients are relatively harmless but have almost no nutritional value:

- Carbonated water, filtered from a municipal water supply and then injected with carbon dioxide gas

- Corn syrup and/or sugar

- Caramel color, made by heating corn syrup

- Phosphoric acid, extracted from phosphate rock with sulfuric acid

- Natural flavors

- Caffeine

The newer soft drinks, however, include a host of chemicals:

- *Aspartame* (NutraSweet), a synthetic, no-calorie sweetener now used in most diet soda pop, not known to be harmful to the general population but dangerous to those few people who cannot metabolize it

- *Saccharin,* a synthetic sweetener made from petroleum or coal-tar oils and sulfuric acid; a suspected human carcinogen known to cause cancer in animals

- *Sodium and potassium benzoate,* preservatives derived from petrochemicals

- *Polyethylene glycol,* a "softener" made from petroleum gases or natural gas

- *Artificial flavors and colors,* derived from coal-tar oils and petroleum

- *Glycerol ester of wood rosin,* a stabilizer extracted from pine using naphtha, a volatile liquid made from coal tar or natural gas

- *EDTA,* a preservative made by mixing sodium cyanide and formaldehyde with ethylenediamine (derived from hydrocarbon gases)

These chemicals, even those not toxic to humans, contribute to our fossil-fuel dependence and add to soft drinks' processing and environmental costs.

Wasteful packaging. In 1987 Americans drank over 37 billion soft drinks in aluminum cans but recycled only half of the cans.[2] Soft-drink containers—whether aluminum, glass, or plastic—must be manufactured from molten material, stamped or molded, sprayed with ink, sealed, and shipped. Glass bottles and aluminum cans can be recycled almost indefinitely, saving raw materials and reducing both manufacturing costs and disposal problems. Plastic bottles (polyethylene terephthalate, or PET) offer the packaging advantage of larger size but are made from fossil fuels and are usually recyclable only once, into a different, nondegradable plastic product.

CHOOSING A PRODUCT
GENERAL GUIDELINES

Healthier ingredients. Look for brands with a minimum of chemicals and additives.

Sensible packaging. Returnable deposit containers (mandatory in some areas) are the best choice, followed by recyclable aluminum or glass. Buy plastic bottles only as your last choice and only if you can recycle them.

TABLE
8

NATURAL-INGREDIENT SOFT DRINKS

Brand	Packaging	Ingredients
Blue Sky Natural Soda	Aluminum	Purified carbonated water, fructose, citric acid, natural flavor
Calistoga Sparkling Water and Fruit Juice	Glass	Sparkling mineral water, pure juice concentrate, high fructose corn syrup, natural fruit flavor
Robert Corr Natural Soda	Aluminum	Purified carbonated water, high fructose corn sweetener, natural flavors and colors
Crystal Geyser Light Seltzer with Juice	Glass	Sparkling water, fructose, concentrated juice, natural flavors, natural malic acid
Crystal Geyser Zonic Herbal Tonic	Glass	Herb tea, concentrated juice, carbonation added
Ginseng Up	Glass	Filtered carbonated water, fructose, natural citric acid, natural ginger, natural color, Il Hwa Korean ginseng tea
Hansen's Natural Soda	Aluminum	Purified carbonated water, high fructose corn syrup, natural flavors, citric acid, caramel color
Health Valley's Gingerale, Sarsaparilla, Old Fashioned Root Beer	Glass	Sparkling spring water, fructose, juices, natural flavorings, molasses, herbal extracts
Mendocino Mineral Juice	Glass	Sparkling water, pure fruit juice concentrate, high fructose corn syrup, citric acid, natural flavors
Old San Francisco All Natural Seltzer	Glass	Carbonated water, high fructose corn syrup, citric acid, natural flavors
Soho Natural Soda	Glass	Carbonated water, high fructose corn syrup, fruit juice, citric acid, fruit extract, natural flavors, grapeskin extract
Dr. Tima Natural Sodas	Glass	Filtered carbonated water, honey, essential oils, juices, citric acid

COMMERCIAL PRODUCTS

Natural-ingredient brands (recommended). Some smaller companies make soft drinks that contain only filtered, carbonated water, high-fructose corn syrup, and natural favors. Table 8 lists many of these simpler, more-natural soft drinks and their ingredients. A final note in their favor: they don't come in plastic bottles.

Old, established brands (not generally recommended). In general the older brands of soft drinks, such as Coke, Pepsi, 7-Up, and Royal Crown, have kept to simpler formulas. While not especially healthy, they avoid most of the synthetic additives found in other soft drinks.

Other major brands (never recommended). These products make extensive use of chemical flavorings, colors, conditioners, stabilizers, and preservatives. They are environmentally costly to manufacture and process, and their ingredients may be harmful to some people.

DO-IT-YOURSELF

Carbonated fruit juice. Make your own soft drink by combining fruit juice with sparkling water.

WISE USE

Container recycling. *Always* recycle your soft-drink containers. Aluminum cans are especially easy—if you're away from home or a recycling bin, just crush the can and carry it back in your pocket or purse.

1. Louis Rukeyser and John Cooney, *Louis Rukeyser's Business Almanac* (Simon & Schuster, 1988), p. 18.
2. "Can Shipments Report, 1987" (Can Manufacturers Institute, 1625 Massachusetts Ave. NW, Washington, DC 20036), p. 5.

WATER, BOTTLED

Finding that tap water often tastes and smells awful, and worrying about contamination, Americans are increasingly turning to the bottle: we now drink over 1.7 billion gallons of bottled water every year.[1]

The health benefits of drinking plenty of clean water are hard to overestimate. Water helps flush out toxins and keeps the kidneys and other organs working properly. A basic rule of thumb: drink four to six glasses a day, not including caffeinated and alcoholic drinks, which can remove more water than they provide. The main advantage of bottled water over most tap water is that it tastes good, which encourages you to drink more.

ENVIRONMENTAL PROBLEMS

Chemical contamination. Water is so easily contaminated—from bacteria, industrial wastes, heavy metals, or organic pollutants—that its purity is often difficult to assess. Even water that tests clean can later become polluted or can get contaminated during bottling—as happened when benzene contamination prompted a worldwide recall of Perrier bottled water in 1989. For water bottled in the United States, the government regulates both water sources and processing methods. Most bottled water, in fact, comes from deep, protected sources free of ongoing contamination.

Long-distance shipping. The costliest environmental problem with bottled water involves shipping it from its source to you. Perrier, for example, is drawn from a spring in France, trucked to a port, freighted across the Atlantic Ocean, and trucked again to your store. When the product being shipped is just *water*, such an effort begins to look environmentally foolish.

Wasteful packaging. Bottled water comes in various-sized containers usually made from glass or plastic. Each container must be manufactured from molten material, molded, sprayed with ink, sealed, and shipped. Glass bottles can be recycled almost indefinitely, saving raw materials and reducing both manufacturing costs and disposal problems. Plastic bottles, such as one-gallon jugs of drinking water, are made from fossil fuels and are usually recyclable only once.

CHOOSING A PRODUCT

GENERAL GUIDELINES

Local sources. Look for water bottled near you to save on transportation. Clean, great-tasting waters are bottled in most parts of North America.

Water quality. If possible, ask the bottler for test results that prove the water is contaminant free. Or ask whether the bottler is certified by the International Bottled Water Association (IBWA). As of 1991 the IBWA requires certified water to test free of 181 contaminants.[2]

Sensible packaging. As with all beverage containers, choose glass bottles in the largest convenient size and reuse or recycle them whenever possible. If you regularly use one- or two-gallon jugs of water in your home, consider replacing them with permanent reusable five-gallon glass bottles. When full a five-gallon glass bottle weighs over 40 pounds and is awkward to carry, so home delivery might be your best solution (check your local yellow pages). Reusable five-gallon plastic bottles are easier for many people to handle than the heavy, breakable glass bottles. Questions have been raised, however, about the leaching of toxic, carcinogenic meythylene chloride from the plastic into the water.[3]

COMMERCIAL PRODUCTS

Spring water *(sometimes recommended).* This product usually comes from a protected well, and is sometimes disinfected with ozone.

Sparkling water *(sometimes recommended).* Sparkling water has been charged with carbon dioxide, either a naturally occurring or a com-

mercially produced gas. The term implies—but doesn't guarantee—a protected, natural water source.

Mineral water *(sometimes recommended).* This water contains naturally occurring minerals in various amounts. The term implies—but doesn't guarantee—a protected, natural water source.

Seltzer or club soda *(not generally recommended).* This beverage is usually just tap water, filtered to some degree and then charged with carbon dioxide gas.

Distilled water *(not generally recommended).* This product has no minerals at all; it is produced through an extremely energy-intensive process of boiling followed by condensation. Since minerals give water its taste, distilled water often seems flat by comparison.

ALTERNATIVES

See Water Filters, p. 157.

WISE USE

Container recycling. *Always* recycle your water containers. Five-gallon jugs are especially efficient and easy to reuse. Small glass bottles and aluminum cans are easy to recycle. Plastic bottles are recyclable but must be sorted by type (see Plastics, p. 34).

1. Michael de Courcy Hinds, "Concern over Water Safety Is Growing," *New York Times* (March 25, 1989).
2. Gina Bellafante, "Bottled Water: Fads and Facts," *Garbage* (January/February 1990), p. 50.
3. Ibid.

HOME CLEANING AND PEST CONTROL

AIR FRESHENERS

Most air fresheners do not "freshen" the air at all; instead, they simply pump more pollutants into it to cover up offensive odors or numb your sense of smell.

ENVIRONMENTAL PROBLEMS

Air pollution. The active ingredients in many air fresheners—as well as the propellants in many of the aerosol versions—are petrochemicals. When used they pollute the air with hydrocarbons, which vaporize relatively easily. Disinfectant air fresheners add small amounts of toxic chemicals, such as the o-phenylphenol in Lysol Disinfectant Spray, that further pollute the air.

Ozone depletion. Some products (such as Control Mist Lime Air Freshener) use 1,1,1-trichloroethane as a solvent. This chemical, like the better-known chlorofluorocarbons, slowly rises to the stratosphere and attacks the thin ozone layer that shields us from solar radiation.

Wasteful packaging. Many air fresheners come in aerosol cans, which are energy-intensive to make, polluting to use, and nonrecyclable. Other products come in wasteful, nonrecyclable plastic dispensers.

CHOOSING A PRODUCT

GENERAL GUIDELINES

Simple, natural ingredients. Look for products based on citrus, herbs, essential oils, or minerals rather than on petrochemicals. If the label doesn't say what the active ingredients are, don't buy the product.

Sensible packaging. Instead of aerosols, wicks, and other nonreusable plastic or metal dispensers, choose reusable spray bottles or paperboard boxes, always in the largest practical sizes.

COMMERCIAL PRODUCTS

Natural-ingredient brands *(highly recommended)*. See Table 9 for a list of products that contain only natural ingredients. You can also order the following products:

- ◆ The Hummer Nature Works, (512) 232-6167, sells cedar-based air fresheners including sachets, potpourri blends, and a mix-it-yourself spray freshener.

- ◆ Will's Wonder, Rt. 1, P.O. Box 197, Gatlinburg, TN 37738, sells an Odor Digester that uses harmless bacteria. It comes in a pump spray bottle.

Major brands *(never recommended)*. All major-brand air fresheners are petroleum derived and pollute the air; they are not an environmentally sound choice.

DO-IT-YOURSELF

Herbs and spices. Try these home remedies instead of using commercial products:

- Simmer fragrant herbs and spices in a pan of water.

- Put cinnamon in a cup of hot water.

- Make potpourri packets by wrapping fragrant herbs in cloth; hang them in rooms with stale air.

Baking soda. Set out dishes of baking soda to absorb odors.

ALTERNATIVES

Good housekeeping. A clean, well-ventilated house seldom needs air fresheners. If you notice a smell, track it down and eliminate the cause. For strong, temporary odors, ventilate the area thoroughly with a fan or by opening doors and windows.

TABLE 9

NATURAL-INGREDIENT AIR FRESHENERS

Brand	Type	Dispenser	Active Ingredients	Warnings
Air Therapy	Liquid	Plastic pump spray bottle	Ions derived from organic essential oils of citrus and herbs	Avoid eye contact; do not ingest; keep from children, flame; avoid plastic
Citrus II	Liquid	Plastic pump spray bottle	Citrus fruit, concentrated citrus oils from peels	Avoid skin and eye contact and flame; keep from plastic, vinyl, varnished surfaces
De-Moist	Powder	Cardboard box or cloth bag	Granular diatomaceous earth, calcium chloride	None listed
Nonscents	Powder	Cardboard shaker	100% natural minerals, no perfume	None listed

ALL-PURPOSE CLEANERS

Most all-purpose cleaners are effective for everyday cleaning chores, but their environmental effects vary widely.

ENVIRONMENTAL PROBLEMS

Harmful ingredients. Most commercial all-purpose cleaners contain either pine oil or ammonia.

- *Pine oil* is a powerful cleaner extracted from pine trees and processed with heat. It is quite flammable. Pine oil's "clean" smell comes from its oils and terpene alcohols; as they evaporate during manufacture and use, they pollute the air with hydrocarbons.

- *Ammonia* is made from natural gas through a complex, heat-intensive process that pollutes both the air and the water. It irritates mucous membranes and is highly flammable.

Unnecessary additives. Most all-purpose cleaners contain added ingredients—usually synthetic chemicals—they don't really need, such as emulsifiers, colors, scents, and two or three detergents instead of one. Many are also heavily diluted with water, adding packaging and transportation costs for a substance already found in every home.

Animal cruelty. Because some ingredients can harm humans, many manufacturers test cleaners on animals, under inhumane conditions; afterward the animals are killed.

Wasteful packaging. Most cleaners come in refillable plastic bottles, often with manual pump sprays. Some, however, still come in aerosol cans, which are energy-intensive to make, polluting to use, and nonrecyclable. Similarly wasteful are throwaway, cleaner-saturated cloths.

CHOOSING A PRODUCT

GENERAL GUIDELINES

Simple, natural ingredients. Pick the mildest, simplest cleaner that will do the job (often plain warm water works well). Choose naturally derived ingredients instead of synthetic chemicals.

Cruelty-free products. Look for cleaners made by companies that do not test products on animals.

TABLE 10
NATURAL-INGREDIENT, CRUELTY-FREE ALL-PURPOSE CLEANERS

Brand	Size	Type	Ingredients
Dr. Bronner's Sal Suds	16 oz.	Concentrate	Castor oil, coconut, pine needle oils
Earth Wise All-Purpose Cleaner	22 oz. 4 oz.	Liquid Concentrate	Water, degreasers, detergent from coconut and palm oil, water softener, quality control agents, mint fragrance
Ecover Cream Cleaner	16 oz. 33.8 oz.	Cream Cream	Finely ground chalk; coconut-oil-based cleaner; liquid soap from palm; coconut; and linseed oil; olay; citrus oil; preservative
Heavenly Horsetail All-Purpose Cleaner	24 oz.	Liquid	Soft water, cocamide DEA, sodium laureth sulfate, sodium chloride, citric acid, olive oil, lemon juice extracts
Keep America Clean All-Purpose Cleaner	16 oz.	Liquid	Biodegradable surfactants, water, coconut-based cleaner, citrus oil, aloe skin conditioner
Kleen All-Purpose Cleaner	32 oz.	Concentrate	Water, linear alkyl sulfonate, ammonium laureth sulfate, sodium citrate, coconut monoethanolamide, linear alcohol ethoxylate, aloe vera, honeysuckle fragrance, methylparaben
Lifeline Natural Cleaner	32 oz.	Liquid	Coco triethanolamine, sodium alkylaryl sulfonate, monoethanolamine, water, citrus oil
Life Tree Home Soap Household Cleaner	16 oz. 32 oz.	Concentrate Concentrate	Purified water, TEA lauryl sulfate, cocamide DEA, fragrance, methyl and propyl paraben, cocoyl
Murphy's Oil Soap	22 oz.	Liquid	Not available
Murphy's Oil Soap Spray	16 oz.	Liquid	Not available
Natus Nature's Maid	8 oz.	Concentrate	Castor oil, emulsifiers, orange oil, natural fragrance
New Age Biodegradeable Household Cleaner	4 oz.	Concentrate	Neutralized caustic soda, petroleum- and coconut-oil-based detergents, citric acid, lemon oil
Professional All-Purpose Spray Cleaner	22 oz.	Liquid	Not available

Sensible packaging. Save packaging by choosing the largest container practical; buy concentrates when possible. If you prefer a spray, don't choose an aerosol; instead, buy a manual-pump bottle and refill it from larger bottles of concentrate, diluting the cleaner with tap water.

COMMERCIAL PRODUCTS

Natural-ingredient, cruelty-free brands *(highly recommended)*. See Table 10 for some effective all-purpose cleaners that are naturally derived, biodegradable, nontoxic, and free of animal testing.

Major brands *(not generally recommended)*. All the major-brand cleaners have undesirable ingredients. If you must buy one, look for one that contains only water, detergent, softener or builder (to increase cleaning ability), and a grease cutter. Ammonia and pine-oil products are needed only rarely, for extra-strong cleaning.

DO-IT-YOURSELF

Soap. Add a few drops of high-quality liquid soap to a gallon of water, or use bar soap on a damp rag.

Vinegar. Add one or two tablespoons of white vinegar to a quart of warm or hot water.

Baking soda. Apply baking soda directly to soiled surfaces and rub with a damp rag, or add baking soda to warm or hot water.

Salt. Apply plain table salt directly to surfaces and rub with a damp rag, or add salt to warm water.

WISE USE

Safe use. Commercial all-purpose cleaners can harm the eyes; take care when opening bottles, pouring, or spraying. Use them in ventilated rooms, and keep them away from heat or flame.

BASIN, TUB, AND TILE CLEANERS

These cleaners are designed to remove mildew, soap scum, and mineral deposits, but many are unnecessarily harsh and polluting.

ENVIRONMENTAL PROBLEMS

Harmful ingredients. Among the common chemicals in major brands are

- *Alkyl dimethyl-benzylammonium chlorides,* highly toxic detergents

- *Sodium hypochlorite,* a toxic chlorine bleaching agent

- *Sodium hydroxide (lye),* a corrosive and strong irritant

- *Phosphoric and sulfuric acids,* both toxic cleaners

Animal cruelty. Because some ingredients can harm humans, many manufacturers test cleaners on animals, under inhumane conditions; afterward the animals are killed.

Wasteful packaging. Some cleaners come in aerosol cans, which are energy-intensive to make, polluting to use, and nonrecyclable.

CHOOSING A PRODUCT

GENERAL GUIDELINES

Natural, nontoxic remedies. Specialized basin, tub, and tile cleaners are rarely necessary. Try the do-it-yourself suggestions first; if they don't work, try safe, mild cleaners made from natural ingredients.

Cruelty-free products. Look for cleaners made by companies that do not test products on animals.

Sensible packaging. Save packaging by choosing the largest container practical. If you prefer a spray, don't choose an aerosol; instead, buy a manual-pump bottle and refill it.

COMMERCIAL PRODUCTS

Natural-ingredient, cruelty-free brands *(highly recommended)*. The following brands are available nationwide:

- Bon Ami Original Cleansing Powder, Bon Ami Polishing Cleanser. Found in many grocery or cleaning-supply stores.

- EarthRite Tub & Tile Cleaner. Buy in grocery and natural foods stores, or call EarthRite, (800) 828-4408, for a nearby distributor.

- Ecover Cream Cleaner. Buy in natural foods stores, or mail order from Ecco Bella, (201) 226-5799.

Major brands *(not generally recommended)*. All major-brand basin, tub, and tile cleaners use toxic, harsh chemicals and should be avoided whenever possible.

DO-IT-YOURSELF

Baking soda. Either dissolve baking soda in water or sprinkle it straight from the box, moisten it with water, and rub it with a damp cloth. It's nonabrasive and good for soap scum and minerals.

Vinegar. Use vinegar straight from the bottle for hard mineral deposits, or mix ¼ cup to 1 quart of vinegar with 1 gallon of water. Great for soap scum and minerals.

Borax. This natural mineral is safer than the harsh chemicals in commercial products, but is toxic if swallowed or inhaled, so use it with care. Scrub borax with a damp sponge. It works well on ceramic tile and porcelain, but will scratch softer surfaces, such as formica and other plastics.

Borax and vinegar. Mix ½ cup vinegar and ½ cup borax in enough warm water to dissolve the borax; make a fresh batch each time. Great for mold and mildew.

WISE USE

Safe use. If you must use a commercial chemical cleaner, ventilate the area well and wear rubber gloves to protect your hands.

DISINFECTANTS

Disinfectants kill microbes, but only temporarily. Most homes, except during outbreaks of highly contagious illnesses, don't require strong disinfectants.

ENVIRONMENTAL PROBLEMS

Harmful ingredients. Many of the ingredients used in commercial disinfectants are both toxic and polluting:

- *Cresol*, a phenol derived from coal tar or petroleum, can be absorbed by humans and pets through the skin, nose, and throat. Once absorbed it can damage the nervous system, liver, kidneys, and other organs.

- *O-phenylphenol*, another phenol, is toxic when swallowed. Found in the popular Lysol Disinfectant Spray, it is made from chlorine, benzene, and caustic soda.

- *Chlorine bleach*, found in household liquid bleach in the form of sodium hypochlorite, is toxic if swallowed and a strong skin and respiratory irritant.

- *Pine oil*, an ingredient in disinfectant all-purpose cleaners, is extracted from pine trees and processed with heat. It is quite flammable. Pine oil's "clean" smell comes from its oils and terpene alcohols; as they evaporate during manufacture and use, they pollute the air with hydrocarbons.

Animal cruelty. Because some ingredients can harm humans, manufacturers test disinfectants on animals, under inhumane conditions; the animals are killed after testing.

Wasteful packaging. Many disinfectants are packaged in aerosol cans, which are energy-intensive to make, polluting to use, and nonrecyclable.

CHOOSING A PRODUCT

GENERAL GUIDELINES

Natural, nontoxic remedies. Before you resort to a commercial product, try using hot water with either a mild all-purpose cleaner or one of the natural disinfectants listed below in Do-It-Yourself. Stronger disinfectants are rarely necessary.

Cruelty-free products. Look for disinfectants made by companies that do not test products on animals.

Sensible packaging. Instead of buying aerosols, look for concentrates you can mix with water. If you prefer a spray, buy a refillable manual-pump bottle.

COMMERCIAL PRODUCTS

Natural-ingredient, cruelty-free all-purpose cleaners *(highly recommended)*. Most good all-purpose cleaners kill germs on contact, making special disinfectants unnecessary. (See Table 10, All-Purpose Cleaners, p. 84.)

Hypo-allergenic disinfectants *(not generally recommended)*. Zephiran is a hospital-grade disinfectant whose active ingredient is benzalkonium chloride. Zephiran is highly toxic in concentrated form, but when diluted (1 part to 750 parts water) it is less irritating to sensitive people than most disinfectants. Pharmacies carry it as a concentrate. Handle it with extreme care.

Major-brand disinfectants *(not generally recommended)*. All major-brand disinfectants contain harmful ingredients; avoid them unless you are trying to control a serious contagious illness. If you must use a strong disinfectant for large surfaces such as floors, consider an all-purpose cleaner containing pine oil, such as Real Pine (30 percent pine oil) or Pine Power (19.9 percent pine oil). Though polluting to make and use, pine-oil cleaners are strong disinfectants with fewer health and environmental risks than petrochemical-based products. For disinfecting utensils and other household items, consider house-hold chlorine bleach dissolved in water, a multipurpose cleaner that leaves less of a residue than pine oil and other major-brand disinfectants.

DO-IT-YOURSELF

Borax. Add ½ cup of borax to a gallon of hot water, mix, and scrub with a damp sponge. Rinse well. You can store the mixture after use, but be sure to label it. This natural mineral is safer than the harsh chemicals in commercial products but is toxic if swallowed or inhaled; use it with care.

Borax and vinegar. To clean mold or mildew, mix ½ cup vinegar and ½ cup borax in enough warm water to dissolve the borax; make a fresh batch each time.

ALTERNATIVES

Good housekeeping. If you keep surfaces clean and dry, and wash them regularly with hot water and a mild all-purpose cleaner, you'll rarely need a disinfectant.

WISE USE

Conservative use. Microbes multiply rapidly, so disinfectants control them for only a short time. For extraordinary situations—such as a highly contagious illness in the home—consult a medical practitioner about the need for disinfectants.

Safe use. Treat all disinfectants as dangerous: use them only in well-ventilated areas, keep them away from flame and heat, and avoid getting them in your eyes or on your skin or mucous membranes.

DRAIN CLEANERS

Stopped-up drains are certainly frustrating, but most commercial drain openers are both dangerous and environmentally unsound—and if they fail to work, they can even compound the problem.

ENVIRONMENTAL PROBLEMS

Harmful ingredients. Chemical drain cleaners contain caustic lye (sodium hydroxide), sulfuric acid, or hydrochloric acid, making them some of the most dangerous household products in general use. Lye, which can kill tissue after only one second of exposure, causes up to 12,000 injuries a year in the United States.[1] Sulfuric or hydrochloric acid can also inflict serious burns.

Water pollution. Chemical cleaners move from the drain into the wastewater, further burdening the treatment facility that must remove these extremely corrosive chemicals and dissolved salts.

Animal cruelty. Because some ingredients can harm humans, many manufacturers test drain cleaners on animals, under inhumane conditions; afterward the animals are killed.

Ozone depletion. Aerosol drain openers that use pressure rather than chemicals contain chlorofluorocarbons (CFCs) as their propellants; CFCs contribute to the destruction of the stratospheric ozone layer that shields us from solar radiation. (Drain openers were exempted from the United States' 1978 ban on CFC use in aerosols.)

CHOOSING A PRODUCT

GENERAL GUIDELINES

Natural, nontoxic remedies. Always try the do-it-yourself formulas or mechanical techniques first; consider chemicals only for the most extraordinary cases.

COMMERCIAL PRODUCTS

Plungers *(highly recommended)*. A plunger is a safe and often effective tool for unclogging drains. Use flat-bottomed plungers to unclog sinks, round-bottomed plungers to unclog toilets. (*Never* use a plunger after trying a chemical cleaner; you could splash and burn yourself.)

Snakes *(highly recommended)*. These long, flexible metal augers are powered by hand or electricity. They are inserted into the clogged pipe and jiggled or rotated until they break up the stoppage. Found at rental or hardware stores, snakes are highly effective and require no special expertise. (Be *extremely* careful using one if you've already tried a chemical opener.)

Pumps *(highly recommended)*. Three mechanical-pump drain openers are available:

- ◆ Pango Modelo Brevattato, from Brookstone, (603) 924-7181, uses a hand-powered pump to shoot pressurized air down a drain.

- ◆ Sinkmaster, from M-P Corp., (313) 834-3200, uses a hand-powered pump to break up material by pumping it up and down.

- ◆ Vacuum Suction Pump (U.S. General, 100 Commercial St., Plainview, NY 11803) uses a hand-powered pump to pull obstructing material back up the pipe.

(If you've already used a chemical opener, use a pump only with *extreme* caution.)

Chemical drain cleaners *(never recommended)*. Not only are these products dangerous and polluting, they are often ineffective as well, compounding your problem: they leave lye or acid sitting in the blocked drain, making your next try at opening it even more hazardous. Well-known lye-based cleaners are Crystal Drano, Double Agent, Lewis Red Devil, Liquid Drano, Liquid Plumr, K-Mart, Mister Plumber, Mr. Roebic, Rooto, and Woolworth. Acid-based cleaners include Instant Power, Rooto Professional, and The Works. (All but Crystal Drano and Lewis Red Devil are liquids, which are more likely to splash on the skin.) Avoid them all. (*Never* use lye- and acid-based cleaners together, or one after the other.)

Pressurized drain openers *(never recommended)*. Drano Instant Plunger and Drain Power are two widely available brands that use ozone-depleting CFC gases to generate pressure; they should be avoided.

DO-IT-YOURSELF

Baking soda and vinegar. For minor blockages and as a regular treatment to keep drains open, pour ¼ cup baking soda down the drain followed immediately by ½ cup white vinegar; cover the drain for a minute and repeat. (*Do not use* after trying a chemical opener.)

Cleaning the P-trap. Clogged sink drains are often blocked in the P-trap, a removable joint that makes a U-turn under the sink before the drain continues downward. Traps catch rising sewer gases as well as hair, food, and other debris. Clean a trap as follows:

1. Bail out any standing water in the sink.

2. Remove any articles from under the sink.

3. Place a pan or washbasin directly under the trap to catch any water.

4. Using a large crescent wrench or pliers, unscrew the joint's connection(s) and slip it off.

5. Clean and replace the trap; be sure to tighten the connections firmly.

(*Do not* attempt this method after trying a chemical cleaner.)

ALTERNATIVES

Prevention. Keep your drains open by taking the following precautions:

- Always keep a strainer in the drain to catch debris.

- Never pour grease or oil down the drain.

- Every one or two weeks, mix 2 tablespoons baking soda, 2 tablespoons salt, and 1½ teaspoons cream of tartar. Pour the mixture down the drain, and follow with very hot and then cold water. (You can also use baking soda and vinegar, as described in Do-It-Yourself.)

WISE USE

Safe use. If you must use a chemical cleaner, be extremely careful:

- Avoid liquid products; liquid lye is especially dangerous and easy to spill.

- Follow the instructions carefully.

- Use as little cleaner as possible.

- If you try a chemical cleaner and it doesn't work, *never* follow it up with a plunger or any other chemicals—even nontoxic ones. You could splash yourself or cause an explosive chemical reaction. Call a plumber or home-repair service instead.

Proper disposal. For a chemical cleaner, make sure the container is empty (if it was a liquid, rinse the container thoroughly), then replace the cap and put it in the trash. Be sure any aerosol cans are empty of pressure before throwing them away.

1. Stephen Brobeck and Anne Averyt, *The Product Safety Book* (E.P. Dutton, 1983), p. 141.

FURNITURE POLISHES

Most commercial polishes let you shine your furniture with very little labor, but they take their toll on the environment.

ENVIRONMENTAL PROBLEMS

Air pollution. Many polishes contain oil, wax, or silicone in petroleum-based solvents that evaporate after application, leaving only the shiny coating. As they evaporate, the solvents release hydrocarbons and other volatile organic (carbon-containing) compounds. These highly reactive gases are air pollutants in their own right and also react with sunlight to form ozone, a serious pollutant and health hazard when found in the lower atmosphere.

Animal cruelty. Because some ingredients can harm humans, many manufacturers test polishes on animals, under inhumane conditions; afterward the animals are killed.

Wasteful packaging. Many furniture polishes come in aerosol cans that are energy-intensive to make, polluting to use, and nonrecyclable. Single-use, throwaway polishing cloths are also extremely wasteful.

CHOOSING A PRODUCT

GENERAL GUIDELINES

Simple, natural ingredients. Look for polishes that use beeswax or natural plant oils instead of petrochemical solvents, oils, or waxes.

Cruelty-free products. Look for polishes made by companies that do not test products on animals.

Sensible packaging. Instead of aerosol cans, choose the largest practical bottles, jars, or tins.

COMMERCIAL PRODUCTS

Natural-ingredient, cruelty-free brands *(highly recommended)*. These products require some rubbing but bring out a lustrous finish, cause no pollution, and involve no animal testing. Livos Plant Chemistry, (505) 438-3448, sells three such products:

- ◆ Alis Furniture Polish
- ◆ Bekos-Bee & Resin Ointment
- ◆ Gleivo Liquid Wax

Look for other brands in better hardware stores or co-ops.

Major brands *(not generally recommended)*. The use of petrochemicals as solvents and coatings makes these products environmentally unsound.

DO-IT-YOURSELF

Oil and vinegar spray. Add 2 tablespoons olive oil and 1 tablespoon white vinegar to 1 quart warm water; mix thoroughly. Suitable for a spray bottle, but works best if slightly warmed first. Rub well after applying.

Oil and lemon juice. For scratches, mix equal parts of olive oil and lemon juice and rub into wood thoroughly with a soft cloth.

WISE USE

Safe use. If you must use a petrochemical furniture polish, use as little as possible, open windows and doors to ventilate the area during and after use, and keep the polish and used rags away from heat or flame.

Proper disposal. Treat all petrochemical polishes as hazardous waste. Never throw away leftover polish; instead, store it in a cool, dry place for hazardous waste collection or take it to a collection site. Call your local waste disposal office for information on hazardous waste collection programs. Be sure any aerosol cans are empty of pressure before throwing them away.

INSECT REPELLENTS

By keeping flies, mosquitoes, and ticks at bay, repellents help us enjoy the outdoors and avoid Lyme disease, encephalitis, and other illnesses. Unfortunately, many repellents are also quite dangerous.

ENVIRONMENTAL PROBLEMS

Toxic ingredients. "Deet" is the harmless-sounding common name for N,N-diethyl-m-toluamide, the active ingredient in most bug repellents. Deet is made from xylene, a toxic petroleum derivative, and other toxic chemicals through a heat-intensive, air-polluting process. Used in industry as a solvent for resins, deet is toxic to swallow and irritating to eyes and mucous membranes. Potential toxic and allergic reactions to deet include slurred speech, trembling, seizures, coma, and death. It is particularly dangerous for infants and children.

Animal cruelty. Because some ingredients can harm humans, many manufacturers test insect repellents on animals, under inhumane conditions; afterward the animals are killed.

Wasteful packaging. Insect repellents often come in aerosol cans, which are energy-intensive to make, polluting to use, and nonrecyclable. Throwaway towelettes are also wasteful.

CHOOSING A PRODUCT

GENERAL GUIDELINES

Nontoxic or less toxic repellents. Try herbal-based, cruelty-free insect repellents first; if they don't work, use chemical repellents with low concentrations of deet.

Cruelty-free products. Look for repellents made by companies that do not test products on animals.

Sensible packaging. Instead of aerosol cans and towelettes, choose lotions or liquids in the largest practical sizes.

COMMERCIAL PRODUCTS

Herbal, cruelty-free insect repellents *(recommended)*. These products use essential oils of citronella, pennyroyal, and other herbs to repel flies, mosquitoes, fleas, and ticks. They are made from natural ingredients, but are potential irritants to some people and should be handled and used with care:

- Bugg Off; available from Wyoming Wild-crafters, (307) 733-6731.

- Green Ban Insect Repellent; buy in natural foods stores or mail order from A Clear Alternative, (713) 356-7031.

- Honeydew Herbal Citronella Insect Screen; mail order from Co-op America, (802) 655-2975.

- No Common Scents Insect Repellent; mail order from No Common Scents, (513) 767-4261.

Look for these or other herbal products in natural foods or outdoor equipment stores, or ask your local drugstore or food store to order them. *(Caution:* pregnant women should avoid using products containing pennyroyal.)

Deet-based insect repellents *(not generally recommended)*. Commercial repellents contain deet in concentrations of up to 100 percent. If you must resort to deet, minimize the risk of skin absorption and possible reactions by choosing a brand with a low deet percentage. The following products are widely available and come in nonaerosol form:

- 6-12 Plus (stick), 9.1 percent deet

- Cutter Insect Repellent (spray), 17.9 percent deet

- Deep Woods Off! (spray), 20 percent deet

Electric bug killers *(never recommended)*. Noisy, visually offensive, and energy-consuming, these devices kill mostly nonpest insects.

ALTERNATIVES

Proper dress. Wear light-colored, long-sleeved shirts and long pants, and avoid using scented products, which can attract mosquitoes.

Habitat control. To prevent mosquito infestations, check your yard and the surrounding area for mosquito-breeding areas of standing water (on the ground, in toys or equipment, or in old tires or containers).

- To help control insects, encourage pest-eating birds and bats; add purple martin houses and bat houses to your backyard.

Limiting time outdoors. Limit your time outdoors around dawn and dusk, when mosquitoes are most active. During tick season, avoid weedy, brushy areas.

WISE USE

Safe use. If you use either deet or herbal repellents, take the following precautions:

- Apply repellents only to your clothing instead of to your skin, if possible.

- Always keep repellents away from your eyes, nose, and mouth.

- Wash repellents from your skin as soon as possible.

- Watch for allergic reactions.

- Avoid using repellents repeatedly over days or weeks.

- Don't use repellents on infants or on small children.

- If pregnant, avoid pennyroyal products.

FOR FURTHER INFORMATION: "Those Damned Mosquitoes" (Massachusetts Audubon Society, South Great Road, Lincoln, MA 01773).

INSECTICIDES, HOUSEHOLD

Americans use about 300 million pounds of chemical insecticides in their homes every year. These compounds are toxic and polluting, and often ineffective, because some insects quickly build up resistance to them.[1]

ENVIRONMENTAL PROBLEMS

Toxic ingredients. Table 11 lists some common but toxic household insecticides. Many people feel safe using such chemicals as long as they don't swallow them, but some pesticides enter the body through the skin or lungs.[2] Once absorbed the chemicals usually enter the bloodstream, bypassing the liver, which could otherwise help detoxify them.[3] The immediate, short-term effects of pesticides—either synthetic or naturally derived—entering the body can include headache, nausea, vomiting, muscle twitching, convulsions, or tremors, as well as skin, eye, or mucous-membrane irritation.[4] If the chemicals are fat-soluble, they can build up in fatty tissue, causing long-term ill effects. Their toxicity and their easy availability (they're often stored under the sink) make pesticides a special threat to children: nationally, pesticides—including insecticides, weed-killers, and rodenticides—are the second-leading cause of child poisonings.[5]

Manufacturing impacts. Not surprisingly, the materials from which chemical insecticides are made are also poisonous; processing them contaminates the air and water and endangers workers' health.

Animal cruelty. Because some ingredients can harm humans, many manufacturers test insecticides on animals, under inhumane conditions; afterward the animals are killed.

Wasteful packaging. Many insecticides come in aerosol cans, which are energy-intensive to make, polluting to use, and nonrecyclable. Even nonaerosol dispensers contain toxic residues that make them unsuitable for recycling and create potential pollution hazards in landfills or incinerators.

CHOOSING A PRODUCT

GENERAL GUIDELINES

Natural, nontoxic remedies. Unless you have an unusually serious infestation, you should be able to control household insects without resorting to toxic chemicals. Try the nonchemical products and alternatives first; if you must use chemicals, begin with the least poisonous.

Sensible packaging. If you must use a chemical product, look for one in a nonaerosol container.

COMMERCIAL PRODUCTS

Insecticidal soaps *(highly recommended).* These products use a simple soap-and-water solution and often work well when applied directly to insects such as ants, aphids, crickets, earwigs, mealybugs, scale, and white flies. The soaps' fatty acids penetrate the insects' membranes and dehydrate the insects. These products are effective yet quite safe for people and pets. Look for Safer Insecticidal Soap and other brands in better hardware and garden-supply stores, co-ops, or natural foods stores, or contact Safer at (800) 423-7544.

Diatomaceous earth *(highly recommended).* Mined from deposits of fossilized, algae-like plants, this soft powder consists mostly of silica and is nontoxic to humans and animals. As they travel about, insects pick up its sharp microscopic particles, which lacerate the insects' waxy protective coating and draw moisture from them, causing rapid dehydration. When spread along insect trails, it kills ants, crickets, fleas, roaches, ticks, weevils, and many other soft-bodied insects. (Note: *Don't* use diatomaceous earth in gardens or flower beds, because it indiscrimi-

TABLE 11

TOXIC HOUSEHOLD INSECTICIDES TO AVOID

Generic or Trade Name	Chemical Names[a]	Contained In
Diazinon	0,0-diethyl 0-(2-isopropyl-4-methyl-6-pyrimidinyl) phosphorothioate	Johnston's No-Roach Spray Ortho Products Real-Kill Ant and Roach Killer
Chlorpyrifos (Dursban, Lorsban)	0,0-diethyl 0-3, 5, 6-trichloro-2-pyridyl phosphorothioate	Bug-out Home Pest Control d-Con Home Pest Control Killer Ortho Flea-B-Gone Raid Home Insect Killer Raid Roach Controller
Propoxur (Baygon, Unden)	Ortho-isopropoxyphenyl-N-methylcarbamate	Ortho Earwig, Roach, and Sowbug Bait Ortho Hornet and Wasp Killer Ortho Pest-B-Gone Ortho Ant, Roach, and Spider Killer Raid Wasp and Hornet Killer
Methoxychlor	Methoxy DDT; DMDT; 2,2-bis (p-methoxyphenol)-l,l,l,-trichloroethane	Black Flag Insect Spray Sergeant's Cat Flea Powder

[a] Some products list ingredients by chemical rather than trade name.

nately kills both pests and beneficial insects.) Look for Fossil Flowers Diatomaceous Earth or Natural Guard Diatomaceous Earth at garden-supply stores, or order Bug and Pest Control from 4-D SUNaturals, (602) 257-1950.

Nonpoisonous flypaper traps (*highly recommended*). Though visually unpleasant, these traps are effective and nontoxic. They are long strips of paper coated with sticky gum resins that trap flies. They're very sticky, so hang them well out of the way. Look for Lure-Fly Fly Catchers, Aeroxon Fly Catchers, or Big Stick Fly Traps in hardware or garden-supply stores.

Boric acid insecticides (*not generally recommended*). Boric acid, made from borax, is somewhat safer than many insecticides but is still toxic to swallow and irritating to the skin. Usually mixed with bait and eaten by insects, boric acid is a stomach poison with one advantage over many of the nerve poisons in other insecticides: insects cannot develop a resistance to it. (They can, however, learn to avoid it.) Look for Drax, made by R Value/West, (818) 798-4000, in better hardware stores.

Pyrethrum insecticides (*not generally recommended*). Certain chrysanthemums native to Ecuador, Kenya, and Japan contain pyrethrum, a natural, toxic insecticide that can be refined into the stronger pyrethrin I, pyrethrin II, cinerin I, and cinerin II. These products kill ants, cockroaches, crickets, fleas, silverfish, and ticks. They quickly break down into harmless substances, but while intact they are toxic to people (and may cause allergic reactions), animals, and aquatic life. Use them only if absolutely necessary and with extreme care. Look for EcoSafe Pyrethrum Insect Powder at better hardware stores, or call EcoSafe at (800) 553-4833.

Chemical insecticides (*never recommended*). Table 11 shows the most dangerous products in common use; they are all quite toxic. Other chemical insecticides have varying degrees of toxicity, but should be avoided if at all possible because of the environmental impacts of their production, use, and disposal.

DO-IT-YOURSELF

Ants. Simply wiping up ants with a wet cloth or sponge can discourage further exploration. If that's not enough, try the following measures:

- Wash counters and floors with a mixture of half vinegar and half water.

- Find out where the ants enter your home (they usually live outside and journey back and forth), and encourage them to stay outside by putting ½ teaspoon of honey near their path. To discourage them from coming in, pour cream of tartar, powdered red chile, paprika, or peppermint across their entry path.

- Use strong mint tea in a refillable spray bottle as a repellent.

- Steep catnip leaves in hot water, cool, and strain for a bottle spray.

- Make your own insecticidal soap solution by adding 1 part liquid soap to 50 parts water; spray it directly on ants.

Beetles and weevils. Beetles and weevils usually infest stored grains such as flour, cereal, and cornmeal:

- Place two or three bay leaves in containers of any foods likely to be infested.

- Freeze the foods for 48 hours before you store them to kill eggs.

Cockroaches. A number of home remedies can help discourage these persistent pests:

- Spread bay leaves around infested areas.

- Kill cockroaches with a hot house; they expire after an hour at 115° F. On a hot day close the windows, turn the furnace on, and leave for a while (be sure to take pets and houseplants with you).

- Trap them: grease the inside of the top of a glass jar, put a piece of banana inside for bait, and lean a ruler against the jar as a gangplank.

- Poison them with borax: thoroughly mix 2 tablespoons flour, 1 tablespoon cocoa, and 4 tablespoons borax and spread the mixture in infested areas but *out* of reach of small children and pets. Borax is toxic; keep it away from your mouth, eyes, and skin.

Fleas. See Flea and Tick Control, p. 271.

Flies. Discourage flies by hanging small bags of clover flowers, crushed cloves, bay leaves, and eucalyptus leaves in doorways.

Houseplant insects. Try these simple, nontoxic measures to combat pests on your houseplants:

- For mealybugs, wipe the infested area every few days with cotton swabs dipped in rubbing alcohol.

- For scale, scrub the affected areas with an old toothbrush and water.

- For spider mites, spray the plants with a hand-pump water bottle every day.

- For white flies, place glue traps near the plants.

Moths. See Mothproofing, p. 96.

Silverfish. To discourage silverfish, keep all areas of your home very dry, or try the following measures:

- Trap them with a mixture of 1 part molasses to 2 parts vinegar. Put it in a jar lid where they enter rooms, such as floor cracks and holes in walls.

- Kill them with a mixture of borax and honey (see Cockroaches for precautions).

Spiders. Don't kill spiders unless they are a serious problem; they kill other undesirable insects and do not infest food. If you must remove them, trap them with a glass and a piece of paper, and put them outdoors.

Termites. Prevent termites through vigilance and periodic maintenance:

- Termites often build tunnels, tan-colored and about ¼-inch around, up the foundation. Check your foundation occasionally from both outside and inside the crawl space, and destroy any tunnels.

- Make sure the soil near the foundation is well drained and dry.

- Remove any scrap wood piles close to the house.

- Never place wooden steps, posts, or supports directly in or on the ground.

- Fill any cracks in the foundation with cement grout.

- Quickly replace any damaged wood, such as foundation plates and floor joists.

- During construction you can place metal shields between the foundation and the wooden sill plate; they act as a physical barrier to termites. Ask building-supply stores or contractors about them.

WISE USE

Good housekeeping. No insecticide—toxic or nontoxic—will work effectively unless you keep your house reasonably clean. Keep counters wiped off, floors swept and mopped, and foods tightly closed and put away.

Proper disposal. Treat any unwanted insecticides as hazardous wastes; the only proper disposal method is incineration under controlled conditions. Store the insecticides carefully for hazardous waste collection, or take them to a collection site. Call your local waste disposal office for information on hazardous waste collection programs.

SEE ALSO: Pesticides, Garden and Lawn, p. 286.

1. Bryan Jay Bashin, "Bug Bomb Fallout," *Harrowsmith* (May/June 1989), p. 43.
2. "Selected Pesticide Residues or Metabolites in Blood or Urine Specimens from a General Population Survey," *Environmental Health Perspectives 48* (1983), pp. 81–86.
3. N. Irving Sax, *Dangerous Properties of Industrial Materials* (Van Nostrand Reinhold, 1984), pp. 3–4.
4. Andrew Watterson, *Pesticide Users' Health and Safety Handbook* (Van Nostrand Reinhold, 1988), pp. 399–407.
5. Bashin, op. cit., p. 114.

MOTHPROOFING

Moths don't eat clothes, but their larvae do. Mothproofing products help repel the moths before they lay their eggs; unfortunately, the most popular mothproofers are environmentally unsound.

ENVIRONMENTAL PROBLEMS

Air pollution. The two most common ingredients in mothballs and other repellents are p-dichlorobenzene (made by chlorinating benzene, a carcinogen) and napthalene, or tar camphor, derived from coal-tar oils or petroleum. These two volatile organic (carbon-containing) compounds are very reactive, vaporize continuously, and pollute the indoor and outdoor air with hydrocarbons.

Toxic ingredients. P-dichlorobenzene is toxic if swallowed and an eye irritant; napthalene is toxic if inhaled.

CHOOSING A PRODUCT

GENERAL GUIDELINES

Natural, nontoxic remedies. Before you resort to chemical repellents, try cedar products or the other suggestions in Do-It-Yourself and Alternatives.

COMMERCIAL PRODUCTS

Cedar moth repellents *(highly recommended).* Moths dislike cedar, and it often repels them quite effectively. Table 12 lists some widely available cedar products.

Chemical moth repellents *(never recommended).* These products all have toxic, polluting ingredients; use them only in extraordinary cases, as a last resort.

TABLE
12

MOTHBALL ALTERNATIVES

Brand	Description	Use	Available At
Cedar Friends in Animal Shapes	Small blocks of cedar	In closets and garment bags	Ecco Bella (201) 226-5799
Cedarscenter Cedar Balls	Small blocks of cedar	In drawers and chests	Better hardware stores
Cedarscenter Cedar Butterflies	Butterfly-shaped pieces of cedar on strings	In closets and garment bags	Better hardware stores
Cedarscenter Cedar Chips	Porous paper packets with cedar shavings	In drawers and chests	Better hardware stores
Texas Moth Balls	Small blocks of cedar	In drawers and chests	Ecco Bella (201) 226-5799

DO-IT-YOURSELF

Cedar repellents. You can make your own cedar repellents; just buy cedar boards at a lumberyard and place them in closets or storage areas, or put cedar shavings in light cloth bags.

Aromatic herbs. Packets of fragrant, aromatic herbs repel moths; lavender, pennyroyal, and peppercorns are all effective. One herbal recipe: fill a cheesecloth bag with equal parts rosemary, mint, and thyme, and 1 to 2 tablespoons cloves.

ALTERNATIVES

Washing and storage. For long-term storage wash all clothes immediately before storing them, to kill any eggs. Then pack them in boxes, sealing the edges with tape.

Cedar chests and closets. These once-common moth-repelling storage areas are both effective and attractive. For long-term storage follow the directions above.

WISE USE

Safe use. If you must use mothproofing chemicals, seal the storage container carefully to keep the vapors from dissipating, and store it away from living areas. When unpacking it, air both the container and the clothes outdoors or in a well-ventilated, unoccupied room.

Proper disposal. Treat all chemical mothproofers as hazardous waste; never place them in the regular trash. Instead, store them safely for hazardous waste collection or take them to a collection site. Call your local waste disposal office for information on hazardous waste collection programs.

RODENT CONTROL

Mice or rats in the home are intolerable, but rodent poisons often create more problems than they solve.

ENVIRONMENTAL PROBLEMS

Toxic ingredients. The poisons that kill rodents are also harmful to people, pets, and wildlife, and poisoned rodent carcasses can kill animals that eat them. Manufacturing these poisons also creates serious air pollution and toxic wastes. Three common rodent poisons are

- *Arsenic trioxide*, a human carcinogen and poison made by smelting copper and lead concentrates, treating the resulting dust with metals, and then condensing it.

- *White phosphorus,* made by heating phosphate rock, sand, and coke in furnaces and condensing the vapors; toxic if swallowed or inhaled, it can also burn skin on contact.

- *Warfarin*, a highly poisonous compound made through a complex process from coumarin, itself toxic and carcinogenic.

Sanitation risks. Because poisoning can take time, dying rodents sometimes crawl into walls or crevices, where their decaying carcasses cause odors and pose health hazards.

Animal cruelty. Some poisons and traps work slowly, subjecting the animals to prolonged suffering before they die.

CHOOSING A PRODUCT

GENERAL GUIDELINES

Nonpoisonous, humane remedies. Use humane traps instead of chemical poisons and cruel traps.

COMMERCIAL PRODUCTS

Live traps *(highly recommended)*. The most humane approach is to trap rodents uninjured and release them well away from buildings and people. Look for these three reusable live traps in better hardware stores:

Brand	Capacity	Materials
Ketch All	2–4 mice	metal
Victor Havahart	1–2 mice	plastic
Victor Tin Cat	4+ mice	metal

Quick-kill traps *(sometimes recommended)*. If you live in an urban area where releasing live rodents is not practical, the next-best method is a quick-kill trap. Some widely available spring-loaded traps are

Brand	Capacity	Materials
Big Snap-E	4+ mice	plastic, metal
Snap-E	1–2 mice	plastic, metal
Victor Standard	1–2 mice	wood, metal

Nontoxic bait *(sometimes recommended)*. Large doses of vitamin D can kill mice and rats by disrupting the calcium levels in their blood. Vitamin D Rat and Mouse Bait, nontoxic to humans and pets, is available as pellets or granules in better hardware stores or by mail order from Gardens Alive! (812) 623-3800.

Cats *(not generally recommended)*. Cats can reduce, if not eliminate, rodent populations. But because they have their own environmental impacts (see Pets, p. 273) and often kill their prey slowly and cruelly, cats are not a sound choice for rodent control.

Poisons *(never recommended)*. Use these products only for an extreme infestation, only for a short period of time, and only after you have tried nontoxic methods.

Glue traps *(never recommended)*. These traps are simply paper smeared with a thick, sticky glue; as the animal struggles it gets more firmly stuck. The glue is nontoxic, so the traps are touted as safe, but they are actually inhumane and wasteful: you can't release the animal from the powerful glue, so you must either let it suffer a slow death or kill it yourself—and then throw away the trap, with the animal still attached.

ALTERNATIVES

Prevention. The best way to combat rodents is to make your house unattractive to them:

■ Keep the floors and counters clean.

■ Keep food stored securely in metal or glass containers.

■ Plug any cracks or holes in the floors and walls.

■ Weatherstrip the bottoms of all exterior doors.

WISE USE

Efficient use. If you have a persistent or serious rodent problem, take a systematic approach:

■ Set five to ten traps at once to eliminate resident rodents quickly and discourage new arrivals.

■ Move the traps around; mice and rats learn quickly.

■ If your traps require bait, change it every day or two; peanut butter, not cheese, is reputed to work best.

Humane use. Use all rodent-control methods as humanely as possible:

■ Check traps often; even quick-kill traps might not kill rodents immediately, but instead hold them entrapped, causing prolonged suffering and slow death from bleeding or dehydration.

■ If you need to kill a rodent quickly, submerge it in a bucket of water; wash the bucket afterward with a mild soap.

Safe use. For maximum safety and sanitation, take the following precautions:

■ If you use traps, keep them reasonably clean (you can clean them outdoors with soap and a hose); store and use them well away from pets or children.

■ If you must use poisons, be extremely careful: store and use them well away from children, pets, foods, or utensils; never place them on counters or in appliances or cabinets. If you must dispose of poisons, treat them as hazardous wastes; seal them tightly and store them in a cool, protected place for hazardous waste collection, or take them to a collection site. Call your local waste disposal office for information on hazardous waste collection programs.

■ Dispose of dead rodents in your regular household trash; wash your hands thoroughly after handling them.

WINDOW AND GLASS CLEANERS

Commercial window cleaners might make an unpopular task slightly easier—but not enough to offset the environmental costs incurred.

ENVIRONMENTAL PROBLEMS

Harmful ingredients. Most window cleaners contain water-soluble ammonia, a poisonous gas or liquid made from fossil fuels through a complex process that uses high pressure and heat. Ammonia is a strong alkali that cuts oils and grease, but it also irritates the eyes and mucous membranes.

Animal cruelty. Because some ingredients can harm humans, many manufacturers test cleaners on animals, under inhumane conditions; afterward the animals are killed.

Wasteful packaging. Water is the main ingredient in most window cleaners, adding substantial packaging and transportation costs for a substance already found in every home. Furthermore, some cleaners come in aerosol cans, which are energy-intensive to make, polluting to use, and nonrecyclable.

CHOOSING A PRODUCT

GENERAL GUIDELINES

Natural, nontoxic remedies. Commercial window cleaners are rarely necessary. Instead, make your own effective, inexpensive cleaner using the do-it-yourself suggestions below.

Cruelty-free products. Look for cleaners made by companies that do not test products on animals.

Sensible packaging. Buy a refillable, manual-pump spray bottle and fill it with homemade cleaner. If you must use a commercial product, avoid aerosol cans and nonrefillable sprayers; instead, buy large bottles and refill your own sprayer.

COMMERCIAL PRODUCTS

Squeegees *(highly recommended)*. These devices, which have handles of various lengths and soft rubber blades for wiping, make streak-free window cleaning fast and simple—even with plain water. Look for them in hardware stores.

Cruelty-free brands *(sometimes recommended)*. Two of these products widely sold in natural foods stores are

- Allens Naturally Glass Cleaner
- Winter White Glass Mate Cleaner

Major brands *(not generally recommended)*. If you prefer a commercial product, choose a vinegar-based (usually green-tinted) rather than an ammonia-based (blue-tinted) cleaner. Some major-brand vinegar cleaners available in pump spray bottles are A & P with Vinegar, Kroger Bright with Vinegar, Safeway White Magic with Vinegar, SOS Glass Works with Vinegar, and Windex with Vinegar.

DO-IT-YOURSELF

Warm water. For lightly soiled windows try plain warm water and a squeegee.

Vinegar. For medium cleaning use vinegar: add 1 to 2 tablespoons to a pint of warm water and mix thoroughly. For extra strength add 1 teaspoon liquid dishwashing detergent.

Rubbing alcohol. In cold weather add 1 tablespoon of rubbing alcohol to homemade cleaner as an antifreeze.

Rags. Newspaper does shine windows, because of its ink, but leaves a pile of soggy, hard-to-recycle paper. Instead of newspaper or paper towels, use clean rags.

WISE USE

Safe use. If you must use ammonia-based window cleaners, use them only in well-ventilated areas. Keep them away from children.

HOME CONSTRUCTION, SYSTEMS, AND REPAIR

AIR CONDITIONERS, HOUSEHOLD

Home air conditioning makes hot weather more bearable and helps filter out allergens and pollutants, but its environmental costs are enormous.

ENVIRONMENTAL PROBLEMS

Energy consumption. Each summer our nation's 50 million central and room air conditioners cause electricity demands to soar. Running a room air conditioner for a summer uses almost as much electricity—nearly 900 kilowatt-hours—as running a refrigerator for an entire year.[1] Air conditioners are becoming increasingly energy efficient, but they are still a major culprit in the government's forecast of rising electricity consumption through the year 2000.[2] Producing the energy to power air conditioners depletes reserves of nonrenewable fossil fuels and creates vast amounts of the chemicals that contribute to acid rain, air pollution, and the greenhouse effect.

Ozone depletion. The coolant in air conditioners (HCFC-22) is a chlorofluorocarbon (CFC) with an added hydrogen atom that causes the molecule to break up in the atmosphere. Because it does not harm the stratospheric ozone as severely as other CFCs, and because no good replacement has yet been found, HCFC-22 was exempted from the 1987 Montreal Protocol limiting CFC use. However, HCFC-22 is considered an unwanted atmospheric chemical because it does cause some ozone depletion; manufacturers are looking for alternatives, anticipating an eventual ban.

Health hazards. Air conditioners not only pollute the outdoor air through their energy use, they can also pollute the indoor air. Despite their dust-removing filters, they can actually recirculate some pollutants and contaminants.[3] The drip pan, which collects moisture removed from the air, can also cause contamination: if water doesn't drain from the pan properly, microorganisms can proliferate and be distributed throughout the home.[4]

CHOOSING A PRODUCT

GENERAL GUIDELINES

Weighing your needs. Decide whether you really need air conditioning and if so, how often. Consider alternatives—fans, ventilation systems, awnings, trees—to reduce or replace your air-conditioner use. When choosing between room or central air conditioners, weigh their advantages and disadvantages carefully:

- *Room air conditioners* are less expensive and easier to install and remove, and they enable you to cool selected rooms. They're less effective for large areas or whole houses, however, and they generate noise in the living space.

- *Central air conditioners* cool your entire home evenly, adapt well to forced-air heating systems, and permit you to choose the correct cooling capacity for your entire home. On the other hand, they're expensive to install and permanent, they're difficult to install if your heating isn't forced air, and they don't do well at cooling only selected rooms.

Energy efficiency. When purchasing a new air conditioner, make your top priority energy efficiency, which varies widely among brands and models. Make sure you check the energy-efficiency rating of any unit you consider.

Cooling capacity. Select a machine with the right cooling capacity—measured in either British thermal units (Btu) per hour, or tons—for your living space. Too large a unit will waste electricity and cost more to run, and won't dehumidify adequately, leaving your home cool and damp. Too small a unit will run too often and won't cool adequately or evenly. To get a simple, do-it-yourself estimate sheet, ask the Association of Home Appliance Manufacturers, (312) 984-5800, for a "Cooling Load Estimate Form."

COMMERCIAL PRODUCTS

Energy-efficient room air conditioners *(recommended).* Look for the Energy Efficiency Rating (EER) on the machine's EnergyGuide Label: generally an EER of 8.5 is good; 10 or higher is excellent. Table 13 lists the most energy-efficient models, rated by cooling capacity and energy use.

Energy-efficient central air conditioners *(recommended).* Central air conditioners receive a Seasonal Energy Efficiency Rating (SEER) but seldom have it displayed on the EnergyGuide Label; ask the dealer or contractor to supply it. A SEER of 12 or more is good; 15 or more is excellent. Table 14 lists the most efficient models, with their cooling capacities. (*Note:* If you replace your outdoor compressor unit with a new, efficient compressor, be sure your indoor blower coil is equally efficient or the system won't operate at optimal energy efficiency.)

ALTERNATIVES

Ventilation. To remove heat from your home without using much electricity, try the following:

- Cool your attic either with roof and gable vents or with convection systems, in which outdoor air enters through openings in the lower roof and exits through vents above.

- Cool parts or all of your home with fans (see Fans, p. 112).

Building design and insulation. If you are building or remodeling your home, keep cooling in mind:

- Plan for adequate ventilation and air flow. Look for do-it-yourself guides to installing effective ventilation systems or contact a building contractor.

- If you can get into your attic, make sure both the rafters and the ceiling joists are well insulated, then add a layer of heat-reflective aluminum foil over the insulation in the rafters.

Look for special fiber-reinforced foil at larger hardware and building-supply stores.

- If you live in a warm climate, paint your house a light color to reflect the sun's heat.

- Shade sunlit windows with awnings.

Landscaping. To cool the outdoor air near your home, plant trees and shrubs nearby, particularly on the south and west sides (but don't let them block prevailing breezes that can help cool your home). Trees and shrubs provide shade and also cool through evaporation; three mature trees shading a house can reduce air conditioner use by 20 to 50 percent (see Trees, p. 291).[5]

WISE USE

Conservative use. Use your air conditioner as little as possible:

- Use it only when the temperature and humidity are too high for alternatives to work.

- Cool only those parts of your home that are in use.

- Pull the shades on windows to prevent the sun from shining in.

- Limit use of ovens and other heat producers.

Regular maintenance. To keep your room or central air conditioner running smoothly and safely, make sure it's well maintained:

- Keep the unit's drain hole and tubes unclogged. If the outside tube doesn't drip regularly whenever the unit is running, shut the machine off and check and clean both the drip pan and the tube. If your unit is difficult to clean, as many are, call a repair service.

- Clean or change the filter regularly.

- Clean the coils yourself or have the machine serviced and cleaned yearly, or whenever dirt accumulates on the coils.

TABLE 13

ENERGY-EFFICIENT ROOM AIR CONDITIONERS

Brand	Model	Energy Efficiency (EER)[a]	Cooling Capacity (Btu/Hr)[b]
115 VOLTS			
Cooling Capacity: Under 5,000 Btu/Hr			
General Electric	ATX04LA	9.0	4,400
	ATM04LA	8.0	4,200
Hotpoint	HTP04LA; KTM04LA	8.0	4,200
Kenmore	106.8790531	8.0	4,950
Cooling Capacity: 5,000 to 5,999 Btu/Hr			
Airtemp	C3R06F2A; G3R06F2A	10.0	5,800
Climatrol	M3R06F2A	10.0	5,800
Fedders	A3R06F2A	10.0	5,800
Friedrich	SQ05H10	10.0	5,600
Hunter	42060005	10.0	5,800
Marta America	W3R06F2A	10.0	5,800
Sharp	AF-508M6	9.5	5,500
	AF-507M6	9.4	5,500
Airtemp	C2G05F2A	9.0	5,250
	C2P05F2A; G2P05F2A	9.0	5,400
Carrier	51AGZ7051; 51BTZ7051; 51ZMB7051; 77ATA0051	9.0	5,400
Climatrol	M2G05F2A	9.0	5,250
	M2P05F2A	9.0	5,400
Crest	15-152	9.0	5,250
	15540	9.0	5,400
Crosley	CCA5E63	9.0	5,200
Emerson Quiet Kool	5DC53	9.0	5,200
Fedders	A2G05F2A	9.0	5,250
	A2P05F2A	9.0	5,400
Friedrich	KP06G10E	9.0	5,900
Frigidaire	A06LE2N; A06LH5N	9.0	5,900
Gibson	AL06A4EYA; AL06A5EYA	9.0	5,900
Hampton Bay	15541	9.0	5,400
Hunter	41054005	9.0	5,400
J.C. Penney	8571705	9.0	5,400
Kelvinator	MH206H1QA	9.0	5,900
Kenmore	106.8760582; 106.8790550	9.0	5,000
Marta America	W2P05F2A	9.0	5,400
Montgomery Ward	5057D; UEE5455	9.0	5,200
Panasonic	CW-501JU	9.0	5,000
Quasar	HQ2052DW	9.0	5,000
Teknika	AM54E	9.0	5,200
	AM53E	9.0	5,300
Whirlpool	ACP552XT1; ACQ052XWO	9.0	5,000
White-Westinghouse	AC062N7A1; AC066N7A	9.0	5,900
Cooling Capacity: 6,000 to 6,999 Btu/Hr			
Emerson Quiet Kool	6DC53	10.0	6,500
Friedrich	SQ06H10	10.0	6,500
Montgomery Ward	UEE5465	10.0	6,500
Sharp	AF-607M6	9.8	6,300

TABLE 13

ENERGY-EFFICIENT ROOM AIR CONDITIONERS *(continued)*

Brand	Model	Energy Efficiency (EER)[a]	Cooling Capacity (Btu/Hr)[b]
Amana	7P2MA	9.5	6,650
General Electric	AME06LA	9.5	6,000
Panasonic	CW-601JU	9.5	6,000
Quasar	HQ2062DW	9.5	6,000
Sharp	AF-608M6	9.5	6,500
Teknika	AM63E; AM64E	9.5	6,300
Carrier	51ZMB7061	9.4	6,200
Panasonic	CW-600HU; CW-601HU	9.1	6,000
Quasar	HQ5061DW; HQ5061DW1	9.1	6,000
Cooling Capacity: 7,000 to 7,999 Btu/Hr			
Friedrich	SS07H10A	11.0	7,200
Sanyo	ES0711	10.2	7,000
Emerson Quiet Kool	7DC73	10.0	7,200
Friedrich	SQ07H10	10.0	7,100
Harvard	7HA720	9.5	7,200
Teknika	AM73E; AM74E	9.5	7,200
White-Westinghouse	AC079N7B1	9.3	7,000
General Electric	ACM08FAT1; ACM08FAX1	9.2	7,900
Hotpoint	KCM08FAT1; KCM08FAX1	9.2	7,900
Airtemp	C2R07F2A; G2R07F2A	9.0	7,000
	C1V08S2A; G1V08S2A	9.0	7,600
Climatrol	M2R07F2A	9.0	7,000
	M1V08S2A	9.0	7,600
Crest	15700	9.0	7,000
Fedders	A2R07F2A	9.0	7,000
	A1V08S2A	9.0	7,600
General Electric	ACS08AA	9.0	7,800
Hampton Bay	15701	9.0	7,000
Hotpoint	KCD08AAT1	9.0	7,800
J.C. Penney	8571713	9.0	7,000
	9467325	9.0	7,600
Kenmore	484.8700730	9.0	7,000
Marta America	W2R07F2A	9.0	7,000
Panasonic	CW-700JU	9.0	7,000
Quasar	HQ2071DW	9.0	7,000
Cooling Capacity: 8,000 to 8,999 Btu/Hr			
Friedrich	SS08H10A	10.5	8,200
Kenmore	106.8770881	9.7	8,000
Teknika	AK83E; AK84E	9.7	8,000
Kenmore	253.8780892	9.6	8,000
	106.8790830	9.6	8,250
Carrier	51CMA1091; 51CMB1091	9.5	8,800
General Electric	AME08FA	9.5	8,000
Panasonic	CW-802JU	9.5	8,000
Quasar	HQ2082DW	9.5	8,000
Whirlpool	ACPS82XS0; ACW082XS0	9.5	8,000
Climette	KAF08E1A	9.4	8,000
Keeprite	KAF08E1A	9.4	8,000
General Electric	AEX08FA	9.3	8,000

(continued on next page)

TABLE
13

ENERGY-EFFICIENT ROOM AIR CONDITIONERS *(continued)*

Brand	Model	Energy Efficiency (EER)[a]	Cooling Capacity (Btu/Hr)[b]
Hotpoint	KEM08FA	9.3	8,000
Panasonic	CW-81A126U; CW-81A12L6U	9.3	8,000
Quasar	HQ2082AW; HQ2083AS	9.3	8,000
Cooling Capacity: 9,000 to 9,999 Btu/Hr			
Carrier	51GMB0091	12.0	9,000
General Electric	ACD09LA	12.0	9,000
Hotpoint	KCD09LA	12.0	9,000
Friedrich	SS09H10A	11.0	9,000
General Electric	AMX09FA	10.5	9,000
Kenmore	253.8780991	10.5	9,000
Sanyo	ES0911	10.4	9,000
Frigidaire	AR09ME5L	9.5	9,200
Gibson	AM09C4EYA	9.5	9,200
Kelvinator	MH309H1QA	9.5	9,200
Montgomery Ward	5159B; 5169C	9.5	9,200
Panasonic	CW-901FU	9.5	9,000
Philco	PAP9P1-9	9.5	9,200
Quasar	HQ2092DW	9.5	9,000
White-Westinghouse	AL095N1A	9.5	9,200
Panasonic	CW-900JU	9.1	9,000
Quasar	HQ2091DW	9.1	9,000
Cooling Capacity: 10,000 to 10,999 Btu/Hr			
Friedrich	SM10H10A	12.0	10,300
General Electric	AVX10FA	11.6	10,000
Panasonic	CW-102VS12L6U	11.6	10,000
Quasar	HQ2102CW	11.6	10,000
Amana	10C2MA	9.6	10,000
Frigidaire	AR10ME5N	9.5	10,000
General Electric	AMD10AA	9.5	10,000
Gibson	AM10C5EY; AM10C6EY	9.5	10,000
Kelvinator	MH310H1QA	9.5	10,000
Montgomery Ward	5189A	9.5	10,000
Panasonic	CW-1001FU	9.5	10,000
Quasar	HQ2102DW	9.5	10,000
White-Westinghouse	AL106N1A	9.5	10,000
Friedrich	D10S1; KS10H10	9.3	10,000
Montgomery Ward	KMJ-5810	9.1	10,000
Panasonic	CW-1000FU	9.1	10,000
Quasar	HQ2101DW	9.1	10,000
Cooling Capacity: 11,000 to 12,999 Btu/Hr			
Sanyo	ES1211	10.4	12,000
Friedrich	SS12H10A	10.0	12,000
General Electric	AMH12AA	9.5	12,000
Hotpoint	KMH12AA	9.5	12,000
Panasonic	CW-1201FU	9.5	12,000
Quasar	HQ2122DW	9.5	12,000
Sharp	AF-1207M6	9.4	12,200
Amana	12C2MA	9.3	12,000

TABLE
13

ENERGY-EFFICIENT ROOM AIR CONDITIONERS *(continued)*

Brand	Model	Energy Efficiency (EER)[a]	Cooling Capacity (Btu/Hr)[b]
Carrier	51CMC1121	9.2	12,000
General Electric	AMD12AA	9.1	12,000
Hotpoint	KMD12AA	9.1	12,000
Montgomery Ward	KMJ-5813	9.1	12,000
Panasonic	CW-1200FU	9.1	12,000
Quasar	HQ2121DW	9.1	12,000
Sharp	AF-1206M6	9.1	12,000
Cooling Capacity: 13,000 to 14,999 Btu/Hr			
Friedrich	SM14H10A	10.5	14,000
Carrier	51GMA1141	10.2	13,500
	51GMB1141	10.2	14,000
General Electric	ACD14AA	10.2	13,500
Kenmore	106.8761492	10.2	14,000
Airtemp	C3L14E2A; G3L14E2A	10.0	14,000
Climatrol	M3L14E2A	10.0	14,000
Crest	15140	10.0	14,000
Fedders	A3L14E2A	10.0	14,000
General Electric	AVD14AA	10.0	14,000
Hampton Bay	15141	10.0	14,000
Hunter	41140005	10.0	14,000
J.C. Penney	8571739	10.0	14,000
Marta America	W3L14E2A	10.0	14,000
Summit	SUM14L	10.0	14,000
230/208 VOLTS **Cooling Capacity: 11,000 to 12,999 Btu/Hr**			
Friedrich	SS11H30A	9.5/9.5	11,000/10,800
Amana	12C3A; B12C3S	9.4/9.4	12,000/11,800
Carrier	51CMD0123	9.2/9.2	12,000/11,800
Emerson Quiet Kool	12DM44	9.2/9.4	12,000/11,700
General Electric	AMD12DA	9.1/9.1	12,000/11,800
Hotpoint	KMD12DA	9.1/9.1	12,000/11,800
Cooling Capacity: 13,000 to 14,999 Btu/Hr			
Friedrich	SS13H30A	9.5/9.5	13,000/12,700
Airtemp	G1M14E7A	9.0/9.0	14,000/14,000
Fedders	T1B14W7A	9.0/9.0	13,500/13,000
Kenmore	253.8791460	9.0/9.0	13,500/13,200
Marta America	W1M14E7M	9.0/9.0	14,000/14,000
Cooling Capacity: 15,000 to 16,999 Btu/Hr			
Carrier	15CMA1153	9.2/9.2	15,000/14,800
Comfort-Aire	WV163HE; WW163	9.0/9.0	16,400/16,200
Friedrich	SS15H30A	9.0/9.0	15,000/15,000
General Electric	ACD15DA; ACS15DA	9.0/9.0	15,000/14,800
	AES15DA	9.0/9.0	15,500/15,100
Hotpoint	KCS15DAX1	9.0/9.0	15,000/14,800
	KES15DA	9.0/9.0	15,500/15,100
Kenmore	106.8771591	9.0/9.0	15,000/14,800

(continued on next page)

TABLE 13

ENERGY-EFFICIENT ROOM AIR CONDITIONERS *(continued)*

Brand	Model	Energy Efficiency (EER)[a]	Cooling Capacity (Btu/Hr)[b]
RCA	YES15DA	9.0/9.0	15,500/15,100
Whirlpool	AC1504XT0	9.0/9.0	15,000/14,800
Cooling Capacity: 17,000 to 19,999 Btu/Hr			
Emerson Quiet Kool	18DD44	10.0/10.0	18,000/17,500
Montgomery Ward	UEE5418	10.0/10.0	18,000/17,500
Friedrich	SL19H30	9.5/9.5	19,000/18,800
Panasonic	CW-1802QU	9.5/9.5	18,000/17,700
Quasar	HQ2182DW	9.5/9.5	18,000/17,700
Sanyo	ES1812	9.5/9.4	18,900/18,500
Carrier	77GMA1183	9.4/9.4	17,600/17,300
Sharp	AF-1807M8	9.3/9.4	18,500/18,300
Carrier	51GMC1183	9.2/9.2	17,600/17,300
	51GMA1183	9.2/9.2	18,000/17,700
Comfort-Aire	WV183HE	9.2/9.1	18,000/17,800
Frigidaire	AR18NS2N; AR18NS5N	9.2/9.2	18,000/17,600
	AR18NS8F	9.2/9.2	18,000/17,700
General Electric	ACS18DB; AED18DA; AES18DA	9.2/9.2	18,000/17,600
Gibson	AK18E2RYA; AK18E4RYA; AK18E5RYA	9.2/9.2	18,000/17,600
Hotpoint	KCS18DB	9.2/9.2	18,000/17,600
Kelvinator	MH418H2SA	9.2/9.2	18,000/17,600
Kenmore	253.8781851; 253.879183; 253.8791830	9.2/9.2	18,000/17,600
Montgomery Ward	5249B; 5257D	9.2/9.2	18,000/17,600
Philco	PAH18P4-9	9.2/9.2	18,000/17,600
RCA	YES18DA	9.2/9.2	18,000/17,600
White-Westinghouse	AS181N2K; AS182N2K; AS186N2K; AS189N2K	9.2/9.2	18,000/17,600
Cooling Capacity: 20,000 to 22,999 Btu/Hr			
Carrier	51GMA1213	9.2/9.2	20,500/20,000
General Electric	ACD21DA	9.2/9.2	20,500/20,000
Hotpoint	KCD21DA	9.2/9.2	20,500/20,000
Crosley	CHD20E63	9.0/9.0	20,000/19,300
Emerson Quiet Kool	20DD44	9.0/9.0	20,000/19,300
Friedrich	D21L3; KL21H30	9.0/9.0	21,000/20,800
Montgomery Ward	UEE5421	9.0/9.0	20,000/19,300
Cooling Capacity: 23,000 to 25,999 Btu/Hr			
Carrier	51GMA1243	9.2/9.2	23,500/23,000
General Electric	ACS24DAT1	9.2/9.2	23,500/23,000
Hotpoint	KCS24DAT1	9.2/9.2	23,500/23,000
Friedrich	SL24H30	9.1/9.1	24,000/23,500
Airtemp	C1K25E7A; G1K25E7A	9.0/9.0	25,000/24,500
Carrier	51HKH2243	9.0/9.0	24,000/23,500
Climatrol	M1K25E7A	9.0/9.0	25,000/24,500
Crest	15250	9.0/9.0	25,000/24,500
Fedders	A1K25E7A	9.0/9.0	25,000/24,500
Hampton Bay	15251	9.0/9.0	25,000/24,500
Marta America	W1K25E7A	9.0/9.0	25,000/24,500

TABLE 13

ENERGY-EFFICIENT ROOM AIR CONDITIONERS *(continued)*

Brand	Model	Energy Efficiency (EER)[a]	Cooling Capacity (Btu/Hr)[b]
Cooling Capacity: 26,000 to 28,999 Btu/Hr			
Comfort-Aire	WV303HES; WW303	9.1/9.0	28,500/27,900
Friedrich	SL28H30A	9.0/9.0	27,500/27,000
Cooling Capacity: 29,000 and over Btu/Hr			
Carrier	51HKB2293	8.7/8.7	29,200/28,800

Source: *1991 Consumer Selection Guide for Room Air Conditioners* (Association of Home Appliance Manufacturers).

[a] Based on the Energy Efficiency Rating (EER). The higher the number, the more efficient the air conditioner. Two EER numbers for one model indicate different operating efficiencies at different voltages.

[b] Btu = British thermal unit, a measure of energy.

■ Have any coolant leaks fixed immediately (don't just have more coolant added).

■ If you have central air conditioning, get the ductwork cleaned periodically to remove molds, dust, and bacteria.

Proper disposal. If you must dispose of an air conditioner, look for a repair shop that uses a "vampire" machine to recapture the coolant.

FOR FURTHER INFORMATION: *Cooling with Ventilation,* by Subrato Chandra, Philip W. Fairey, and Michael Houston (Superintendent of Documents, U.S. Government Printing Office, Washington, DC 20402-9325). "Consumer Selection Guide for Room Air Conditioners" (Association of Home Appliance Manufacturers, 20 N. Wacker Dr., Chicago, IL 60606). "Directory of Central Air Conditioners and Heat Pumps" (Air Conditioning and Refrigeration Institute, 1501 Wilson Blvd., Arlington, VA 22209). *1991 Consumer Guide to Home Energy Savings,* by Alex Wilson (American Council for an Energy-Efficient Economy, 1990).

1. "Major Appliance Industry Facts Book" (Association of Home Appliance Manufacturers, 20 N. Wacker Dr., Chicago, IL 60606) 1987, pp. 40–45.
2. "Annual Energy Outlook, 1989" (Energy Information Administration, Department of Energy, Forrestal Bldg., El-231, Washington, DC 20585), pp. 24–25.
3. Richard A. Wadden and Peter A. Scheff, *Indoor Air Pollution* (John Wiley, 1983), p. 166.
4. R. B. Gammage and S. V. Kaye, eds., *Indoor Air and Human Health* (Lewis Publishers, 1985), p. 141.
5. R. Neil Sampson, American Forestry Association, quoted in "Queries & Quandaries," *Harrowsmith* (September/October 1989), p. 106.

TABLE
14

ENERGY-EFFICIENT CENTRAL AIR CONDITIONERS

Brand	Condensing Unit Model Number	Coil Model Number	Energy Efficiency (SEER)[a]	Cooling Capacity (Btu/Hr)[b]
Cooling Capacity: approximately 2.0 tons[c]				
Trane	TTX724A	TWV739E15-C	13.45	26,400
	TTX724A	THD080A9V3+TXF73655+BAY24X045	13.40	25,800
	TTX724A	TWH739E15-C	13.40	26,400
American Standard	ATN024A	THD080A9V3+TXF73655+BAY24X045	13.35	25,600
	ATN024A	TUC08089V3+TXC73655+BAY24X045	13.00	25,800
Lennox	HS22-261V-1P	CB15-41-1P+LB53081CD	13.00	25,400
	HS22-261V-1P	CB19-26-1P+LB53081CD	12.90	24,000
	HS22-261V-1P	CBH19-26-1P+LB-53081CD	12.90	24,000
	HS22-211V-1P	CB19-21-1P+LB53081CF	12.85	20,800
	HS22-211V-1P	CBH19-21-1P+LB+53081CF	12.85	20,800
Rheem	RAJA-024JA	RHQA-08+RCTB-A024	12.85	23,600
	RAJB-024JA	RHQA-08+RCTB-A024	12.85	24,600
	UAJA-024JA	UHQA-08+RCTB-A024	12.85	24,600
	UAJB-024JA	UHQA-08+RCTB-A024	12.85	24,600
Trane	TTX724A	TWH739P15-C	12.80	26,400
York	H2CH024S06	G1UT036	12.80	24,800
	H2CH024S06	G2CN030	12.80	24,800
Cooling Capacity: approximately 2.5 tons				
Trane	TTS730A	TUC08089V3+TXC73655	15.70	30,800
	TTS730A	TDC08089V3+TXC73655	15.70	30,800
Lennox	HS22-311V-1P	CB15-41-1P+LB53081CD	13.50	31,400
Trane	TTX730A	TWV739E15-C	13.45	32,000
	TTX730A	TWH739E15-C	13.40	31,800
American Standard	ATN030A	TWV739E15-C	13.35	32,200
Lennox	HS22-311V-1P	C14-41-1FF+LB53081CD	13.25	32,000
Coleman	9430G911	9435E833K	13.20	29,600
	9430G911	3736-823K	13.20	29,600
American Standard	ATN030A	THD080A9V3+TXF73655+BAY24X045	13.15	31,000
Amana	ZRCF30U01D	SCFC36A0VD	12.95	30,400
Coleman	9430G911	9435E833	12.95	29,600
Lennox	HS22-311V-1P	CB19-31-1P+LB53081CD	12.90	31,200
	HS22-311V-1P	CBH19-31-1P+LB-53081CD	12.90	31,200
	HS22-311V-1P	CBH19-26-1P+LB-53081CD	12.85	29,800
	HS22-311V-1P	CB19-26-1P+LB53081CD	12.85	29,800
Amana	ZRCF30U01D	ABCH360MBM	12.80	29,000
	ZRCF30U01D	SCFC30H0HD	12.80	29,800
Coleman	9430G911	3736-823	12.80	29,600
Amana	ZRCF30U01D	ABCH3000MC	12.70	29,800
	ZRCF30U01D	ABCH3600MC	12.70	29,800
American Standard	ATN030A	TUC080B9V3+TXC736S5+BAY24X045	12.70	31,000
Amana	ZRCF30U01D	SCFC24A0VD	12.65	29,200
American Standard	ATN030A	TWV739P15-C	12.65	32,200
Lennox	HS22-311V-1P	C14-26-1FF+LB53081CD	12.65	30,200
	HS22-311V-1P	CB18-41-3P+LB53081CD	12.65	30,600
	HS22-311V-1P	CBS18-41-3P+LB-53081CD	12.65	30,600
American Standard	ATN030A	TDC080B9V3+TXC736S5+BAY24X045	12.60	30,800
	ATN030A	THD080A9V3+TXF36S5	12.60	31,000
	ATN030A	TWH739P15-C	12.60	32,000
Trane	TTX730A	TWV739P15-C	12.60	31,800

TABLE 14

ENERGY-EFFICIENT CENTRAL AIR CONDITIONERS *(continued)*

Brand	Condensing Unit Model Number	Coil Model Number	Energy Efficiency (SEER)[a]	Cooling Capacity (Btu/Hr)[b]
Cooling Capacity: approximately 3.0 tons				
Trane	TTS730A	TWV739E15-C	16.90	33,200
	TTS730A	TWH739E15-C	16.90	33,200
	TTS736A	TWV739E15-C	16.20	39,000
	TTS736A	TWH739E15-C	16.20	39,000
	TTS736A	TUC080B9V3+TXC736S5	15.45	36,000
	TTS5736A	TDC080B9V3+TXC736S5	15.45	36,000
Lennox	HS14-411V-6P	CB15-41-1P	15.00	40,000
	HS14-413V-6Y	CB15-41-1P	15.00	40,000
Goodman (GMC, Janitrol, Franklin)	CTS36-1	A50-XX+EEP	14.00	40,000
American Standard	ATN036A	TWH064E15-C	13.85	40,000
Trane	TTX736A	TWH064E15-C	13.80	39,500
American Standard	ATN036A	TWV064E15-C	13.75	40,000
Trane	TTX736A	TWV064E15-C	13.75	39,000
Lennox	HS22-411V-1P	CB15-41-1P+LB53081CB	13.35	37,800
American Standard	ATN036A	TWH739E15-C	13.30	37,600
	ATN035A	TWE060A	13.30	37,800
Lennox	HS14-411V-6P	C14-41-1FF	13.30	38,000
	HS14-413V-6Y	C14-41-1FF	13.30	38,000
Trane	TTX736A	TWV739E15-C	13.30	37,800
Cooling Capacity: approximately 4.0 tons				
Trane	TTS748A	TWV064E15-C	15.15	49,500
	TTS748A	TUC100B9V5+TXC0,TXC754S	15.00	46,500
	TTS748A	TUC100B9V5+TXC,TXA064S	15.00	48,500
	TTS748A	THD100A9V5+THX060S	15.00	48,500
	TTS748A	TDC120B9V5+TXC0,TXC754S	14.50	46,000
	TTS748A	TDC120B9V5+TXC,TXA064S	14.50	48,500
Lennox	HS14-511V-6P	CB15-65-1P	14.00	52,000
	HS14-513V-6Y	CB15-65-1P	14.00	52,000
Trane	TTX742B	TWH064E15-C	13.75	45,000
American Standard	ATN042A	TWH064E15-C	13.70	45,000
Trane	TTX742B	TWV064E15-C	13.60	45,000
	TTX748A	TWE090A	13.60	52,000
American Standard	ATN042A	THD100A9V5+TXH060S5+BAY24X045	13.35	44,500
Lennox	HS14-511V-6P	CB15-46-1P	13.20	49,500
	HS14-513V-6Y	CB15-46-1P	13.20	49,500
Trane	TTX742B	TUC100B9V5+TXC064S5+BAY24X045	13.15	44,000
	TTX742B	TUC100B9VS+TXA064S5+BAY24X045	13.15	44,000
American Standard	ATN042A	TUC100B9V5+TXC064S5+BAY24X045	13.10	44,000
	ATN042A	TUC100B9V5+TXA064S5+BAY24X045	13.10	44,000
Lennox	HS14-511V-6P	CB15-41-1P+LB53081CB	13.00	49,500
Trane	2-TTX724A	TWH062E15-C	13.00	51,000
	TTX748A	TWH064E15-C	13.00	52,000

Source: *1991 Consumer Guide to Home Energy Savings* (American Council for an Energy-Efficient Economy).

[a] Based on the Seasonal Energy Efficiency Rating (SEER). The higher the number, the more efficient the air conditioner.
[b] Btu = British thermal unit, a measure of energy.
[c] One ton = approximately 12,500 Btu per hour.

FANS

Fans generate moving air that wicks perspiration and heat from your skin; they can also vent heat and pollutants from your living space.

ENVIRONMENTAL BENEFITS

Energy conservation. Fans need very little electricity to do their job: a three-speed, 18-inch-diameter table fan draws about 80 watts at high speed, less than one-sixth the energy required by a very small room air conditioner. A whole-house fan draws only 350 to 700 watts, while a small central air conditioner draws at least 2,000 watts.

ENVIRONMENTAL PROBLEMS

Indoor air pollution. Fans stir up dust particles; the smaller particles are easily inhaled and can cause allergic reactions or respiratory irritation.

Safety hazards. Because their blades move at such high speeds, all fans are potentially hazardous to children, pets, and adults. Fans can overheat or be overturned, creating possible fire hazards.

CHOOSING A PRODUCT

GENERAL GUIDELINES

Weighing your needs. When deciding what type of fan to buy, consider your climate, your cooling needs, and the particular features of your home. If you're building a new house, consider adding a whole-house fan instead of air conditioning. Ceiling fans are easy to add to existing rooms, while room and window fans have the advantage of portability.

Quality. Choose high-quality fans that will last longer and work more efficiently.

Safety. To minimize the hazards of high-speed fan blades, choose models with secure safety grilles and keep fingers and other objects away from the blades.

COMMERCIAL PRODUCTS

Ceiling fans *(highly recommended)*. Out of the way and very efficient, ceiling fans move a lot of air for the energy they use. They sometimes require special wiring, but often can be installed by homeowners or tenants with basic tools and skills. Some features to watch for:

- Sealed bearings and smooth, continuous power flow ensure quiet, reliable performance.

- Variable speeds help you find the most comfortable degree of air flow. A reversing capability can switch the direction of air flow: in hot weather you can direct air downward to cool you off; in cold weather you can pull air up, forcing warm air near the ceiling back down.

- Built-in or optional add-on lights turn the fan into a light fixture as well.

Portable room fans *(highly recommended)*. These fans are the most versatile, cooling you directly with their breeze. Look for the following features:

- A well-made fan should run quietly and have a grille that securely covers the blades.

- Variable speeds and an oscillating feature provide the best all-around cooling.

- If dust is a problem, look for fans with changeable paper filters, which remove dust particles very effectively.

Whole-house fans *(highly recommended)*. Typically installed in the ceiling to draw air into the attic, these large fans can replace all the indoor air in a house every minute or two, cooling the home dramatically. Whole-house fans should be installed by a professional; call a heating and cooling contractor for information. Look for these features:

- A fused safety switch prevents fires caused by overheating.

- A thermostat wired to the fan's switch turns the fan on and off automatically, keeping the temperature in the house within a suitable range and saving electricity.

Window fans (*highly recommended*). These fans operate on the same principle as whole-house fans but are smaller and portable. A 20-inch-diameter window fan, venting to the outside, can exchange all the air in a 20-by-12-foot room every minute. Models are available either as window-mount units only or as convertible box fans for portable use. Look for these features:

- Variable speeds and reversing capability provide versatile cooling options.

- Built-in safety switches automatically shut off the power if the fan tips over.

WISE USE

Safe, efficient use. To get the most out of your fans, follow these guidelines:

- *Ceiling fans* should be mounted securely at a safe height and properly wired. If you have doubts about the wiring, consult a professional electrician.

- *Portable room fans* should be set on a stable surface, away from pets and children. Make sure the safety grille is secure (newer grilles are removable for cleaning).

- *Whole-house fans* draw more electricity than other fans and should be installed safely and wired correctly. When the fan is in operation, be sure to leave windows open so it can effectively pull air through the house, and so it doesn't draw exhaust gases back through your chimney.

- *Window fans* should be placed in windows securely—away from small children, pets, and draperies—and unplugged when it rains. Be sure to block off the whole window opening, placing cardboard around the fan if necessary, for maximum air-pulling efficiency.

FOR FURTHER INFORMATION: *Cooling with Ventilation*, by Subrato Chandra, Philip W. Fairey, and Michael Houston (Superintendent of Documents, U.S. Government Printing Office, Washington, DC 20402-9325).

FAUCETS AND SHOWERHEADS

Between 30 and 40 percent of the water we use indoors in our homes flows through a sink faucet or showerhead.[1] Fortunately, you can minimize this water use.

ENVIRONMENTAL PROBLEMS

Wasteful water use. Most faucets run water at a wasteful three to five gallons per minute; most showerheads, at five to eight gallons. These devices affect our water supplies in three ways:

- They deplete the supplies available in rivers, lakes, wells, and underground aquifers.

- They increase the amount of water that must be purified at a treatment facility before it is piped to your home.

- They add to the wastewater that must be treated before being released.

Energy consumption. Much of the water that passes through your faucets or showerheads is heated, usually with energy that comes from burning nonrenewable fossil fuels. Wasting water often means wasting energy, too.

CHOOSING A PRODUCT

GENERAL GUIDELINES

Water efficiency. Make efficient water use a high priority. If your faucets do not have aerators, add them. If you have older, standard-flow showerheads, replace them with newer low-flow models.

COMMERCIAL PRODUCTS

Low-flow faucet aerators *(highly recommended)*. Aerators screw onto the faucet stem and, by mixing air with the water, can cut water flow by about 60 percent with little noticeable reduction of pressure. You can buy aerators designed for kitchens, bathrooms, and laundry rooms in any hardware store. Some models have handy on-off levers for adjusting the water pressure.

Low-flow showerheads *(highly recommended)*. These products can also cut water flow by up to 60 percent without sacrificing comfort. Many brands and styles of fixed and hand-held showerheads are available, including some with optional spray patterns. Most employ aerators, but some use pulsing pressure instead, for a massage effect. All low-flow showerheads use three gallons or less per minute, and some use as little as one. Look for them in hardware or plumbing-supply stores, or call for catalogs from Ecological Water Products, (401) 849-4004; Interbath, (818) 369-1841; or Real Goods Trading Co., (800) 762-7325.

♦ One brand of showerhead, Rainshower, not only conserves water but also removes most of the chlorine in it before it touches your skin. (A 15-minute shower is estimated to expose the body to more chlorine absorption than drinking eight glasses of the same water.) Available from Real Goods Trading Co., (800) 762-7325.

Standard showerheads *(never recommended)*. Designed and built in an age when water conservation was not an issue, these devices are environmentally unsound. Do not buy showerheads unless they are clearly labeled "low flow."

WISE USE

Proper installation. Faucet aerators and low-flow showerheads screw on to existing fittings and can be installed with simple tools. If an old showerhead does not come off easily, secure the pipe above it with a pipe wrench and try again.

- If your home has inadequate plumbing lines, low-flow showerheads can cause scalding when someone flushes a toilet while a shower is running. Before you install the new showerhead, flush a toilet while running the shower at a normal temperature. If the shower temperature rises significantly, consider getting a plumber to install larger water lines.

Water conservation. Even if you have low-flow faucets and showerheads, you can save additional water and energy with these simple practices:

- Don't leave the faucet running unnecessarily, such as while you shave, brush your teeth, or wash dishes.

- Don't use hot water when cold or warm will do.

- Take short showers instead of baths or long showers.

- Replace leaky faucets, washers, or seals promptly.

1. Diane MacEachern, *Save Our Planet: 750 Everyday Ways You Can Help Clean Up the Earth* (Dell, 1990), p. 53.

HEAT EXCHANGERS

Heat exchangers are an efficient way to remove indoor air pollution from tightly weatherproofed homes. They vent out stale indoor air and pull in outdoor air, which is presumably cleaner. The exchanger transfers heat between the outgoing and incoming air.

ENVIRONMENTAL BENEFITS

Cleaner indoor air. Well-insulated, tightly-sealed homes save energy but pose a potential risk to their inhabitants' health: drafty houses naturally vent smoke, gases, and other pollutants, but well-sealed houses accumulate them. An energy-efficient heat exchanger vents the home properly without losing the warmth or coolness of its heated or air-conditioned air.

Energy conservation. Heat exchangers require virtually no power beyond that needed to run their fans, so they consume far less electricity than they save. In winter they transfer 50 to 70 percent of the heat from the outgoing air to the incoming air. In summer they do the reverse, transferring heat from the incoming to the outgoing air.

CHOOSING A PRODUCT

GENERAL GUIDELINES

Weighing your needs. If you are concerned about indoor air quality, particularly if you live in a tightly sealed building, contact either your local government or a professional, such as a reputable heating and cooling contractor. Be sure to choose the right kind of heat exchanger for your home's specific needs.

COMMERCIAL PRODUCTS

Retrofit heat exchangers *(highly recommended).* These smaller units can be installed in existing homes; they're placed in windows, walls, or vents. The most common, simplest, and least efficient type is a fixed-plate system, which has metal, plastic, or paper partitions that transfer heat from outgoing to incoming air. A less common but more efficient type has a wheel that rotates slowly through the incoming and outgoing air, passing heat from one to the other. The following companies make retrofit heat exchangers:

- ◆ Berner International Corp., (412) 658-3551

- ◆ Mitsubishi Electric Sales, Inc., (714) 220-2500

- ◆ NuTone Division, Scovill Housing Group, (800) 543-8687

New-construction heat exchangers *(highly recommended).* Also called heat-recovery ventilators, these more elaborate systems ventilate entire homes, using either rotary-wheel heat exchangers or even more efficient heat pipes. The pipes run between the incoming and outgoing air and are filled with an HCFC refrigerant (similar to that in air conditioners) that evaporates at the warm end and condenses at the cool end, transferring heat. The following companies make heat-recovery ventilator systems for new homes:

- ◆ Airxchange, (617) 871-4816

- ◆ American Aldes Ventilation Corp., (813) 351-3441

- ◆ Berner International Corp., (412) 658-3551

- ◆ Nortron Industries Ltd., (416) 670-2500

- ◆ NuTone Division, Scovill Housing Group, (800) 543-8687

DO-IT-YOURSELF

Home-built exchangers. You can build your own simple but effective heat exchanger; for construction information write to Northern Scientific, Inc., P.O. Box D, Minot, ND 58702.

FOR FURTHER INFORMATION: Contact your local energy-conservation office.

HEATING, ELECTRIC

Electric heating systems are cheap and easy to install and are necessary where natural gas and other fuels aren't available. Unfortunately, they're also inefficient and expensive to operate.

ENVIRONMENTAL PROBLEMS

Energy consumption. Electricity is only one-third as efficient as natural gas at converting fuel into heat. Natural gas needs only to be piped, with little filtering or treatment, to your home, where it is burned in your furnace to produce heat. Electricity, on the other hand, must be generated, usually by burning fossil fuels to turn steam-driven turbines—a process that depletes fossil-fuel supplies and causes serious air pollution. Then the electricity is transmitted over long distances, during which up to 10 percent of the voltage is lost. Once in your home the electricity is inefficiently converted *back* into heat using resistance coils.

Indoor air pollution. The electric baseboard heater, preferred over forced-air heating by some allergy-sufferers, can actually create allergic problems. The hot coils "fry" dust, dander, and particles from carpets and fabrics, sending fumes and allergenic particles into the air.[1]

Safety hazards. Electric space heaters create an ongoing danger of burns and electric shock; if they malfunction, lack safety features, or are used improperly, they can easily start fires.

CHOOSING A PRODUCT
GENERAL GUIDELINES

Weighing your needs. Because of its energy inefficiency, avoid electric heating for your home if at all possible. If you must use electric heaters, make sure you pick the right type for your particular heating needs. Some types, for example, are best for quick, temporary heating of a small area, while others are best for slower, long-term warming of a whole room.

Safety. Make safety a high priority. If you buy an electric heater, look for good quality, an Underwriters' Laboratories (UL) inspection tag, and safety features—particularly protective grilles to keep objects away from the coils, and a switch that shuts the heater off if it tips over.

COMMERCIAL PRODUCTS

Portable heaters *(sometimes recommended).* These heaters can be useful either for heating a small space or for warming one room when the overall house temperature is kept low. There are four types of portable heaters:

- *Convection heaters* use electrical resistance to heat coils or wires, which then warm the air around them. These heaters usually have a fan and a thermostat, and they work best for heating a room quickly. Convection heaters can be fire hazards, so make sure you buy one with a tip-over switch.

- *Liquid-filled heaters* use oil or water to radiate heat through natural convection. They have no fan and are slow to warm up, so they work best for long-term, supplementary heating. Liquid-filled heaters can be fire hazards, so check for a tip-over switch.

- *Radiant heaters* don't warm the air; instead, they warm nearby people and objects with directly radiated heat. The standard type has a reflector mounted behind resistance coils; in the quartz type the coils are inside a tall, thin glass tube. Both types usually have fans to add some convection heating. Radiant heaters are best for quickly, temporarily warming people in one area of a room. They can be fire hazards, so check for a tip-over switch.

- *Ceramic heaters*, a slightly different form of convection heater, use ceramic disks instead of metal coils as their heating elements. The disks create a steadier energy flow that, their manufacturers claim, improves efficiency. This claim has not been proven, but the

machines do have one plus: they operate at fairly low temperatures, creating less of a fire hazard. They are slow to warm, so they are best for long-term, supplementary heating.

Baseboard heaters *(not generally recommended).* Most homes that rely on electricity for their primary heat use baseboard heaters, which are simply enclosed resistance coils. They have no fans; heat moves into the room by natural convection. Baseboard heaters are difficult to keep clean and can cause allergy problems.

WISE USE

Regular maintenance. To minimize pollution and keep your heaters operating smoothly, keep them well maintained:

- Keep heaters clean and free of dust.

- Oil fan motors according to the manufacturer's directions.

Safe use. To avoid fire or injury, follow these precautions:

- Make sure permanent units are properly wired and grounded.

- Place portable heaters on stable surfaces, away from children and pets.

- Keep all heaters well away from any flammable materials.

- *Never* use extension cords with heaters.

Energy-efficient heating. If you must use electric heat, try to reduce your overall heating needs:

- Insulate and weatherproof your home thoroughly. This is by far the most important way to reduce your heating needs. Tightly insulated homes do create some risk of indoor air pollution and radon buildup, but you can always install a heat exchanger to vent the indoor air (see Heat Exchangers, p. 115; Insulation, p. 141).

- If you have baseboard heaters, install programmable thermostats in each room or group of rooms, so you can heat rooms selectively. Programmable thermostats let you preset temperatures for different times of the day or week. With electric heating these devices pay for themselves quickly.

- Keep indoor temperatures as low as you comfortably can.

1. Alfred Zamm and Robert Gannon, *Why Your House May Endanger Your Health* (Simon & Schuster, 1980), p. 139.

HEATING, GAS

Natural gas is not only the cheapest and most popular home-heating fuel, it is also the most environmentally sound—second only to solar heating. Composed mainly of methane, natural gas is fairly simple to extract, needs little refining, and burns cleanly, producing far less air pollution—including the greenhouse gas, carbon dioxide—than do other fuels.

ENVIRONMENTAL PROBLEMS

Fossil-fuel consumption. Despite its advantages, natural gas is still a nonrenewable fossil fuel. The government forecasts increases in natural gas supplies through the year 2000, but energy specialists predict declining supplies in the next century and point out that any new sources will be harder to reach and more expensive.[1]

Pipeline hazards. Natural gas can be transported only by pipe. These pipelines disrupt natural habitats, both during and after their construction, and present a constant danger of leaks, explosions, and fires.

Indoor air pollution. Leaks from fittings, a malfunctioning furnace, or an inadequate or blocked chimney can introduce toxic gases or combustion byproducts into the home, creating a potentially serious health hazard.

Safety hazards. Just as large gas pipelines do, the small lines that service a home present a danger of leaking fumes, explosions, and fire.

CHOOSING A PRODUCT

GENERAL GUIDELINES

Weighing your needs. Analyze your home's heating needs carefully to determine the type of furnace and heating capacity you require. (Heating capacity is measured in British thermal units, or Btu, per hour.) An energy audit might be helpful.

Energy efficiency. Make energy efficiency a top priority. Before you buy a gas furnace or heater, check the energy efficiency figure (Annual Fuel Utilization Efficiency, or AFUE) shown on its yellow EnergyGuide label. Gas furnaces vary widely in their efficiency—from 60 to almost 100 percent—depending on their type and features.

COMMERCIAL PRODUCTS

Energy-efficient furnaces and boilers *(highly recommended)*. The most efficient gas-fired furnaces (for forced-air heating) and boilers (for hot-water or steam heating) are *condensing* units, which have an additional heat exchanger to extract otherwise-wasted heat from exhaust gases. Their exhaust is so cool it can be vented through a simple plastic or metal pipe instead of a chimney. Although they are fairly expensive and sometimes difficult to install (especially in existing homes), they have AFUE ratings of over 90 percent and save money over the long term.

Energy-efficient noncondensing furnaces and boilers have special power burners, outdoor-air intakes, and other features that can increase their AFUE rating to 80 percent or more. If you can't get a condensing unit, these are your best alternative.

Table 15 lists the most energy-efficient gas furnaces, Table 16 the most energy-efficient gas boilers for hot-water systems, and Table 17 the most energy-efficient gas boilers for steam systems. All three tables include both condensing and noncondensing models.

Add-on equipment for existing furnaces *(recommended)*. The following items, available through heating contractors or by special order, can be retrofitted to older gas furnaces and boilers to increase efficiency:

- *Power burners* use a fan to control air flow through the burner during combustion. The energy savings are 10 to 20 percent.

- *Automatic vent dampers* close the flue whenever the burner shuts off, preventing heat from escaping. The energy savings are up to 10 percent.

- *Modulating aquastats* for hot-water systems adjust boiler temperatures to suit outside temperatures, allowing the boiler to run cooler during warmer months. The energy savings are 5 to 10 percent.

- *Electronic ignitions* replace the gas-burning pilot lights still found on some old models. The energy savings are up to 5 percent.

Energy-efficient room heaters *(sometimes recommended)*. You can use these heaters to retrofit a home with gas heat when other options are not practical. They install directly in the home's living space, either in a wall or as free-standing units. Table 18 lists the most energy-efficient models available.

Conventional furnaces and boilers *(never recommended)*. Given the widespread availability of more energy-efficient systems, these expensive-to-run and environmentally unsound models should be avoided.

WISE USE

Proper installation. To ensure both safety and efficiency, gas furnaces and boilers must be professionally installed by an insured, bonded contractor, who will check carefully for the following:

- Gas leaks from pipes, fittings, or the furnace or boiler itself.

- Sufficient air supply for combustion; many condensing furnaces require a separate, unobstructed supply of outdoor air.

- Proper venting; for conventional furnaces or boilers that includes a fire-resistant chimney or stack.

- For condensing furnaces, an unobstructed, acid-resistant outlet for draining water vapor.

TABLE 15

ENERGY-EFFICIENT GAS FURNACES

For Forced-Air Heating Systems, Natural or Propane Gas

Brand	Model	Energy Efficiency (AFUE%)[a]	Heating Capacity (Btu/Hr)[b]
Heating Capacity: 37,000 to 53,000 Btu/Hr			
Carrier	58SXA040-FG; 58SX040-BC; 58SX040-FG	96.6	40,000
Day & Night	398AAW030040; 398AAZ030040	96.6	40,000
Payne	398AAW030040; 398AAZ030040	96.6	40,000
Pulse	G14Q3-40-	96.2	38,000
Armstrong	EG6E40DC13	95.4	38,000
GlowCore	UGR040D13	95.4	38,000
Pulse	GSR14Q4-50-	95.0	47,000
	GSR14Q3-50-	94.8	47,000
Heil	NUGS050AF	94.6	47,000
Kenmore	867.769050	94.6	47,000
Tempstar	NUGK050AF	94.6	47,000
Williamson	WU47-05-3N	94.6	47,000
Dayton	3E436B	94.0	46,000
Heil	NUGK050MF	94.0	46,000
Kenmore	867.769412	94.0	46,000
Tempstar	NUGK050MF	94.0	46,000
Williamson	WU47-05-2	94.0	46,000
Bryant	398BAZ036060-L	93.5	41,000
Carrier	58SXB060-GG-L	93.5	41,000
Day & Night	398BAZ036060-L	93.5	41,000
	TUC040B924A	93.3	38,000
XL90	TUC040B924A	93.3	38,000
GlowCore	DGX040D13	93.2	37,000
American Standard	BLU040K930B	93.0	38,000
Heil	NUGK040KF	93.0	37,000
Kenmore	867.769452; 867.769460	93.0	37,000
Tempstar	NUGK040KF	93.0	37,000
XL90	BLU040K930B	93.0	38,000
Heating Capacity: 54,000 to 74,000 Btu/Hr			
Kenmore	867.769060	96.6	68,000
Olsen, Airco	HDS 70M	94.2	67,000
Bryant	398BAW036060	93.6	59,000
Carrier	58SXB060-CC	93.6	59,000
	58SXB080-GG-L	93.5	54,000
Bryant	398BAZ060100-L	93.5	68,000
	398BAZ036080-L	93.5	59,000
	398BAZ036060-L	93.5	54,000
Day & Night	398BAZ060100-L	93.5	68,000
	398BAZ036080; 398BAW036080	93.5	59,000
	398BAZ036080-L	93.5	54,000
Olsen, Airco	HDS 80M (90/80M)	93.5	67,000
Kenmore	867.769470	93.4	67,000
Armstrong	EG6E0DC14	93.3	56,000

TABLE
15

ENERGY-EFFICIENT GAS FURNACES *(continued)*
For Forced-Air Heating Systems, Natural or Propane Gas

Brand	Model	Energy Efficiency (AFUE%)[a]	Heating Capacity (Btu/Hr)[b]
Century	GZD-A60-D3.5N	93.3	56,000
Comfort-Aire, Reclaimer	GZD-A60-D3.5NX	93.3	56,000
GlowCore	UGR060D14	93.3	56,000
Intertherm, Miller	RFYDC-060A14E	93.3	56,000
Ruud	UGKA-06EA-F*; UGKA-06NA-F*	93.3	56,000
American Standard	AGUH060A012*IN	93.1	56,000
Comfortmaker	CGUH060A012*IN	93.1	56,000
Heating Capacity: 75,000 to 93,000 Btu/Hr			
Olsen, Airco	HDS 90M	94.0	86,000
Williamson	C217-08-NOAH	94.0	80,000
Olsen, Airco	HCS2-90(M)	93.7	84,000
Bryant	398BAW036080	93.6	79,000
Carrier	58SXB080-BC	93.6	79,000
Day & Night	398BAW036080	93.6	79,000
Bryant	398BAZ036080	93.5	79,000
Carrier	58SXB080-GG	93.5	84,000
Day & Night	398BAZ036080	93.5	79,000
Olsen, Airco	HCS2-81 (M)	93.2	75,000
Heating Capacity: 94,000 to 111,000 Btu/Hr			
Amana	EGHW100DC3	93.9	94,000
Bryant	398BAZ042100-L; 398BAZ060100-L	93.5	99,000
Carrier	58SXB100-HG; 58SXB100-LG	93.5	99,000
Day & Night	398BAZ060100	93.5	99,000
Pulse	G14Q4/5-100	93.5	95,000
Heating Capacity: 112,000 to 149,000 Btu/Hr			
Fraser-Johnston, Luxaire	PANU-LD20N160A	92.6	149,000
	PANU-LD20N140A; PBNU-LD20N140A	92.6	131,000
	PANU-LD16N120A; PBNU-LD16N120A	92.6	112,000
York	P1UDD20N15201A	92.6	149,000
	P1UDD20N13301A; P2UDD20N13301	92.6	131,000
	P1UDD16N11401A; P2UDD16N11401	92.6	112,000

Source: *Consumer's Directory of Certified Efficiency Ratings for Residential Heating and Water Heating Equipment* (Gas Appliance Manufacturers Association, 1990).

[a] Based on Annual Fuel Utilization Efficiency (AFUE). The higher the number, the more efficient the furnace.

[b] Btu = British thermal unit, a measure of energy.

TABLE 16

ENERGY-EFFICIENT GAS BOILERS
For Hot-Water Heating Systems, Natural or Propane Gas

Brand	Model	Energy Efficiency (AFUE%)[a]	Heating Capacity (Btu/Hr)[b]
Heating Capacity: 36,000 to 46,000 Btu/Hr			
Weil-Mclain	AHE-45	85.3	38,000
Bryant	237AAW002042; 237AAY002042	84.5	36,000
Carrier	61SWB042; 61SWD042	84.5	36,000
Crown	XE-2	84.5	36,000
Day & Night	237AAW002042; 237AAY002042	84.5	36,000
Dunkirk	XE-2	84.5	36,000
Metzger	XE-2	84.5	36,000
Payne	237AAY002042	84.5	36,000
Pennco	FS-2	84.5	36,000
Kenmore	229.964421; 229.964122	84.5	36,000
Heating Capacity: 47,000 to 81,000 Btu/Hr			
Hydrotherm	A-50 B	90.4	47,000
EnerRoyal	60H; 60HC; 60HW; 60HWC	87.0	52,000
Heatmaker	60H; 60HC; 60HW, 60HWC	87.0	52,000
Weil-Mclain	VHE-3	87.0	59,000
Burnham	XG-2003A-PV	86.5	54,000
Weil-Mclain	AHE-60	85.5	51,000
Peerless	PDE-065	84.8	56,000
Slant/Fin	GG-75HEDS	84.7	64,000
Heating Capacity: 82,000 to 116,000 Btu/Hr			
Hydrotherm	A-100 B	90.4	88,000
Weil-Mclain	VHE-4	87.1	87,000
Burnham	XG-2004A-PV	85.3	82,000
	XG-2004AV	84.8	82,000
Peerless	PDE-097	84.4	83,000
Heating Capacity: 117,000 to 272,000 Btu/Hr			
Hydrotherm	A-150 B,C	90.5	132,000
	M-300	90.1	272,000
Weil-Mclain	VHE-6	87.4	147,000
	VHE-5	87.3	117,000

Source: *Consumer's Directory of Certified Efficiency Ratings for Residential Heating and Water Heating Equipment* (Gas Appliance Manufacturers Association, 1990).

[a] Based on Annual Fuel Utilization Efficiency (AFUE). The higher the number, the more efficient the boiler.

[b] Btu = British thermal unit, a measure of energy.

TABLE 17

ENERGY-EFFICIENT GAS BOILERS
For Steam-Heating Systems, Natural or Propane Gas

Brand	Model	Energy Efficiency (AFUE%)[a]	Heating Capacity (Btu/Hr)[b]
Heating Capacity: 88,000 to 146,000 Btu/Hr			
Axeman-Anderson	108PGU	83.5	116,000
Burnham	XG-4004; XG-4005	83.5	88,000
Axeman-Anderson	74PG	82.5	114,000
	87PG	82.1	129,000
Heating Capacity: 147,000 to 190,000 Btu/Hr			
Burnham	XG-4006	83.3	147,000
Axeman-Anderson	108PG; 128PGU	82.4	159,000
Heating Capacity: 191,000 to 245,000 Btu/Hr			
Axeman-Anderson	149PGU	82.6	201,000
	149PG; 128PG	81.8	191,000
Bryant	235BAW007299	81.5	245,000
	235BAY007280	81.5	229,000
Carrier	61BSB299	81.5	245,000

Source: *Consumer's Directory of Certified Efficiency Ratings for Residential Heating and Water Heating Equipment* (Gas Appliance Manufacturers Association, 1990).

[a] Based on Annual Fuel Utilization Efficiency (AFUE). The higher the number, the more efficient the boiler.

[b] Btu = British thermal unit, a measure of energy.

Regular maintenance. To keep your furnace or boiler running at its best, you need to maintain it:

- Check the burner flame periodically. It should be mostly blue with a lighter blue cone in the center; if it isn't, call a professional to adjust it.

- If you have a forced-air furnace, change the filters frequently and clean the ducts periodically to avoid dust buildup.

- Lubricate the blower and motor once a year; check the instruction manual and look for oil ports or grease cups.

- Vacuum the blower blades once a year. Unscrew the panel covering the blower, unbolt the blower, and remove it for cleaning.

- Clean and service hot-water and steam systems regularly.

- With condensing furnaces, periodically check the air supply line (if there is one) and the water-vapor drainage line for blockages.

Safe use. To operate your furnace safely, remember the following points:

- If you suspect a minor gas leak, check by pouring a small amount of soapy water around each joint; bubbles indicate a leak. If you can't track it down, call the gas company for assistance.

- If you smell a strong gas odor, leave the house *immediately* (don't create a spark by turning on a light or dialing your phone) and call the gas company or fire department.

- If you start getting frequent headaches, notice a slight exhaust odor, or have any other reason to suspect your furnace is not venting properly, call a service contractor immediately to test it.

TABLE 18

ENERGY-EFFICIENT GAS WALL-MOUNTED HEATERS
For Natural or Propane Gas

Brand	Model	Energy Efficiency (AFUE%)[a]	Heating Capacity (Btu/Hr)[b]
Heating Capacity: 19,000 to 27,000 Btu/Hr			
Empire	PH-20	91.1	19,000
Suburban	DNV-25GS	75.6	19,250
Warm Morning	LSC35PB	75.2	24,570
Heating Capacity: 28,000 to 38,000 Btu/Hr			
Kenmore	629.756830	77.5	32,000
Dayton	3E477B	77.0	32,000
Forsair	400DVI	76.5	32,000
Suburban	DWW-40EA	76.5	32,000
Forsair	435FEI	75.6	28,000
Suburban	DNV-40GS	75.6	30,800
	UWW-35EA	75.6	28,000
Dayton	3E473B	75.5	32,000
	3E472B7	75.5	28,000
Kenmore	629.756820	75.5	28,000
Forsair	400DVX	75.4	32,000
Martin-Aire	MDVX40B	75.4	32,000
Suburban	DWW-40PA	75.4	32,000
Warm Morning	LSC50PB	75.1	36,432
Heating Capacity: 39,000 to 48,000 Btu/Hr			
Kenmore	629.756870	77.5	44,000
Martin-Aire	MDV155B	77.5	44,000
Forsair	550DVI	76.5	44,000
Suburban	DWW-55EA	76.5	44,000
Forsair	455FEI	76.0	44,000
Martin-Aire	MFE155B	76.0	44,000
Suburban	DWW-55PA; UWW-55EA	76.0	44,000
Perfection	CV750IPL-A	75.4	39,950
Warm Morning	LSC65PB	75.2	47,483

Source: *Consumer's Directory of Certified Efficiency Ratings for Residential Heating and Water Heating Equipment* (Gas Appliance Manufacturers Association, 1990).

[a] Based on Annual Fuel Utilization Efficiency (AFUE). The higher the number, the more efficient the heater.

[b] Btu = British thermal unit, a measure of energy.

Using other gas appliances such as ranges and dryers can cause a furnace chimney to "downdraft," sucking exhaust gases into your home, so be sure to run these appliances during the test.

Energy-efficient heating. Save energy and money by using your furnace as little as possible:

- Insulate and weatherproof your home thoroughly; this is by far the most important way to reduce your heating needs. Tightly insulated homes do create some risk of indoor air pollution and radon buildup, but you can always install a heat exchanger to vent the indoor air (see Heat Exchangers, p. 115; Insulation, p. 141).

- Install a programmable thermostat that lets

you preset temperatures for different times of the day or week.

- Close off vents or radiators in unused rooms.

FOR FURTHER INFORMATION: "Oil and Gas Heating Systems" (Massachusetts Audubon Society, South Great Road, Lincoln, MA 01773-9988).

1. "Annual Energy Outlook, 1989" (Energy Information Administration, Department of Energy, Forrestal Bldg., El-231, Washington, DC 20585), pp. 20–23.

HEATING, KEROSENE

Kerosene heaters are cheap to buy, cheap to run, and very portable; though rarely used to heat whole homes, they're popular as space heaters or secondary heaters. But they're also dangerous and environmentally unsound.

ENVIRONMENTAL PROBLEMS

Fossil-fuel consumption. Kerosene is made by distilling petroleum, a nonrenewable fossil fuel. Obtaining, refining, shipping, and using kerosene pollutes the land, air, or water at every step. Environmentally, kerosene rates between electricity and natural gas: it is more difficult and polluting to refine than gas, but more energy efficient than electricity.

Air pollution. Kerosene is usually burned right in the home, with no outside venting, and can seriously pollute indoor air. The fuel itself is toxic to inhale; if burned incompletely it produces poisonous carbon monoxide. Kerosene stoves can also produce nitrogen dioxide, sulfur dioxide, and unsafe levels of carbon dioxide.[1] All these gases add to outdoor air pollution once they escape from the building.

Safety hazards. Though newer heaters start fewer fires than earlier models, they still get hot enough to cause thousands of contact burns every year.[2]

CHOOSING A PRODUCT
GENERAL GUIDELINES

Weighing your needs. Consider a kerosene heater only if you have a well-ventilated area such as a garage or shed that needs occasional heating. To minimize indoor air pollution and health hazards, do not buy kerosene heaters for any living space unless it has a proper ventilation system.

COMMERCIAL PRODUCTS

Kerosene heaters *(not generally recommended).* Because of their numerous environmental problems, kerosene heaters should be avoided whenever possible. If you must buy one for economic or fuel-supply reasons, install a ventilating system (consult a heating and cooling contractor for advice) and look for a model with the following features:

- *Multistage combustion,* which burns the fuel more completely

- *A temperature control,* so you can control the unit's heat output

- *A safety tip-over switch* that shuts the heater off if it falls over

- *Safety grilles and guards* to protect against accidentally touching the flame or hot surfaces

WISE USE

Safe use. If you must use a kerosene heater, follow these safety precautions:

- Burn only low-sulfur, K-1 type kerosene.

- Never lower the wick to cut the flame size or heat output; this increases air pollution.

- Use the stove only in well-ventilated spaces such as a garage (preferably with a door or window partially open), a fan-ventilated workspace, or a living area with a specially designed ventilation system (for which you need a contractor).

1. "Nitrogen dioxide and sulfur dioxide": R. B. Gammage and S. V. Kaye, eds., *Indoor Air and Human Health* (Lewis Publishers, 1985), p. 28; "Carbon dioxide": Edward Calabrese and Michael Dorsey, *Healthy Living in an Unhealthy World* (Simon & Schuster, 1984), p.124.
2. Stephen Brobeck and Anne Averyt, *The Product Safety Book* (E.P. Dutton, 1983), p. 237.

HEATING, OIL

About 12 percent of American homes are heated with oil, an environmentally unsound fuel.[1]

ENVIRONMENTAL PROBLEMS

Fossil-fuel consumption. Fuel oil is distilled from petroleum, a nonrenewable fossil fuel. Obtaining, refining, and transporting fuel oil pollutes the air, land, or water at every step.

Air pollution. Oil is not a clean-burning fuel. It generates far more hydrocarbons and particulates than does the most popular home-heating fuel, natural gas.

CHOOSING A PRODUCT

GENERAL GUIDELINES

Comparing oil and gas. If you heat your home with oil, look into natural gas as an alternative. You might find that gas is now available and relatively cheap in areas where it was once unavailable or expensive. Gas heating systems are far more efficient than oil.

Energy efficiency. If you must use oil, make energy efficiency a top priority. If your home has an old (or inefficient) oil furnace or boiler, replace or improve it as soon as possible. Look for Annual Fuel Utilization Efficiency (AFUE) ratings on new furnaces' EnergyGuide labels.

COMMERCIAL PRODUCTS

Energy-efficient furnaces and boilers *(highly recommended).* Special features and designs can improve the energy efficiency of oil-fired furnaces (for forced-air heating) and boilers (for hot-water or steam heating) by at least 10 percent. The most energy-efficient oil furnaces and boilers are *condensing* units, which have an additional heat exchanger to extract otherwise-

TABLE 19

ENERGY-EFFICIENT OIL FURNACES
For Forced-Air Heating Systems

Brand	Model	Energy Efficiency (AFUE%)[a]	Heating Capacity (Btu/Hr)[b]
Heating Capacity: 57,000 to 74,000 Btu/Hr			
Yukon	U-70-0-03	88.9	64,000
	H-70-0-02	87.8	63,000
EnerRoyal	ERCF 56	86.7	59,000
	ERHB56 SF	86.3	58,000
Yukon	85-100-1500	86.2	58,000
EnerRoyal	ERLB56 SF;	86.0	58,000
	ERLB56 SFR		
Thermo Pride	OL2-56-V	85.6	57,000
Williamson	R164-07-3, 4	85.1	59,000
Heating Capacity: 75,000 to 82,000 Btu/Hr			
EnerRoyal	ER75 HB;	86.7	75,000
	ER75 FF		
	ER75 RF	86.5	75,000
Olsen, Airco	HTL 80B	86.2	77,000
	WTL 80A	86.1	77,000
	WTL 90A	86.0	77,000
	BCL 80S	86.0	76,000
EnerRoyal	ERHB73 SF	86.0	75,000
	ERLB73 SFR	85.8	75,000
	ERCF 73; ERLB73 SF	85.7	75,000
Heating Capacity: 83,000 to 97,000 Btu/Hr			
Yukon	U-90-0-03	89.1	83,000
Olsen, Airco	BCL 90S	86.5	89,000
	HTL 90B	86.1	88,000
Thermo Pride	OL5-85-V	86.1	83,000
	OT5-85-V	85.5	83,000
EnerRoyal	ERHB84 SF;	85.2	86,000
	ERCF84		
	ERLB84 SF	85.1	86,000
Heating Capacity: 98,000 to 146,000 Btu/Hr			
Olsen, Airco	BCL 120S	86.7	119,000
	WTL 105A	86.0	105,000
	WTL 100A;	86.0	99,000
	BCL 100S		
	HTL 100B	86.0	98,000
Williamson	1454-17	86.0	146,000
	T164-15	85.6	114,000
	1454-14	85.5	118,000
EnerRoyal	ER116 HB	85.2	115,000
	ER116 FF	85.1	116,000
	ERLB95 SFR	85.0	98,000
Williamson	R164-15-3,4	85.0	119,000

Source: *Consumer's Directory of Certified Efficiency Ratings for Residential Heating and Water Heating Equipment* (Gas Appliance Manufacturers Association, 1990).

[a] Based on Annual Fuel Utilization Efficiency (AFUE). The higher the number, the more efficient the furnace.

[b] Btu = British thermal unit, a measure of energy.

TABLE 20

ENERGY-EFFICIENT OIL BOILERS
For Hot-Water Heating Systems

Brand	Model	Energy Efficiency (AFUE%)[a]	Heating Capacity (Btu/Hr)[b]
Heating Capacity: 87,000 to 120,000 Btu/Hr			
Crown	CTPR-3	87.6	92,000
EnerRoyal	ERO-40; ERO-40C	87.0	87,000
Thermo-Dynamics	BY-75	87.0	91,000
Vaillant	F70, F75-40	87.0	87,000
Axeman-Anderson	74NPO-U	86.5	105,000
Peerless	JO/JOT-TWO75-W	86.5	92,000
Heating Capacity: 121,000 to 152,000 Btu/Hr			
Crown	CTPR-4	87.5	130,000
Axeman-Anderson	87NPO-U	87.2	134,000
EnerRoyal	ERO-50,ERO-50C	86.7	121,000
Vaillant	F70, F75-50	86.7	121,000
Axeman-Anderson	74NPO	86.6	133,000
Heating Capacity: 153,000 to 183,000 Btu/Hr			
Axeman-Anderson	108NPO-U	87.4	153,000
Crown	CTPR-5	87.4	167,000
Axeman-Anderson	128NPO-U	87.3	183,000
Columbia	TE-153	86.8	153,000
Axeman-Anderson	108NPO	86.5	181,000
Vaillant	F70, F75-60	86.5	156,000

Source: *Consumer's Directory of Certified Efficiency Ratings for Residential Heating and Water Heating Equipment* (Gas Appliance Manufacturers Association, 1990).

[a] Based on Annual Fuel Utilization Efficiency (AFUE). The higher the number, the more efficient the boiler.

[b] Btu = British thermal unit, a measure of energy.

wasted heat from exhaust gases. Their exhaust is so cool it can be vented through a simple plastic or metal pipe instead of a chimney. Condensing oil-fired units are hard to find, fairly high-priced, and sometimes difficult to install, but they have AFUE ratings of over 90 percent and save money in the long run. For more information on condensing oil-fired furnaces, contact these companies:

♦ Bard Manufacturing Co., (419) 636-1194

♦ Dornback Furnace and Foundry, (216) 946-1600

♦ Lennox Industries, Inc., (214) 980-6000

♦ Magic Chef Air Conditioning Co., (419) 483-4840

♦ Yukon Energy Corp., (612) 633-3115

For information on condensing oil-fired boilers, contact Weil-McLain, (219) 879-6561.

Energy-efficient, noncondensing oil furnaces and boilers use automatic vent dampers and other features to save fuel. These systems, which are much more common than condensing units, have AFUE ratings of 85 percent or more. Table 19 lists the most efficient noncondensing oil furnaces, Table 20 lists the most efficient noncondensing oil boilers for hot-water systems, and Table 21 lists the most efficient noncondensing boilers for steam systems.

Add-on equipment for existing furnaces and boilers *(recommended).* The following items,

TABLE 21

ENERGY-EFFICIENT OIL BOILERS
For Steam Heating Systems

Brand	Model	Energy Efficiency (AFUE%)[a]	Heating Capacity (Btu/Hr)[b]
Heating Capacity: 79,000 to 101,000 Btu/Hr			
Columbia	TE-91	86.4	91,000
	CSF-365	86.0	79,000
Utica	SF-365	86.0	79,000
H.B. Smith	8-S/W-3L	85.8	91,000
Peerless	JO/HOT-TWO75-S	84.2	91,000
H.B. Smith	BB-14-S-3L	83.7	89,000
Burnham	V-73S	83.0	89,000
Heating Capacity: 102,000 to 134,000 Btu/Hr			
Columbia	TE-122	86.4	122,000
	CSF-4100	86.0	120,000
Utica	SF-4100	86.0	120,000
H.B. Smith	8-S/W-4L	85.9	131,000
	89-S/W-3H	85.6	102,000
Slant/Fin	L30PZ	84.1	134,000

Source: *Consumer's Directory of Certified Efficiency Ratings for Residential Heating and Water Heating Equipment* (Gas Appliance Manufacturers Association, 1990).

[a] Based on Annual Fuel Utilization Efficiency (AFUE). The higher the number, the more efficient the boiler.

[b] Btu = British thermal unit, a measure of energy.

available through heating contractors or by special order, can be retrofitted onto older oil furnaces and boilers to increase efficiency:

- *Flame-retention burners* are designed to generate more heat with a slightly smaller flame. The energy savings are 10 to 20 percent.

- *Automatic flue dampers* close the flue whenever the burner shuts off, preventing heat from escaping. The energy savings are 3 to 15 percent.

- *Modulating aquastats* for hot-water systems adjust boiler temperatures to suit outside temperatures, allowing the boiler to run cooler during warmer months. The energy savings are 5 to 10 percent.

- *Smaller fuel nozzles* (called "derating") make a furnace run longer to generate the same amount of heat, saving fuel and cutting heat losses that occur when the furnace is off. The energy savings are 5 percent.

- *Secondary heat exchangers* extract additional heat from exhaust gases. They can be added to both boilers and forced-air furnaces; their energy savings vary, depending on the furnace, but they are usually cost effective. Two companies that make them are

  ◆ Heat Extractor, Inc., (617) 321-2300

  ◆ Heatsaver, Dumont Industries, (207) 933-4811

Conventional furnaces and boilers *(never recommended)*. Given the widespread availability of more energy-efficient systems, these expensive-to-run, environmentally unsound models should be avoided.

WISE USE

Proper installation. To ensure both safety and efficiency, oil furnaces and boilers must be professionally installed by an insured, bonded contractor, who will check carefully for the following:

- Proper venting; for conventional furnaces and boilers that includes a fire-resistant chimney or stack.

- Sufficient air supply for combustion; many condensing furnaces require a separate, unobstructed supply of outdoor air.

- For condensing furnaces, an unobstructed, acid-resistant outlet for draining water vapor.

Regular maintenance. To keep your furnace or boiler running at its best, get it serviced *every year* and maintain it properly:

- If you can smell oil, your system needs a tune-up.

- If you have a forced-air furnace, change the filters frequently and clean the ducts periodically to avoid dust buildup.

- Clean and service hot-water and steam systems regularly.

- With condensing furnaces, periodically check the air-supply line (if there is one) and the water-vapor drainage line for blockages.

Safe use. If you start getting frequent headaches, notice a slight exhaust odor, or have any other reason to suspect your furnace or boiler is not venting its toxic exhaust gases properly, call a service contractor immediately to check it.

Energy-efficient heating. Save energy and money by using your furnace or boiler as little as possible:

- Insulate and weatherproof your home thoroughly; this is by far the most important way to reduce your heating needs. Tightly insulated homes do create some risk of indoor air

pollution and radon buildup, but you can always install a heat exchanger to vent the indoor air (see Heat Exchangers, p.115; Insulation, p. 141).

- Install programmable thermostats to preset temperatures for different times of the day or week.

- Close off vents and radiators in unused rooms.

FOR FURTHER INFORMATION: "Oil and Gas Heating Systems" (Massachusetts Audubon Society, South Great Road, Lincoln, MA 01773-9988).

1. "Oil: Cheap, but for How Long?" *Practical Homeowner* (October 1986), p. 68.

HEATING, SOLAR

Using only glass, insulating materials, and possibly a fan or a pump, solar heating systems can warm your home with the sun, using little or no electricity and generating almost no pollution.

ENVIRONMENTAL BENEFITS

Renewable, nonpolluting energy. Solar heating gets its power from a free, limitless energy source—the sun. Using solar energy avoids the environmental damage caused by traditional sources of energy: the contamination risks and radioactive wastes associated with nuclear power; the destruction of riverine ecosystems caused by hydroelectric dams; and most important of all, the pollution and resource depletion caused by burning nonrenewable fossil fuels.

CHOOSING A PRODUCT

GENERAL GUIDELINES

Weighing your needs. Before deciding on solar heating, you'll need to assess both your house and your heating needs and options. Important factors to consider are whether it's a new or older home; how well it's designed and insulated; its orientation and access to sunlight; what your climate is like; and what backup fuel sources are available. A home solar-energy audit is recommended; arrange one through your city or county energy office, professionals in solar energy construction, or heating and cooling contractors who do solar work.

Thorough research. Because there are so many types of solar heating systems available, you should either research the subject yourself or hire a reputable consultant or contractor. For information on solar heating and names of consultants and contractors, contact your city or county energy office and the Better Business Bureau.

Weighing costs. Solar systems cost far more to install than other home-heating systems. But once installed, they are basically free to operate, saving you significant fuel costs for as long as you own the home—and as fossil-fuel costs rise, the payback period shortens. Even so, solar heating is an investment more in ecology and good sense than in short-term economics.

COMMERCIAL PRODUCTS

Windows *(highly recommended).* Well-insulated, south-facing windows act as solar collectors, so installing thermopane (double- or triple-glazed) windows with insulated curtains that retain heat at night is a relatively easy way to use the sun's heat. You can get good-quality thermopane windows in all sizes, shapes, and types from better building-supply stores.

Passive solar systems *(highly recommended).* Passive solar systems use no energy except the sun's; they have large south-facing areas of glass and heat-storage materials that absorb, retain, and slowly radiate solar heat. The heat-storage materials—typically brick, stone, concrete, earth, or water—are placed in the floor, in containers or enclosures, or in separate walls usually built of brick or stone. Ideally, the storage area is in direct winter sunlight; if not, it can be designed to receive the sun's heat through natural convection.

Active solar systems *(highly recommended).* Active systems use fans or pumps to transport collected solar heat from one part of the house to another. Some use liquid exchangers; others blow warm air through vents. These systems are sometimes complicated and require careful maintenance, but they work well in many homes not suited to passive systems.

Add-on solar collectors *(highly recommended).* You can buy (or build) an add-on solar collector and attach it to your home's southern wall; on sunny days it will collect solar heat and send warm air through vents into your home, with minimal disruption of the home's interior.

Sunspaces *(sometimes recommended)*. These add-on solar enclosures, which are usually all glass and measure about 9 by 12 feet, can bring abundant heat into a home when the sun is shining and can create bright new living spaces. However, glass is a poor insulator, and in cold, cloudy weather all-glass sunspaces can lose more heat than they generate when it's sunny; they must be regularly shut off from the rest of the home to realize any energy savings. But if well situated for solar access and controllable for heat loss, these add-on units are an easy way to go solar. High-quality manufacturers of pre-packaged sunspaces include the following:

♦ Andersen Corporation, (800) 426-4261

♦ Sun Room Company, (800) 426-2737

♦ Sunspace, Inc., (800) 877-7901

♦ Vegetable Factory, (800) 221-2550

DO-IT-YOURSELF

Window installation. With basic skills and tools you can install south-facing windows or add-on collectors yourself. Follow local building codes carefully; if you have questions, ask your city or county building permit officials for advice. Building-supply stores offer many models of thermopane windows and can provide help and installation advice.

WISE USE

Proper installation. To work properly solar heating systems must be designed and installed very carefully. Professional installation or advice is strongly recommended unless you are installing windows or add-on collectors.

Careful insulation. Solar heating makes sense only *after* you have reduced your heating needs as much as possible by thoroughly insulating and weatherproofing your home.

Monitoring radon levels. Radon is a naturally occurring radioactive gas emitted by some soils

and other earth-based construction materials, such as bricks and rock, which are often used as the thermal mass in passive solar heating. Radon can build up in homes to dangerous levels, increasing the risk of lung cancer and other health problems. Radon is not a common problem in solar-heated homes, but you should check for it if the problem is common in your area. Test kits are inexpensive and simple to use; for more information call the Environmental Protection Agency at (800) 633-8372. You can also install a heat exchanger to vent the indoor air (see Heat Exchangers, p. 115; Insulation, p. 141).

FOR FURTHER INFORMATION: "Solar Ideas for Your Home or Apartment" (Massachusetts Audubon Society, South Great Road, Lincoln, MA 01773-9988). *Home Energy: Your Best Options for Solar Heating and Cooling, Wood, Wind, and Photovoltaics,* by Dan Halacy; Rodale Press, 1984. *Real Goods Catalog* (Real Goods Trading Company, 966 Mazzoni St., Ukiah, CA 95482).

HEATING, WOOD

Wood is somewhat messy, bulky, and time-consuming to use for home heating, but it is also inexpensive in many regions and has one environmental advantage: it is a completely renewable fuel source.

ENVIRONMENTAL PROBLEMS

Firewood harvesting impacts. Most firewood comes from dead or dying trees, but some comes from trees that are perfectly healthy. Besides storing carbon dioxide and producing much of the oxygen we breathe, trees—particularly hardwoods, which are much valued for firewood— are a source of food and shelter to wildlife. Even downed and dead trees are vital to forest ecosystems; they provide shelter for small creatures and keep the forest floor untrampled. Woods cleared of downed trees sometimes, for example, become overrun by deer, which can deplete foods needed by other creatures.

Air pollution. Using wood heat creates serious outdoor and indoor air pollution problems.

- *Outdoors,* burning green firewood causes extreme air pollution, because the water in the wood prevents complete burning. But burning even dead, dry wood pollutes the air with particles of soot and dust and carbon monoxide, an invisible but poisonous gas. The soot and dust are quite visible; in fact, they make up nearly 20 percent of the particles in some cities' winter haze.[1]

- *Indoors,* wood smoke buildup can raise levels of two well-known carcinogens, polycyclic aromatic hydrocarbons and benzopyrene, the latter to several times its outdoor level.[2]

Safety hazards. Woodstoves in the living space can cause contact burns, fires from sparks or cinders, or chimney fires, which occur when creosote deposits in the smokestack ignite.

CHOOSING A PRODUCT

GENERAL GUIDELINES

Weighing your needs. Wood heat usually works best as a home's second heating source or as occasional heat for one or two rooms. Before you buy, consider your home's heating needs, your lifestyle, and the variety of available options:

- Self-standing woodstoves, available in dozens of different models and styles, are ideal for limited use.

- An existing fireplace is often a good spot for an efficient woodstove or fireplace insert.

- Wood furnaces can efficiently heat a larger space and serve as a home's primary heat source.

- If you dislike the mess and work of using firewood, consider a pellet stove or insert, which eliminates most of the trouble.

Energy efficiency and low pollution. Whichever type of woodburning device you buy, save wood and prevent air pollution by choosing a high-efficiency model—one with an efficiency rating of 75 percent or better. Many companies now make clean-burning stoves, fireplace inserts, and furnaces that actually surpass current federal standards for emissions. To compare the efficiency and emission levels of different models, look for their Environmental Protection Agency (EPA) rating tags.

Environmentally sound fuel. Before you choose a stove, look into the kinds and sources of fuel available in your area:

- The best suppliers are those that use dead, diseased, or downed trees, collected locally to save transportation costs.

- The type of fire you want determines the best choice of woods: more expensive hardwoods make a hotter, longer-burning fire; cheaper, more plentiful softwoods heat the stove quickly but do not last as long.

- Wood pellets, made from wood scraps, are available in some areas; they're more expensive but burn cleanly, are environmentally sound, and can be used with special automatic feeders for continuous heat.

COMMERCIAL PRODUCTS

Energy-efficient woodstoves and fireplace inserts *(highly recommended)*. Catalytic combustors (which lower the combustion temperature of gases so they burn more completely) and better designs have made woodstoves 30 percent more energy efficient and 60 percent cleaner-burning than they were 20 years ago.[3] A high-efficiency fireplace insert is essentially an efficient, clean-burning woodstove designed to fit into a fireplace opening. Increasingly strict federal emissions limits for fireplace inserts are expected to save 700,000 cords of firewood (about 1,100 square miles of forest) each year, and prevent the release of 436,000 tons of airborne particulates.[4] Some stoves and inserts, however, do even better than the federal standards. Table 22 lists some of the cleanest-burning units available; they all produce less than half the particulates permitted by law after 1990.

Pellet woodstoves *(highly recommended)*. A newer technology uses thousands of pounds of pressure to compress waste wood into small, very dry cylinders. These cylindrical pellets are clean-burning, easy to handle, and environmentally sound—a good use of wood byproducts. Pellets require special stoves with automatic feeders; Table 22 lists the cleanest-burning models available. Make sure pellets are available in your area before you buy a pellet woodstove.

Energy-efficient woodburning furnaces *(highly recommended)*. Rare, but quite practical, these systems can deliver heat to most or all of a house, something a woodstove can't do. They use either forced air or hot water to distribute the heat, have larger fireboxes than woodstoves, and are controlled by adjusting the amount of wood and the air flow into the firebox. For a list of manufacturers, call the Wood Heating Alliance, (202) 857-1181, or a local heating contractor. *Note:* not all wood furnaces are highly efficient; check their efficiency before

you buy.

Standard fireplace inserts *(not generally recommended)*. Usually just simple shells with glass doors, regular fireplace inserts are not covered by federal emissions regulations. They improve the energy efficiency of fireplaces only threefold, to about 30 percent, far below the 75 percent or greater efficiency of woodstove-style inserts.

Fireplaces *(never recommended)*. The standard fireplace, though it looks cozy and warm, can actually pull more heat from a home than it delivers; the best efficiency you can hope for is 10 percent. Fireplaces should be avoided in all new construction; existing fireplaces should be either carefully sealed off or replaced with an energy-efficient insert.

WISE USE

Proper installation. Many house fires are caused by improperly installed woodstoves, so consult a professional about installation. If you install one yourself, follow local codes and the manufacturer's instructions to the letter. Take these basic safety precautions:

- Leave 36 inches of clearance between stove sides and unprotected walls or ceilings; 18 inches for stovepipes. For closer installation, place fireproofing materials between the stove and the walls.

- Protect floors under free-standing stoves with sheet metal or masonry.

- Use masonry or insulated metal chimneys outside, rather than stovepipe, to prevent creosote buildup.

- Install guardrails to keep young children and pets away from the hot stove (or look for models that are safe to touch when in operation).

Regular maintenance. To burn wood cleanly and prevent chimney fires, keep the firebox rel-

TABLE
22

THE CLEANEST-BURNING WOODSTOVES[a]

Brand	Model	Type[b]	Emissions (Grams/Hr)
Thermic	Crossfire: FS-1	P, F	0.5
Vermont Castings	Defiant Encore: 0028	F	0.6
Welenco Manufacturing	Welenco P-1000W	P, F	0.7
Pyro Industries	Whitfield Pellet Fireplace	P, F	1.0
Vermont Castings	Intrepid II: 1303	F	1.0
Pyro Industries	Whitfield WP-1	P, F	1.3
Consolidated Dutchwest	Large Federal Convection Heater	F or I	1.6
Woodcutters Manufacturing	Blaze King: KEJ 1101	F	1.9
HearthStone	HearthStone III:C	F	2.0
Sierra Manufacturing	Evolution 8000TE	F	2.2
Woodcutters Manufacturing	Blaze King Insert: KEI 1300	I	2.2
Derco/Grizzly Stoveworks	Super Achiever FPI: 2 LEX	F or I	2.4
England's Stove Works	Englander 24FC	F	2.4
Martin Industries	Sahara AH51, ASH1B	F	2.4
Russo Corporation	W-25C	F	2.4
England's Stove Works	Englander 2BIC	F	2.5
Sierra Manufacturing	Ambassador 4700TE	I	2.5
Woodcutters Manufacturing	Royal Heir: RHT-2200	F	2.5
	Royal Heir: RHT-2250	I	2.5
Consolidated Dutchwest	Extra Large Federal Convection Heater	F or I	2.6
Luap Associates	Convector Eagle 2001	P, F	2.6
England's Stove Works	Englander 28CC	F	2.7
Orley's Manufacturing	Cougar G225	F	2.7

Source: "Guide to EPA Certified Stoves," *Woodheat '89: A Guide to Wood, Gas, Pellet and Coal Fires*, 1988-89 (Gilford Publishing).

[a] Shown are those with particulate emissions of no more than half the 1990 federal limit.

[b] F = Freestanding; I = Fireplace Insert; P = Pellet.

atively free of ashes and the stovepipes clear of soot and creosote buildup.

Safety equipment. Fire is always a hazard with wood heat. Make sure you have the following items:

- A smoke detector, preferably hard-wired rather than battery powered

- A fully charged fire extinguisher (nonhalon), stored near your stove or fireplace

- Proper tools for loading and cleaning the stove, including an ash rake, a small shovel, a log pike, and thermal gloves

- Other safety devices, such as a flue-overheating alarm and fire-extinguishing flares for chimney fires

Proper fuel. For safe, efficient wood heat, use good-quality fuel:

■ Burn only wood that has been dried for at least six months. Burning green or moist wood creates air pollution, robs heat, and leaves creosote and soot in your chimney, creating a serious fire hazard.

■ Never burn painted or treated scrap wood; it can release toxic fumes.

■ Never burn paper (except a small amount to start a fire) or plastics; both cause pollution and some plastics emit toxic fumes.

Before you buy firewood, think carefully about the kinds available. Each species differs in how it's harvested and how well it burns. Heat values for wood are measured in British thermal units (Btu) per cord (128 cubic feet of wood). Mixing different types of wood can help you start and prolong fires.[5]

■ The highest heat values (24 to 31 million Btu/cord) and longest burning times belong to hardwoods such as oak, beech, maple, hickory, and ash. But cutting down hardwoods—even deadwood—in certain areas causes significant ecological damage.

■ Medium heat values (20 to 24 million Btu/cord) belong to most pines, Douglas fir, juniper, red cedar, sycamore, American elm, magnolia, and chestnut. The pines and Douglas fir are the next-best choices after hardwoods; they ignite easily and can burn for quite a while in efficient stoves.

■ The lowest heat values (16 to 20 million Btu/cord) belong to Ponderosa, white, and sugar pines; red, noble, and balsam fir; aspen; spruce; willow; poplar; and cottonwood. Best for starting fires, these woods give off heat immediately and burn very quickly.

FOR FURTHER INFORMATION: "Home Heating with Wood and Coal" (Massachusetts Audubon Society, South Great Road, Lincoln, MA 01773-9988).

1. "Wood Smoke Pollutes Our Environment" (American Lung Association of Colorado, 1600 Race St., Denver, CO 80206), p. 1.

2. "Polycyclic aromatic hydrocarbons": R. B. Gammage and S. V. Kaye, eds., *Indoor Air and Human Health* (Lewis Publishers, 1985), p. 28; "Benzopyrene": Edward Calabrese and Michael Dorsey, *Healthy Living in an Unhealthy World* (Simon & Schuster, 1984), p. 122.

3. "Wood, Down but Not Out," *Practical Homeowner* (October 1986), p. 75.

4. "The Clean Burn," *Practical Homeowner* (January 1988), p. 79.

5. "Heating with Wood" (Department of Energy, Forrestal Bldg., E1-231, Washington, DC 20585), p. 4.

HEAT PUMPS

Electric heat pumps extract heat from air and move it indoors or outdoors as the need arises, working as heaters in the winter and air conditioners in the summer.

ENVIRONMENTAL PROBLEMS

Energy consumption. Heat pumps use energy twice as efficiently as do the coils or wires found in other electric heating systems, but they are still less efficient than gas heat. Although heat pumps also function as air conditioners, thus requiring only one household system instead of two, they are actually 10 to 15 percent *less* efficient than good central air conditioners.

CHOOSING A PRODUCT

GENERAL GUIDELINES

Weighing your needs. Before you decide whether to get a heat pump, carefully assess your house, climate, heating and cooling needs, and alternative fuels. If you live in a climate with warm winters and hot summers, have a well-insulated house, and do not have access to natural gas, you might benefit from a heat pump. The pumps do *not* work well in extended sub-freezing temperatures.

Energy efficiency. If you do get a heat pump, make energy efficiency your top priority. There are two measures of heat pump efficiency to consider: the Seasonal Energy Efficiency Rating (SEER) measures the unit's overall cooling efficiency, and the Heating Season Performance Factor (HSPF) measures its overall heating efficiency. If you live in a hot climate, cooling efficiency might be the most important factor; in a cooler climate, heating efficiency might be more important.

COMMERCIAL PRODUCTS

Energy-efficient heat pumps *(sometimes recommended).* Always compare SEER and HSPF ratings to find the most energy-efficient unit. Table 23 lists the most energy-efficient heat pumps available in the United States.

Standard heat pumps *(never recommended).* Given the availability of more energy-efficient, better-built, and better-designed models, these heat pumps should be avoided.

FOR FURTHER INFORMATION: "Heat, Cool, and Save Energy with a Heat Pump" and "Directory of Central Air Conditioners and Heat Pumps" (Air Conditioning and Refrigeration Institute, 1501 Wilson Blvd., Arlington, VA 22209). *1991 Consumer Guide to Home Energy Savings,* by Alex Wilson; American Council for an Energy-Efficient Economy, 1990.

TABLE
23

ENERGY-EFFICIENT CENTRAL HEAT PUMPS

Brand	Outdoor Unit Model Number	Indoor Unit Model Number	Cooling Efficiency (SEER)[a]	Cooling Capacity (Btu/Hr)[b]	Heating Efficiency (HSPF)[c]	Heating Capacity (Btu/Hr)
Cooling Capacity: approximately 1.5 tons[d]						
Coleman	3718-611	3718-833	11.30	19,400	8.00	20,200
Lennox	HP22-211-1P	CB19-21-1P+ LB-34792BE	12.85	19,800	7.90	19,000
	HP22-211-1P	CBH19-21-1P+ LB-34792BE	12.85	19,800	7.90	19,000
	HP22-211-1P	CB19-26-1P+ LB-34792BE	12.85	19,800	7.90	19,000
	HP22-211-1P	CBH19-26-1P+ LB-34792BE	12.85	19,800	7.90	19,000
	HP22-211-1P	CH16-41-1FF+ LB-34792BE	11.90	19,700	7.60	19,700
	HP22-211-1P	C16-41-1FF+ LB-34792BE	11.70	19,400	7.45	19,500
	HP22-211-1P	CR16-41-2FF+ LB-34792BE	11.70	19,400	7.45	19,500
Cooling Capacity: approximately 2.0 tons						
Carrier	38QE92430	38QE02430+ 40QE02430	13.35	24,000	8.75	25,800
Lennox	HP22-261-1P	CB19-31-1P+ LB-34792BE	13.60	24,800	8.40	24,000
	HP22-261-1P	CBH19-31-1P+ LB-34792BE	13.60	24,800	8.40	24,000
	HP22-261-1P	CB19-26-1P+ LB-34792BE	13.25	24,400	8.20	24,000
	HP22-261-1P	CBH19-26-1P+ LB-34792BE	13.25	24,400	8.20	24,000
Coleman	3724-911	6932-DUVO	11.10	23,400	8.20	24,400
	3724-911	3724-833	11.30	23,800	8.00	24,800
Cooling Capacity: approximately 2.5 tons						
Trane	TWS730A	TWV739E15-C	16.40	31,800	8.70	29,600
	TWS730A	TWH739E15-C	16.40	31,800	8.70	29,600
Lennox	HP21-311-1P	CB19-31-1P+ LB-34792BG	13.40	31,000	8.65	31,200
	HP21-311-1P	CBH19-31-1P+ LB-34792BG	13.40	31,000	8.65	31,200
	HP21-311-1P	CB19-41-1P+ LB-34792BG	13.00	30,800	8.55	31,000
	HP21-311-1P	CBH19-41-1P+ LB-34792BG	13.00	30,800	8.55	31,000

TABLE 23

ENERGY-EFFICIENT CENTRAL HEAT PUMPS *(continued)*

Brand	Outdoor Unit Model Number	Indoor Unit Model Number	Cooling Efficiency (SEER)[a]	Cooling Capacity (Btu/Hr)[b]	Heating Efficiency (HSPF)[c]	Heating Capacity (Btu/Hr)
Cooling Capacity: approximately 3.0 tons[d]						
Carrier	38QE93630	38QE03630+ 40QE03630	14.05	36,800	9.05	35,400
Trane	TWS736A	TWV739E15-C	15.20	37,600	8.75	34,600
	TWS736A	TWH739E15-C	15.20	37,600	8.75	34,600
	TWX736A	TWH064E15-C	12.85	40,000	8.65	34,600
	TWX736A	TWV064E15-C	12.80	39,500	8.60	34,400
American Standard	TWA036A	TWH064E15-C	12.00	42,000	8.55	36,400
Cooling Capacity: approximately 3.5 tons						
Trane	TWS748A	TWV064E15-C	15.05	48,000	9.40	43,500
	TWS748	TWH064E15-C	15.05	48,000	9.40	43,500
Rheem	RPGB-048JA	RHQA-16+RCQB-B048	11.25	47,500	8.70	49,000
	RPGB-042CA	RHQA-16+RCQB-B042	11.25	47,500	8.70	49,000
	RPGB-048DA	RHQA-16+RCQB-B048	11.25	47,500	8.70	49,000
Ruud	UPGB-048JA	UHQA-16+RCQB-B048	11.25	47,500	8.70	49,000
	UPGB-048CA	UHQA-16+RCQB-B048	11.25	47,000	8.70	49,000
	UPGB-048DA	UHQA-16+RCQB-B048	11.25	47,500	8.70	49,000
Rheem	RPGB-048JA	RCQB-B048	10.95	47,000	8.60	49,500
	RPGB-048CA	RCQB-B048	10.95	47,000	8.60	49,500
	RPGB-048DA	RCQB-B048	10.95	47,000	8.60	49,500
Ruud	UPGB-048CA	RCQB-B048	10.95	47,000	8.60	49,500
	UPGB-048DA	RCQB-B048 LB-34792BG	10.95	47,000	8.60	49,500
	HP22-461-1P	CH19-51-1+B19- 51-1P+LB-34792BG	12.80	42,000	8.50	42,000

Source: *1991 Consumer's Guide to Home Energy Savings* (American Council for an Energy-Efficient Economy).

[a] Based on the Seasonal Energy Efficiency Rating (SEER). The higher the number, the more efficient the heat pump.

[b] Btu = British thermal unit, a measure of energy.

[c] Based on the Heating Season Performance Factor (HSPF). The higher the number, the more efficient the heat pump.

[d] One ton = approximately 12,500 Btu per hour.

HUMIDIFIERS

Humidifiers disperse water into the air, increasing its relative humidity. Humid air is easier to breathe (especially if you have certain respiratory problems), helps control static electricity, and keeps you warmer in winter. Humidifiers do, however, have drawbacks.

ENVIRONMENTAL PROBLEMS

Health hazards. Running a poorly maintained humidifier, especially in a tightly sealed home, can cause serious air contamination:

- Microorganisms can multiply quickly in a humidifier's water reservoir and, in some models, be ejected into the air, triggering or aggravating illnesses.

- Molds and other microorganisms grow on household surfaces and dust mites proliferate in overly humid air.

- Dust left by minerals in the water, especially hard tap water, can cause respiratory problems for sensitive people. A poorly cleaned humidifier filled with plain tap water can raise particulate levels in a closed bedroom to nearly 50 times the federal standards for outdoor air.[1]

CHOOSING A PRODUCT

GENERAL GUIDELINES

Weighing your needs. If you have a tightly sealed home (which retains moisture) and do not live in a dry climate, you might not need a humidifier. You might want to consider one, however, if during the winter your nose or throat always feels dry or you're always chilly.

Weighing contamination problems. Consider the potential indoor air pollution problems of each type of unit before you buy:

Type	Contamination potential
Warm mist	Less likely to spew microbes into the air; does not create mineral dust
Cool mist	Can eject bacteria and live molds into the air; creates some mineral dust
Ultrasound	Produces no live molds but some bacteria; can raise mineral dust to high levels indoors

COMMERCIAL PRODUCTS

Ultrasound humidifiers *(highly recommended)*. By far the most popular type, these humidifiers are quiet and can humidify just as well as a warm-mist unit but use only a fraction of the electricity—40 to 45 watts. They can contaminate the air with bacteria and mineral dust particles, however, unless they are used with a demineralizer or distilled water and cleaned every day.[2] Ultrasound humidifiers come in both portable sizes for single rooms, and console units that can disperse 5 to 15 gallons of water every 24 hours. A console unit can humidify an entire home if its output is distributed properly.

Demineralizers *(highly recommended)*. Separate demineralizers, which can reduce the mineral dust problem, are available for all three types of humidifiers. They either attach to the water supply or fit inside the humidifier itself and filter out minerals before the water enters the unit. Many humidifier manufacturers make demineralizers designed for their products; the cost per gallon of water, based on filter life, runs from 30 cents to over a dollar.

Warm-mist humidifiers *(not generally recommended)*. This type of humidifier heats water into steam, mixes it with air, and releases it as an invisible warm mist. Unfortunately, it uses a lot of electricity to boil the water—up to 400 watts. It is, however, the least polluting type.[3]

Cool-mist humidifiers *(not generally recommended)*. These units break up water into tiny drops that are sprayed into the air. They use relatively little electricity but are most likely to contaminate the air. Most cool-mist humidifiers are small tabletop models.

DO-IT-YOURSELF

Evaporation. During heating season, set pans of water near radiators or forced-air vents or in other warm spots; change the water and clean the pans daily.

WISE USE

Regular maintenance. Careful maintenance is essential for controlling any humidifier's bacteria and mold problem. Airborne microbes will quickly contaminate standing water, so you must clean the reservoir *daily* and rinse it with a mild bleach-and-water solution.

Mineral-free water. Mineral dust is a major problem with both cool-mist and ultrasound humidifiers, so use mineral-free water. Distilled water has no mineral content at all, but it is extremely energy-intensive to produce and comes in wasteful plastic jugs, making it an environmentally unsound choice. Using a demineralizer is preferable.

Careful use. The healthiest, most comfortable indoor humidity level is between 30 and 50 percent. Too much humidity can encourage microorganism growth and even damage your home itself by peeling the wallpaper and rotting the wood. If you see condensation on your windows in cold weather, your home is too humid.

FOR FURTHER INFORMATION: "Humidifiers," *Consumer Reports,* September 1988.

1. Jane E. Brody, "Personal Health," *New York Times* (December 22, 1988).
2. "Humidifiers," *Consumer Reports* (September 1988), p. 589.
3. George Brandsberg, "Breathing Easy," *Practical Home-owner* (November 1989), p. 76.

INSULATION

Insulation is one of the most environmentally important consumer products because it keeps your house warm in winter and cool in summer. Types of insulation vary widely, however, in their effectiveness and safety.

ENVIRONMENTAL BENEFITS

Energy conservation. Insulating materials have low thermal conductivity: heat moves through them much more slowly than through most other building materials. Because home heating and cooling systems are major energy consumers, insulation's ability to conserve warm or cool indoor air without using any energy makes it essential to overall energy conservation.

ENVIRONMENTAL PROBLEMS

Health hazards. Each of the four major types of insulation—urea-formaldehyde foam, polyfoam, cellulose, and fiberglass or rock wool—carries health risks:

- *Urea-formaldehyde foam* has a long history of health hazards: it was banned in 1982 after thousands of complaints, but the ban was later overruled. The foam, which is usually blown into existing walls, releases formaldehyde fumes that can irritate the nose, throat, and eyes, especially in the years right after installation. High concentrations, like those found in some tightly sealed homes, can cause coughing, wheezing, and chest constriction. Long-term exposure to high concentrations can cause cancer.[1] (See Wise Use, below, for ways to deal with formaldehyde pollution.)

- *Polyfoam* is made from polystyrene, polyurethane, or polyisocyanurate, all fossil-fuel derivatives. Once installed and sealed from

141

the living space by a vapor barrier and dry-wall, polyfoams are considered relatively stable and nonpolluting. Polyurethane, however, emits toxic fumes when burned, making it lethal during a fire.

- *Cellulose* is made from old paper, newspaper, or wood materials treated with powdered fire retardants such as boric acid and ammonium sulfate, which can cause health problems if they enter the living space through wall or ceiling openings. The cellulose itself, if moist, can attract molds.

- *Fiberglass or rock wool* is made from molten glass or minerals. Contact with tissue can cause itching and irritation, so the insulation should be handled with care during installation. Fiberglass is believed to be stable and nontoxic once installed.

Fire hazards. Polyfoams are extremely flammable, even when a fire retardant is used, and can turn a small fire into a catastrophic one.[2]

Air pollution and ozone depletion. Both urea-formaldehyde foam and the polyfoams are made from petroleum and natural gas through complicated processes that cause serious air pollution. Ozone-destroying chlorofluorocarbons (CFCs) were once used as the blowing agent for all rigid foam; some manufacturers still use them, but many others have now switched to HCFCs, which cause about one-twentieth the damage to the stratospheric ozone layer. HCFCs do pollute the air, however, and will probably be banned in the future.

CHOOSING A PRODUCT

GENERAL GUIDELINES

Energy audit. Before you insulate your home, have an energy audit done by your local energy-conservation office or a reputable insulation or weatherization contractor. The audit will assess your insulation options and needs as well as possible weatherproofing methods for doors and windows, furnace efficiency, and other conservation factors. You can also do an energy audit yourself: just ask your local utility company or energy-conservation office for information.

High R-value. The resistance value (R-value) of an insulating material indicates its ability to impede heat flow. The best energy-efficient standard for most homes is R-19 for walls and R-30 for ceilings.

Safety. Choose a product that won't be hazardous to your health once it's installed.

Superinsulation. This is not so much a type of insulation as a combination of careful building techniques and quality materials. Consider superinsulation if you are building a new home or remodeling your present one. See For Further Information, below.

COMMERCIAL PRODUCTS

Fiberglass or rock wool *(highly recommended).* Insulating value: 1 inch = R-3.0 to R-3.8. Fiberglass and the very similar rock wool (made from naturally occurring minerals or metal ore slag) are good insulating choices for both environmental and safety reasons. However, meeting recommended R-values with them often requires using wider framing materials (for example, 2 x 8 wall studs instead of 2 x 4s), double-framing, or other special construction methods. Both fiberglass and rock wool are commonly available in easy-to-install batts and blankets and as loose fill that can be poured or blown (as loose fill, fiberglass may have a lower R-value per inch, depending on the product). Fiberglass also comes in rigid boards with an insulating value per inch of about R-4.4. The batts, blankets, and loose fill generate airborne particles during installation that can irritate the skin, eyes, and respiratory tract, so installers should wear adequate protection. Once sealed off from the living space, fiberglass and rock wool insulation is quite stable, does not absorb moisture, and has good fire resistance.

Cellulose *(sometimes recommended).* Insulating value: 1 inch = R-2.8 to R-4.0. Cellulose loose-fill insulation can be poured or blown into attics or through holes in existing walls or other closed spaces; it can also be sprayed directly onto masonry walls or similar surfaces, with special equipment. Often made from recycled newspapers, cellulose has the best R-value of any loose-fill insulation and is well-suited for application to attics. But cellulose must be carefully sealed off from the living space and from any possible moisture, which can be absorbed by the insulation, causing it to deteriorate. Cellulose is also rated only fair for fire resistance. Cellulose generates dust when it is poured or blown, so wear protective equipment (particle mask, glasses or goggles, gloves) during installation.

Reflective aluminum foil (sometimes recommended). Insulating value: 1 layer = R-6.4 to R-11. This product comes in long rolls of very thin material (less than ½-inch thick), composed of two or three layers of aluminum foil, which reflect heat very effectively, bonded to layers of polyethylene insulation. It must be specially installed with ¾-inch of air space on both sides. This air space, if not carefully sealed, can lead to air infiltration, which greatly lowers the R-value; in a fire, the air space can become a pathway for spreading the flames quickly throughout a structure. Aluminum foil is most effective when placed on the underside of roofs, to keep homes cool in hot climates.

Polystyrene foam. (sometimes recommended). Insulating value: 1 inch = R-3.6 to R-5.0. Generally available only in rigid boards, polystyrene is derived from the petrochemicals ethylene and benzene through a complex, polluting process. Polystyrene (marketed as Styrofoam by Dow Chemical Co.) comes in two versions, expanded (EPS) and extruded. Extruded is more expensive but is also much stronger and more moisture resistant, and has a higher R-value. It works well as sheathing for masonry walls, above and below ground. Both expanded and extruded polystyrene are highly combustible and must be well protected from all heat sources. Installation poses no special risks (except as a fire hazard) but must be done carefully to prevent empty spaces that can greatly diminish its effective R-value.

Polyurethane, polyisocyanurate foam (not generally recommended). Insulating value: 1 inch = R-5.8 to R-7.7. Both these products are made from petrochemical isocyanates through complex, polluting processes. They are widely available as rigid boards, though polyurethane can also be foamed in place for unusual structures or hard-to-reach places. Despite their high R-values (the highest of all commercially available insulators) these products should be considered only for special applications, or for sheathing masonry walls, foundations, etc., when other materials are unsuitable. Both are highly flammable; polyurethane releases toxic fumes when burned.

Urea-formaldehyde foam (never recommended). This type of insulation causes serious, health-endangering air pollution, and should not be used under any circumstances.

WISE USE

Proper installation. There are many tricks to installing insulation correctly, in either an old or a new home, including use of vapor barriers, proper ventilation, and working around wiring. If you plan to install it yourself, do some homework first. For safety's sake, always wear a particle mask, eye protection, gloves, a long-sleeved shirt, and a hat. Unless you're certain you can install it safely and correctly, hire a licensed contractor.

Adequate ventilation. To prevent indoor air pollution, a tightly insulated house must be adequately vented. Contact your local energy office or a heating and cooling contractor for information about testing your home's air quality and venting ability.

Monitoring radon levels. Radon is a naturally occurring radioactive gas emitted by some soils and rock. In some parts of the country it builds up in homes, increasing risks of lung cancer and other serious health problems. For more information on radon, contact the Environmental Protection Agency at (800) 633-8372.

Reducing formaldehyde contamination. If you already have urea-formaldehyde insulation in your home, you might want to check the formaldehyde level; call 3M at (612) 426-0691 and ask about the 3M 3720 Formaldehyde Monitor. You can reduce formaldehyde in several ways:

- Sealing the insulated walls, ceilings, or floors with caulk or special coatings can keep fumes from infiltrating the living space (see Particleboard and Plywood, p. 152, for paints and sealers that block formaldehyde).

- Ventilating the living space removes the gases. Heat exchangers make effective, energy-efficient ventilators. (See Heat Exchangers, p. 115).

- Dehumidifying the indoor air can lower formaldehyde levels by up to 50 percent; you can get dehumidifiers at department and hardware stores.

FOR FURTHER INFORMATION: Contact your local utility companies and energy conservation offices. "All About Insulation," "Contractor's Guide to Finding and Sealing Hidden Air Leaks," and "Superinsulation" (Massachusetts Audubon Society, South Great Road, Lincoln, MA 01773-9988). *The Superinsulated Home Book,* by J.D. Ned Nisson and Gautam Dutt; John Wiley & Sons, 1985.

1. W. J. Fisk et al., *Indoor Air Quality Control Techniques* (Noyes Data Corporation, 1987), p. 10.
2. N. Irving Sax and Richard J. Lewis, Sr., eds., *Hawley's Condensed Chemical Dictionary,* 11th ed. (Van Nostrand Reinhold, 1987), p. 584.

PAINTS AND FINISHES

There are many types of paints and finishes, but all contain three basic ingredients: resins that bind to the surface after drying; solvents or water in which the resins are dissolved; and pigments and fillers that add color, texture, and finish. Paints and finishes are essential—they brighten, color, and protect surfaces—but they also cause considerable pollution.

ENVIRONMENTAL PROBLEMS

Fossil-fuel depletion. The resins in alkyd or oil-based products, which dry to a hard, glossy finish, are made from alcohols and petroleum or coal-tar oils through a complex, heat-intensive process. The resins in latex or water-based products, which dry to a softer, flatter finish, are acrylic or vinyl derivatives of petrochemicals. Producing either type of resin pollutes the air, soil, and water and depletes nonrenewable resources.

Air pollution. Paints, varnishes, lacquers, thinners, and solvents used by consumers account for 3.4 percent of the ozone-causing hydrocarbons, or volatile organic compounds (VOCs), released into our nation's air every year.[1] Paints and sealers—particularly alkyd products, with their solvents made from petroleum or coal tars—pollute the air as they dry. The VOCs they release react with nitrogen oxides and sunlight to produce ozone, which at ground level is an air pollutant that is toxic to inhale and a serious lung irritant. Latex paints and finishes create far less air pollution because they use water instead of petrochemical solvents.

Health hazards. Both alkyd and latex paints give off harmful vapors and can contain toxic metals:[2]

- Concentrated *vapors from alkyd solvents* can cause dizziness, lightheadedness, nausea, headaches, and even long-term illness.

- *Acrylic and vinyl resins* in latex paints can give off irritating vapors.

- *Mercury,* a toxic metal used in latex paints to control mildew, has now been banned in interior paints; exterior paints that contain mercury must say so on the label.

- *Lead,* a toxic metal often used as a pigment in oil-based paints until the 1960s, is now banned; today's pigments are relatively safe. Old lead paint, however, still poses a serious danger if stripped or sanded (see Paint Thinners, Solvents, and Removers, p.148).

Disposal problems. Paints and finishes make up a large portion of our nation's nonindustrial hazardous wastes. If they end up in a landfill, their toxic ingredients can pollute groundwater. And if they are poured down the drain they can bypass or overtax water treatment facilities and pollute downstream water.

Wasteful packaging. Cans of aerosol spray paint, popular and easy to use, are energy-intensive to make, dangerously polluting to use, highly flammable, and nonrecyclable. Regular paint cans are also nonrecyclable because of their toxic residues.

CHOOSING A PRODUCT

GENERAL GUIDELINES

Weighing your needs. Before buying any paint or finish, do some homework to determine the best product for the job. Call paint professionals, both painters and salespeople, for advice. Make it clear you are looking for water-based, environmentally sound products that perform well. Some painters now specialize in using nontoxic materials.

Less-toxic ingredients. Make latex paints, stains, and sealers your first choice; if you must use an alkyd product, choose one with a low percentage of solvent.

Quality. Always select the best quality products available. They usually perform better and last

longer, reducing the need for repainting or refinishing.

Sensible packaging. Buy the largest containers practical if you are sure you will use all the contents. Avoid aerosols whenever possible.

COMMERCIAL PRODUCTS

Nontoxic products *(highly recommended).* Four companies market specially formulated nontoxic products. These products are relatively expensive and are used primarily by people with allergies and chemical sensitivities, but are also of interest to anyone looking for naturally based paints and finishes:

- Livos PlantChemistry, (505) 438-0199, distributes interior and exterior paints plus a wide variety of stains, lacquers, shellacs, polishes, adhesives, thinners, cleaners, and art supplies.

- Murco Wall Products, (817) 626-1987, makes nontoxic interior flat latex and latex gloss enamel paint.

- AFM Enterprises, (714) 781-6860, makes water-based semigloss enamel.

- AURO, available from Sinan Co., (916) 753-3104, makes naturally derived organic paints, varnishes, and other finishes.

Latex paints *(recommended).* Environmentally, latex paints are a wiser choice than alkyds, but for certain applications alkyds look better or last longer. Latex paints are also less water resistant, an important factor in bathrooms and kitchens and on outdoor furniture. Latex paints are improving all the time, however, and despite their problems offer important advantages over alkyds for do-it-yourselfers: they perform very well on flat-finished surfaces such as interior walls; apply easily with either brushes or rollers; "sag" less after application; clean up easily with water; and produce less air pollution in the working or living space.

For high quality look for these three features:

- *A high percentage of solids* (35 to 45 percent, instead of 25 to 30 percent)

- *A 100 percent acrylic resin* (without added vinyl acetate or vinyl chloride, which are cheaper and less effective)

- *A high percentage of titanium dioxide,* an expensive pigment with good "hiding" (covering old colors) ability

Many surfaces that are typically covered with glossy alkyd paints, including wood trim, cabinets, and furniture, can instead be covered with more environmentally sound latex semigloss paints. Among the best interior semigloss latex paints are

- ◆ Benjamin Moore Regal Aquaglo Series 333

- ◆ Fuller-O'Brien Double AA Series 214XX

- ◆ Fuller-O'Brien Ful-Flo Series 614XX

- ◆ Kelly-Moore Acry-Plex Series 1650

- ◆ Sherwin-Williams Classic 99

- ◆ Sherwin-Williams Superpaint

Latex stains and clear sealers *(recommended).* Relatively new, latex stains and clear sealers are still harder to find than latex paint, but are gaining in popularity. They perform very well if used appropriately and applied correctly. Some brands are available nationwide:

Product	Use
Aqua Fabulon	Interior floor finish
Benjamin Moore	Interior clear sealer
Duron; Bond-n-Seal; Muralo; Stain Stopper	Exterior primers
Flame-Stop	Exterior fire-retardant sealer
Okon	Exterior sealers for various surfaces
Pace; Crystal Aire I	Interior sealers
Pace-Creme	Interior stains
Pittsburgh Paints	Exterior solid-color stains, interior semitransparent stains
Pratt & Lambert	Various stains and sealers
Samuel Cabot; Sherwin-Williams	Exterior stains

Alkyd paints *(not generally recommended).* Alkyd paints' hardness, durability, and lustrous appearance make them the logical choice for some applications—outdoor furniture, for example—despite their environmental drawbacks. If you need to use an alkyd paint, look for the following characteristics by checking labels and asking salespeople:

- *Low VOC content.* Some states now limit VOC content, and some low-VOC products are now sold nationwide.

- *High quality.* A high ratio of solids (resin and pigment) to solvent is the best indication of quality. Price is also a rough guide: more expensive brands tend to be less polluting, better looking, and longer lasting.

Alkyd penetrating finishes *(not generally recommended).* These products, which soak into wood and leave a nonglossy finish, are easy to apply and recoat, but are less resistant to abrasion than surface finishes. Most are made from vegetable oils in a mineral spirits solvent. For exteriors consider these low-VOC products:

- ◆ Minwax reformulated Watco Exterior Wood Finish

- ◆ Darworth Cuprinol Deck Stain, No. 10 Green Wood Preservative, and No. 20 Clear Wood Preservative

- ◆ Sikkens Cetol DEK, for wood decks

- ◆ Weather-Master wood preservatives

Alkyd surface finishes *(not generally recommended).* These products do not soak into wood; instead they form a tough, protective coating on the surface. Common products include polyurethane, shellac, lacquer, varnish, epoxy finish, and Swedish finish. All except shellac pollute the air when applied and sometimes long after, and all are extremely flammable and must be handled and stored with great care.

- *Shellacs* contain an insect resin dissolved in alcohol rather than petroleum solvents, so they release fewer fumes. They are suitable only for interiors and discolor from spills more easily than other coatings. One product, Target, made by Wm. Zinnser & Co., has an added resin to make it more durable.

- *Polyurethane* and *epoxy coatings* are notorious for the fumes emitted by their petrochemical resins and solvents.

- *Lacquers* and *varnishes* use naturally derived resins, but also use strong petrochemical solvents.

- *Swedish finishes,* such as Glitsa, use a toxic urea-formaldehyde resin and should be avoided.

As with alkyd paints, if you must use any alkyd surface finishes, look for a high ratio of solids to solvent and a low VOC level.

DO-IT-YOURSELF

Interior whitewash. This homemade formula works better on drywall than on wood. (Lime is caustic, so wear gloves and eye protection and avoid getting it on your skin.)

1. Add 5 pounds of hydrated lime to 1 gallon of water, stir, and let sit overnight.

2. Add powdered pigment to create the desired color (remember, paint will dry to a lighter color).

3. Add 1½ pounds of salt to 2 quarts of warm water, stir, and pour into the lime mixture.

4. Dampen the surface before painting; apply paint in thin coats. Stir continually during application.

ALTERNATIVES

Linseed oil. Made from seeds of the flax plant, nontoxic linseed oil preserves and protects exterior wood and adds a soft, golden color. It takes time to dry, because it has no solvent. You can buy linseed oil at paint and hardware stores.

WISE USE

Safe use. When applying paints or finishes, particularly alkyd products, take the following precautions:

- If you must first remove old paint, see Paint Thinners, Solvents, and Removers, p. 148.

- Rent or buy an organic-vapor respirator with an activated carbon or charcoal filter to absorb harmful vapors.

- Ventilate the area during and after application to speed drying and minimize your exposure to vapors.

- Never use products labeled "exterior" for interior applications; they are likely to have toxic ingredients not suitable for indoors.

- Wear rubber gloves. Skin can easily absorb toxic compounds.

- Follow the manufacturer's instructions carefully.

- When cleaning up latex paints, wash brushes and tools in a utility sink rather than outside to avoid contaminating soil and groundwater.

- For cleaning up alkyd paints, see Paint Thinners, Solvents, and Removers, p. 148.

Proper disposal. When finished with a paint job, be sure to follow these disposal guidelines:

- Instead of discarding leftover paints or finishes, find other uses for them: sell them at a yard sale; donate them to a church or charity group; or give them to friends.

- *Never* pour any paint or finish—either latex or alkyd—down a drain, gutter, or sewer, or onto the ground.

- *Never* put any paint in trash that is going to a landfill or an incinerator.

- Don't open cans of alkyd products to let them evaporate before disposal, as some writers advocate; doing so badly pollutes the air. You can evaporate latex paints safely, but evaporation takes a long time, so keep them away from children, pets, and wildlife.

- Never throw out paints and finishes; instead store them for hazardous waste collection, or take them to a collection site. Call your local waste disposal office for information on hazardous waste collection programs.

- Until you can dispose of them properly, seal paints tightly and store them away from heat.

FOR FURTHER INFORMATION: "New Age Finishes" and "The Fine Print," by Walt Gozdan, *Practical Homeowner* (April 1990), pp. 60-83. "Interior Latex Paints," *Consumer Reports* (May 1991), pp. 335-339.

1. Gina Kolata, "How Much Is Too Much to Pay to Meet Standards for Smog?" *New York Times* (April 3, 1989).
2. Don Best, "Using Floor Finishes Safely," *Practical Homeowner* (February 1988), p. 84.

PAINT THINNERS, SOLVENTS, AND REMOVERS

Though they are useful for cleaning up or removing paints, these products are also some of the most dangerous of all consumer goods on the market.

ENVIRONMENTAL PROBLEMS

Toxic ingredients. Vapors from chemical paint thinners, solvents, and removers are easily inhaled or absorbed through the skin and pose major health hazards. Most of the products are toxic if inhaled, and fumes can quickly build to unsafe levels in an enclosed space. And because most of the products do not cause immediate burns, many users are casual about getting them on their skin, unaware of the dangers of absorption. Health hazards of specific products vary widely and are included in the Commercial Products section, below.

Air pollution. Most chemical thinners, solvents, and removers contain petroleum-derived hydrocarbons. When their volatile organic compounds (VOCs) evaporate, they contribute to general air pollution and react with sunlight to create ozone, which is toxic and a lung irritant.

Fire danger. Except for methylene chloride, most thinners, strippers, and solvents are extremely flammable; even rags used to apply them can combust spontaneously if the rags are placed in a container before they are dry. And heat devices for removing paint can start fires, even when used with care.

CHOOSING A PRODUCT

GENERAL GUIDELINES

Weighing your needs. Make sure you pick the right product for the job:

- For cleaning and thinning, select a thinner or solvent that will work well but minimize environmental and health risks.

- Before attempting to remove old paint, make sure removal is necessary and will be successful. Paint sinks so deeply into some softwoods, for example, that complete removal is nearly impossible. Have the paint tested to see if it contains lead. If you must remove lead paint yourself, use only approved methods (less-toxic chemical strippers and some heat tools are best).

Less-toxic remedies. Try the less-toxic products first, resorting to the more toxic ones only as a last resort.

Sensible packaging. Large containers—whether metal or plastic—are *not* the best choice when buying these products, because storage is hazardous; buy only the amounts you will use in the near future.

COMMERCIAL PRODUCTS

Less-toxic natural paint thinner *(highly recommended)*. Leinos-Citrus Thinner uses a citrus-based solvent made from orange peels to make a less toxic, low-odor substitute for mineral spirits and turpentine. It works both as a cleaner and degreaser and as a thinner for paints and finishes. The American distributor is Livos PlantChemistry, (505) 438-3448.

Heat paint-removal tools *(recommended)*. These devices use heat to strip old paint and are highly effective, though they must be used very carefully. Look for them at rental and painting-equipment stores:

- *Heat torches* are blow torches and should be used *only* by professionals. They work quickly and effectively but are serious fire hazards.

They create temperatures high enough to vaporize lead, so they should *not* be used to remove lead paint.

- *Heat guns* look similar to hair dryers, but blow air hot enough to remove paint and burn wood. They work well on moldings, railings, and curved surfaces. They are *not* safe, however, for hollow surfaces such as frame siding, because they can blow hot air into crevices and start slow, smoldering fires. Heat guns operate at much lower temperatures than torches and are sometimes suitable for removing lead paint since they do not vaporize the heavy metal. They do produce some fumes and should be used with respirator masks and other safety precautions.

- *Heat plates* consist of a simple electric coil mounted on a hand-held plate. They work best on large flat areas and, unlike heat guns, are less likely to start fires behind hollow surfaces. They still present a fire hazard, however, and must be used carefully. Like heat guns, they are sometimes useful for removing lead paint, though many safety precautions must be taken.

Less-toxic chemical paint removers *(sometimes recommended)*. If you must use a paint remover, consider a less-toxic, less-flammable product such as:

- *Safest Stripper*, made by 3M. Instead of methylene chloride, methanol, and other toxics, this product uses the much less volatile dimethyl adipate and dimethyl glutarate. For best results, leave Safest Stripper on paint overnight. Available in better hardware stores, or call 3M, (612) 426-0691, for more information.

- *Peel-Away 1* and *Peel-Away 6*, made by Dumond Chemicals. Neither contains methylene chloride. Peel-Away 1 is a solvent-free, biodegradable paste that is applied to old paint then covered with a cloth to control evaporation. The paint comes off when the cloth is removed. Peel-Away 1 is free of vapors but caustic and dangerous to eyes and skin. A new

149

solvent-free product, Peel-Away 6, works the same way but is not caustic. For more information, contact Dumond Chemicals, Inc., (212) 869-6350.

Chemical thinners and solvents *(not generally recommended)*. The most common types of thinners and solvents are hydrocarbon-based products that create polluting, hazardous vapors. They should be used very carefully and only when absolutely necessary.

- *Acetone* is a petrochemical derivative with very high solvent power. It is extremely flammable but only moderately toxic, and its vapors, though dangerous, are the least harmful among these products. It is the fastest-evaporating solvent, which limits its usefulness for tasks such as cleaning brushes, and it dissolves plastics. Often used for thinning epoxies, it will dissolve two-part epoxy before the epoxy sets up.

- *Benzene, toluene,* and *xylene* are aromatic hydrocarbons, toxic and flammable. Their solvent power is high. Benzene is carcinogenic and highly toxic and should be avoided under all circumstances. Toluene and xylene are central nervous system depressants and eye and throat irritants, but they are less toxic than benzene. They are also very versatile and can be used to thin almost anything: paints, stains, lacquers, polyurethanes, and epoxies. Toluene is also an excellent degreaser.

- *Lacquer thinner* is a blend of alcohols and petrochemicals. Toxic and flammable, this high-strength solvent is designed specifically to thin and clean lacquer.

- *Methyl ethyl ketone* is a petrochemical derivative with very high solvent power. Toxic to inhale and extremely flammable, it is similar to acetone but evaporates much more slowly. It can be reduced with water and used to thin epoxies.

- *Mineral spirits,* such as VM & P naphtha, are petrochemicals that are both flammable and toxic. Vapors can cause eye irritation, nausea, loss of coordination, and other symptoms. They have the lowest solvent strengths among the petrochemical products, but are usually adequate for cleaning and thinning alkyd paints, stains, varnishes, and finishes.

- *Turpentine* is made from the gum of living pine trees but is still a hydrocarbon, toxic if swallowed and capable of burning the skin or eyes. Turpentine has low solvent power (slightly higher than that of mineral spirits) and a slower evaporation rate, and leaves a slight residue upon drying. It thins oil-based products.

Chemical paint removers *(never recommended)*. Methylene chloride, the most popular and effective ingredient in paint strippers, is carcinogenic, toxic, narcotic, and capable of seriously burning eyes and skin. If absorbed into the body—through inhalation, for example—it forms toxic carbon monoxide, making it especially dangerous for people with heart or respiratory conditions. Other common ingredients in chemical strippers include toluene, discussed above, and methanol. Methanol, another petrochemical derivative, is both toxic if swallowed and extremely flammable, and is particularly dangerous if used with methylene chloride. Avoid chemical strippers if at all possible; if you must use one, either hire a professional or take the safety precautions listed under Wise Use.

ALTERNATIVES

Dipping. If you need to strip paint from furniture or other movable items, have it done professionally. Most professionals dip all but the most delicate items into a vat of solvent rather than spraying or brushing it on; dipping is usually safer and environmentally cleaner.

Sanding. Sanding, scraping, and wire-brushing old paint can be effective and less-toxic removal methods, depending on the paint. None of these methods should be used for lead paint, because they produce fine, inhalable particles of the toxic metal.

WISE USE

Safe use. If you must remove old paint, follow these precautions:

- Hire professionals if feasible, and make sure they use safe techniques and equipment. If you must do the work yourself *exercise extreme caution.*

- Try to determine whether any of the paint is an alkyd over 20 years old; if so it probably contains lead, especially if it is white or light-colored. To be certain, have a sample tested; call your local health department for information.

- If the paint contains lead and you must remove it yourself, ask a professional or the health department for detailed safety precautions. Leave intact paint alone; remove only chipping or peeling paint. Never remove lead paint while children or pregnant women are present.

- Rent or buy an organic-vapor respirator, with activated carbon or charcoal filters to absorb harmful vapors.

- Wear protective clothing, including long sleeves, solvent-resistant rubber gloves, and eye goggles.

- Ventilate the space with fans while you are working.

- Follow the manufacturers' instructions carefully.

- Never use paint thinner or any solvent to clean your skin. Instead, use moisturizing cream or lotion to soften the paint, then wash with soap and a scrubber.

Reuse and proper disposal. If you use mineral spirits, turpentine, and similar solvents to clean brushes and other tools, you can reuse the solvents many times. After cleaning, put the liquid in a covered container, let the paint settle to the bottom, and carefully pour the solvent through a cloth filter and back into its original container. If you must dispose of thinner, solvents, or removers, treat them as hazardous wastes and follow these guidelines:

- Rags or paper with solvents on them must be *completely* dry before you put them in a closed container, such as a trash can or plastic bag, or they might spontaneously combust.

- *Never* pour any of these products down a drain, gutter, or sewer, or onto the ground, or put them into trash going to a landfill or incinerator.

- Do not evaporate solvents as a method of disposal; their evaporating hydrocarbons pollute the air.

- Tightly seal containers of unwanted solvents, thinners, and removers and store them in a secure, cool place for a hazardous waste collection, or take them to a collection site. Call your local waste disposal office for information on hazardous waste collection programs.

FOR FURTHER INFORMATION: "The Basics of Stripping Paint," by Patricia Poore, and "Restoration Health Hazards," by Bill O'Donnell, *The Old House Journal* (January/February 1988); pp. 38-49.

PARTICLEBOARD AND PLYWOOD

Americans buy 25 billion square feet of particleboard and plywood every year.[1] Made of small scraps or thin sheets of wood glued together, these and other composite wood products are popular and inexpensive, but they have hidden health and environmental costs.

ENVIRONMENTAL PROBLEMS

Health hazards. The glue used in most interior particleboard, plywood, and other composites is urea-formaldehyde resin with extra formaldehyde added for faster drying. The "free" formaldehyde slowly outgasses over several years, contributing to indoor air pollution, or "sick building syndrome," and causing eye, nose, and throat irritation.[2] Particle-composite products are worse offenders than plywood because they contain more urea-formaldehyde resin. Outdoor plywood and composites contain a somewhat stabler glue, phenol-formaldehyde, but it too outgasses over time.

Manufacturing impacts. Urea-formaldehyde resin is made from petroleum and natural gas through a complicated process and is then converted to glues using intense heat, high pressure, and added catalysts and formaldehyde. The entire process depletes nonrenewable fossil-fuel supplies and causes air and water pollution. The major ingredients include ammonia, which is extremely toxic, and formaldehyde, a carcinogen; both are strong air contaminants.

CHOOSING A PRODUCT

GENERAL GUIDELINES

Weighing your needs. Before you buy household goods such as furniture, toys, shelving, or paneling, find out whether they contain particleboard; if they do, decide whether their value is really worth the pollution. When you buy construction materials, use plywood or solid wood instead of particle-composite materials whenever possible.

COMMERCIAL PRODUCTS

Plywood *(recommended)*. Most plywood is made from thin sheets of wood cut by rolling a tree against a saw blade. The sheets are layered and glued with a small amount of either urea- or phenol-formaldehyde resin, depending on whether they are to be used indoors or out. Alternating layers have their grains at right angles to each other, making the sheet stronger and less likely to split or sag than solid wood when used over large areas. Many kinds of plywood are available: interior or exterior; softwood or hardwood; plain, sanded, or textured finishes; paneling or sheathing; high quality or low quality. Plywood's low price and structural strength make it ideal for exterior sheathing; it can be replaced by solid wood or other materials such as drywall for many other uses.

Formaldehyde-free sheet goods *(sometimes recommended)*. Some manufacturers make composite wood products that are based on petrochemical resins but use no formaldehyde; you can find or order them at better building-materials stores:

- ◆ *Iso-Board,* a particleboard made without urea-formaldehyde, for general-purpose use

- ◆ *Homasote 440 Carpet Board,* made without urea-formaldehyde but with a mildew-resistant chemical, for carpet underlayment

- ◆ *Wonderboard,* a lightweight concrete board reinforced with fiberglass, for underlayment of tile or other hard flooring

Particleboard and other composite products *(not generally recommended)*. There are three main types of particle-composite sheets made with polluting formaldehyde-based resins:

- *Particleboard* is made with small wood chips. It is flat, dense, and stable when dry and not overloaded, but it expands when damp and, if used for shelving, will warp under heavy loads. It is used primarily indoors as subflooring, as underlayment for cabinets and counters, and in furniture and toys. Inspect wood furniture and similar goods closely, looking underneath or inside to see whether the wood is actually just a veneer over particleboard.

- *Waferboard* (sometimes called flakeboard or chipboard) is made with larger wood chips and flakes, glued with a phenol-formaldehyde resin that better withstands moisture. It is used primarily for exterior sheathing as a cheaper substitute for plywood.

- *Hardboard* (fiberboard) is made from tiny wood fibers that form a dense sheet with a flat, hard surface finish. It is often used as utility-grade paneling indoors or as paintable exterior siding. Medium-density fiberboard is used in furniture and cabinets.

Less polluting substitutes, such as solid wood, plywood, and sheetrock or drywall, are available for all three types of composite products.

WISE USE

Safe use. Minimize pollution from formaldehyde fumes as much as possible by taking these steps:

- If you're having a home built, consider using plywood instead of particleboard.

- If you suspect a formaldehyde problem in your existing home or office, test the air with a 3M 3720 Formaldehyde Monitor from the 3M Company, (612) 426-0691.

- If you are exposed to formaldehyde fumes from new construction or household items, look into sealing the accessible surfaces and improving the building's ventilation. The following sealers work well for formaldehyde:

- Aqua Fabulon, an acrylic water-based coating

- Auro Particleboard Fume Sealer and Clear Wood Sealer

- DeGrayco Particleboard Sealer

- Dennyfoil or similar metal-foil laminates, which are impervious to gases

- Falima F paint

- Right On Crystal Aire Shellac, for dry surfaces only

FOR FURTHER INFORMATION: "Healthy Building," by Mark Alvarez, *Practical Homeowner* (February 1987), pp. 30-35.

1. *1989 U.S. Industrial Outlook* (Department of Commerce, 1989), pp. 5–12, 14.
2. R. B. Gammage and S. V. Kaye, eds., *Indoor Air and Human Health* (Lewis Publishers, 1985), p. 182; W. J. Fisk et al., *Indoor Air Quality Control Techniques* (Noyes Data Corporation, 1987), p. 11.

TOILETS

Few household fixtures are more essential than the toilet—or more wasteful of water. More than a third of all household water goes down the toilet.[1]

ENVIRONMENTAL PROBLEMS

Wasteful water use. Standard toilets use 5 to 8 gallons of water to flush an average of only one to three cups of waste. In areas with water shortages, this heavy use of water depletes the total available supply. Even in areas with plentiful water, this use overburdens water treatment facilities, which must purify water for flushing toilets to drinking-water quality and then purify the wastewater for release. Because of the high volume of water used, both tasks are often performed inadequately. For example, only slightly over half of American wastewater treatment facilities remove all the suspended solids, phosphorus, and nitrogen polluting the wastewater.[2]

CHOOSING A PRODUCT

GENERAL GUIDELINES

Water conservation. When you choose a new toilet or consider replacing an old, water-wasting one, make water conservation a top priority. Look into buying a new, ultra-low-flush toilet; if a new toilet isn't feasible, install a water-saving device in your old one.

COMMERCIAL PRODUCTS

Ultra-low-flush toilets *(highly recommended).* Also called low-consumption or simply low-flush, these toilets use no more than 1.6 gallons of water. Some models use simple gravity, as conventional toilets do, along with a tank and bowl designed to use the falling water more effectively. Other "turbo-charged" models com-

press air in a special trap when water flows into the unit; the air then adds velocity (and sometimes extra noise) to the flush. Eventually, all new American toilets will be ultra-low-flush; some areas already require them in new construction. Table 24 lists ultra-low-flush toilets and some of their important features. Two features to consider on any new toilet are drainline carrying distance and water-seal size:

- *Drainline carrying distance* is the distance over which a toilet can flush wastes—to avoid drainline clogging, it must be far enough to reach a main sewer line. All the models in Table 24 meet American National Standards Institute specifications: 100 ¾-inch balls must travel 40 feet in a 4-inch sewer line with a ¼-inch drop per foot. If you think your drainline is longer or has less of a drop, look for models—usually air-pressurized types—with a higher rated distance.

- The *water seal* is the surface area of the water sitting in the bowl, which to some people is important for aesthetic reasons. Many ultra-low-flush toilets have small water seals that increase water efficiency but make it harder for flushing to clean the bowl completely. A second flush often removes any residue, but defeats the efficiency of the toilet. (A simple wipe with a long-handled brush also works well and wastes no water.) In general the more expensive, air-pressurized toilets have the largest water seals.

Water-saving devices *(sometimes recommended).* If you can't replace your existing toilet, consider these products, which you can add to an existing toilet:

◆ An *adjustable flush* valve that regulates the water during flushing and refilling; made by the Geberit Manufacturing Company, (800) 225-7217.

◆ A *water-saving replacement tank* that fits on most standard toilets; also made by Geberit.

◆ The Mini Flush Watersaver, a device that regulates the water released from the tank during flushing by adjusting the

TABLE
24

ULTRA-LOW-FLUSH TOILETS

Brand	Manufacturer	Gallons Per Flush	Flush Mechanism	Water Seal Size (in.)
Allegro	Mansfield Plumbing Products (419) 938-5211	1.6	gravity	5×7
Aqualine	U.S. Brass (800) 872-7277	1.5	gravity, flush valve	4×5
Atlas	Universal-Rundle (800) 245-1753	1.5 or less	gravity	$7\frac{1}{4} \times 4\frac{3}{4}$
Cascade	Mansfield Plumbing Products (419) 938-5211	1.6	gravity, flush valve	$9 \times 9\frac{1}{2}$; $5 \times 5\frac{1}{2}$
Crane-Miser	Crane Plumbing (312) 864-7600	1.6 or less	gravity	$9 \times 8\frac{5}{8}$; $11 \times 8\frac{5}{8}$
Econo-miser	Crane Plumbing (312) 864-7600	1.5	air pressure	$9 \times 8\frac{5}{8}$; 12×10
Flush-o-matic	Sanitation Equipment (416) 738-0055	0.25	mechanical trap seal	varies
Hydro Miser	Peerless Pottery (800) 457-5785	1.6	gravity	$8\frac{1}{4} \times 8\frac{3}{4}$; 9×9
Madera Aquameter	American Standard (800) 821-7700	1.6	gravity	12×8
Micro-flush	Microphor (800) 358-8280	0.5	compressed air, water	$12\frac{1}{4} \times 10\frac{1}{2}$
New Cadet Aquameter	American Standard (800) 821-7700	1.5	air pressure	12×8
Pearl	Water Conservation Systems (800) 462-3341	1 cup	biodegradable chemicals	N/A
Plebe Aquameter	American Standard (800) 821-7700	1.5	gravity	$5 \times 5\frac{1}{8}$
Quantum	Mansfield Plumbing Products (419) 938-5211	1.5	air pressure	10×12
Santa Fe	Artesian Plumbing Products (419) 522-4211	1.6–1.9	gravity	7×8
Toto	Microphor (800) 358-8280	1.6	gravity	$8 \times 7\frac{1}{2}$
Turbo-flush 4700	Briggs (813) 878-0178	1.6	air pressure	$15 \times 11\frac{1}{2}$
Ultra Flush	Gerber Plumbing Fixtures (312) 675-6570	1.6	air pressure	12×10
Ultra-One/G	Eljer Plumbingware (214) 881-7177	1.4	siphon jet, gravity	$4\frac{1}{2} \times 6$
Veneto US 9710	Porcher (800) 338-1756	1.5	gravity	$5 \times 5\frac{1}{2}$; 8×9
Wellworth Lite	Kohler (800) 456-4537	1.5	gravity	8×9

Source: Excerpted from *GARBAGE Magazine* (January/February 1990) issue, Brooklyn, New York.

flush valve; made by the Mini Flush Company, (714) 993-7332.

Water-saver toilets *(not generally recommended)*. The terms "water-saver," "water-miser," and "low-flush" have all been applied to toilets that use about 3.5 gallons of water per flush, 30 to 50 percent less than a conventional model. These toilets have a conventional design but a smaller tank. With ultra-low-flush toilets now improved in quality and competitive in price, there is no sound reason to compromise on a water-saver toilet instead.

Conventional toilets *(never recommended)*. These toilets are inexcusably wasteful, using 5 gallons of water in the tank and another 1 or 2 gallons in the bowl. The worst conventional toilets fill the tank and the bowl at the same time; the large tank takes longer to fill, and extra water simply runs through the bowl until the tank is full. If you have such a toilet, consider replacing it.

DO-IT-YOURSELF

Bottles and dams. Many hardware stores sell rubber damming devices you can fit into a regular tank to reduce water use. Or, you can fill one or two plastic bottles—gallon or half-gallon size—with water and set them in the tank. Just make sure the toilet still flushes adequately. *Never* use bricks or other materials that will decompose over time; they might clog the water lines.

ALTERNATIVES

Composting toilets. These toilets use no water at all and can even, under carefully controlled conditions, produce compost suitable for garden use. Their maintenance requires some diligence, and they are tightly restricted in many communities. One well-known manufacturer is Composting Toilet Systems, (509) 447-3708.

WISE USE

Water conservation. Flushing human wastes is essential for sanitary reasons, but some people flush more often than necessary.

Regular maintenance. Leaky toilets waste water. To check for a leaky toilet, add a little natural food coloring to the tank and notice whether colored water appears in the bowl. If the tank does leak, check to see whether the floating ball is adjusted to the proper water level or whether the handle is sticking, or replace the seal at the bottom of the tank.

Proper waste disposal. *Never* flush anything but your own wastes and toilet paper, which is designed to break down quickly. Anything else will have to be filtered out at the treatment plant—if it doesn't clog up your sewer line first.

FOR FURTHER INFORMATION: "A Buyer's Guide to Ultra-Low-Flush Toilets," *Garbage* (January/February 1990), pp. 16-23.

1. "Low-flush Toilets," *Consumer Reports* (July 1990), p. 466.
2. *Environmental Quality 1987–88* (Council on Environmental Quality, 1987), p. 313.

WATER FILTERS

Treating our nation's tap water to make it safer or more palatable has become an industry totaling nearly $4 billion a year in equipment sales and supplies. Water filters can remove any contaminants your tap water might contain, but some filtering systems work far better than others.

ENVIRONMENTAL PROBLEMS

Recontamination. Carbon filters are very popular and effective, but if they are not maintained regularly, they can recontaminate water with the very pollutants they are supposed to remove.

Hazardous wastes. Activated carbon filters can concentrate toxic substances in their disposable cartridges, generating hazardous wastes.

Energy consumption. Most water filters use no electricity, but one popular system, the distiller, uses a lot of electricity to boil the water.

Wasteful water use. Reverse-osmosis units waste 6 to 8 gallons of water for every gallon of pure water they produce. This waste depletes available supplies and adds to the burden of the water treatment facilities that must purify both the incoming water and the wastewater.

CHOOSING A PRODUCT

GENERAL GUIDELINES

Water testing. Before you can know which type of filter to buy, you must know what contaminants your water contains. Some companies that market filters offer tests themselves, but independent information sources and testers are more objective and reliable:

- If your water comes from a municipal supply, engineers at the water treatment facility can tell you what substances the water might contain.

- If your water comes from a well, cistern, or other untreated source, county or state water-conservation agencies can provide information on regional problems and testing. Many agencies will perform the most basic test—for coliform bacteria—at little or no cost.

- Local independent water-testing labs can do in-depth testing; ask city or county agencies for their names.

- Mail-in labs do testing nationwide and will consult about specific problems. Well-known labs include

  ◆ Hydro-Analysis Associates, Inc., (800) 622-6462

  ◆ WaterTest Corporation, (800) 426-8378

  ◆ Aqua Associates, Inc., (201) 227-0422

Weighing your needs. To choose the right filter, you must consider three factors:

- The types of contaminants you need to remove. Table 25 shows the different types of filtering systems and what they can remove.

- The filter's location and maintenance. Some filters are permanently installed under or on the sink; others simply screw onto the faucet or operate as free-standing units.

- The capacity, which is determined by the projected life of the filter.

Other considerations are cost, ease of installation, and availability of replacement parts or filter cartridges.

COMMERCIAL PRODUCTS

Activated-carbon filters *(highly recommended).* Carbon filters come in two types: granular and solid block.

- *Granular* filters consist of carbon granules or powder packed into a canister. Water running through them sometimes causes channeling, lessening their filtering ability.

TABLE 25

FINDING THE RIGHT WATER FILTER

Water Contaminants Removed	Granular Carbon	Solid-Carbon Block	Reverse Osmosis	Distillation	Ultraviolet Light	Ion Exchanger	Water Softener
Bacteria		variable	✔	✔	✔		
Nitrates			✔	✔		✔	
Inorganic chemicals (arsenic, barium, cadmium, lead, mercury, selenium)		variable	✔	✔			
Synthetic organic chemicals (pesticides, herbicides, PCBs, industrial solvents)	✔	✔					
Trihalomethanes	✔	✔					
Turbidity (cloudiness)		✔		✔			
Bad taste	✔	✔	✔	✔			
Bad odors	✔	✔	✔				
Stains and colors	✔	✔	✔			✔	variable
Hardness			✔	✔			✔
Sodium			✔	✔			

Source: Craig Canine, "Distilling the Essence," *Harrowsmith* (September/October 1989).

- *Solid-block* filters use a solid piece of carbon. They do not form channels and in tests do better than granular filters at removing chlorine and halogenated organics such as chloroform.[1] Some manufacturers claim that they can also remove bacteria, but not all industry specialists agree. (Under certain conditions carbon filters can actually grow bacteria.)

- *Countertop* and *under-the-sink* versions of both granular and block filters improve the taste of water and effectively eliminate two of the most dangerous types of contaminants, synthetic organic chemicals and trihalomethanes.

- *Faucet-mount* and *pour-through* units are the least expensive; their small filters make them most suitable for improving the flavor of relatively clean urban tap water, not for removing harmful substances.

Table 26 lists effective granular and solid-block carbon water filters.

Reverse-osmosis filters (ROs) *(sometimes recommended)*. These systems use water pressure in the pipes to filter water through a porous membrane; they are complicated and expensive, and waste water. ROs, which are usually combined with activated-carbon filters, remove heavy metals, dissolved minerals, nitrates, salt, bacteria, and some viruses. This combined system is the best choice for seriously contaminated water—but only that which is too polluted for carbon-block filters. In testing by Rodale Product Testing, the Culligan H-82C, available from Beatrice Water Conditioning, (708) 285-6000, removed more contaminants and wasted less water.[2]

Ultraviolet lamps *(sometimes recommended)*. These devices expose the water to an ultraviolet

TABLE 26

HIGH-QUALITY ACTIVATED-CARBON WATER FILTERS

Manufacturer	Model	Type	Filter
Ametek (Sears #34201)	CCF-201	Under sink	Granular
Amway	E-9230	Under sink, countertop	Block
Culligan	SuperGard THM	Under sink	Granular
Cuno AquaPure	AP-CRF	Under sink	Granular
Ecowater	Water Master	Under sink	Block & granular
Filterite	CF-10	Under sink	Granular
General Ecology	Seagull IV X1-F	Under sink	Block
Hurley	II	Countertop	Granular
Kinetico	MAC	Under sink	Granular
Neolife	Water Dome #500-32	Countertop	Block

lamp, killing bacteria and viruses but removing no other pollutants. They use little energy and are useful for well water with a high bacteria count but no other serious contaminants.

Lead-removal filters *(sometimes recommended)*. If lead is the only contaminant in your tap water, you can use filters that are specially designed to remove it:

◆ Selecto Lead Out-20 works with activated alumina and has a 15,000-gallon filter life. Widely available at hardware and plumbing supply stores.

◆ Filter Pure's CT-M, a countertop unit, uses an oxidation-reduction media to remove lead very effectively; it also filters out chlorine and some organic chemicals. Available at better hardware and plumbing supply stores, or from Real Goods Trading Co., (800) 762-7325.

Radon removers *(sometimes recommended)*. Radon is a naturally occuring radioactive gas that can contaminate water from deep wells in radon-rich areas of the United States (see Environmental Glossary). Though not considered dangerous to drink, radon can be released from water—during showers, for example, or when running the faucet—into the air, where it may

pose a threat. Two companies that make expensive but effective radon-removing equipment for the home are

◆ Lowry Engineering, (207) 948-3790

◆ North East Environmental Products, (603) 298-7061

Distillers *(not generally recommended)*. Distillers boil the water, then condense the steam back into cleaner water. They can remove all pollutants except trihalomethanes and organic chemicals such as pesticides, herbicides, and solvents. If combined with a carbon filter, a distiller becomes a complete filtering system. Distilled water tastes bland because it lacks minerals. The lack of minerals also makes the water a stronger solvent, one that can actually leach essential minerals from the body. The biggest environmental problem with distillers is their heavy electricity use—3 to 4 kilowatt-hours per gallon of water—which makes them unacceptable except as a last resort. One product tested by Rodale Product Testing that did well is Shetland Distil-Clear, made by the Shetland Co., (617) 884-7744.[3]

Ion exchangers *(not generally recommended)*. Designed specifically to remove nitrates, these expensive systems use special resins called anion exchangers. Nitrates are dangerous because the body converts them into nitrites, which can interfere with oxygen transport. Installing a new, deeper well or a reverse-osmosis system are better ways to remove them.

Water softeners (*not generally recommended*). These complicated systems reduce mineral deposits by circulating water through tanks that exchange "hard" ions, such as calcium and magnesium, for "soft" sodium ions. By removing these minerals, water softeners can increase the cleaning ability of soaps and detergents and reduce tub and sink residues. Water softeners have no health benefits and may add sodium to the treated water. Most models use some electricity; all pollute wastewater with brine.

WISE USE

Proper installation. Most under-the-sink units must be plumbed into the cold water line, a job for either an experienced do-it-yourselfer or a professional plumber.

Regular maintenance. Follow these guidelines to keep your filter clean and working effectively:

- Keep your filter current. Follow the manufacturer's instructions for cleaning the equipment and changing the filter.

- When you change a filter, mark the date of the next change on a calendar or on the unit.

- When you replace a carbon filter, flush water through it for several minutes to remove loose particles.

Safe use. Make sure your filter doesn't add to the contamination problem:

- If you have a carbon filter, run some water through it every morning before using it (see the manufacturer's instructions).

- Let the water run through a carbon filter as slowly as possible to enhance the carbon's filtering power.

- Never run hot water through a filter; it may loosen contaminants.

Proper disposal. Instead of throwing old carbon filters in the trash, save them for a hazardous waste collection. Call your local waste disposal office for information on hazardous waste collection programs.

FOR FURTHER INFORMATION: "Buying a Water Treatment Unit," Environmental Protection Agency (800) 426-4791. "Distilling the Essence: A Trustworthy Guide to Home Water Filters," by Craig Canine, *Harrowsmith* (September/October 1989), pp. 78-87. *Water Treatment Handbook,* by Rodale Product Testing (Northeast Publishing, P.O. Box 571, Emmaus, PA 18049).

1. Rodale Product Testing, *Water Treatment Handbook* (Northeast Publishing, P.O. Box 571, Emmaus PA 18049), p. 29.
2. Ibid., p. 32.
3. Ibid., p. 31.

WATER HEATERS

Americans buy millions of residential water heaters every year—4 million gas and 3.3 million electric.[1] It's unfortunate that electric heaters are so popular, because they use much more energy than gas heaters do.

ENVIRONMENTAL PROBLEMS

Energy consumption. As a fuel, electricity is much less efficient than natural gas because it must first be generated by a power plant, then reconverted back into heat in the home, while gas needs only to be lightly processed and piped directly to the home. Providing hot water for a family of four using a gas heater, for example, takes about 36,000 cubic feet of gas a year, while an electric heater uses about 6,000 kilowatt-hours of electricity—which would require 60,000 cubic feet of gas to generate at a power plant.[2] This extra gas use wastes a valuable, nonrenewable resource and pumps about 3,000 pounds of carbon dioxide, the greenhouse gas, into the air.[3]

Pipeline hazards. Though much more efficient than electricity, natural gas for water heaters must be transported by pipeline to the home. These pipelines disrupt natural habitats, both during and after their construction, and present a constant danger of leaks, explosions, and fires.

Safety hazards. Just as large gas pipelines do, the small lines in your home that service your gas water heater present a danger of leaking fumes, explosions, and fire.

CHOOSING A PRODUCT

GENERAL GUIDELINES

Energy efficiency. When you buy a water heater, make energy efficiency a top priority.

The yellow EnergyGuide label on each new water heater shows its average operating costs per year—the higher the amount, the greater the energy use.

Correct capacity. With storage, or tank, water heaters, size is an important factor in efficiency. A tank that's too large wastes energy heating water that is never used, and its large surface area loses a lot of heat. The best measure of capacity, however, is not the unit's tank size but its "first hour rating," the number of gallons of hot water it will deliver in one hour of high use after the tank is fully heated. Some heaters have smaller tanks but larger burners, which enable them to deliver more hot water per hour than models with larger tanks. To decide what capacity is best, evaluate your household's peak demands for hot water.

COMMERCIAL PRODUCTS

Solar water heaters *(highly recommended)*. Solar water heaters perform very well when the sun shines but usually require a gas or electric backup system for cold, cloudy days. A typical solar heater has a roof-mounted collector and an exchanger that transfers the solar heat to a water tank. A solar system costs several thousand dollars to install, but the total costs—including buying the system and paying for backup heating energy over its 20-year average life span—are nearly 40 percent *less* than that of purchasing and using an electric water heater.[4] Because solar water heaters vary widely, it's important to know which kind of system will work best in your home. Consider getting your home evaluated by your local energy office or a contractor before shopping for a solar water heater. The following companies manufacture solar water-heating systems:

- American Energy Technologies, Inc., (904) 284-0552

- American Solar Network, Ltd., (703) 620-2242

- FAFCO, Inc., (415) 363-2690

- Radco Products, Inc., (805) 928-1881

- Sage Advance, (503) 485-1947

◆ Solar Development, Inc., (407) 842-8935

◆ Sun Earth, Inc., (714) 984-8737

◆ Thermo Dynamics, Ltd. (Canada), (902) 468-1001

Demand (tankless) water heaters *(highly recommended)*. These heaters, which come in both electric and gas versions, have a small unit that heats the water just before it leaves the tap, eliminating the storage tank (and the wasted heat that constantly escapes from it). They cannot match the flow of hot water from a tank system, but many people find them quite adequate. Although a demand heater costs up to twice as much to buy as a cheap gas storage heater, it saves hundreds of dollars in total costs over its lifetime. The following major manufacturers will send their catalogs on request:

◆ Aquavac, (914) 964-9180

◆ Controlled Energy Corp., (802) 496-4436

◆ Hot Water Generators, Inc., (713) 492-1713

◆ H2OT, Inc., (800) 247-3619

◆ In-Sink-Erator, (414) 552-7303

◆ Low Energy Systems, (303) 388-7718

◆ Pacific Thermal Systems, (509) 453-2355

◆ Paloma Industries, Inc., (312) 595-8778

◆ Pecbras Co., (800) 826-7070

◆ Rinnai America Corp., (213) 618-8550

◆ Thermar Corp., (203) 452-0500

Heat traps *(highly recommended)*. Consider a heat trap when installing a new heater (many energy-efficient heaters have one built in). This one-way valve, which is installed in the pipe directly above the heater, allows water to flow through but stops the heat radiating from the tank. Heat traps can also be retrofitted to older tanks, but it's a job for a plumber.

Gas water heaters *(recommended)*. All new gas water heaters must meet minimum energy-efficiency standards and have an Energy Factor (a basic measure of efficiency) of from 0.56 for 30-gallon tanks to 0.51 for 60-gallon tanks. However, the most efficient models available easily beat these standards (see Table 27).

Heat-pump water heaters *(recommended)*. These heaters, which are suitable for climates without severe winters, extract heat from either the outdoor air or the earth itself and carry it through refrigerant lines to the water tank. Although they use ozone-threatening chlorofluorocarbons as refrigerants and require the complex machinery of a heat pump, these machines are *three times* more efficient at producing hot water with electricity than is an ordinary electric water heater. See Table 28 for air-based models available nationwide. (See also Heat Pumps, p. 137.)

Oil water heaters *(not generally recommended)*. These water heaters have an average efficiency rating slightly lower than that of gas heaters, and they burn #2 heating oil, a messier, more polluting fuel. Still, if fuel oil is readily available in your area and natural gas isn't, and if you already must use fuel oil to heat your home, an oil-fired water heater is a better choice than an electric one. Table 29 lists the most efficient models.

Electric water heaters *(not generally recommended)*. As with gas, electric heaters must now meet new minimum Energy Factor standards: 0.91 for 30-gallon tanks to 0.87 for 60-gallon tanks. Table 30 lists models that far exceed the standards.

WISE USE

Proper installation. Make sure your gas water heater is adequately vented to the outdoors with an unobstructed, vertical metal stack that meets all local building codes.

TABLE 27

ENERGY-EFFICIENT GAS WATER HEATERS
For Propane or Natural Gas

Manufacturer[a]	Model	Energy Efficiency[b]	Storage Capacity (Gallons)	1st Hour Rating (Gallons)[c]
Storage Capacity: 29 to 39 gallons				
American Appliance	DVPB35[d]	.86	34	147
Bock	40 HE-N; 40 HE-X	.65	38	71
Bradford-White	M-III-403T5CN-7; M-III-403T5CX-7	.65	38	71
Lochinvar	HEN040	.65	38	71
U.S. Water Heater	M-III-R403T5CN-9; M-III-R403T5CX-7	.65	38	71
American Appliance	N2F363T	.64	30	61
Bradford-White	M-III-303T5CN-7; M-III-303T5CX-7	.64	29	64
Mor-Flo	N2F363T	.64	30	61
Rheem	21VR30-5; 21VR30-5N; 21VR30-5P; 21XR30-5; 21XR30-5N	.64	30	52
U.S. Water Heater	M-III-R303T5CN-7; M-III-R303T5CX-7	.64	29	64
American Appliance	N363S	.63	30	55
	N363T	.63	30	61
Craftmaster	30	.63	30	61
Enterprise	CRNX30	.63	30	61
Mor-Flo	GVN363S	.63	30	55
	GVN363T	.63	30	61
A.O. Smith	PGCS-30T	.63	30	56
Allied	215331	.62	39	71
American Appliance	GVN2F363T	.62	30	61
Craftmaster	CRN2FB30	.62	30	61
Mor-Flo	2F90-333T	.62	30	52
	GVN2F363T	.62	30	61
Rheem	44V40-1EM; 44V40-1; 44V40-1N; 44V40-1P; D4V40-1; D4V40-1N; D4X40-1; D4X40-1N; D4V40-1P; D4X40-1P; PT40-1; PT40-1N; PT40-1P; MT40-1; MT40-1N	.62	39	71
	21W30-5; 21W30-5N	.62	30	52
American Appliance	2F90-333T	.61	30	52
	GVN363S	.61	30	55
	GNV363T	.61	30	61
Bradford-White	M-II-40T5LN-9; M-II-40T5SN-9	.61	38	67
Craftmaster	CRNV30	.61	30	61
Enterprise	CRNV30	.61	30	61
Mor-Flo	GVN363T	.61	30	61
Pay-N-Pack	121032	.61	30	52
Reliance	5 30 NOMDS6-W	.61	30	50
	5 30 NADS6-W; 5 30 NODS6-W	.61	30	53
	5 30 NGRT6-W;	.61	30	56

(continued on next page)

TABLE 27

ENERGY-EFFICIENT GAS WATER HEATERS *(continued)*
For Propane or Natural Gas

Manufacturer[a]	Model	Energy Efficiency[b]	Storage Capacity (Gallons)	1st Hour Rating (Gallons)[c]
	5 30 NGRT6-2W;			
	5 30 NKRT6-W;			
	5 30 NKRT6-2W			
A.O. Smith	PCGS-30	.61	30	56
	FGC-30; PGC-30	.61	30	64
State Industries	PRV 30 NOMDS6-W	.61	30	50
	PRV 30 NODS6-W;	.61	30	53
	PRV 30 NADS6-W			
	PRV NORT6-W;	.61	30	56
	PRV NORT6-2W;			
	TV 30 NKRT6-W;			
	TV 30 NKRT6-2W			
Superbo	GV2F8333T	.61	30	52
U.S. Water Heater	M-II-RG40T5LN-9;	.61	38	67
	M-II-RG40T5SN-9			

Storage Capacity: 40 gallons

Marathon	MG40345; MG40345H	.74	40	77
Sears, Roebuck	449.330410;	.74	40	77
	449.330430			
American Appliance	N463V	.72	40	86
Craftmaster	N463V	.72	40	86
Mor-Flo	N463V	.72	40	86
American Appliance	463SV	.63	40	65
	N2F463T	.63	40	72
Craftmaster	40	.63	40	72
Mor-Flo	463SV	.63	40	65
	N2F463T	.63	40	72
American Appliance	N463S	.62	40	66
	N463T	.62	40	72
Apollo	A5 40 40.0NXRT8-2W	.62	40	73
Craftmaster	2F90-433T	.62	40	63
Dayton	3E534J	.62	40	72
Enterprise	CRNX40	.62	40	72
Mor-Flo	2F90-433T	.62	40	63
	GXN463X	.62	40	66
	GXN463T	.62	40	72
Reliance	5 40 NXRTL8-2W;	.62	40	73
	5 40 NXRT7-2W			
Rheem	21VR40-5; 21VR40-5N;	.62	40	61
	21VR40-5P; 21XR40-5;			
	21XR40-5N; 21XR40-5P			
A.O. Smith	PGCS-40T	.62	40	66
State Industries	SEV 40 NXRTL8-2W;	.62	40	73
	SEV 40 NXRT6-2W			
American Appliance	GVN2F463T	.61	40	72
Apollo	A5 40 40.0NXRT8-W;	.61	40	73
	A5 40 40.0NXRT8-2			
Craftmaster	2F90-433T	.61	40	72
Mor-Flo	GVN2F463T	.61	40	72

TABLE 27

ENERGY-EFFICIENT GAS WATER HEATERS (continued)
For Propane or Natural Gas

Manufacturer[a]	Model	Energy Efficiency[b]	Storage Capacity (Gallons)	1st Hour Rating (Gallons)[c]
Reliance	5 40 NXRTL8-W; 5 40 NXRTL8-2; 5 40 NXRT7-W; 5 40 NXRT7-2	.61	40	73
Sears, Roebuck	153.338101; 153.338131; 153.338420	.61	40	73
State Industries	SEV 40 NXRTL8-W; SEV 40 NXRTL8-2; SEV 40 NXRT6-W; SEV 40 NXRT6-2	.61	40	73
Storage Capacity: 50 gallons				
Marathon	MG50345; MG50345H	.71	50	85
Sears, Roebuck	449.330510; 449.330530	.71	50	85
Bock	50 HE-N; 50 HE-X	.62	50	81
Bradford-White	M-III-503S5CX-7	.62	50	81
Lochinvar	HEN050	.62	50	81
U.S. Water Heater	M-III-R503S5CN-7; M-III-R503S5CX-7	.62	50	81
American Appliance	N2F563T	.61	50	81
Craftmaster	50	.61	50	81
Mor-Flo	N2F563T	.61	50	81

Source: Consumer's Directory of Certified Efficiency Ratings for Residential Heating and Water Heating Equipment (Gas Appliance Manufacturers Association, 1990).

[a] Most manufacturers sell water heaters under many different brand names.

[b] Based on the Energy Factor, a measure of overall energy efficiency. The higher the number, the more efficient the heater.

[c] The amount of hot water delivered in one hour, starting with a full tank of hot water.

[d] This model designed for combination space and water heating.

Regular maintenance. To keep your water heater running efficiently, follow these guidelines:

- Every few months drain 2 to 3 quarts of water from the tank's utility faucet to remove sediment and improve efficiency.

- Have gas or oil heaters serviced periodically. With gas, check the flame; if it is burning cleanly, it will be bright blue, not orange or yellow.

Energy-efficient use. No matter what type of water heater you use, follow these important conservation tips:

- Try turning the thermostat down. For small households, this makes little difference in comfort and a big difference in energy use. Lowering the thermostat from 140° to 115° F reduces energy use by up to 30 percent.

- Insulate the tank (unless it's a well-insulated model) with a snug fiberglass cover. You can cut energy use by up to 10 percent.

TABLE 28

ENERGY-EFFICIENT HEAT-PUMP WATER HEATERS

Manufacturer[a]	Model	Energy Efficiency[b]	Storage Capacity (Gallons)	1st Hour Rating (Gallons)[c]
Reliance	5 82 1AHP4/1HP-3, 3-4	3.1	82	81
State Industries	SS8 82 1AHP4/CHP-3, 3-4	3.1	82	81
Therma-Stor	TS-HP-80-HRA	3.1	80	72
	TS-HP-120-18-30	3.1	120	111
Reliance	5 52 1AHP4/1HP-3, 3-4	3.0	52	54
State Industries	SS8 52 1AHP4/CHP-3, 3-4	3.0	52	54

Source: *Consumer's Directory of Certified Efficiency Ratings for Residential Heating and Water Heating Equipment* (Gas Appliance Manufacturers Association, 1990).

[a] Most manufacturers sell water heaters under many different brand names.

[b] Based on the *Energy Factor*, a measure of overall energy efficiency. The higher the number, the more efficient the heater.

[c] The amount of hot water delivered in one hour, starting with a full tank of hot water.

TABLE 29

ENERGY-EFFICIENT OIL WATER HEATERS

Manufacturer[a]	Model	Energy Efficiency[b]	Storage Capacity (Gallons)	1st Hour Rating (Gallons)[c]
Bock	32PP	.63	32	131
Bradford-White	F-I-305E50EZ	.61	30	120
Carlin	RCG-30EZ	.61	30	120
Ford	FG3016EZ	.61	30	120
Rheem	OGL-30EZ	.61	30	120
Bock	30ES	.60	28	109

Source: *Consumer's Directory of Certified Efficiency Ratings for Residential Heating and Water Heating Equipment* (Gas Appliance Manufacturers Association, 1990).

[a] Most manufacturers sell water heaters under many different brand names.

[b] Based on the *Energy Factor*, a measure of overall energy efficiency. The higher the number, the more efficient the heater.

[c] The amount of hot water delivered in one hour, starting with a full tank of hot water.

TABLE
30

ENERGY-EFFICIENT ELECTRIC WATER HEATERS

Manufacturer[a]	Model	Energy Efficiency[b]	Storage Capacity (Gallons)	1st Hour Rating (Gallons)[c]
Storage Capacity: 20 gallons				
Heat Transfer	ES-20	.98	20	16
Rheem	81SX20DT; 81SX20ST; 81SV20DT; 81SV20ST	.97	20	32
Ruud	MES20-1T; MES20-2T; PES20-1T; PES20-2T	.97	20	32
Storage Capacity: 30 gallons				
Marathon	MP30245	.98	30	42
Reliance	1 30 10PT6-W	.98	30	38
Sears, Roebuck	153.310360; 449-310310	.98	30	39
	449-320310	.98	30	46
Reliance	8 30 2ART6-W; 5 30 2ART4-W; 5 30 2KRT6-W 5 30 20RT6-W; 5 30 20RT7-2W	.97	30	42
Rheem	81SX30DT; 81SX30ST; 81SV30DT; 81SV30ST	.97	30	35
	81G-30D; 81GV30D; 81GV30S; 81GX30D; 81GX30S; H1XG30-1; H1VG30-1; H1VG30-2	.97	30	41
Richmond	8SV30-1T,H1SV30ST; 8SV30-2T,H1SV30ST; 8SX30-1T,H1SX30ST; 8SX30-2T,H1SX30DT	.97	30	35
	8VG30-1,H1VG30S; 8VG30-2,H1VG30D; 8XG30-1,H1XG30S; 8XG30-2,H1XG30D	.97	30	41
Ruud	MES30-1T; MES30-2T; PES30-1T; PES30-2T	.97	30	35
	MEG30-1; MEG30-2; PEG30-1; PEG30-2	.97	30	41
State Industries	CD5 30 20RT6-W; PV 30 20RT7-2W; SD15 30 2ART6-W; SD8 30 2ART6-W; SS8 30 2ART4-W; TD5 30 2KRT6-W; TCL 30 2LRT6-W	.97	30	42
Storage Capacity: 40 to 42 gallons				
Bradford-White	M-III-30R5SS-12	.97	42	42
Sears, Roebuck	449-314410	.97	40	45
	153.310460	.97	40	47
	449-310410	.97	40	49
	449-320410	.97	40	56

(continued on next page)

TABLE 30

ENERGY-EFFICIENT ELECTRIC WATER HEATERS *(continued)*

Manufacturer[a]	Model	Energy Efficiency[b]	Storage Capacity (Gallons)	1st Hour Rating (Gallons)[c]
State Industries	TCL 40 2LRT6-W	.97	40	50
U.S. Water Heater	M-III-RE30R5SS-12	.97	42	42
Bradford-White	M-III-40T5SS-12	.96	40	50
Marathon	MP40238	.96	40	49
	MP40245	.96	40	52
	MP40255	.96	40	56
Reliance	5 40 2ART4-W; 5 40 20RT7-2W; 5 40 2XRT4-W	.96	40	49
	5 40 2KRT6-W; 5 40 20RT6-W; 8 40 2ART6-W	.96	40	50
Rheem	81G-40D; 81GV40S; 81GX40D; 81GX40S; H1XG40-1; H1VG40-1; H1VG40-2	.96	40	49
Richmond	8VG40-1,H1VG40S; 8VG40-2,H1VG40D; 8XG40-1,H1XG40S; 8XG40-2,H1XG40D	.96	40	49
Ruud	MEG40-1; MEG40-2; PEG40-1; PEG40-2	.96	40	49
State Industries	PV 40 20RT7-2W; SEV 40 2XRT4-W; SS8 40 2ART4-W	.96	40	49
	CD5 40 20RT6-W; SD15 40 2ART6-W; SD8 40 2ART6-W; TD5 40 2KRT6-W	.96	40	50
Sutherland	CL81GX40D	.96	40	49
Vaughn	M-40	.96	40	54
Storage Capacity: 50 to 60 gallons				
Bradford-White	M-III-50T5SS-12	.96	50	59
Marathon	MX50155S; MX50255S	.96	50	58
	MX60130, MX60230	.96	60	59
	MX60138; MX60238	.96	60	63
	MX60145; MX60245	.96	60	66
	MX60155; MX60255	.96	60	70
Rheem	81G-52D; 81GV52S; 81GX52D; 81GX52S	.96	52	57
	81GV52D; H1XG52-1; H1VG52-1; H1GV52-2	.96	50	57
Richmond	8VG52-1,H1VG52S; 8VG52-2,H1VG52D; 8XG52-1,H1XG52; 8XG52-2,H1XG52D	.96	52	57
Ruud	MEG52-1	.96	52	57
	MEG52-2; PEG52-1; PEG52-2	.96	50	57

TABLE 30

ENERGY-EFFICIENT ELECTRIC WATER HEATERS *(continued)*

Manufacturer[a]	Model	Energy Efficiency[b]	Storage Capacity (Gallons)	1st Hour Rating (Gallons)[c]
Sears, Roebuck	449-310510	.96	52	59
	449-320510	.96	52	66
Sutherland	CL81GX52D	.96	50	57
U.S. Water Heater	M-III-RE50T5SS-12	.96	50	59
Vaughn	M-50	.96	50	61
Storage Capacity: 75 to 85 gallons				
Marathon	MX75130; MX75230	.97	75	71
	MX75138; MX75238	.97	75	75
	MX75145; MX75245	.97	75	78
	MX75155; MX75255	.97	75	82
	MX85130; MX85230	.97	85	83
	MX85138; MX85238	.97	85	87
	MX85145; MX85245	.97	85	90
	MX85155; MX85255	.97	85	94
A.O. Smith	PEH-80	.95	80	79

Source: *Consumer's Directory of Certified Efficiency Ratings for Residential Heating and Water Heating Equipment* (Gas Appliance Manufacturers Association, 1990).

[a] Most manufacturers sell water heaters under many different brand names.

[b] Based on the *Energy Factor*, a measure of overall energy efficiency. The higher the number, the more efficient the heater.

[c] The amount of hot water delivered in one hour, starting with a full tank of hot water.

- Insulate the pipes. Stores carry special insulated wrapping for the hot water pipes coming from the heater.

- Consider a timer. Especially if you have an electric heater, installing a timer that turns the system off at night and on again in the morning can save energy and pay for itself in under a year. Gas heaters have a pilot light that burns even when the tank is shut off; the savings with a timer are not as dramatic but do add up.

- Use low-flow showerheads and aerator faucets. A low-flow showerhead can cut hot-water use by up to 15 percent and pay back its cost in months. (See Faucets and Showerheads, p. 114.)

- Replace washers on leaky faucets.

- Wash clothes in warm or cold water instead of hot, and always use cold water to rinse.

FOR FURTHER INFORMATION: Directory of Certified Water Heater Efficiency Ratings (ETL Testing Laboratories, Industrial Park, Cortland, NY 13045). *1991 Consumer Guide to Home Energy Savings*, by Alex Wilson; American Council for an Energy-Efficient Economy, 1990.

1. "Statistical Highlights" (Gas Appliance Manufacturers Association, 1990).
2. "Energy Facts 1987" (Energy Information Administration, Department of Energy, Forrestal Bldg., EI-231, Washington, DC 20585), p. 54.
3. Mark Deluchi et al., "Transportation Fuels and the Greenhouse Effect," *Transportation Research Record 1175* (1988), p. 39.
4. Alex Wilson, *1991 Consumer Guide to Home Energy Savings* (American Council for an Energy-Efficient Economy, 1990), p. 156.

WATER, TAP

Most Americans get their tap water from municipal treatment facilities, but about 40 million drink water from their own wells.[1] Tap water comes from a wide variety of sources—rivers, creeks, reservoirs, lakes, and groundwater aquifers—and its purity varies just as widely.

ENVIRONMENTAL PROBLEMS

Harmful contaminants. The Environmental Protection Agency has identified more than 700 pollutants found in tap water.[2] Below are just a few of the most prevalent:

- *Microbes,* including bacteria, viruses, and protozoans such as *Giardia*

- *Nitrates,* which cause oxygen-metabolism problems and are suspected carcinogens

- *Organic* and *inorganic pollutants* known to cause a wide range of serious diseases, including cancer

- *Toxic, nondegradable heavy metals* such as mercury, lead, and cadmium

- *Trihalomethanes,* suspected and known carcinogens created from the chlorine used in water treatment plants

- *Radionuclides,* including radon, uranium, and synthetic substances

The sources of contamination are numerous. Among them are

- *Agriculture,* which pollutes rivers and lakes with nitrates from fertilizers and livestock waste

- *Industry,* which produces numerous water pollutants and is a major source of four toxic, nondegrading heavy metals: lead, cadmium, chromium, and copper

- *Urban stormwater runoff,* which carries chemicals, oils, grease, garbage, and dirt from city streets into ground and surface waters

- *Municipal water treatment plants,* often so overwhelmed by the pollutants and huge volumes of water they must treat that they discharge inadequately treated water

- *Water supply lines* and *indoor pipes,* whose toxic contaminants, such as lead from old pipes and lead solder on copper tubing, can leach into the water flowing through them

Cities deal with the pollution problem by using chlorine and 10 to 60 other chemicals to make the water safe for drinking. According to tests, the chlorine itself has no short-term health effects, but it can react with other substances in the water to form trihalomethanes and other carcinogens.[3] (Chlorine also gives the water a harsh, dry aftertaste and a foul odor.)

Bacterial contamination. Water from some individual wells and small systems has a high bacteria count. A 1984 study revealed that 28 percent of rural homes used water with coliform bacteria levels that exceeded the federal limit.[4] These bacteria are common in the intestines and are not harmful at normal levels, but can signal the presence of other harmful bacteria and viruses.

Wasteful water use. Most faucets run water at a wasteful 3 to 5 gallons per minute and most showerheads at 5 to 8 gallons per minute. This heavy use depletes the supplies in rivers, lakes, wells, and underground aquifers; increases the amount of water that must be purified before being piped to your home; and adds to the wastewater that must be treated for release.

WISE USE

Water testing. Have your water tested for contaminants, preferably by an independent testing lab rather than by a water filter company that will try to sell you its product. Depending on the results, you have three options:

- Keep drinking your tap water. (If its taste discourages you from drinking the recommended four to six glasses per day, however, consider another option.)

- Purchase a water filter system (see Water Filters, p. 157).

- Buy bottled water for drinking (see Water, Bottled, p. 78).

Reducing household water pollution. To reduce the burden placed on wastewater treatment plants, use household products that cut down on water pollution (see specific product entries for recommendations).

Water conservation. Make sure you use water as efficiently as possible:

- Take short showers instead of baths or long showers.

- Replace washers on leaky faucets.

- Install aerator faucets and low-flow showerheads (see Faucets and Showerheads, p. 114).

- Get an ultra-low-flush toilet, or install a device to reduce your old toilet's water use (see Toilets, p. 154).

- Use water-efficient dishwashers and washing machines, and choose the right water level and cycle for each load (see Dishwashers, p. 179; Washing Machines, p. 213).

- Don't wash your car unnecessarily, and use as little water as possible when you do.

- Cut back on hosing down driveways, sidewalks, and patios; sweep them instead.

- Don't water your lawn unnecessarily (see Lawns, p. 283).

- Collect rainwater for gardens and plants.

- Use drip irrigation for gardens rather than spraying or sprinkling.

FOR FURTHER INFORMATION: "Water Efficiency for Your Home: Products Which Save Water, Energy, and Money" (Rocky Mountain Institute, 1739 Snowmass Creek Rd., Snowmass, CO 81654). "The Water Wheel: A Guide to Home Water Conservation" (Water Conservation Systems, Inc., Damonmill Square, Concord, MA 01742).

1. Craig Canine, "Testing the Waters," *Harrowsmith* (September/October 1989), p. 80.
2. "Water Treatment Handbook" (Northeast Publishing, P.O. Box 571, Emmaus, PA 18049), pp. 9–13.
3. Ibid., p. 10.
4. Jonathan King, *Troubled Water* (Rodale Press, 1985), p. 154.

KITCHEN APPLIANCES
AND PRODUCTS

COFFEE FILTERS

About three-quarters of America's coffee drinkers use convenient—but wasteful—paper filters to make their brew.[1]

ENVIRONMENTAL PROBLEMS

Water and soil pollution. Most coffee filters are made from white paper that has been bleached with chlorine gas during manufacture. The gas reacts with wood compounds to form precursors to the toxic dioxin TCDD, a carcinogen and the active ingredient in Agent Orange. TCDD from the bleaching process has been found in waters and land near paper mills, causing potential risks to ecosystems and wildlife.[2]

Dioxin contamination. TCDD also shows up in the bleached paper products themselves. Paper plates, for example, have been found to contain up to ten parts dioxin per trillion parts paper. Although this amount is small, the Environmental Protection Agency believes that *any* level of exposure carries risks for humans.[3] Coffee filters might be far riskier than paper plates because hot water passing through them can dissolve chemicals and add them to your coffee. The Food and Drug Administration estimates that heavy use of bleached coffee filters can result in a 5 to 10 percent increase in daily dioxin consumption.[4]

CHOOSING A PRODUCT

GENERAL GUIDELINES

Reusability. Use cloth or metal filters that can be washed and reused.

Safety. If you must use paper filters, choose an unbleached type that will not expose you to dioxin contamination.

COMMERCIAL PRODUCTS

Metal filters *(highly recommended)*. These filters are made of a fine metal mesh; they're reusable, easy to clean, and quite effective. Look for Braun's 23-carat-gold, cone-shaped filter and other brands in gourmet, coffee, and department stores.

Cloth filters *(highly recommended)*. These simple, inexpensive filters work well with pour-through cones. You must rinse them by hand after each use and boil them periodically to get them really clean, but they save paper and money and add no taste to the coffee. Look for them in natural foods and coffee stores, or order them from

◆ Clothcrafters, (414) 876-2112

◆ Ecco Bella, (201) 226-5799

◆ Seventh Generation, (800) 456-1177

Unbleached paper filters *(recommended)*. These light brown filters are just as sanitary and effective as bleached filters; the only difference is their color. They come in various sizes for both cones and automatic machines. Several brands are sold nationwide in coffee and kitchenware stores:

◆ Ashdun Industries, C.A.R.E. Coffee Filters, (201) 944-2650

◆ Melitta Coffee Filters, Natural Brown, (800) 451-1694

◆ PurePaper Company Coffee Filters, (415) 524-8079

◆ Rockline Natural Brew Coffee Filters, (414) 459-4160

Bleached paper filters *(never recommended)*. Some bleached paper filters do make good-tasting, sediment-free coffee, but their environmental impact and health risks make them a poor choice.

DO-IT-YOURSELF

Homemade cloth filters. You can make your own cloth filter from unbleached muslin; wash it after each use with warm water but no soap, and boil it periodically.

ALTERNATIVES

Plunger/filters. The plunger/filter is a cylindrical glass pot that holds hot water and coffee mixed together. When the brew looks dark enough, you push down a plunger attached to a fine, washable metal screen that holds the grounds on the bottom. Look for Bodun or Melior products in gourmet, coffee, and department stores.

Espresso/cappuccino makers. These electric machines make very strong, rich coffee by using water pressure to strain coffee through a washable metal filter.

1. Associated Press, "Study: Boiled Coffee Raises Cholesterol, Filtered Doesn't," *Boulder Daily Camera* (November 23, 1989).
2. Peter von Stackleberg, "White Wash: The Dioxin," *Greenpeace Magazine* (March/April 1989), p. 7.
3. Ibid.
4. Janet Raloff, "Dioxin: Paper's Trace," *Science News* (February 18, 1989), p. 105.

DETERGENTS, DISH

Despite the popularity of automatic dishwashers, three out of five households still use a liquid dish detergent every day—with some serious environmental consequences.

ENVIRONMENTAL PROBLEMS

Water pollution. The cleaning agents in dish detergents are surfactants, usually derived from petroleum. Although most surfactants are biodegradable, they still pollute wastewater with organic (carbon-containing) compounds, dissolved salts, and foam, which must be either removed by wastewater treatment plants or released to pollute downstream water.

Unnecessary additives. Besides surfactants, many dishwashing detergents contain the following ingredients, which require petroleum or mineral resources to manufacture and which pollute wastewater:

- *Sodium chloride* or *potassium chloride*, used as thickeners

- *Ethyl alcohol*, a liquifier

- *Foaming agents*, added to increase foaming for aesthetic reasons

- *Opacifiers*, for creaminess

- *Dyes* and *fragrances*

Animal cruelty. Because some ingredients can harm humans, many manufacturers test detergents on animals, under inhumane conditions; afterward the animals are killed.

Wasteful packaging. Most detergents are diluted with up to 70 percent water, adding significant packaging and transportation costs for a substance already found in every home.

TABLE 31

SIMPLE-INGREDIENT, CRUELTY-FREE DISHWASHING DETERGENTS

Brand	Ingredients
Allens Naturally	Linear alkylbenzene sulfonate, cocamide DEA, sodium laureth sulfate, sodium chloride, citric acid, preservative
Dr. Bronner's Sal Suds	Castor oil, coconut, pine needle oils
Earth Wise	Water, degreasers, detergents from coconut and palm kernel oil, water softener, quality control agents, mint fragrance, aloe vera
Ecover Dishwashing Liquid	Coconut-oil-based cleaner, milk whey, sea salt, citrus oil, calendula and chamomile extracts, citrus acid, biodegradable preservative
E.Z. Maid	Water, laureth sulfate, nonionic surfactant N-96, coconut oil, sodium chloride
Keep America Clean Dishwashing Liquid	Biodegradable surfactants, natural lemon oil, aloe vera
Kleer Dishwashing Detergent	Water, linear alkyl sulfonate, ammonium laureth sulfate, cocamide DEA, aloe vera, lime fragrance, methyl paraben
Professional Liquid Dishwashing Detergent	Not available
Shaklee Satin Sheen Dishwashing Liquid	Not available

CHOOSING A PRODUCT

GENERAL GUIDELINES

Simple, natural ingredients. Read ingredient labels to find simple formulas that use naturally derived compounds instead of synthetic chemicals; if the ingredients aren't listed, don't buy the product.

Cruelty-free products. Choose detergents made by companies that do not test products on animals.

Sensible packaging. Look for concentrated detergents that provide the most cleaning power per bottle, and choose the largest containers practical.

COMMERCIAL PRODUCTS

Simple-ingredient, cruelty-free brands *(highly recommended).* Table 31 lists nationally distributed nonphosphate dish detergents made with simpler or more naturally derived ingredients; most are highly concentrated and all are cruelty free. Look for them in natural foods stores and co-ops.

Major brands *(not generally recommended).* At present, no major-brand detergent is environmentally sound; they all have unnecessary chemicals, are diluted, and are tested on animals. Some list their surfactants as biodegradable, but most surfactants are.

DO-IT-YOURSELF

Mild soap. A gentle liquid soap, such as castile, can clean dishes and cut grease well, without suds.

Plain water. Unless the dishes are greasy or oily, plain warm or hot water cleans them very well—especially if you soak them first.

DETERGENTS, DISHWASHER

Automatic dishwasher detergents tend to be harsher and more complex than regular dish detergents because they use chemicals (and lots of hot water) to do what your hands would do: scrub.

ENVIRONMENTAL PROBLEMS

Water pollution. Many of the ingredients in dishwasher detergents cause water pollution:

- *Phosphates* disrupt water ecology by providing too much nutrition for algae and other plants, which proliferate wildly and quickly die. As they decompose the plants use up oxygen needed by fish and other marine life. Phosphates break up in fast-moving waters but can badly damage lakes, estuaries, and slow-moving rivers.

- *Other cleaning agents,* such as surfactants, chlorine bleach, sodium carbonate, and sodium hydroxide (lye), leave chemicals that must either be removed by wastewater treatment plants or released to pollute downstream water.

- *Processing and aesthetic agents,* such as sodium sulfate, sodium silicate, perfumes, and colorants, add dissolved salts to wastewater that complicate wastewater treatment.

Animal cruelty. Because some ingredients can harm humans, many manufacturers test detergents on animals, under inhumane conditions; afterward the animals are killed.

Wasteful packaging. Liquid gel detergents come in plastic bottles made from nonrenewable petroleum. The gels are less concentrated than powdered detergents, so you use more packaging per wash.

CHOOSING A PRODUCT

GENERAL GUIDELINES

Simple formulas. Look for no- or low-phosphate formulas with few ingredients.

Cruelty-free products. Choose detergents made by companies that do not test products on animals.

Sensible packaging. Choose a concentrated product in the largest container practical—preferably one you can recycle locally.

COMMERCIAL PRODUCTS

Simple, cruelty-free brands *(highly recommended)*. These concentrated products are not tested on animals and have simpler formulas than those of the major brands. Look for them in natural foods stores or order them directly:

♦ Allens Naturally powder (medium phosphate, 4-lb. box); order from Allens Naturally, (313) 453-5410.

♦ Clean and Green liquid (no phosphate, 32-oz. or 1-gal. plastic bottle); order from Ecco Bella, (800) 888-5320.

♦ Ecover powder (no phosphate, 33.8-oz. box); order from Mercantile Food Company, (203) 544-9891.

♦ Kleer III powder (low phosphate, 32-oz. box) and Kleer II liquid (no phosphates, 32-oz., 64-oz., 128-oz. plastic bottles); order from The Compassionate Consumer, (718) 445-4134.

♦ Professional powder (no phosphate, 5-lb. box); order from A Clear Alternative, (713) 356-7031.

♦ Seventh Generation gel (no phosphate, ½-gal. or 1-gal. plastic bottle); order from Seventh Generation, (800) 456-1177.

♦ Shaklee powder (low phosphate, 47-oz. box); order from Shaklee, (800) 426-0766.

Major brands *(not generally recommended)*. Many major-brand liquids and powders are available, but none stands out as environmentally sound. Powders come in recycled paperboard boxes but contain polluting phosphates. Liquid gels contain about 30 to 50 percent less phosphates than powders do (phosphates tend to be unstable in liquids) but come in wasteful plastic bottles.

DO-IT-YOURSELF

Washing soda and borax. Dishwashers are finicky machines, designed to be used only with commercial detergents. However, you might try equal amounts of washing soda (sodium carbonate) and borax (handle both substances carefully; they're irritating to skin and eyes and harmful if swallowed). Add a little regular dishwasher detergent if necessary.

DISHWASHERS

You might be surprised to learn that on average a dishwasher uses less water (10 gallons) than you would use washing the same dishes by hand and rinsing them with running water (15 to 17 gallons). Since about half of American households—nearly 43 million—have them, however, dishwashers do have an environmental impact.[1]

ENVIRONMENTAL PROBLEMS

Energy consumption. Most of the energy dishwashers use goes toward heating the 8 to 14 gallons of water required for each wash. Some dishwashers have booster water heaters built in, but others require keeping the entire home's hot water at 140° F, which wastes energy continuously. Besides hot water needs, a dishwasher draws 0.6 to 1.1 kilowatt-hours of electricity per wash (enough to burn a compact-fluorescent light bulb for up to 75 hours); the exact amount depends on its efficiency and whether it dries dishes with heat.[2]

Water pollution. Because dishwashers cannot match the scrubbing power of hands, they require more and stronger detergents, usually with added phosphates, than hand washing. The chemicals in dishwasher detergents pollute wastewater. (See Detergents, Dishwasher, p.177.)

CHOOSING A PRODUCT

GENERAL GUIDELINES

Weighing your needs. Consider whether you really need a dishwasher and if so, what size and options are best suited to your home and your lifestyle.

Energy efficiency. As with all major appliances, make energy efficiency a top priority. Check EnergyGuide labels; these bright yellow sheets tell you at a glance what each machine's yearly energy bill will be, based on an average electric rate. Comparing this figure among models will help you find the most energy-efficient unit.

Quality. Always look for high-quality construction and performance; a high-quality machine will cost more initially, but save money and energy over time and have a longer usable life.

COMMERCIAL PRODUCTS

Energy-efficient dishwashers *(recommended).* If you have decided you need a dishwasher, look for the most energy-efficient models. Make sure they have the following energy-saving features:

- *A booster water heater* is a small built-in heater that raises the temperature of the machine's incoming water, allowing you to set your home's hot-water heater at an energy-saving, lower temperature.

- *No-heat drying* uses regular room air instead of heated air to dry dishes. It takes somewhat longer but saves electricity.

- *Multiple wash cycles* let you select the right cycle for each dishwashing load, using less or more water as necessary. Some machines also feature a "rinse and hold" short cycle for storing dirty dishes until the washer is full.

Table 32 lists the most energy-efficient dishwashers. All are available nationwide except the expensive but high-quality, German-made AEG, model Favorit 525i, which is imported by Andi-Co Appliances in New Jersey, (201) 225-8837.

Standard dishwashers *(never recommended).* These wasteful models, built without the energy-saving features listed above, should be avoided.

WISE USE

Energy-efficient use. Save energy by using your dishwasher efficiently:

TABLE 32

ENERGY-EFFICIENT DISHWASHERS

Manufacturer	Model	Energy Use (kWh/cycle)	Annual Energy Cost ($)[a]	Water Preheat
Compact (holds fewer than eight place settings)				
Caloric	DUS314	1.983	49	yes
Frigidaire	DW1800L; DW1805K	1.983	49	yes
Peerless	DW1842	1.983	49	yes
Sears, Roebuck & Co.	14385; 14480; 14485; 14305; 17305; 17385	1.983	49	yes
W.C.I.	DU18J4	1.983	49	yes
Whirlpool	DU1800XT	1.983	49	yes
White-Westinghouse	SU180M; SC186M	1.983	49	yes
Standard (holds more than eight place settings)				
A.E.G.	Favorit 665i	1.600	40	yes
In-Sink-Erator	Classic Supreme	2.150	53	yes
Caloric	DCS416; DUS406	2.169	54	yes
Modern Maid	DDW155; DDW160	2.169	54	yes
Caloric	DUS409	2.230	55	yes
Modern Maid	DDW195	2.230	55	yes
Frigidaire	DW100D	2.300	57	yes
Gibson	SU24P3; SU24P4	2.300	57	yes
Montgomery Ward	UC01005B; UC01026B; UC01034B; UC01035B; UC01038B	2.300	57	yes
Tappan	61-1127-1; 61-1137-10	2.300	57	yes
White-Westinghouse	SU210J	2.300	57	yes
Frigidaire	DW220D	2.307	57	yes
Kelvinator	DWU2005D	2.307	57	yes
White-Westinghouse	SU330J	2.307	57	yes
Whirlpool	DU9000XT	2.358	58	no
Frigidaire	DW4400D; DW4500F; DW5500F; DWF600E	2.377	59	yes
Gibson	SU24C7; SU2459	2.377	59	yes
Kelvinator	DWU7025	2.377	59	yes
Montgomery Ward	UC01066B; UC01077B	2.377	59	yes
Tappan	61-1147-10; 61-1157-10	2.377	59	yes
Whirlpool	DP8700XT; DU8500XT; DU8550XT; DU8570XT; DU8700XT; DU8750XT; DU8900XT; DU8950XT; GDP8700XT	2.387	59	no
	DU9100XT; DU9200XT; DU9400XT; DU9450XT	2.399	59	no

Source: *1991 Consumer Guide to Home Energy Savings* (American Council for an Energy-Efficient Economy).

[a] Based on average use and electricity cost at 7.7¢ per kilowatt-hour.

- Don't install it next to your refrigerator; its heat will make the refrigerator work harder. If you must install them next to each other, put insulation between them.

- Scrape dishes, but don't rinse them; most dishwashers are designed to clean unrinsed dishes, so rinsing just wastes water and energy.

- Wait for a full load before starting a cycle.

- To save hot water use the shortest wash cycle possible.

- Use the air-dry selector, which saves energy by shutting off the heat during the dry cycle. At the end of the drying cycle, open the door.

- Better yet, skip the drying cycle altogether: simply stop the machine at the end of the rinse cycle, and open the door.

- In summer avoid running the dishwasher during the heat of the day, especially if you have air conditioning.

Safe use. When you unload the dishwasher, don't reach down into the bottom, where the heating element is located, until the machine has had time to cool.

Regular maintenance. To keep a dishwasher working well, make sure it's clean and well maintained:

- Clean the filter when necessary (most dishwashers now have self-cleaning filters).

- Keep the door seals clean.

- Occasionally clean the interior with vinegar: just set a full cup of vinegar on the rack and run a regular cycle with no dishes or soap.

FOR FURTHER INFORMATION: 1991 Consumer Guide to Home Energy Savings, by Alex Wilson; American Council for an Energy-Efficient Economy.

1. "Major Appliance Industry Facts Book, 1988 Data Update Supplement," (Association of Home Appliance Manufacturers, 20 N. Wacker Dr., Chicago, IL 60606), p. 5.
2. "Dishwashers Plain and Fancy," *Consumer Reports* (May 1990), p. 343.

FOOD WRAPS AND BAGS

Food wraps and bags are useful for keeping foods fresh, but they vary widely in both performance and environmental soundness.

ENVIRONMENTAL PROBLEMS

Wasteful use of resources. Considering their short usable life span, food wraps and bags are very resource-intensive to make:

- *Aluminum foil* requires bauxite ore and lots of electricity. Bauxite mines, many of which are in third-world countries, cause water pollution, soil degradation, and loss of wildlife habitat. Reducing the bauxite to alumina pollutes water and creates mineral wastes. Generating electricity has numerous problems of its own, especially air pollution and depletion of nonrenewable fossil fuels.

- *Plastic wraps* and *bags* are made from petroleum and natural gas; their manufacture depletes these nonrenewable fossil fuels and pollutes the air and water.

- *Waxed paper* has as its base a high-strength, chemically processed paper, the manufacture of which pollutes the air and water. The paper is then coated with petrochemical waxes, another petroleum derivative.

Harmful ingredients. Some plastic wraps contain polyvinyl chloride or polyvinylidine chloride; their plasticizers can migrate into foods, especially fatty foods, with potentially harmful effects. Polyvinyl chloride can also contaminate food with vinyl chloride, a toxic carcinogen.[1]

Disposal problems. Of the three types of food wrap, only aluminum foil can be recycled easily. Plastic wraps made of polyethylene are potentially recyclable (as are all pure polyethylene plastics) but are rarely recycled in practice. Waxed paper, because of its coating, cannot be recycled.

CHOOSING A PRODUCT

GENERAL GUIDELINES

Weighing your needs. Select the right food wrap for the specific purpose, weighing the type of food to be stored and the need for short-term or long-term storage or use in an oven or microwave.

Reusable or recyclable material. Select a food wrap you can reuse many times or recycle instead of throwing away.

COMMERCIAL PRODUCTS

Aluminum foil *(highly recommended)*. Aluminum foil is strong, wraps tightly, seals well, and is easy to recycle. It holds up well in ovens and freezers and can easily be washed and reused many times. It is also a very effective oxygen barrier, so it keeps fatty and oily foods from turning rancid. Aluminum foil does have two disadvantages: it can't be used in microwaves, and it shouldn't be used with acidic foods, which can react with the metal. Heavy-duty foil is by far the best choice; strong and thick, it has the longest usable life.

Plastic food storage bags *(sometimes recommended)*. The best food storage bags are the large, heavy, polyethylene bags designed for both freezer use and ordinary storage. They are very strong and seal in moisture well; however, they are not very effective oxygen barriers, so they are unsuitable for fatty, oily foods. Avoid the smaller sandwich bags, which are easy to tear and hard to reuse. Look for the more expensive brands such as Pathmark Heavy Duty Freezer, Ziploc Freezer, and Glad-Lock Freezer bags; they are strong and easy to seal, and can be washed and reused many times.

Plastic wrap *(not generally recommended)*. Most plastic wraps are low-density polyethylene (LDPE) films that cling to food and seal in moisture quite well. They are not very strong, however, and their poor resistance to oxygen makes them unsuitable for fatty foods. Three major brands do resist oxygen: Saran Wrap, made of polyvinylidine chloride, and Reynolds Wrap and Borden Sealwrap, both made of polyvinyl chloride. Unfortunately, their toxic vinyl chloride and various plasticizers can contaminate foods, particularly if they're used in microwaves. All polyethylene-film wraps are virtually identical in material and performance; if you must use them, look for the best bargains and reuse them as often as possible.

Waxed paper *(not generally recommended)*. Although stronger than plastic films, waxed paper has few other advantages for food storage: it does not cling to food, so it doesn't seal in moisture well; and it isn't a good barrier to oxygen, so it doesn't work for fatty foods. Waxed paper is also hard—though not impossible—to reuse, because washing is difficult. Waxed paper is nonrecyclable, but some companies tout their products as biodegradable; unfortunately, little degrades in a modern landfill.

Cellophane bags *(never recommended)*. Used mostly for packaging prepared foods, cellophane food storage bags recently have been marketed as alternatives to plastic. Although biodegradable and made from a renewable resource (trees), cellophane has no other advantages: it is weak and easily torn or punctured, hard to reuse, poor at sealing food, and nonrecyclable. Even its manufacture is harmful, requiring some of the harshest chemicals used by the paper industry.

ALTERNATIVES

Reclosable containers. A much better choice than any food wrap is a glass or heavy plastic container with a good lid; it can be washed and reused indefinitely.

WISE USE

Safe use. Whenever possible, avoid using plastic wrap or waxed paper in a microwave. When you do use them, keep the wrap at least one inch above the food and leave an opening for moisture to escape. Never use anything but aluminum foil in a conventional oven.

Proper disposal. Clean aluminum foil before recycling it with your aluminum cans; look for recycling programs for polyethylene wrap or bags.

1. N. Irving Sax and Richard J. Lewis, Sr., eds., *Hawley's Condensed Chemical Dictionary,* 11th ed. (Van Nostrand Reinhold, 1987), p. 946.

MICROWAVE OVENS

About 75 percent of American homes have a microwave oven. Microwaves save not only time and effort, but also lots of energy; they use about 60 percent less energy than conventional or toaster ovens do.[1]

ENVIRONMENTAL PROBLEMS

Safety hazards. Microwave ovens do present a number of potential safety hazards:

- *Radiation.* Microwave ovens heat food by using microwave radiation to "excite" the water molecules in the food, which in turn generates heat. Early microwave ovens sometimes leaked potentially harmful radiation, often from improperly sealed doors. Newer models, however, have better door seals and sensors to detect improperly sealed doors; tests of these newer machines have found emissions to be very low, less than half the federally allowed limit.[2]

- *Burns.* Poorly vented covered dishes can build up steam while cooking and burn you when you open them.

- *Bacterial contamination.* Microwaves cook unevenly, so food that is cooked well on the inside might not be hot enough on the surface to kill harmful bacteria. This problem is of special concern with chicken (which can carry salmonella), pork (trichinosis), and fish (parasite larvae).[3]

- *Plastic contamination.* If plastic coverings or containers come in contact with food during cooking, the plasticizers that make them flexible can leach into the food.

Wasteful packaging. The proliferation of "microwaveable" foods has led to some very wasteful packaging practices. Many such foods come in throwaway cooking dishes and multiple layers of packaging, usually made of nonrecyclable materials.

CHOOSING A PRODUCT

GENERAL GUIDELINES

Weighing your needs. Consider which optional features (a turntable, temperature probe, easy-to-use controls) and what kind of oven (microwave only or microwave/convection) are best suited to your kitchen and your cooking needs.

Energy efficiency. There is little variation in energy efficiency among the models of microwave ovens. Size, however, is important: a full-sized machine uses up to 50 percent more electricity than a small one.

Quality. A well-built microwave oven will probably last longer and perform better; look for the best manufacturers' warranties.

Sensible packaging. Avoid microwaveable products packaged in wasteful single-serving portions and throwaway containers.

COMMERCIAL PRODUCTS

Subcompact/compact microwave ovens *(highly recommended)*. These relatively inexpensive ovens have an oven capacity of 0.5 cubic feet or less for subcompacts and about 0.7 cubic feet for compacts. Most draw 400 to 500 watts of electricity, offer fewer options than mid- or full-sized ovens, and are best for heating snacks, leftovers, and small meals.

Mid-sized or full-sized microwave ovens *(highly recommended)*. These ovens have from 0.7 and 1.5 cubic feet of oven space and draw 600 to 700 watts of power. They have a variety of optional features and can cook large portions of food quickly.

Microwave/convection ovens *(highly recommended)*. With oven sizes of 0.9 to 1.5 cubic feet and 600 to 750 watts of power, these ovens combine microwave cooking with regular thermal heat to produce classic baked dishes—tender on the inside, crispy on the outside. Using both microwave and thermal heat lowers the

energy savings over a conventional oven to about 20 percent (from about 60 percent with microwave only). Still, 20 percent is a significant energy savings. Some microwave/convection ovens use a fan to circulate hot air around the food; others let the heat circulate by itself. Both use regular heat to do the types of cooking that microwave energy can't do. The ovens can be used in microwave mode, in convection mode, or in combination. Many optional features are available.

WISE USE

Energy-efficient use. Use a microwave only for cooking and reheating; using it to defrost food wastes electricity.

Safe use. To avoid any danger of burns, radiation, or contaminated food, take these precautions:

- Read the manufacturer's instructions carefully.

- Don't stay near the oven any more than necessary while it's on, especially if you're pregnant.

- Keep children away from the machine until they are old enough to understand fully the hazards of using it.

- Keep the door seals clean so the door will close tightly.

- Use microwave-safe glass or ceramic dishes. Never cook foods in plastic, as plasticizers and other chemicals can leach into the food. (Although some plastic food containers and wraps are labeled "microwaveable," that doesn't mean they've been tested or approved by any agency.)

- Never put metal in a microwave; it can spark.

- If you're using covered dishes, allow steam to escape; ideally, leave an opening in the cover during cooking.

- Never fat-fry foods in a microwave; moisture can cause the oil to spatter.

- If you're cooking chicken, pork, or fish, be sure the food is thoroughly done, both inside and out, to avoid food poisoning.

1. "Microwave/Convection Ovens," *Consumer Reports* (September 1989), p. 580.
2. "Is Radiation from Microwave Ovens Hazardous?" *Consumer Reports* (November 1985), p. 647.
3. "Small Microwave Ovens," *Consumer Reports* (November 1989), p. 693.

OVEN CLEANERS

Oven cleaning is an ugly chore if you let it go too long. Most commercial oven cleaners are good at removing baked-on grunge, but they're also extremely hazardous.

ENVIRONMENTAL PROBLEMS

Harmful ingredients. Most chemical oven cleaners use caustic lye (sodium hydroxide) as their active ingredient. Lye can severely damage the eyes, skin, nose, or throat on contact.

Indoor air pollution. Oven cleaners can badly pollute indoor air with their harsh active ingredients and, in aerosol products, with their propellants. One study, for example, showed that nonmethane hydrocarbons, potential carcinogens, rose from only 4 or 5 parts per million to more than 80 just after a common oven cleaner was used, and didn't return to normal for seven hours.[1]

Animal cruelty. Because some ingredients can harm humans, many manufacturers test oven cleaners on animals, under inhumane conditions; afterward the animals are killed.

Wasteful packaging. Many oven cleaners come in aerosol cans, which are dangerous to use because of the large amounts of caustic lye they spew out, energy-intensive to manufacture, and completely nonrecyclable.

CHOOSING A PRODUCT

GENERAL GUIDELINES

Natural, nontoxic remedies. First try the nontoxic do-it-yourself methods; if those don't work, try the less toxic commercial products before you even consider lye-based cleaners.

COMMERCIAL PRODUCTS

Noncaustic chemical oven cleaners *(sometimes recommended)*. Easy-Off Oven Cleaner, which comes in a lemon, noncaustic formula, uses heat to help clean the oven and comes in a plastic spray bottle. It is widely available in food and hardware stores. Do not confuse it with Easy-Off's lye-based product.

Caustic chemical oven cleaners *(never recommended)*. All the lye-based products are dangerous and polluting, particularly those in aerosol cans. Avoid them if at all possible.

DO-IT-YOURSELF

Regular cleaning. If you clean the oven often, you'll avoid hard-to-clean buildups of burnt foods. Wipe the oven with a damp sponge (and a mild soap if necessary) after each use.

Baking soda. Make a paste of baking soda, water, and a little mild soap, and apply it when the oven is cool. Let it sit for several hours, then scrub with a soft, plastic scrubber that will not damage the oven's porcelain surface. Repeat if necessary.

Salt. Salt is also an effective cleaner. Either pour it on fresh spills and wipe them up, or sprinkle it on the oven surface and scrub with a damp sponge.

Ammonia. For stubborn stains that defy salt or baking soda, pour ¼ cup ammonia in a shallow nonaluminum pan and add a small amount of water. Put the pan on the bottom shelf and leave it overnight, then scrub with a soft plastic scrubber. *Caution:* ammonia is less caustic than lye but still harsh; open a window if possible and leave the room while the ammonia is working.

WISE USE

Safe use. If you must use a caustic cleaner, follow the instructions carefully. Wear rubber gloves and eye protection and ventilate the room.

Proper disposal. If you must dispose of leftover oven cleaner, either flush it down the drain or, better yet, store it for hazardous waste collection or take it to a collection site. Call your local waste disposal office for information on hazardous waste collection programs. Be sure any aerosol cans are emptied of pressure before throwing them away.

1. Edward Calabrese and Michael Dorsey, *Healthy Living in an Unhealthy World* (Simon & Schuster, 1984), p. 118.

PRESSURE COOKERS

Pressure cookers are low-tech, energy-efficient cooking devices that can shorten cooking times by at least half—often much more. For cooking large quantities, pressure cookers can even outpace microwave ovens, and the short cooking time ensures that foods retain their nutrients and flavors.

ENVIRONMENTAL PROBLEMS

Safety hazards. Early pressure cookers sometimes blew up if the lids were not fastened properly. All modern cookers, however, have safety valves or vents designed to release pressure long before an accident occurs. Many models also feature lid locks that keep you from opening the pot until all pressure is released.

CHOOSING A PRODUCT

GENERAL GUIDELINES

Weighing your needs. A pressure cooker is an excellent choice if you like to cook large batches of such foods as soups, beans, sauces, stews, and vegetables. Most models come in three sizes: 4, 6, and 8 quarts. The 6-quart size is a good compromise; it handles both large and small quantities well.

Safety. Look for cookers with a safety lid lock, not just a button to indicate that pressure remains in the pot. All cookers now come with safety valves that will blow if the pressure gets too high.

Quality. The best-quality cookers have tight seals and easy-to-find replacement parts, and are made of stainless steel rather than aluminum. Aluminum affects the taste and color of some foods, especially acidic ones.

COMMERCIAL PRODUCTS

High-quality stainless-steel pressure cookers *(highly recommended)*. Presto, T-Fal, and Cuisinart all make excellent stainless-steel cookers. Look for them in department and kitchenware stores.

Lower-quality aluminum pressure cookers *(not generally recommended)*. Aluminum cookers are less durable and more likely to affect the quality of the food; bypass them if high-quality stainless-steel brands are available.

WISE USE

Safe and efficient use. To get the best results from your pressure cooker, remember the following guidelines:

- Follow the manufacturer's instructions carefully.

- To avoid a clogged vent during cooking, never overfill the cooker, and always presoak foods such as dried beans when the instructions say to do so.

- Don't try to open the cooker until the pressure-indicating button drops.

Regular maintenance. Thoroughly clean the cooker, including the safety valve, after each use. Check the gaskets and seals periodically, and replace them if they are damaged or cracked.

RANGES, COOKING

Almost all American households have either a freestanding or a built-in cooking range; unfortunately, 60 percent of them are energy-wasting electric ranges, rather than efficient gas.[1]

ENVIRONMENTAL PROBLEMS

Energy consumption. Electric stoves are only about one-third as energy-efficient as gas stoves, since they must convert electrical energy into heat energy—reversing the process that created the electricity in the first place. Natural gas, in contrast, is simply pumped from the ground, processed slightly, and piped into the home ready to burn. Consumers pay only about a third more on their utility bills to operate electric ranges; the high environmental costs of generating the electricity—air and water pollution, acid rain, greenhouse gases, wildlife habitat destruction, nuclear contamination and waste, and fossil-fuel depletion—are hidden.

Indoor air pollution. The open flame on gas ranges can pollute indoor air. Incomplete burning produces poisonous carbon monoxide, and even complete burning can produce nitrogen dioxide, another hazardous pollutant.[2] According to tests, gas stove use can raise indoor levels of carbon monoxide and nitrogen dioxide to several times their norm.[3]

Pipeline hazards. Natural gas can be transported only by pipe. These pipelines disrupt natural habitats, both during and after their construction, and present a constant danger of leaks, explosions, and fires.

Safety hazards. Just as large gas pipelines do, the small lines that service a gas range in the home present a danger of leaking fumes, explosions, and fire. In extreme circumstances gas ranges can be quite dangerous. Older or poorly installed stoves can leak gas, pilot lights can blow out, and faulty controls can allow an oven

to fill with gas before it lights, creating a danger of poisoning or explosion.

CHOOSING A PRODUCT

GENERAL GUIDELINES

Weighing your needs. Choose a stove that fits your kitchen design, your cooking needs, and your lifestyle. Unless you do a lot of baking, for example, you might not need a range with a full-sized oven; instead, you could get a space-saving cooktop and an energy-efficient microwave/convection oven.

Energy efficiency. When choosing a range, make energy efficiency a top priority. If natural gas is available in your area, consider buying a more efficient gas range instead of an electric. Ranges and cooktops do not have EnergyGuide labels that show their average energy use, so look for energy-saving features:

- *Good insulation*—including in the oven door, where it is sometimes skipped in cheaper models—is a real energy-saver.

- *Convection ovens* use a fan to circulate the hot air around the oven, cooking food more evenly and quickly.

- A *glass window* in the oven door lets you see how food is cooking without opening the door and losing heat.

- *Self-cleaning ovens* are *not* very energy-efficient since they use large amounts of heat to vaporize baked-on grime. In electric ovens, for example, running the self-cleaning cycle consumes 5 to 7 kilowatt-hours of electricity, enough to run a 6-inch stove burner for four hours. (See Oven Cleaners, p. 185, for non-toxic ways to clean your oven.)

Quality. High-quality ranges perform better, last longer, and have better oven insulation.

COMMERCIAL PRODUCTS

Energy-efficient gas ranges and cooktops *(highly recommended).* In addition to the energy-saving features listed above, look for electric ignition instead of pilot lights. A distant second to electric ignition are low-heat-input pilot lights; they burn cleaner and use less energy than old-style pilots, which should be avoided.

Energy-efficient electric ranges and cooktops *(recommended).* Look for the energy-saving features listed above, and choose the burner type that best fits your needs:

- *Induction heating elements* create heat directly in the metal of the pan rather than in the burner. They can cut electricity use by up to 50 percent and are the most effective energy-conserving option available on electric stoves. They are expensive, however, and require that you use only flat-bottomed steel or iron cookware.

- *Ceramic-glass burner units,* which have flat glass surfaces with conventional heating elements underneath, are easy to clean and use less energy than coiled or solid-disk burners, but they cost more to buy and require flat-bottomed cookware.

- *Halogen heating elements* with ceramic glass covers heat up instantly and clean easily and, like ceramic-glass burners, use less energy than coil or solid-disk burners. Flat-bottomed cookware is required.

- *"Power-saver" elements* are coils that can be partially heated to fit smaller pans.

Standard gas or electric ranges *(never recommended).* These wasteful models, built without the energy-saving features listed above, should be avoided.

ALTERNATIVES

Microwave ovens. Unless you do a lot of baking, a microwave or microwave/convection oven and a cooktop might meet your cooking needs just as well as a range, saving both money and energy (see Microwave Ovens, p. 183).

WISE USE

Proper installation. To function efficiently and safely, a range must be correctly installed:

- Don't install a range next to a refrigerator; the stove's heat will make the refrigerator work harder.

- Gas ranges *must* be vented with a fan that vents to the outdoors. Fans that simply filter and recycle the air back indoors do not eliminate toxic gases in the stove's exhaust.

- Electric stoves draw a heavy power load. Make sure they're correctly wired and grounded and on an adequate circuit.

Regular maintenance. To keep your range in good working order, make sure it's well maintained:

- Periodically check oven door gaskets for a tight seal. With the oven off and the door closed, try to slide a piece of paper between the gasket and metal; if it slides through, replace the gaskets to stop heat loss.

- Keep the entire stove clean—including the oven—to prevent cooked-on deposits (see Oven Cleaners, p. 185).

- Keep all vent filters clean and the fan oiled and working well.

- Check gas ranges periodically for leaking gas by swabbing a soap-and-water solution around all the joints; if you see bubbles, the stove is leaking.

- Check the burner flame of gas ranges for color, which should be blue, not yellow; if necessary, have a serviceperson adjust it.

- Periodically inspect the wiring and burners on electric ranges. Replace damaged wiring or elements promptly.

Safe use. Reduce risks of indoor pollution and fire by taking the following precautions:

- Whenever you cook with a gas stove, run the exhaust fan.

- Keep a fire extinguisher and a box of baking soda near the stove.

Energy-efficient use. Take the following steps to save energy when you cook:

- Defrost foods before cooking them.

- Fit the pot size to the burner size.

- Cover pots and pans whenever you can.

- Place aluminum foil under electric burners to reflect heat upwards.

- Use a toaster oven or microwave instead of the range's oven whenever possible.

- Preheat your oven for as short a time as possible.

- When you bake, use ceramic (tempered) glass pans; they'll cook food at 25 degrees lower in the same amount of time.

- When you're baking, avoid opening the oven door.

- Turn oven or electric burners off a few minutes early; the food will keep cooking.

- If you use a self-cleaning oven, try to run the cleaning cycle only immediately after you bake, to make use of the oven heat.

1. "Major Appliance Industry Facts Book," (Association of Home Appliance Manufacturers, 20 N. Wacker Dr., Chicago, IL 60606) 1987, p. 5.
2. W. J. Fisk et al., *Indoor Air Quality Control Techniques* (Noyes Data Corporation, 1987), p. 208.
3. Edward Calabrese and Michael Dorsey, *Healthy Living in an Unhealthy World* (Simon & Schuster, 1984), p. 121; R. B. Gammage and S. V. Kaye, eds., *Indoor Air and Human Health* (Lewis Publishers, 1985), p. 307.

REFRIGERATORS AND FREEZERS

Refrigerator/freezers are our most popular home appliance, found in 99.9 percent of American households. Unfortunately, they are also the biggest energy users in most homes, slightly edging out air conditioners.[1]

ENVIRONMENTAL PROBLEMS

Ozone depletion. By far the best coolant available, the chlorofluorocarbon CFC-12 is cheap, nontoxic, very effective, long lasting and, when contained within the refrigerator's tubing, safe. But when released into the air—from leaks, or during disposal or repair—it slowly rises up to the stratosphere and destroys the earth's vital ozone shield. Refrigerators also use CFCs as insulating foam; the average unit has $2\frac{1}{2}$ pounds of CFC-11 in its walls.[2] Manufacturers are looking for alternative coolants and insulation.

Energy consumption. Though their energy efficiency has vastly improved since the early 1970s, American refrigerators are still quite wasteful. The average American refrigerator uses nearly 1,000 kilowatt-hours of electricity per year, while the average Japanese machine, which is smaller, well-designed, and well-built, uses only 500 kilowatt-hours.[3] Congressional mandates have encouraged manufacturers to keep increasing efficiency, and many units on the market now do far better than the national average.

CHOOSING A PRODUCT
GENERAL GUIDELINES

Weighing your needs. If your present unit was made before 1980, consider replacing it; a refrigerator made in 1978, for example, uses 45 percent more electricity than one made today. Carefully consider the size and features your household needs. Smaller machines tend to use less energy and fewer CFCs, but if you need more capacity, using one larger unit is far more efficient than adding a second smaller one.

Energy efficiency. When you buy a refrigerator or freezer, make energy efficiency a top priority. Look for EnergyGuide labels, required on all models, that show the average yearly operating cost. Refrigerators last a long time, so you'll actually save money by choosing a higher-priced, energy-efficient model that will run economically. The most energy-efficient units also contain less CFC coolant—about half as much as inefficient machines.[4] For extra energy efficiency, look for power-saver switches that let you turn off the small heater added to many models to prevent moisture buildup on the surface in humid climates.

COMMERCIAL PRODUCTS (REFRIGERATOR/FREEZERS)

Energy-efficient single-door refrigerator/freezers *(highly recommended)*. If you need only a small unit, consider this simple, energy-saving style. These units, which range from tiny compacts to models with 15 cubic feet of space, use the least energy and offer few options. Some models must be manually defrosted, which saves energy; others offer either automatic or slightly more efficient partial-automatic defrosting (the freezer compartment must be manually defrosted). Table 33 lists the most energy-efficient models available.

Energy-efficient double-door, top-freezer refrigerator/freezers *(highly recommended)*. These refrigerator/freezers feature either automatic or partial-automatic defrost and range in capacity from 11 to 25 cubic feet. Their energy efficiency varies tremendously, so study energy-use figures carefully before you buy. Efficient models have good insulation, high-quality components, and few options (such as automatic ice service); Table 33 lists the most efficient models available. The most efficient refrigerator/freezers are made by Sun Frost. They come with 4 to 19 cubic feet of space and partial-automatic defrost. Though expensive and hard to find,

these machines are three times more energy efficient than the best major brands. Call Sun Frost at (707) 822-9095 for information and dealerships in your area, or call for the Real Goods Trading Company catalog at (800) 762-7325.

Double-door, side-by-side refrigerator/freezers *(never recommended)*. Side-by-side refrigerator/freezers are stylish, often loaded with options, and a bit more convenient for storing frozen foods, but they use up to a third more electricity than top-freezer refrigerators with the same capacity. Avoid this energy-wasting style whenever possible.

COMMERCIAL PRODUCTS (FREEZERS)

Energy-efficient chest freezers *(highly recommended)*. The top-loading chest freezer is up to 30 percent more efficient than an upright (front-loading) freezer of the same size, because of better insulation and design (when the freezer is open, cold air tends to sink and stay in). It is slightly less convenient, however, because it requires more floor space, foods are harder to organize, and you must bend over to store and retrieve food. See Table 34 for the most efficient chest freezers available.

Energy-efficient upright freezers *(sometimes recommended)*. Upright freezers are less energy-efficient than chest freezers, but if you want an upright because of space requirements or convenience, look for a relatively efficient model (see Table 34). Sun Frost makes super-efficient freezers also; see the information on Sun Frost, above.

Standard freezers *(never recommended)*. These wasteful models, built without energy-saving features, should be avoided.

WISE USE

Proper installation. To ensure that your refrigerator or freezer runs well, see that it's correctly installed:

TABLE
33

ENERGY-EFFICIENT REFRIGERATORS

Brand	Model	Capacity (Cubic Ft.)	Annual Energy Use (kWh)	Annual Energy Cost ($)[a]
REFRIGERATORS Single Door, Manual Defrost				
Storage Capacity: less than 2.5 cu. ft.				
Aquarius	AER2-1*	2.1	274	22
Oasis	OER2-1*	2.1	274	22
Absocold	AR021M	1.7	323	26
General Electric	SC2S	1.7	323	26
	TA2	1.8	323	26
Hotpoint	SSD2C	1.7	323	26
Kenmore	89715*0	1.5	323	26
	99017*0	1.7	323	26
Sanyo	SR4807	1.5	323	26
	SR4990X	1.7	323	26
Storage Capacity: 2.5 to 9.4 cu. ft.				
Absocold	AR061M*	5.6	286	23
Sanyo	SR5017	5.6	286	23
Absocold	AR031M	2.5	323	26
Kenmore	89725*0; 8992540	2.5	323	26
Sanyo	SR6907; SR6917	2.5	323	26
Daewoo	DR-090UF	2.8	336	27
Emerson	DR-090UF; OR-300	2.8	336	27
Panasonic	NR-303WG; NR-303WH	2.6	336	27
	NR-504WG; NR-504WH	5.0	336	27
Storage Capacity: 9.5 to 13.0 cu. ft.				
Absocold	AR101M*	9.5	410	33
Kenmore	8600010	9.5	410	33
Sanyo	SR1018	9.5	410	33
Kenmore	86611*0	11.6	485	39
Sanyo	SR1058	11.6	485	39
Frigidaire	D-13F*-0	13.0	498	40
General Electric	TA11SL	10.6	498	40
Hotpoint	SSD11CK	10.6	498	40
Kelvinator	SSX130EM1*	13.0	498	40
Kenmore	83810*	10.5	498	40
White-Westinghouse	RC131LC*0; RC131LL*0	13.0	498	40
REFRIGERATORS Single Door, Automatic Defrost				
Storage Capacity: less than 13.0 cu. ft.				
Absocold	AR031A*1	2.3	336	27
Sanyo	SR4017	3.6	373	30
Marvel	61AR	6.1	448	36
Absocold	AR021A*1	1.7	460	27
Marvel	58RIAD	5.8	597	48
Storage Capacity: 13.0 to 17.5 cu. ft.				
Wood's	OR48; WR48	17.3	435	35
Gibson	RC13M2*S2D	13.0	498	40
Kitchen Aid	KRRF 15XT**0*	15.0	697	56
Gibson	RM18F6*S1F	17.5	808	65

TABLE 33

ENERGY-EFFICIENT REFRIGERATORS *(continued)*

Brand	Model	Capacity (Cubic Ft.)	Annual Energy Use (kWh)	Annual Energy Cost ($)[a]
Kelvinator	AMK175EN2*	17.5	808	65
Frigidaire	FPEM-18F*-0	17.5	821	66
White-Westinghouse	RA186MC*0	17.5	821	66

REFRIGERATOR/FREEZERS Top Freezer, Partial Automatic Defrost
Storage Capacity: Less than 10.2 cu. ft.

Brand	Model	Capacity (Cubic Ft.)	Annual Energy Use (kWh)	Annual Energy Cost ($)[a]
Sun Frost[b]	RF-4	4.0	62	5
Kenmore	8992940	2.9	448	36
Sanyo	SR1487	2.9	448	36

Storage Capacity: 10.2 to 14.4 cu. ft.

Brand	Model	Capacity (Cubic Ft.)	Annual Energy Use (kWh)	Annual Energy Cost ($)[a]
Sun Frost[b]	RF-12	12.0	128	10
Frigidaire	FCD-12TF*-1	12.0	572	54
Kenmore	86801*0	10.6	659	53
Sanyo	SR1158; SR1159; SR1190	10.6	659	53
Admiral	RT11H5	10.2	697	56
Holland	RT11H	10.2	697	56
Magic Chef	RT11H	10.2	697	56
Montgomery Ward	HMG10570	10.2	697	56
Norge	RT11H	10.2	697	56
Warwick	RT11H	10.2	697	56
Gibson	RT12C2*S2B	12.0	709	57
White-Westinghouse	RT120GC*4; RT120GL*4; RT120LC*0; RT120LL*0	12.0	709	57
General Electric	TB13SL	13.4	746	60
Hotpoint	CTA13CL	13.4	746	60
Kenmore	83831*	13.7	746	60
Frigidaire	FCD-14TF*-0; FCD-14TF*-1	14.0	771	62
White-Westinghouse	RT142GC*5	14.0	771	62
	RT142GL*5	14.3	771	62

Storage Capacity: 14.5 to 19.0 cu. ft.

Brand	Model	Capacity (Cubic Ft.)	Annual Energy Use (kWh)	Annual Energy Cost ($)[a]
Sun Frost[b]	RF-16	16.0	205	16
Sun Frost[b]	RF-19	19.0	282	23
General Electric	TB15SL	14.6	771	62
Hotpoint	CTA15CL	14.6	771	62
Kenmore	83851*	14.5	771	62
Magic Chef	RB15E-1P; RB15G	14.6	771	62

REFRIGERATOR/FREEZERS Bottom Freezer, Partial Automatic Defrost
Storage Capacity: less than 10.0 cu. ft.

Brand	Model	Capacity (Cubic Ft.)	Annual Energy Use (kWh)	Annual Energy Cost ($)[a]
General Electric	TI4AK	3.9	547	44
Samsung	FS-150IM	3.9	547	44

REFRIGERATOR/FREEZERS Top Freezer, Automatic Defrost
Storage Capacity: 10.0 to 13.9 cu. ft.

Brand	Model	Capacity (Cubic Ft.)	Annual Energy Use (kWh)	Annual Energy Cost ($)[a]
Absocold	AR111F*1	10.0	721	58
Kenmore	8660210; 8660280; 86802*0; 96004*0	10.0	721	58
Sanyo	SR1258; SR1290	10.0	721	58

(continued on next page)

TABLE 33

ENERGY-EFFICIENT REFRIGERATORS *(continued)*

Brand	Model	Capacity (Cubic Ft.)	Annual Energy Use (kWh)	Annual Energy Cost ($)[a]
Frigidaire	FPI-811TF; FPI-11TLF	11.0	759	61
Gibson	RD11F**V; RT11F**V	11.0	759	61
White-Westinghouse	RT114L	11.0	759	61
Kenmore	86923*0	12.0	771	62
	86922**	11.6	784	63
Whirlpool	ET12LK*W*0*	11.6	784	63
Frigidaire	FPD-12TF*-0	12.0	796	64
Gibson	RT12F3*S2B	12.0	796	64
Kelvinator	TSX120EN1*	12.0	796	64
Kenmore	86923*0	12.0	796	64
Whirlpool	ET12AK*S*0*	11.6	808	65

Storage Capacity: 14.0 to 14.4 cu. ft.

Brand	Model	Capacity (Cubic Ft.)	Annual Energy Use (kWh)	Annual Energy Cost ($)[a]
General Electric	TBX14AM; TBX14DM; TBX14SM; TBXY14LM; TBXY14SM	14.4	784	63
Hotpoint	CTX14AM; CTX14CM; CTX14EM; CTXY14CM; CTXY14LM	14.4	784	63
Kelvinator	96045*0; 97045*0	14.4	784	63
RCA	MTX14EM	14.4	784	63
Amana	TM14M; TM14M1; TM14N	14.2	821	66
White-Westinghouse	RT140LC*1	14.0	821	66

Storage Capacity: 14.5 to 16.5 cu. ft.

Brand	Model	Capacity (Cubic Ft.)	Annual Energy Use (kWh)	Annual Energy Cost ($)[a]
Kelvinator	TPK160BN4*	16.0	771	62
Kenmore	86960*1; 86962*0; 87960*1; 87962*0; 87962*2; 87962*3	16.0	771	62
General Electric	TBX16AM; TBX16DM; TBX16SM; TBX16ZM; TBXY16DM; TBXY16SM	15.6	796	64
Hotpoint	CTX16AM; CTX16CM; CTX16EM; CTX16GM; CTXY16CM	15.6	796	64
Kelvinator	96065*0; 97065*0	15.6	796	64
RCA	MTX16EM	15.6	796	64
Caloric	GFD150-1*3; GFD150-1*5	14.5	833	67
Gibson	RT15F4*U2B; RT15F4*U2D	14.5	833	67
Kelvinator	TSK145PN1*; TSK145PN2*	14.5	833	67
Kenmore	86952*4; 87952*2; 87952*3	14.5	833	67
Philco	PGTN156*AO; TPRD15A61*0	14.5	833	67
White-Westinghouse	RT153HC*2; RT153HL*2; RT153LC*0; RT153LC*2; RT153LL*0; RT154LC*1; RT154LC*2; RT154LL*1; RT154LL*2	14.5	833	67

TABLE
33

ENERGY-EFFICIENT REFRIGERATORS *(continued)*

Brand	Model	Capacity (Cubic Ft.)	Annual Energy Use (kWh)	Annual Energy Cost ($)[a]
Storage Capacity: 16.6 to 20.5 cu. ft.				
Frigidaire	FPD-17TF*-0; FPD-17TIF*-0; FPD-17TIF*-1; FPE-17TF*-0; FPI-17TF*-0; FPZ-17TF*-0	16.6	771	62
Gibson	RT17F3*U3A; RT17F3*U3B; RT17F9*U3B	16.6	771	62
White-Westinghouse	RT174ZC-1	16.6	771	62
Frigidaire	FPCE-19TF*-0; FPCI-29TF*-0; FPCI-19TIF*-0; FPCI-19TIF*-1	18.6	846	68
	FPCI-18TIE*-1	18.0	846	68
Gibson	RT17F2*T3B; RT17F6*T3B; RT17F6*T3C; RT17F7*P3A; RT17F9*T3C	16.6	846	68
Kelvinator	TPK180ZN1*	18.0	846	68
Kenmore	83877*2; 83877*3	16.6	846	68
Philco	PGTN175*A0; PGTN175*A1; PGTN176*A0; PRD17A61*0; PRD17A61*1; YPRD17A61*0	16.6	846	68
Tappan	95-1757-**-2; 95-1757-**-3; 95-1787-**-3; 95-1787-**-4	16.6	846	68
White-Westinghouse	RT171MC*0; RT173MC*0; RT175MC*0; RT176MC*0; RT177MC*0; RT179MC*0;	17.0	846	68
	RT174LC*1	16.6	846	68
Storage Capacity: 20.6 to 22.4 cu. ft.				
Philco	PGTN218*A0; PRD21A61*0; RD21L8*MR0; TPRD21A61*0	20.6	945	76
Tappan	95-2187-**-5	20.6	945	76
White-Westinghouse	RT215MC*0; RT215MC*2; RT216JC*2; RT216JC*3; RT216MC*0; RT216MC*1; RT216MC*2; RT217JC*2; RT217MC*0; RT217MC*1; RT217MC*2; RT218JC*2; RT218MC*0; RT218MC*1; RT219MC*0; RT219MC*1; RT219MC*2	20.6	945	76
Kenmore	86515*4; 87515*4; 87924**; 87926**	20.6	958	77
Admiral	NT21L9; NT21L9A	20.9	970	78
Crosley	CNT21V8	21.0	970	78
Hotpoint	CTX22GM	21.7	970	78
Jenn-Air	JRT212; JRT216	21.0	970	78
Kelvinator	96027*0; 97027*0	21.6	970	78
Magic Chef	RB21K*-4A	20.9	970	78
Montgomery Ward	HMG21594; HMG21904	21.0	970	78
Norge	NNT219K	21.0	970	78
RCA	MTX22GM	21.7	970	78

(continued on next page)

TABLE 33

ENERGY-EFFICIENT REFRIGERATORS *(continued)*

Brand	Model	Capacity (Cubic Ft.)	Annual Energy Use (kWh)	Annual Energy Cost ($)[a]
Storage Capacity: 22.5 to 24.8 cu. ft.				
Maytag	RTD23A	22.5	1,007	81
Admiral	NT23L9; NT23L9A	22.5	1,032	83
General Electric	TBX25ZL; TBX25ZM	24.8	1,032	83
	TBX24KL	23.7	1,032	83
	TBX24ZL	23.6	1,032	83
Hotpoint	CTX25GL	24.8	1,032	83
	CTX24EL; CTX24GL	23.7	1,032	83
Jenn-Air	JRT232	22.6	1,032	83
	JRT236	22.5	1,032	83
Kenmore	86857*; 86956*; 87857*; 87956*	24.8	1,032	83
	86044*; 86046*; 87044*; 87046*	23.6	1,032	83
Magic Chef	RB23K*-4A; RB23K*-4AF; RB23K*-4AFL	22.5	1,032	83
Montgomery Ward	HMG23802	22.5	1,032	83
Norge	NNT239K	22.6	1,032	83
REFRIGERATOR/FREEZERS Bottom Freezer, Automatic Defrost **Storage Capacity: 19.0 to 19.1 cu. ft.**				
Frigidaire	FPES19BD**; FPES19BID**	19.1	1,070	86
Kenmore	86793**; 86993**	19.0	1,070	86
Whirlpool	EB19MK*S*0*	19.1	1,070	86

Source: *1990 Consumer Selection Guide for Refrigerators and Freezers* (The Association of Home Appliance Manufacturers).

[a] Average energy cost per year, based on an electricity cost of 8.04¢ per kilowatt-hour.

[b] Information on these models is provided by the manufacturer and is based on a room air temperature of 70° F. For more information, contact Sun Frost, P.O. Box 1101, Arcata, CA 95521; (707) 822-9095.

*Different numbers may appear here to denote variations in decorations, color, or door swing.

■ Make sure the machine is on a level surface and that the condenser coils at the back are several inches from the wall, to allow adequate circulation.

■ Don't install a refrigerator or freezer next to a cooking range or dishwasher; the heat will make the refrigerator work harder.

Regular maintenance. To keep your refrigerator or freezer in good working order, make sure it's well maintained:

■ Keep the condenser coils clean (dust and dirt will insulate them slightly, interfering with their cooling). On most machines the coils are at the back and easy to reach. On others,

however, they are at the bottom; to clean them you must unplug the machine, remove the food, remove the drip pan underneath, tape the door closed, and tilt the unit slightly to one side.

■ If you have a manual-defrost freezer, defrost it regularly. Frost over ¼-inch thick makes the motor work harder to keep the freezer cold.

■ Check the door seals and replace them if necessary. Starting at the top, place a sheet of paper under the seal and close the door; the paper should be held tightly at each point.

CFC conservation. If your refrigerator or freezer needs repair, make sure you choose a repair service with a CFC-capturing unit. Whirlpool now has a device that removes the CFC coolant, holds it while the repairs are done, and then returns it to the machine; this system is now being used to repair the following brands:

- Whirlpool, (800) 253-1301

- Roper, (800) 447-6437

- KitchenAid, (800) 422-1230

Energy-efficient use. To make sure your unit runs as efficiently as possible, follow these guidelines:

- Check the inside temperature regularly, using a thermometer. Refrigerators should be at 38° to 42° F; freezers at 0° to 5° F. A machine kept 10 degrees colder uses up to 25 percent more energy.

- Use the "power-saver" switch to turn off the small heaters that evaporate condensation in the refrigerator walls. Unless you live in a humid climate, you probably need the heaters only in the summer, if at all.

- Avoid opening the door unnecessarily or leaving it open for long periods.

Proper disposal. To keep CFC coolants from escaping into the air, *never* take a refrigerator or freezer to the dump when you discard it. Instead, call one of the following for advice:

- Your local waste disposal office

- Appliance Recycling Centers of America, (612) 291-1100 (they have pickup centers in Atlanta, Cleveland, Milwaukee, St. Louis, and St. Paul, and they might be able to refer you to a center in your area)

- A Whirlpool dealer, (800) 253-1301

- The Environmental Protection Agency, (202) 382-4627

If you must store an unused refrigerator or freezer, remove the door or otherwise secure it to keep children from getting trapped inside.

FOR FURTHER INFORMATION: *1991 Consumer Guide to Home Energy Savings,* by Alex Wilson; American Council for an Energy-Efficient Economy, 1990. "1991 Directory of Certified Refrigerators and Freezers" (Association of Home Appliance Manufacturers, 20 North Wacker Dr., Chicago, IL 60606).

1. "Major Appliance Industry Facts Book" (Association of Home Appliance Manufacturers, 20 N. Wacker Dr., Chicago, IL 60606) 1987, p. 40.
2. John Holusha, "The Next Refrigerator May Take a Step Back," *New York Times* (March 4, 1989).
3. Matthew Wald, "Why Americans Consume More Energy to Produce Less," *New York Times* (March 12, 1989).
4. Ibid.

TABLE 34

ENERGY-EFFICIENT FREEZERS

Brand	Model	Capacity (Cubic Ft.)	Annual Energy Use (kWh)	Annual Energy Cost ($)[a]
CHEST, Manual Defrost				
Storage Capacity: 14.8 to 20.2 cu. ft.				
Admiral	C17HE	16.5	435	35
Crosley	C17HE	16.5	435	35
Magic Chef	C17HE	16.5	435	35
Admiral	C15HS	14.8	460	37
Crosley	C15HS	14.8	460	37
General Electric	CB15DL	14.8	460	37
Hotpoint	FH15CL	14.8	460	37
Magic Chef	C15HS	14.8	460	37
Whirlpool	EH150F*V*0*	14.8	460	37
Wood's	*C42	14.8	460	37
General	GC15	14.8	473	37
Storage Capacity: 20.3 to 21.7 cu. ft.				
Admiral	C20HE	20.3	510	41
Crosley	C20HE	20.3	510	41
Magic Chef	C20HE	20.3	510	41
Admiral	C22HS	21.7	585	47
Crosley	C22HS	21.7	585	47
Magic Chef	C22HS	21.7	585	47
Whirlpool	EH220F*V*0*	21.7	585	47
Wood's	*C62	21.7	585	47
General	GC20	20.4	622	50
UPRIGHT, Manual Defrost				
Storage Capacity: 10.0 to 15.9 cu. ft.				
Sun Frost[b]	F-10	10.0	250	20
Amana	ESU13D	13.0	585	47
Coronado	UG13A	13.3	609	49
Frigidaire	UF-13N-L*1	13.3	609	49
General Electric	CA13DL-D	13.3	609	49
Gibson	FV13M2WSFH	13.3	609	49
Hotpoint	FV13CL-D	13.3	609	49
Imperial	UG13A	13.3	609	49
Kelvinator	UFS133FM3W	13.3	609	49
Kenmore	20321; 20328	13.3	609	49
Marquette	UG13A	13.3	609	49
Montgomery Ward	FFT43159-0; FFT43359-0	13.3	609	49
Tappan	98-1348-002	13.3	609	49
White-Westinghouse	FU134LRW3	13.3	609	49
Amana	ESU15D	15.0	647	52
Storage Capacity: 16.0 to 18.9 cu. ft.				
White-Westinghouse	FU168LRW3	16.1	609	49
	ESU17D	17.0	697	56
Coronado	UG16A	16.0	709	57
Frigidaire	UF-16N-L*1; UFS16N-W*1	16.0	709	57
General Electric	CA16DL-D	16.0	709	57
Gibson	FV16M4WSFE; FV16M6WVFC; FV16M8WWFC; FV16M9WXFA	16.0	709	57

TABLE 34

ENERGY-EFFICIENT FREEZERS *(continued)*

Brand	Model	Capacity (Cubic Ft.)	Annual Energy Use (kWh)	Annual Energy Cost ($)[a]
Hotpoint	FV16CL-D	16.0	709	57
Imperial	UG16A; UL1647ECW1	16.0	709	57
Kelvinator	USF160FM3W	16.0	709	57
Kenmore	20621; 20628; 20631; 20638	16.0	709	57
Marquette	UG16A	16.0	709	57
Montgomery Ward	FFT46159-0	16.0	709	57
Tappan	98-1668-002	16.0	709	57
White-Westinghouse	FU161LRW3	16.0	709	57
Storage Capacity: 19.0 to 21.2 cu. ft.				
Sun Frost[b]	F-19	19.0	456	37
Whirlpool	EV190F*S*0; EV190F*W*0	19.2	721	58
Frigidaire	UFS19N-L*1	19.3	734	59
General Electric	CA19DL-D	19.3	734	59
Gibson	FV19M2WVFC; FV19M8WWFC	19.3	734	59
Hotpoint	FV19CL-D	19.3	734	59
Imperial	UL2075ECW1	19.3	734	59
Kenmore	20938	19.3	734	59
Montgomery Ward	FFT49269-0	19.3	734	59
White-Westinghouse	FU196LRW3	19.3	734	59
Coronado	UG21A	21.2	771	62
Frigidaire	UF-21N-L*1	21.2	771	62
General Electric	CA21DL-D	21.2	771	62
Gibson	FV21M2WSF; FV21M8WSFE; FV21M9WXFA	21.2	771	62
Hotpoint	FV21CL-D	21.2	771	62
Imperial	UG21A; UL2164ECW1; UL2483ECW1	21.2	771	62
Kelvinator	UFP212FM3W	21.2	771	62
Marquette	UG21A	21.2	771	62
Montgomery Ward	FFT49669-0	21.2	771	62
Tappan	98-2188-002	21.2	771	62
White-Westinghouse	FU211LRW3; FU218LRW3	21.2	771	62
Wood's	*U60	20.9	796	64

Source: *1991 Consumer Guide to Home Energy Savings* (American Council for an Energy-Efficient Economy).

[a] Based on average use and electricity cost at 7.7¢ per kilowatt-hour.

[b] Information on these models is provided by the manufacturer and is based on a room air temperature of 70° F. For more information, contact Sun Frost, P.O. Box 1101, Arcata, CA 95521; (707) 822-9095.

*Different numbers may appear here to denote variations in decoration, color, or door swing.

LAUNDRY APPLIANCES
AND PRODUCTS

BLEACHES

All bleaches, both chlorine and nonchlorine, use oxidizing agents to remove stains from fabric. They differ greatly, however, in their strength, added ingredients, potential damage to fabrics, and environmental effects.

ENVIRONMENTAL PROBLEMS

Harmful ingredients. The active ingredients in commercial bleaches are potent, dangerous substances. Liquid chlorine bleaches contain sodium hypochlorite, which is toxic to swallow and a strong irritant. If mixed with other acidic or ammonia-based household cleaners, it can form deadly chlorine or chloramine gas. Most nonchlorine bleaches use sodium perborate or hydrogen peroxide, both less damaging to tissue than chlorine but still toxic to swallow. Using bleach in the laundry room provides many opportunities for accidental contact with eyes, skin, or mouth.

Unnecessary additives. Many nonchlorine bleaches contain extra ingredients such as water softeners, surfactants, processing aids, and perfumes. These chemicals are often either unnecessary or already in laundry detergents; their production requires additional resources and energy and their disposal complicates wastewater treatment.

Water pollution. Of the commercial bleaches only pure hydrogen peroxide, which breaks down quickly to hydrogen and oxygen, is relatively nonpolluting. Most commercial, multiple-ingredient laundry bleaches pollute wastewater with dissolved salts, surfactants, and other carbon compounds that require special treatment to remove. Some bleaches also use phosphates, which can disrupt water ecology by causing algae to proliferate. All these ingredients add to the substances wastewater treatment plants must either remove, if they can, or release downstream as water pollutants.

Animal cruelty. Because bleach ingredients are hazardous to humans, many manufacturers test them on animals, under inhumane conditions; afterward the animals are killed.

CHOOSING A PRODUCT

GENERAL GUIDELINES

Weighing your needs. Choose a bleach that matches the type of fabric and the degree of whitening, brightening, or disinfecting you need.

- Chlorine bleach, suitable only for certain white and light-colored fabrics, should be used only occasionally for whitening or disinfecting.

- All-fabric, nonchlorine bleach brightens colored fabrics and removes some stains. It also should be used only periodically.

- Avoid detergents with added bleach—they do not allow you to use bleach selectively.

Simple, less-toxic ingredients. When possible choose bleaches with simple ingredients and formulas; they are less hazardous and less polluting than more complex bleaches.

Cruelty-free products. Look for bleaches made by companies that do not test products on animals.

Sensible packaging. Whether you buy bleach in a paperboard box or a plastic jug, always select as large a container—and as concentrated a product—as practical, and recycle it if possible.

COMMERCIAL PRODUCTS

Simple, cruelty-free nonchlorine bleaches *(recommended)*. These products contain hydrogen peroxide with few additives. They can brighten colored fabrics, but they are not especially good for whitening and offer little disinfecting power beyond that of the detergent (which is adequate for most laundry needs). Winter White makes both a powdered bleach, which contains only sodium carbonate and peroxyhydrate, and a liquid bleach, which contains only detergent and hydrogen peroxide. Look for them in natural foods stores, co-ops, and some grocery stores, or order from A Clear Alternative, (713) 356-7031.

Simple, major-brand nonchlorine bleaches *(sometimes recommended)*. Clorox 2 Liquid Bleach, which contains only hydrogen peroxide as its active ingredient and propylene glycol as a processing aid, is probably the least polluting major-brand bleach. Clorox does test on animals, however.

Multiple-ingredient, major-brand nonchlorine bleaches *(not generally recommended)*. Most major-brand nonchlorine bleaches have very similar formulas to detergents, with surfactants, water softeners, enzymes, processing aids, and perfumes added to a bleaching agent, usually sodium perborate. These bleaches brighten colored fabrics and remove some stains, but do not excel at whitening fabrics. (Their strong formulas do add some disinfecting power, however.) Producing and disposing of these complex products causes environmental damage, so they should be used rarely, if at all. Phosphate-containing brands such as White Magic and Biz Bleach should be avoided altogether.

Chlorine bleaches *(not generally recommended)*. Chlorine-based bleaches usually contain sodium hypochlorite in water and do well at both whitening fabrics and disinfecting. Chlorine bleach is a harsh, toxic chemical, so use it only when you need to whiten and disinfect certain types of fabrics, such as white cotton or synthetic fabrics. To avoid fading, discoloration, and fiber damage, never use it on

- Colored fabrics of any kind

- Wool, silk, mohair, or alpaca

- Delicate clothing or fabrics

Always check the cleaning instructions for new clothing before using chlorine bleach.

ALTERNATIVES

Washing soda. If your detergent simply needs a booster, try adding plain sodium carbonate, widely available as Arm & Hammer Washing Soda, instead of powdered all-fabric bleach. (Be careful, however; washing soda can irritate the skin, eyes, and mucous membranes.)

Borax. Borax (sodium borate) can help brighten laundry and clean some stains; just add a small amount with your detergent. (But keep it away from your eyes, skin, and mucous membranes.)

WISE USE

Conservative use. Use all laundry bleaches sparingly and only when you need them for specific cleaning tasks.

Safe use. To prevent injuries when using bleaches, take the following precautions:

- Avoid getting bleach on your skin or in your eyes or mouth.

- Use chlorine bleach only in well-ventilated areas, to avoid harming your mucous membranes and lungs.

- *Never* mix chlorine bleach with any other household chemicals, such as window, toilet-bowl, or all-purpose cleaners. Mixing chlorine bleach with ammonia or acids can quickly produce deadly fumes.

Container recycling. Whether you use paperboard boxes or plastic bottles, recycle them if possible.

DETERGENTS, LAUNDRY

Detergents, because they rinse away without leaving the "scum" that soap often leaves on laundry, have become a huge industry—nearly 7 billion pounds are manufactured in the United States every year—with an equally huge environmental impact.[1]

ENVIRONMENTAL PROBLEMS

Water pollution. Several laundry-detergent ingredients are water pollutants:

- *Phosphates* soften water and boost a detergent's cleaning power. They are not completely removed by wastewater treatment plants, however, so they end up in downstream water. Though quickly broken up in fast-moving water, phosphates can severely damage the ecology of lakes, estuaries, and slow-moving rivers by serving as nutrients for algae, which proliferate and then die off, consuming oxygen needed for aquatic life. Many states have banned or limited phosphates, but they are still found in many commercial detergents.

- *Surfactants,* or surface active agents, are the main ingredients in detergents; they lift dirt off fabrics during the wash cycle. Older surfactants, called ABS or "hard" detergents, are not biodegradable and have been largely replaced in commercial detergents by LAS (linear alkyl sulfonate) and other surfactants, all petroleum derived. Although they do eventually break down, LAS surfactants still pollute wastewater with foam, mineral salts, and organic chemicals that require special wastewater treatment. If the chemicals are not broken down completely during wastewater treatment, they enter downstream water, where they continue to degrade, using up essential oxygen in the water as they do so.

- *Other ingredients,* such as enzymes, processing aids, stabilizers, bleaches, other whiteners and brighteners, perfumes, and colorants, add more mineral salts and organic chemicals to wastewater, burdening wastewater treatment facilities and polluting downstream water.

Unnecessary additives. Many ingredients commonly found in laundry detergents—fillers, bleaches, enzymes, perfumes, and colorants—are often unnecessary or only occasionally useful. They pollute water after disposal, and their production depletes nonrenewable petroleum and mineral reserves.

Safety hazards. Sodium carbonate, or washing soda, is a typical replacement for phosphate. Though less polluting, it is irritating to eyes, skin, and mucous membranes.

Animal cruelty. Because some ingredients can harm humans, manufacturers often test detergents on animals, under inhumane conditions; afterward the animals are killed.

Wasteful packaging. Some detergents come in small, single-use packets made of plastic or foil—an extraordinary waste of resources for such a minor convenience.

CHOOSING A PRODUCT

GENERAL GUIDELINES

Nonphosphate detergents. Read labels carefully to find detergents that contain no phosphates.

Appropriate surfactants. Choose a detergent with the right surfactants for your laundry needs. The three major types of surfactants have very different capabilities:

- *Anionic surfactants* remove dirt and soil, but not oils, from cotton, wool, silk, and linen; they need hot, "soft" water for best results and are high-sudsing.

TABLE 35

SIMPLE-INGREDIENT, CRUELTY-FREE NONPHOSPHATE LAUNDRY DETERGENTS

Brand	Type	Surfactant	Water Softener	Stabilizing Agents	Processing Agents	Bleaches, Whiteners	Perfumes, Colors
Allens Naturally	Liquid	■ A,N	O	O	■	O	O
Country Safe	Powder	■ N	?	?	?	■	O
Co-op	Powder	■ A,N	■	■	■	■	■
Earth's Choice	Liquid	■ A,N	■	■	■	■	■
Ecover	Liquid	■ A,N	■	■	■	O	✻
Ecover	Powder	■ A,N	■	■	■	■	✻
Keep America Clean	Liquid	■ A,N	?	?	?	O	✻
Lifeline	Liquid	■ A,N	O	O	■	O	✻
Life Tree	Liquid	■ A,N	O	O	✻	O	✻
Nu-Wash	Powder	■ A,N	■	■	■	■	■
Power Plus	Liquid	■ N	O	O	O	O	O
Professional	Liquid	?	■	?	■	?	?
Professional	Powder	■ N	■	?	■	?	?
Winter White	Liquid	■ A,N	O	O	■	O	✻
Winter White	Powder	?	■	■	■	■	■

✻ = Natural ingredient   O = None   ■ = Chemical   A = Anionic   N = Nonionic   ? = Not available

- *Nonionic surfactants* remove oily stains from synthetic fabrics, work in harder water, and are low-sudsing.

- *Cationic surfactants*, the most expensive, soften water as well as clean. They are also germicidal and should be used only when disinfecting is necessary.

Simple formulas. Avoid unnecessary additives in detergents; read labels carefully to see whether products contain nonessential bleaches, brighteners, perfumes, or colorants. (Bleaches and brighteners should always be added separately so you can use them selectively.)

Cruelty-free products. Look for detergents made by companies that do not test products on animals.

Sensible packaging. Choose a concentrated product in as large a container as practical—preferably a container you can recycle locally.

COMMERCIAL PRODUCTS

Simple-ingredient, cruelty-free nonphosphate detergents *(highly recommended).* Available in both liquids and powders, these detergents are free of unnecessary chemicals or use naturally derived substitutes. They are phosphate-free and not tested on animals. Table 35 lists some nationally distributed brands sold at grocery and natural foods stores and co-ops, and by mail order.

Major-brand nonphosphate detergents *(not generally recommended).* All major-brand liquid detergents are phosphate-free (phosphates cause stability problems in liquids); the phosphate content of powdered detergents varies. Different states permit different percentages of phosphates, so examine labels carefully before you buy. Most major-brand manufacturers stamp the boxes lightly with one of three codes: *0*, indicating 0.5 percent phosphate or less; *L*, for 0.5 to about 6.5 percent; or *P*, for 6.5 to about 8.0 percent. Look for those clearly labeled *non*phosphate. Most major brands also contain unnecessary ingredients and are tested on animals.

Phosphate detergents *(never recommended).* Not all lakes and streams are vulnerable to algae build-up from phosphate pollution, which is why phosphates are not banned nationwide. Unless you know where your wastewater goes and whether phosphates could cause damage, however, it is best to avoid them. Phosphates might not help much anyway: Consumers Union testing has found phosphate-containing detergents "only slightly more effective" than non-phosphate ones.[2]

DO-IT-YOURSELF

Soap. Mild soap cleans and rinses well if you have soft water. (Soaps also pollute water, however, so the simpler the better.) Try this formula for detergent-free washing:

■ Let the machine fill with water. Pour ⅓ cup washing soda (sodium carbonate) into the water and let it dissolve, add the clothes, and pour in 1½ cups of soap flakes or liquid soap (less if it's concentrated).

■ With harder water, add ¼ cup vinegar during the first rinse.

■ Fabrics washed previously in detergents will have a residue you must remove before washing in soap: just run the laundry through a regular wash cycle using ¼ cup washing soda to remove the residue.

■ The most popular brand of soap flakes, Ivory Snow, is not pure soap; it also contains a fabric whitener and a perfume, and its manufacturer, Proctor & Gamble, tests on animals. Look instead for concentrated pure castile or coconut-oil soaps sold in bulk at natural foods stores and co-ops, or order Suds Soap from Ecco Bella, (201) 226-5799.

WISE USE

Conservative use. Carefully measure the detergent for each washload, following the manufacturer's instructions. If clothing is badly soiled, pretreat it with a little detergent or stain remover rather than adding extra detergent to the entire wash (see Stain Removers, p. 210).

Safe use. Keep all detergents away from your eyes, mouth, and skin. Make sure liquid detergents, which can accidentally squirt into one's eyes, are kept out of childrens' reach.

Container recycling. Whether you use paperboard boxes or plastic bottles, recycle them if possible.

1. *1989 U.S. Industrial Outlook* (Department of Commerce, 1989), p. 15-1.
2. *1989 Buying Guide Issue* (Consumers Union, 1988), p. 78.

DRY CLEANERS

Some fabrics that can't be washed easily or safely with water and detergent are "dry" cleaned instead with chemical solvents and detergents. This process cleans well but seriously pollutes the air.

ENVIRONMENTAL PROBLEMS

Air pollution. All the major dry-cleaning solvents—perchloroethylene, trichloroethylene, naphtha, Stoddard solvent—are made from petrochemicals through complex distillation processes, then transported to users in barrels. Highly reactive, these hydrocarbon-based solvents emit fumes during their manufacture and use and contribute greatly to air pollution, especially ozone formation. (Although ozone high in the stratosphere shields the earth from lethal solar radiation, it is a serious pollutant near ground level.)

Health hazards. The solvents pose health risks directly to people who work with them and indirectly to the population at large. Both trichloroethylene, a suspected carcinogen, and perchloroethylene, an irritant to eyes and skin, are just as toxic as carbon monoxide.[1] The ozone pollution to which dry-cleaning solvents contribute also has health effects: it impairs lung function, especially during exercise and in children.[2]

Wasteful packaging. The superthin polyethylene bags in which dry cleaners encase clothing are an example of resource waste: their useful lifetime is only a few hours; they can't be reused for any other purpose; and they are extremely difficult to recycle.

CHOOSING A PRODUCT

GENERAL GUIDELINES

Washable fabrics. Avoid buying fabrics that require dry cleaning. Instead, choose natural fabrics that can be machine washed on a gentle cycle, then ironed or steam pressed.

Alternative cleaning methods. Even fabrics that can't be easily machine washed need not necessarily be dry cleaned. Try commercial laundries, gentle-cycle machine washing, or hand washing (see Alternatives section).

COMMERCIAL SERVICES

Low-polluting dry cleaners *(sometimes recommended).* All current dry-cleaning methods use petrochemical solvents, so none is environmentally sound. If you must use a dry cleaner, however, look for one that advertises that it is non- or low-air-polluting, indicating that it has installed pollution-control equipment.

Traditional dry cleaners *(never recommended).* If possible, avoid dry cleaners that have not installed pollution-control equipment.

ALTERNATIVES

Stain removal. You can reduce the frequency of dry cleanings by spot-cleaning stains on otherwise unsoiled fabrics (see Stain Removers, p. 210).

Commercial laundries. Look for a high-quality laundry that hand washes or delicately machine washes fine fabrics; ask their advice about tailored clothing or other special items.

Hand washing. Many delicate fabrics can be hand washed instead of dry cleaned. Try hand washing bulky items (such as drapes) yourself, letting them dry, then taking them to a laundry or dry cleaner for steam pressing. Check garments' care labels for washing advice; here are some general guidelines:

- *Acetate.* Soak in warm water that contains dissolved soap or laundry detergent. Squeeze gently, rinse in lukewarm water, and air dry without clothespins.

- *Acrylic.* Dissolve nonionic-surfactant laundry detergent (see Detergents, Laundry, p. 204) in warm water, and soak garments. Do not rub or wring. Rinse in lukewarm water and air dry.

- *Cotton.* Same procedure as for acetate; iron while still damp.

- *Polyester.* Same procedure as for acrylic.

- *Rayon.* Same procedure as for acetate; iron while still damp.

- *Silk.* Soak in cold water with a mild soap (such as castile or coconut-oil soap) or dishwashing detergent, with a little vinegar. Do not rub or wring; instead, rinse with cold water and use a towel to absorb water. Air dry without clothespins.

- *Wool.* Use lukewarm water with either mild soap and a little vinegar or dishwashing detergent. Soak, then drain off water, handling item gently. Rinse twice in lukewarm water. "Block" or reshape damp garment to its original size and air dry on a towel.

Machine washing. Do not use regular laundry detergents on delicate fabrics; many contain enzymes that attack the protein in fabrics such as wool and silk. Most detergents are also too alkaline, damaging fibers over time. Instead, use delicate-fabric detergents—for example, Cool Wash (made by Winter White, with no animal testing) or major brands such as Delicare or A&P Wool Wash (Woolite is too alkaline). Always use the gentle cycle and keep the water temperature lukewarm or cool.

Machine drying. To dry fine fabrics in a dryer, keep the heat at 110° F or less. Use the shortest cycle possible to minimize wear and tear.

1. N. Irving Sax and Richard J. Lewis, Sr., eds., *Hawley's Condensed Chemical Dictionary,* 11th ed. (Van Nostrand Reinhold, 1987), pp. 886, 1176.
2. *Air Quality Management Plan* (Southern California Association of Governments, 1989), pp. 1–4.

DRYERS, CLOTHES

Two-thirds of American households have a clothes dryer, making it the third most popular appliance (after refrigerators and washing machines).[1] Unfortunately, most dryers are heated inefficiently with electricity rather than with gas.

ENVIRONMENTAL PROBLEMS

Energy consumption. Electricity is the most wasteful (and usually the most expensive) fuel for heating any appliance because of the many steps necessary to generate and transmit it; inefficiency and energy losses occur at every step. Using natural gas to heat appliances is far more efficient. Here's a simple comparison: drying 10 pounds of laundry requires about 10,000 British thermal units (Btu, a basic measure of heat). To supply 10,000 Btu a gas dryer burns 10 to 15 cubic feet of gas, whereas an electric dryer uses up to 3 kilowatt-hours of electricity, which would require *30* cubic feet of gas to generate.[2] With 44 million electric dryers in use,[3] the total wasted gas equals 10 percent of all the natural gas burned to generate electricity in the United States each year.[4]

Pipeline hazards. Natural gas pipelines disrupt natural habitats, both during and after their construction, and present a constant danger of leaks, explosions, and fires.

Safety hazards. With gas dryers, the pipelines that bring gas into your home present a danger of leaking fumes, explosions, and fire.

CHOOSING A PRODUCT

GENERAL GUIDELINES

Energy efficiency. If natural gas is available in your area, consider a gas dryer instead of an electric one. You'll save money as well as energy and recover the difference in purchase price in as little as a year. But no matter whether you buy gas or electric, make energy efficiency a top priority. EnergyGuide labels are not required for dryers, so look for the specific, energy-saving features described below.

COMMERCIAL PRODUCTS

Moisture-sensing gas dryers *(highly recommended)*. For top energy efficiency, look for a gas dryer with a moisture sensor, often available on higher-quality models. Not to be confused with the less-efficient temperature sensor, a moisture sensor actually monitors the laundry's dampness and shuts the dryer off when the laundry is dry. Manufacturers use many different terms for both moisture and temperature sensors, so ask salespeople and check product literature for details and for current model numbers, which change continually. Moisture-sensing cycles use about 15 percent less energy than timed cycles. General Electric, Maytag, Sears, and Whirlpool all make gas dryers with moisture sensors.

Temperature-sensing gas dryers *(recommended)*. These dryers have sensors that measure the exhaust air temperature to determine when clothes are dry. Cheaper and less efficient than moisture sensors, but more common, temperature sensors save 5 to 10 percent of the energy used in a timed cycle.

Moisture-sensing electric dryers *(sometimes recommended)*. If natural gas is not available or practical, get an electric dryer equipped with a moisture sensor (see description in Moisture-sensing gas dryers, above). General Electric, KitchenAid, Maytag, Sears, and Whirlpool all make electric dryers with moisture sensors.

Temperature-sensing electric dryers *(never recommended)*. These dryers are cheaper to buy than moisture-sensing dryers, but they use so much electricity that their operating costs far surpass those of a more efficient machine.

ALTERNATIVES

Air drying. For small loads skip the dryer altogether and use a drying rack instead. Drying racks fold up for easy storage and can dry lighter fabrics overnight, using no energy. Consider using a clothesline, outdoors during warm weather and indoors year-round. Vermont Country Store sells heavy-duty retractable clotheslines and several types of drying racks; (802) 362-2400.

WISE USE

Proper installation. To ensure efficient, safe operation, make sure your dryer is correctly installed:

- Install it in a heated part of your house to conserve energy.

- If you have gas service—natural, liquified petroleum, or propane—make sure you get a dryer that burns the right kind.

- An electric dryer draws a lot of electricity; make sure it's correctly wired and on an adequate circuit.

- Both gas and electric dryers should be vented outdoors, despite the temptation to capture the warm, moist air during cold weather. Exhaust fumes from gas dryers vented indoors can be toxic; those from electric dryers can cause particulate pollution. The vents should be of rigid, straight, metal tubing that doesn't trap heat or allow lint to build up (accumulated lint can cause the dryer to overheat, seriously damaging it).

Energy-efficient use. Make sure you use your dryer as efficiently as possible:

- Don't mix light and heavy clothing in the same load; the machine will keep running until the heavy items are dry.

- Keep the lint filter clean.

- Check the vent occasionally for lint buildup.

Safe use. To operate your dryer safely, remember the following points:

- If you start getting frequent headaches, notice a slight exhaust odor, or have any other reason to suspect your gas dryer is not venting properly, call a service contractor immediately to check it.

- If you suspect a minor gas leak, check by pouring a small amount of soapy water around each joint; bubbles indicate a leak. If you can't track it down, call the gas company for assistance.

- If you smell a strong gas odor, leave the house *immediately* (don't create a spark by turning on a light or dialing your phone) and call the gas company or fire department.

1. "Major Appliance Industry Facts Book, 1988 Data Supplement" (Association of Home Appliance Manufacturers, 20 N. Wacker Dr., Chicago, IL 60606), p. 5.
2. Based on calculations from "Energy Facts 1987" (Energy Information Administration, Department of Energy, Forrestal Bldg., EI-231, Washington, DC 20585), p. 54.
3. "Major Appliance Industry Facts Book," op. cit., p. 29.
4. "Energy Facts 1987," op. cit., p. 24.

STAIN REMOVERS

Stain removers are handy for spot-cleaning clothing and fabric, but the toxic petrochemicals used in some products are environmentally destructive.

ENVIRONMENTAL PROBLEMS

Harmful ingredients. Many stain removers contain the following solvents, all made from petroleum:

- *Stoddard solvent*, *naphtha*, and *toluene* are toxic, flammable air pollutants.

- *Perchloroethylene*, a chlorinated hydrocarbon, is an eye and skin irritant and an air pollutant.

- *1,1,1-trichloroethane* (methyl chloroform) is an eye and skin irritant, an air pollutant, and an ozone-depleting chemical.

Animal cruelty. Because some ingredients can harm humans, many manufacturers test stain removers on animals, under inhumane conditions; afterward the animals are killed.

Wasteful packaging. Some spot cleaners come in aerosol spray cans, which are costly to manufacture, polluting to use, and nonrecyclable.

CHOOSING A PRODUCT

GENERAL GUIDELINES

Appropriate removal methods. Make sure you know what a specific stain is and how to remove it. Different stains require different methods of treatment; you can actually make some worse by using the wrong removal method.

Nontoxic remedies. Try nontoxic methods and products before turning to harsh, environmentally destructive chemicals.

Cruelty-free products. Look for stain removers made by companies that do not test products on animals.

Sensible packaging. Avoid any product packaged in an aerosol can. Instead, choose liquids or manual-pump sprays.

COMMERCIAL PRODUCTS

Cruelty-free, nontoxic chemical stain removers *(recommended).* Some manufacturers make stain removers that are effective, yet contain no petrochemical solvents. The following are also cruelty-free:

- Granny's Soil Away; order from The Allergy Store, (800) 950-6202

- Winter White Liquid Pre-Spot; order from A Clear Alternative, (713) 356-7031

Toxic chemical stain removers *(not generally recommended).* These solvent-containing products are hazardous and polluting and should be used only as a last resort. *Never* use stain removers containing 1,1,1-trichloroethane: Carbo Chlor Spot Remover, Carbona Spot Lift, Carbona Spot Remover, Dyo Spot Remover, Energine Cleaning Fluid, Tectron Tie Cleaner, Texize K2r Spotlifter, Tru-Test Solvent Spotter.

DO-IT-YOURSELF

Less-toxic removal methods. Below is a list of some common stains, and natural or less-toxic methods for removing them. Try the first method listed; if it doesn't work, go on to the next. Always treat stains as soon as possible.

- *Blood:*
  1. Soak in cold water and rinse.
  2. Rub with a paste of cornstarch and cold water.
  3. Use mild soap or hydrogen peroxide (hydrogen peroxide bleaches clothes; test an inconspicuous spot for color-fastness first).
  4. Soak in borax and cold water.

- *Chocolate:*
  1. Soak in cold water, then wash in a mild soap-and-water solution.

2. Soak in borax and cold water.
3. Soak in bleach and cold water (test an inconspicuous spot for color-fastness first).

- *Coffee:*
  1. Soak in cold water, then in hot water.
  2. Rub with a mixture of egg yolk and lukewarm water.
  3. Soak in borax and cold water.

- *Egg, cream, or milk:*
  1. Soak in cold water, then rinse.
  2. Soak in mild soap with cold water.

- *Fruit, fruit juice, or wine:*
  1. Pour salt on stain.
  2. Pour boiling water on stain.
  3. Soak in milk, then wash.

- *Grass:*
  1. Soak in mild soap and cold water.
  2. Pour on a mixture of isopropyl alcohol (70 percent) and cold water.
  3. Pour on a small amount of turpentine, then rinse immediately and thoroughly in cold water.

- *Grease:*
  1. Soak in warm or hot water with mild soap.
  2. Add dry baking soda after soaking.
  3. Soak in cold water, then in milk.
  4. Squeeze on lemon juice.
  5. Pour on a small amount of hydrogen peroxide (test fabric for color-fastness first).
  6. Pour on a 50/50 mixture of ammonia and water.

- *Ink:*
  1. Pour on cold water, apply a paste of lemon juice and cream of tartar, let dry for an hour, then wash.

- *Lipstick:*
  1. Rub on shortening or cold cream, then wash with sodium carbonate (washing soda).

- *Mildew:*
  1. Soak in cold water, then pour on a mixture of strong soap and salt, place in sunlight, and repeat if necessary.

■ *Mud and soil:*
   1. Soak in borax and cold water, then wash.
   2. Rub with solution of 1 tablespoon sodium carbonate (washing soda) in 1 cup warm water.

■ *Paint:*
   1. For latex, soak in warm water and soap.
   2. For alkyd enamel, pour on mixture of water and isopropyl alcohol (70 percent), then rinse.

■ *Perspiration:*
   1. Rub on solution of lemon juice or white vinegar and water.

■ *Rust:*
   1. Pour on lemon juice, then rub with salt and dry in sunlight.

■ *Scorches:*
   1. Boil scorched area in mixture of milk and soap.

■ *Tea:*
   1. Pour on boiling water, then wash.

■ *Urine:*
   1. Rub on solution of baking soda and water, rinse in warm water, then wash.

■ *Wax:*
   1. Scrape off wax, and heat stain with warm iron through blotting paper (paper towels or tissue).
   2. Pour on isopropyl alcohol (70 percent).

WISE USE

Prompt treatment. Always treat a stain as soon as possible, before it sets permanently.

Safe use. If you must use chemical products, follow the manufacturers' instructions to the letter; many products are flammable as well as toxic.

Proper disposal. *Never* throw any solvent-based product in the trash or pour it on the ground or down a drain. Instead, store it safely for a hazardous waste collection, or take it to a collection site. Call your local waste disposal office for information on hazardous waste collection programs. Be sure any aerosol cans are empty of pressure before throwing them away.

WASHING MACHINES

Washing machines are found in about 70 percent of American households, making them second only to refrigerators in popularity. Most of the 60 million machines in use, however, are energy-wasting top-loading machines rather than more efficient front-loaders.[1]

ENVIRONMENTAL PROBLEMS

Energy consumption. About 90 percent of the energy used by a washer goes toward heating the water, so a machine's efficiency is measured by how much water it uses to clean a load of laundry. Producing the energy needed yearly to run an average top-loading washer four times a week, using water supplied by an electric water heater, releases roughly 1,500 pounds of carbon dioxide, the greenhouse gas, and 12 pounds of sulfur dioxide, a serious air pollutant that causes acid rain.[2]

Water use and pollution. Washers use large amounts of water and detergent, depleting water reserves and increasing demands on water treatment facilities. A top-loader uses 35 to 45 gallons of water for a regular cycle and an extra 5 to 10 gallons for a permanent press cycle. The more water the machine uses, the more detergent it needs, even for the same amount of laundry. The extra detergent aggravates one of our nation's most severe water pollution problems—treating the nearly 7 billion pounds of laundry detergent rinsed down the drain every year.[3]

CHOOSING A PRODUCT

GENERAL GUIDELINES

Weighing your needs. If yours is a small household, you might not need a standard-sized washer; many energy-efficient compacts are now available.

Water and energy efficiency. Look for a machine that will meet your needs but use as little water and energy as possible. EnergyGuide labels required on all machines show their average yearly operating costs and make it easy to compare different models. Look for the following water-, energy-, and pollution-saving features on both front- and top-loading washers:

- *A water-level control* adjusts the amount of water for small, medium, and large loads; some models have a continuous control that lets you pick any level.

- *A water-temperature control* gives you multiple options for using cold, warm, or hot water during different cycles, letting you pick the best temperatures for each load.

- *A "save" feature* allows you to save and reuse lightly soiled wash water if you have a double laundry sink.

- *A speed control* lets you pick the machine's agitation and spin speeds. High-speed spinning extracts more water, saving drying time.

COMMERCIAL PRODUCTS

Front loaders *(highly recommended).* Front-loading tumblers have slightly smaller capacities than top-loading agitators but work well except for very large loads. They do not fill with water (nor do they beat the laundry to clean it), saving at least half the hot water a top loader would use. Front loaders also use 25 to 50 percent less detergent. One American manufacturer, White Consolidated Industries, makes high-quality front loaders sold by Gibson, Sears, and White-Westinghouse (see Table 36). AEG, a German company, makes three expensive but high-quality front-loading models sold by Andi-Co Appliances in New Jersey, (201) 225-8837.

Compact top loaders *(recommended).* Compact washers, which have capacities of 16 gallons or less, are available only as top loaders, but make sense for small households with little space. They are 10 to 20 percent more water-

TABLE 36

ENERGY-EFFICIENT WASHING MACHINES

Manufacturer	Model	Annual Energy Use (kWh)	Annual Energy Cost ($)[a]
Standard Front-Loading Machines (over 16-gallon capacity)			
Gibson	WS 27 M6-V	286	22
Sears, Roebuck	4988	286	22
White-Westinghouse	LT250L; LT700L; LT800L; LT150L	286	22
Compact Top-Loading Machines (less than 16-gallon capacity)			
General Electric	118	649	50
Kelvinator	AW1201	649	50
Philco	C6M2	649	50
White-Westinghouse	550	649	50
Montgomery Ward	6009	675	50
Frigidaire	441	688	53
	462; LC120; LC248	688	53
Gibson	24F2; 24F4	688	53
Magic Chef	L10A	688	53
Philco	44-2409	688	53
Tappan	44-2408; 44-2409	688	53
White-Westinghouse	SM115; SM230	688	53
Standard Top-Loading Machines (over 16-gallon capacity)			
Frigidaire	WL	675	52
White-Westinghouse	LA271	675	52
Maytag	A212ST	678	52
	A10*T	836	64
	A112T; A183T; A190T; A21*T; A28*T; A312T	840	65
	A512ST; A612ST	853	66
Amana	LWD553	857	66
Kelvinator	701; AW700	857	66
Tappan	46-28*0	857	66
Whirlpool	26186*1; 2619211; 2619501; 2624271	870	67

Source: *1991 Consumer Guide to Home Energy Savings* (The American Council for an Energy-Efficient Economy).

[a] Based on average use and electricity cost at 7.7¢ per kilowatt-hour.

*Different numbers may appear here to denote differences in decoration or color.

and energy-efficient than larger top loaders; Table 36 lists the most efficient models.

Standard top loaders *(not generally recommended)*. The top-loading washer, though it is convenient to use and has a large capacity, also has an inefficient design. Its deep tank must completely fill with water twice (once to wash, once to rinse), and the agitator blades pummel the laundry. See Table 36 for the most efficient models available.

ALTERNATIVES

Wringer washers. The Speed Queen, the original washing machine, with its power wringer over the tub to extract rinse water, is still available and quite efficient. For information call the Real Goods Trading Company, (800) 762-7325.

WISE USE

Proper installation. To ensure efficient, safe operation, make sure your washer is correctly installed:

- Avoid installing it in an unheated space, to prevent damage during cold weather.

- Install the machine as close to the hot water heater as possible to minimize heat loss from the hot water pipes. Insulate the pipes to further reduce heat loss.

- Be sure the machine is level and that all electrical and water connections are secure.

Regular maintenance. Prevent problems by keeping your washer in good working order:

- Clean the lint filter as recommended by the manufacturer.

- Wash the machine itself, empty, with 1 cup of white vinegar in cold water. Monthly cleaning removes buildups of minerals and chemicals left by detergents in the pipes, tubing, and moving parts.

Energy-efficient use. Maximize your energy savings by taking the following measures:

- Try washing with cold water, using a detergent designed for cold-water or all-temperature wash (Ecover and Winter White are all-temperature products). With top loaders, sprinkle the detergent into the wash water after the machine is filled and agitating to prevent the detergent from clumping.

- Always rinse with cold water; it rinses better than warm or hot water and saves energy.

FOR FURTHER INFORMATION: *1991 Consumer Guide to Home Energy Savings,* by Alex Wilson; American Council for an Energy-Efficient Economy, 1990.

1. "Major Appliance Industry Facts Book" (Association of Home Appliance Manufacturers, 20 N. Wacker Dr., Chicago, IL 60606) 1987, p. 29.
2. "Washing Machines," *Consumer Reports* (March 1989), p. 190; "Nucleus" (Union of Concerned Scientists, 26 Church St., Cambridge, MA 02138), p. 5; World Resources Institute, *World Resources 1988–89* (Basic Books, 1988), p. 164.
3. *1989 U.S. Industrial Outlook* (Department of Commerce, 1989), p. 15-1.

MISCELLANEOUS
HOUSEHOLD
PRODUCTS

BATTERIES, HOUSEHOLD

Household batteries have become a familiar part of our American lifestyle; each year we buy 3 billion to run flashlights, tape players, cameras, and dozens of other consumer goods.[1] The manufacture and disposal of batteries, however, takes a terrible toll on the environment.

ENVIRONMENTAL PROBLEMS

Manufacturing impacts. A typical zinc-carbon flashlight battery is composed of the following parts:

- *Zinc*, the negative electrode; made by roasting ores and using electrolysis or distillation

- *Compressed carbon* or *graphite*, the positive electrode; made from petroleum through a series of industrial processes

- *Manganese dioxide*, the depolarizer; made either through electrolysis or by heating manganese oxide

- *Ammonium chloride paste*, the electrolyte; often mined from deposits in the western United States

The steps required to bring you batteries—extracting and processing the raw materials, forming them into metal-clad batteries, charging and packaging them, and transporting them to your local store—use energy and cause many forms of pollution, just to deliver a tiny amount of electricity.

Hazardous wastes. Because it's made with toxic heavy metals such as zinc, manganese, lithium, nickel, cadmium, or mercury, the household battery presents a formidable waste disposal problem. The heavy metals are basic elements that can never be broken down or made nontoxic. When its useful life—often a few hours or less—is finished, the battery will likely end up either in a landfill, where its metals

can leach into groundwater, or in an incinerator, where it will add toxic metals to airborne emissions and ash. Theoretically, household batteries can be recycled, but because they are difficult to sort and collect in bulk and their different metals must be processed separately, they are rarely recycled in practice.

Wasteful packaging. Many batteries are sold in oversized, mixed-materials packages that waste paper and plastic and are extremely difficult to recycle.

CHOOSING A PRODUCT

GENERAL GUIDELINES

Weighing your needs. Though not suitable for all purposes, rechargeable batteries can often substitute for disposables, with less ecological damage. Your choice of battery depends on your need:

- For high-power devices such as tape players and toys, rechargeable batteries work well. A single charge cannot deliver the same length of use as does a disposable, so rechargeables are best suited to devices where the battery is easy to remove and recharge.

- For devices that are difficult to access and might remain unused for long periods of time, such as flashlights, smoke alarms, and garage-door openers, disposable batteries are usually necessary, because rechargeable batteries lose about 1 percent of their capacity every day and self-discharge in about 90 days.

COMMERCIAL PRODUCTS

Rechargeable batteries *(recommended)*. Even though they are made from nickel and cadmium, which are toxic, carcinogenic heavy metals, rechargeable batteries still reduce toxic wastes and save money. Battery-recycling programs are rare, so increasing use of rechargeable batteries is causing levels of nickel and cadmium in the wastestream to skyrocket. One rechargeable battery, however, replaces 65 to

TABLE 37

BATTERY CHARGERS
For Use with Nickel-Cadmium Rechargeable Batteries

Brand	Method	Battery Capacity	Recharge Time
SunWatt[a]	Solar	6 AA *or* 3 C and 2 D	1 to 2 days sunlight
Eveready (quick charger)	Electric	2 to 10 AAA, AA, C, or D *or* 1 to 4 9-volt	1 to 7 hours
General Electric (small size)	Electric	2 AAA, AA, C, or D *or* 1 9-volt	8 to 16 hours
General Electric (medium size)	Electric	2 to 4 AAA, AA, C, or D *or* 1 to 2 9-volt	8 to 16 hours
General Electric (large size)	Electric	2 to 8 AAA, AA, C, or D *or* 1 to 2 9-volt	8 to 16 hours
General Electric (quick charger)	Electric	Up to 8 AAA, AA, C, or D *or* 1 9-volt	1 hour

[a] Can be ordered from Co-op America, (802) 658-5507.

150 alkaline and even more zinc-carbon throw-aways, all of which contain heavy metals. Rechargeables save money, too: General Electric calculates that someone who uses 75 AA disposable batteries a year would save $321.50 over a four-year period by using rechargeables.[2] Nickel-cadmium batteries require a special charger that plugs into any wall socket and, depending on the model, recharges them in 1 to 16 hours (a solar model is also available). See Table 37 for makes and models of chargers.

Rechargeable flashlights (recommended). These flashlights each contain a large, long-life nickel-cadmium battery and a recharging unit that plugs into an electrical outlet. The large size of the internal battery makes its useful life much longer than those of regular rechargeable batteries. Some rechargeable flashlights are available nationwide:

♦ Black & Decker Spotlighter

♦ Brinkmann Home/Auto Rechargeable Light

♦ First Alert Rechargeable Lantern

♦ First Alert Rechargeable Work Light

♦ First Alert Rechargeable Flashlight

Disposable batteries (not generally recommended). These products are wasteful and polluting. If you must use them, make sure you choose the best type for your needs:

■ *Zinc-carbon* batteries are the standard, most inexpensive type. They come in most sizes except button-shaped, and in both regular and heavy-duty strength. Regular are for items such as remote controls; heavy-duty are best for clocks and photoflash equipment.

■ *Alkaline* batteries are much more expensive than zinc-carbon, but deliver higher power and have four to five times the shelf life. They are your best choice for smoke alarms and emergency flashlights.

■ *Lithium* batteries, long used in cameras, are now also available in AA size. Their maker, Eveready, claims they have twice the power and shelf life of alkaline AA batteries at less than twice the price.

■ *Button-shaped* batteries, used for calculators, watches, and other very low-power devices, are often made with mercury or silver. Choose

219

silver oxide when possible; their average useful life is 15 to 20 percent longer than that of mercuric oxide batteries. Real Goods Trading Co., (800) 762-7325, now offers a solar charger for button-type batteries. The small, lightweight unit can be attached to a window with a suction cup; it recharges in two to six hours.

ALTERNATIVES

Non-battery-powered items. The best way to avoid using toxic, disposable batteries is to buy items that don't require them:

- Calculators—solar-powered, light-powered, or electric (see Calculators, p. 223)

- Cameras—manually wound film and controls

- Clocks—wind-up or electric

- Smoke detectors—hard-wired (safer than battery-run smoke detectors, which can fail due to dead batteries)

- Toys—wind-up or otherwise human-powered

- Watches—wind-up, self-winding, or light-powered

WISE USE

Proper use. To get the maximum from batteries, follow these guidelines:

- Use batteries sparingly, regardless of type.

- Never mix different types of batteries (for example, alkaline with zinc-carbon) or new batteries with old.

- Use wall-socket adapters instead of batteries to run devices whenever possible.

- Before discarding a "dead" battery, make sure it is really dead and not just dislodged from the terminals.

- Since rechargeables lose their charge even when not in use, be sure to put them only in products that do not require a long-life charge.

Battery recharging. Follow the manufacturer's instructions for recharging carefully. It is best to wait until a battery is completely drained before recharging it; otherwise it might not be able to draw on power below the partial charge level it had previously drained to.

Recycling and disposal. Ask your local waste disposal office about what to do with batteries. You might be able to recycle some batteries in your area, particularly mercury or silver-based button batteries. One New York company, Mercury Refining Co., (800) 833-3505, accepts all types of household batteries and recycles those with mercury, silver, or nickel-cadmium. The company also consults with local community groups and agencies on battery recycling programs.

When disposing of batteries, treat them as hazardous waste—don't discard them with your regular trash; instead, save them for hazardous waste collection or take them to a collection site.

1. Matthew L. Wald, "Improving Batteries: Big Hurdles," *New York Times* (June 14, 1989).
2. "Rechargeable Batteries" (General Electric, Nela Park, Cleveland, OH 44112).

BLANKETS AND COMFORTERS

Blankets and comforters not only keep us warm at night, they also permit us to turn down our thermostats and save energy. Most blankets and comforters work by retaining our own body heat, but electric blankets add heat instead, using energy and creating health hazards.

ENVIRONMENTAL PROBLEMS

Health hazards. Studies of electric blankets have revealed an increased risk of cancer in children whose mothers slept under the blankets during early pregnancy. Some researchers have suggested that the blankets' mild electromagnetic fields—to which users are exposed for long periods and at close proximity—are responsible.[1]

Safety hazards. On an average of every three days, somewhere in the United States electric blankets cause a fire because of faulty manufacturing or misuse.[2]

Wasteful use of resources. Electric blankets waste energy, especially since electricity is the most inefficient source of heating energy. Both electric and nonelectric blankets are often made of synthetic fabrics derived from nonrenewable petroleum.

CHOOSING A PRODUCT

GENERAL GUIDELINES

Weighing your needs. Choose a blanket that is light and supple, yet warm enough to keep you comfortable at your bedroom's average nighttime temperature. It should also be easy to clean, needing only machine or hand washing instead of dry cleaning.

Natural-fiber products. Instead of electric blankets, look for well-made, natural-fiber blankets and comforters that keep you warm while using no energy.

Quality and longevity. High-quality blankets and comforters are the warmest, most comfortable, and longest-lasting. Both blankets and comforters should be well-stitched, evenly woven, and made of durable fabric. The best comforters are stitched in a quilted (karo) pattern that keeps the fill fluffy and evenly distributed.

COMMERCIAL PRODUCTS

Cotton blankets *(highly recommended).* Cotton blankets are sturdy, comfortable, and suitable for use in all but the coldest temperatures. Easy to machine wash and dry, cotton is ideal for people with allergies or chemical sensitivities. (Multiple washings remove residues of dyes or agricultural chemicals.)

Wool blankets *(recommended).* Wool is a better insulator than cotton, so wool blankets are excellent for cold temperatures. You might need to use several layers, however, to equal a comforter's warmth, and the heaviness of the layers might get uncomfortable. The process of raising and shearing sheep has a greater environmental impact than growing cotton does, and many wool blankets must be dry cleaned, causing air pollution. Look for machine-washable blankets whenever possible.

Natural-fill comforters *(sometimes recommended).* Among all the materials used as fill, the warmest by far is down, the superlight fluff from geese or ducks (or sometimes chickens or turkeys). Other natural fills are mixtures of down and feathers, silk, or lamb's wool; they are warm, but heavier than pure down. Unfortunately, down is collected by either killing the animals or plucking them and leaving them to live a miserable existence until they are slaughtered for meat. Eiderdown comforters, the warmest of all, are now scarce and unaffordable because the eider duck has become an endangered species. Cotton comforter covers are a slightly better choice than durable but petroleum-derived polyester covers.

Synthetic-fiber comforters *(sometimes recommended)*. Though not as warm as down, polyester fill performs well and lasts a long time. The warmest polyester fibers have hollow cores; their tradenames are Hollofil II, Quallofil, and Kodofil. Cotton comforter covers are a slightly better choice than durable but petroleum-derived polyester covers.

Synthetic-fiber blankets *(not generally recommended)*. Synthetic blankets, which are usually made of polyester, are inexpensive, reasonably warm, and long-lasting. They have no great advantages over wool or cotton, however, that would offset the disadvantages of their petrochemical origin. If you do purchase a synthetic blanket, make sure it's machine washable.

Electric blankets *(never recommended)*. There is nothing environmentally sound or practical about electric blankets; down or fiberfill comforters are just as warm and use no energy.

WISE USE

Safe use. If you must use an electric blanket, take the following precautions:

- Keep the blanket flat, unfolded, and uncovered when it's in use.

- Never sit or lie on the blanket when it's in use.

- Watch for signs of wear and tear that could break or expose wires.

- Do not dry clean the blanket; the solvents could damage the wiring.

- Pregnant women and children should avoid using electric blankets unless further research proves them safe.

Regular cleaning. Keep all blankets and comforters clean to avoid the buildup of dust, dust mites, or mold.

FOR FURTHER INFORMATION: "Keeping Warm in Bed," *Consumer Reports* (November 1989), pp. 706-716.

1. "EPA Suspects ELF Fields Can Cause Cancer," *Science News* (June 30, 1990), p. 405.
2. "Electric Blankets and Mattress Pads," *Consumer Reports* (November 1989), p. 712.

TABLE
38

LIGHT-POWERED CALCULATORS

Brand	Model	Number of Functions[a]	Battery Also?
Casio	JW-8M	5	Yes
	SL-100W	5	No
	HS-8G	6	No
	FX-451M	132	Yes
	FX-115N	154	Yes
Ima	LC-672; LC-70H	6	Yes
	LC-900	6	No
Royal	CBC 80	5	Yes
Sharp	EL-24313	6	No
Texas Instruments	TI 307	5	No
	TI 1706 III; TI 1768; TI 1795	6	No
	TI 36	89	No

[a] First six functions: add, subtract, multiply, divide, percentage, square root.

CALCULATORS

Solid-state circuitry and silicon chips have made possible today's fast, tiny, and amazingly cheap calculators—some of which are more environmentally sound than others.

ENVIRONMENTAL PROBLEMS

Hazardous wastes. Modern calculators are small and require very little power, but many still use batteries. Usually made of zinc or mercury, batteries are toxic, very difficult to recycle, and hazardous to incinerate or bury in a landfill, and their toxic ingredients last forever (mercury and zinc are elements and cannot decompose).

CHOOSING A PRODUCT

GENERAL GUIDELINES

Light power. Instead of investing in batteries, choose from the wide range of light-powered calculators now available; they come in many styles and include most options and capabilities (except printing).

Quality. A high-quality calculator will perform well and last much longer than one that is cheaper and not as well made.

COMMERCIAL PRODUCTS

Light-powered calculators *(highly recommended)*. Almost any light source—the sun, indirect daylight, or even an electric lamp—is enough to run the tiny microcircuits of light-powered calculators. Some come with optional battery features, but you don't necessarily need to buy the battery. Light-powered calculators are available with many options—an adjustable display, large keys, a folding style, or business-card size—and functions ranging from the basic five (addition, subtraction, multiplication, division, percentages) to an advanced 154 that include calculus. Table 38 lists some widely available light-powered calculators, some with the optional battery feature.

Plug-in calculators (*recommended*). If you want a calculator that prints a running tape of calculations or one with a very large display, look for one you can plug into an electrical outlet. When in use the calculator pulls only a tiny amount of electricity, and you'll avoid wasteful and inconvenient batteries.

Battery-powered calculators (*never recommended*). These calculators are powered solely by batteries, which are wasteful, polluting, and a nuisance to change. Avoid these products if at all possible.

FIRE EXTINGUISHERS

These home safety items are essential—especially in the kitchen, where two-thirds of all household fires start. Make sure, however, that you buy extinguishers that are safe for the environment.

ENVIRONMENTAL PROBLEMS

Ozone depletion. Many fire extinguishers use halon chemicals, fluorocarbons that are similar to CFCs (chlorofluorocarbons) but are even more destructive to the stratospheric ozone that shields the earth from solar radiation. Producing, testing, and using halon fire extinguishers contributes about 12 percent of our nation's share of ozone destruction.[1] Despite their extraordinary environmental damage, these products have not yet been banned because they are so effective for fighting fires in certain situations.

Wasteful packaging. Over time fire extinguishers lose their propellant through leakage. Most extinguishers can be recharged, but a few models cannot—they must be discarded, wasting energy and resources.

CHOOSING A PRODUCT
GENERAL GUIDELINES

Weighing your needs. Choose an extinguisher that's right for the type and size of fire that might start in a particular space. All fire extinguishers carry a rating, using the letters A, B, and C, that shows their ability to put out different types of fires:

- *A* for trash, wood, and paper fires

- *B* for liquids, grease, and oil fires

- *C* for electrical fires

Extinguishers come in several sizes. Numbers are used along with the ABC ratings to show how many square feet of coverage a unit can provide during a fire. All extinguishers are available with easy-access wall mounts.

Halon-free products. When buying a new fire extinguisher, look for dry-chemical or non-halon types.

Rechargeability. Some fire extinguishers cannot be recharged with propellant; buy only rechargeable models.

COMMERCIAL PRODUCTS

Dry-chemical extinguishers *(highly recommended)*. These extinguishers typically use monoammonium phosphate (for type A fires) and sodium carbonate (for type B and C fires). Both chemicals are potential irritants but are not considered toxic when used to extinguish fires under most conditions; neither harm the ozone layer after use. They are very effective at putting out fires, though careful cleanup of the powder may be necessary afterward. There is little variation among brands. Most extinguishers slowly lose their propellant charge, usually over several years, and must be recharged by a dealer. Some nonrechargeable units on the market are designed to be thrown away when the propellant is exhausted; avoid these wasteful products. To be sure you're getting the right product,

- Check for the terms *dry chemical* or *dry powder* on the label.

- Check for *rechargeability* by finding specific recharging instructions on the canister label or in the accompanying product literature.

Halon-based extinguishers *(never recommended)*. These extinguishers—often painted white (instead of red) by major manufacturers such as Pittway and Kidde—use halons: tiny inert particles that can snuff out flames without soiling or damaging sensitive electronic equipment, as dry powders might. Thus halon-based extinguishers are often used in commercial computer rooms, but they are not necessary in most households. Though they destroy the stratospheric ozone layer, they are otherwise safe and nonreactive and are therefore sometimes used

by fire fighters, or in aircraft or other tightly enclosed spaces. Unless you have a specific, compelling need for halon fire extinguishers, avoid them.

WISE USE

Proper location. Fire fighters recommend wall-mounting an extinguisher in an obvious location—such as near a main door—but sufficiently out of the way to avoid accidentally knocking it over. Typical places for fire extinguishers are

- In the kitchen near the stove or a doorway

- Near the wood stove, furnace, or heater

- In the basement, near the stairs or a light switch

- In the garage or shop, near the doorway

- In each car, near the driver's seat

Regular maintenance. Periodically check the propellant charge on every fire extinguisher. Some models have a button you must push down; when it doesn't pop back up, the unit is empty. Others have easy-to-read gauges. When your extinguisher needs recharging, call the dealer or your local fire department for a recharging location near you.

Safe use. To extinguish a fire safely, follow these steps:

1. Stand about 6 feet from the flames.

2. Hold the extinguisher upright.

3. Remove the safety pin and engage the handle or trigger.

4. Aim at the base of the fire, using a side-to-side motion.

5. If you begin to have trouble breathing, give up your fire-fighting efforts and leave the area *immediately*.

1. "Can We Repair the Sky?" *Consumer Reports* (May 1989), p. 324.

FURNITURE

Furniture uses no energy and seems quite benign. But in reality it can pollute indoor air and create fire hazards, and its production and disposal often has serious environmental effects.

ENVIRONMENTAL PROBLEMS

Manufacturing impacts. Furniture contains a wide variety of materials that cause an equally wide range of environmental impacts:

- *Soft plastic foams* and *foam cushions* are often still made with CFC-11—one of the worst of the ozone-depleting chlorofluorocarbons. Manufacturers are looking for alternatives.

- All *plastic foams* (polyurethane, polyethylene, vinyl polymers) and *synthetic fabrics* (nylon, polyester) are made from petroleum and other nonrenewable fossil fuels. Manufacturing them uses numerous chemicals and large amounts of energy and causes air and water pollution.

- *Cotton* and *wool*, while preferable to synthetics, have their own environmental effects: lots of pesticides are used to grow cotton (partly because it is not a food crop), and raising sheep can damage the land's natural ecology.

- *Exotic woods*, popular for their richly colored grains, come from exotic places—mostly rainforests. Harvesting these woods has aggravated the massive, ongoing destruction of the world's vital rainforests.

Indoor air pollution. Outgassing from plastics, chemical stain repellents, mothproofers, and formaldehyde durable-press treatments can pollute the indoor air with vapors that can irritate the eyes and mucous membranes or otherwise affect sensitive individuals.

Fire hazards. Most plastics and plastic foams are combustible (some extremely so) even when treated with a chemical fire-retardant; many also release poisonous fumes when they burn.

Disposal problems. Furniture, with its mixture of materials, is bulky, hard to recycle, and slow to decompose. Furniture and furnishings make up 4.5 percent of our nation's entire municipal wastestream—slightly more than all plastic products combined.[1]

CHOOSING A PRODUCT

GENERAL GUIDELINES

Natural materials. Instead of plastics and synthetic fabrics, look for natural fibers and domestic woods.

Durability. Though expensive to buy, high-quality furniture lasts longer than cheaper products, saving you money and reducing the environmental impact over time.

Easy care. Avoid the need for chemical coatings and plastics on upholstery by choosing furniture that is easy to clean and by using slipcovers you can remove and wash easily.

Used furniture. To save resources and money, look for used furniture at second-hand and antique stores, garage sales, flea markets, estates sales, and through want ads.

COMMERCIAL PRODUCTS

North American woods *(highly recommended).* At least 19 species of wood—both harder deciduous woods and softer conifers—grown on this continent are used for indoor and outdoor furniture. Logging certain stands might cause environmental damage, but overall the following species are not overlogged:

Ash	Pecan
Beech	Ponderosa pine
Birch	Red gum
Black gum	Red oak
Black walnut	Soft maple
Butternut	Sugar maple

Cherry	Sycamore
Cypress	White oak
Elm	Yellow popular
Hackberry	

Wicker and rattan *(highly recommended)*. Usually made from the rattan palm, this distinctive woven furniture comes from plentiful sources and can last a long time if well maintained.

Futons *(highly recommended)*. Futons, basically cotton cushions that can be placed on wooden frames, are popular for chairs, sofas, and beds. Some futons are made entirely of cotton batting; others have a plastic foam core in the middle. All-cotton futons are not as spongy as those with plastic foam, but are still firm and comfortable. Futon chairs and sofas come in a wide variety of designs, and most have removable, washable covers and are easy to dust and vacuum.

Natural fabrics *(highly recommended)*. Slipcovers and upholstery made of cotton or wool are far superior environmentally to synthetics. Although cotton canvas is not as strong as nylon for outdoor furniture, it lasts many years if properly cared for. Be aware that some natural fabrics are chemically treated to resist stains; check the labels or ask a salesperson for details.

Metal *(recommended)*. Metal frames and tubing—aluminum, iron, or steel—are little better than plastic from a manufacturing viewpoint; the metals industries consume lots of energy and generate air and water pollution. Metal has great strength and longevity, however, which makes it superior in actual use to plastics, especially for outdoor furniture. Some metals can also be recycled, depending on their type, their paint or coatings, and the local recycling market.

Overstuffed upholstery *(not generally recommended)*. Modern overstuffed chairs or sofas use thick plastic foam and synthetic fabrics that have numerous environmental problems. The design itself also causes problems: the nonremovable cushions and covers, which are hard to clean, can trap dirt and breed dust mites.

Redwood *(not generally recommended)*. This tree, which is famous for its color and water resistance and popular in outdoor furniture, grows only in tiny areas along the West Coast. Redwood has been overlogged for decades, and many environmental groups have urged consumers to avoid or limit their redwood use.

Particleboard and plywood *(not generally recommended)*. Cheap furniture, especially tables and desks, might look like solid wood from a distance, but is usually particleboard or plywood covered with a thin veneer of plastic or real wood. Outgassing of formaldehyde from these products—especially particleboard—makes them unsafe in the home; they are also environmentally unsound to manufacture (see Particleboard and Plywood, p. 152). Plywood outgasses less than particleboard, requires much less resin to make, and may be suitable in items for which solid wood is not practical or available.

Exotic woods *(never recommended)*. Because logging has aggravated rainforest destruction, the Rainforest Action Network (RAN) has called for a permanent boycott of all tropical-hardwood furniture. The following woods are often used in furniture and should be boycotted:[2]

Exotic Wood	Origin
Afrormosia	West Africa
Bocote	Central and South America
Canarywood	South America
Cocobolo	Central America
Jatoba	Mexico, Central and South America
Mahogany	South America
Purpleheart	Central and South America
Ramin	Southeast Asia
Red Meranti	Malaysia
Spanish Cedar	South America
Teak	Southeast Asia

Imported finished wood products must be labeled with their country of origin, but imported raw wood that is assembled here does not. If the wood isn't clearly labeled, ask a salesperson or store manager (see Exotic Wood Products, p. 19).

Plastic *(never recommended)*. There is simply nothing good to say about plastic furniture: it is flammable; it can pollute the indoor air when new; it is made from nonrenewable petroleum;

it will never degrade in a landfill and will create toxins if incinerated; and it is virtually non-recyclable.

WISE USE

Proper maintenance. To preserve your health and extend your furniture's life span, follow these guidelines:

- If you have new furniture made of synthetic material, ventilate the room well for the first few weeks.

- Vacuum upholstered furniture regularly to stop dust and dirt buildup; use nontoxic cleaners for stains and shampooing.

- Reupholster and refinish old furniture to extend its life and beauty and delay its trip to the landfill.

Recycling and disposal. Make disposal the absolute last resort. Better options are to

- Ask whether family or friends could use your unwanted items.

- Sell your old furniture through newspaper want ads or a yard sale.

- Call your local United Way to ask where you can donate furniture, or donate it directly to a Goodwill, Salvation Army, or other thrift store.

- Ask a church or community group if they need furniture.

1. *Environmental Quality 1987–88* (Council on Environmental Quality, 1987), p. 10.
2. "Tropical Rainforests and the Timber Trade" (Boulder Rainforest Action Group, Campus Box 207, University of Colorado, Boulder, CO 80309).

LIGHT BULBS

The incandescent bulb hasn't changed much in 75 years: it's a cheap, primitive, energy-wasting anachronism. Fortunately, modern technology is finally catching up.

ENVIRONMENTAL PROBLEMS

Energy consumption. More than one-fifth of all the electricity America consumes goes for lighting, yet much of this is wasted in our crude incandescent bulbs: a current passes through a bit of tungsten wire inside a glass bulb, turning most of its energy into heat, not light.[1] Incandescent bulbs are so wasteful—and the nation's use of natural lighting is so neglected—the Rocky Mountain Institute has calculated that we could improve our overall lighting efficiency by an amazing 92 percent.[2] Generating the electricity now wasted by inefficient lighting has tremendous environmental consequences, from fossil-fuel depletion to air pollution.

Health hazards. Lengthy exposure to artificial light has long been considered unhealthy for people. Seasonal affective disorder, for example, characterized by seasonal bouts of depression, increased appetite, and cravings for carbohydrates, is now being attributed to hormonal imbalances caused by too little natural light.[3] Fluorescent light bulbs contain toxic mercury vapor; breaking a relatively new bulb indoors can cause the risk of inhaling poisonous mercury.

Disposal problems. The mercury in fluorescent bulbs and lamps (up to 15 milligrams per unit) begins as a vapor but during use breaks down into solids that are deposited on the inner surface.[4] If a bulb is buried in a landfill and broken, the mercury—one of the most toxic substances in general use—on the glass can eventually migrate to the groundwater. Even incandescent bulbs present a disposal problem: they cannot be recycled because of their mixed materials, so they must be sent to a landfill.

LIGHT BULB COMPARISON

TABLE 39

Type	Fits Most Fixtures?	Energy Rating[a]	Lifetime (Hours)	Color Rating[b]	Dimmable?	Relative Price	Lamp Noise	Safety Issues
Standard Incandescent	Yes	12-19	750-1,000	93	Yes	—	Negligible	Fragile bulbs
Compact Fluorescent	Yes; some types too large	35-60	7,500-10,000	82 (average)	Most are not	20-50 x standard incandescent	Unlikely	Mercury contamination possible if bulb breaks
Standard Fluorescent	Yes	50-82	15,000-24,000	45-55	No	3-6 x standard incandescent	More likely	Mercury contamination possible if bulb breaks
Tri-Chromatic Fluorescent	No; special fixture needed	89-93	12,000-20,000	75-85	No	7-10 x standard incandescent	Unlikely	Mercury contamination possible if bulb breaks

Source: Peter Weiss, "Lighting the Way Towards More Efficient Lighting," Home Energy (January/February 1989).
[a] Relative efficiency based on a comparison of lumens and wattages for all types. The higher the number, the more efficient the bulb.
[b] Based on the Color Rendering Index, which gauges how objects look in light. The higher the number, the more comfortable the light.

CHOOSING A PRODUCT

GENERAL GUIDELINES

Weighing your needs. Choose proper lighting, either natural and artificial, for specific areas and needs in your home. Task lighting for working or reading should be direct and sufficiently bright, with a minimum of glare. Background lighting can be indirect and less bright.

Energy efficiency and longevity. When suitable, replace incandescents with compact fluorescent or fluorescent tube lamps for huge energy savings and much longer usable life spans. Before you buy any fluorescent bulb, check the package for a rated lumens power and an estimated bulb life; all high-quality bulbs will list these ratings.

Warm color or full-spectrum light. Avoid the glare of standard fluorescents by using tri-chromatic or full-spectrum lights; choose compact fluorescents with a warm color range that nearly matches that of incandescents.

COMMERCIAL PRODUCTS

Compact fluorescent lights (highly recommended). Compact fluorescent bulbs generate light very close to the warm, comfortable color of incandescent bulbs. A small fitting called a ballast, which is sold either attached to each bulb or separately, adapts compact fluorescents to any incandescent-bulb socket. Compact fluorescents are best for lights that are left on for an hour or more, not connected to a dimmer switch, and not in outdoor or enclosed fixtures (except for specially designed models). Fairly complicated to manufacture, compact fluorescents are expensive (up to $25 each), but actually cost $25 less than incandescents over their lifetime because they last up to ten times longer and use only one-third to one-fifth the electricity. They also have environmental benefits: using an 18-watt compact fluorescent instead of a 75-watt incandescent will, over its lifetime, prevent the release of 1,000 pounds of carbon dioxide and 20 pounds of sulfur diox-

TABLE 40

COMPACT FLUORESCENT BULBS

Brand	Description	Electricity Use (Watts)	Replaces Incandescent (Watts)	Average Lifetime (Hours)
Incandescent, for comparison	$4\frac{1}{4}'' \times 2\frac{1}{4}''$ bulb with base	25–100	——	750–1000
General Electric	$6.4'' \times 3.8''$ bulb with base	15	60	9,000
	$6.8'' \times 2.9''$ twin tube	15	60	9,000
Marathon	$6.9'' \times 3''$ bulb with base	15	60	9,000
	$6.9'' \times 3.7''$ bulb with base	15	60	9,000
Osram	$5\frac{11}{16}'' \times 2\frac{1}{4}''$ twin tube	7	25	10,000
	$5\frac{11}{16}'' \times 2\frac{1}{4}''$ twin tube	11	40	10,000
	$6\frac{7}{8}'' \times 2\frac{1}{4}''$ twin tube	15	60	10,000
	$8\frac{3}{16}'' \times 2\frac{1}{4}''$ twin tube	20	75	10,000
	$5\frac{7}{8}'' \times 2\frac{3}{10}''$ quad tube	12.5	40	10,000
	$6\frac{1}{2}'' \times 2\frac{3}{10}''$ quad tube	16	60	10,000
Panasonic	$6.5'' \times 3.1''$ bulb with base	15	60	9,000
	$7.4'' \times 3.0''$ quad tube	18	75	9,000
	$7.8'' \times 2.1''$ quad tube	27	100	9,000
Philips	$7\frac{3}{16}'' \times 2\frac{1}{2}''$ quad tube	18	75	10,000
Satco	$5\frac{5}{8}'' \times 3\frac{1}{4}''$ bulb with base	15	60	8,000
	$6\frac{1}{2}'' \times 3\frac{1}{4}''$ bulb with base	16	60	9,000
Sylvania	$5\frac{13}{16}'' \times 2\frac{1}{8}''$ quad tube	18	75	10,000

ide by a coal-fired power plant.[5] Table 39 compares the features of compact fluorescents and standard incandescents. Be sure to check lamp or fixture sizes before purchasing. Try better hardware and lighting-supply stores for the integral models (ballast and bulb in one unit) listed in Table 40, or try these supply houses:

- A Brighter Way, (800) 369-9360, sells Osram and Philips lighting products.

- Energy Federation (EFI), (508) 875-4921, sells General Electric, Osram, Panasonic, Philips, and Sylvania products.

- Jade Mountain, (800) 442-1972, (303) 449-6601, carries Philips lights.

- Real Goods Trading Co., (800) 762-7325, sells Osram and Panasonic products.

- Rising Sun Enterprises, (303) 927-8051, offers Osram and other products.

- White Electric Co., (800) 468-2852, (415) 845-8534, sells Satco and Philips lights, with a minimum order of 12.

A Brighter Way and Rising Sun Enterprises carry both integral and modular (ballast and bulb are sold separately for greater savings and efficiency) products. Residential lighting fixtures, such as those mounted on walls or ceilings, are now available for compact fluorescents from Lightolier, (201) 864-3000, and Staff Lighting, (914) 691-6262.

Energy-saving switches (highly recommended). To further reduce energy use, consider installing these devices:

- *Dimmer switches* (for incandescents only) save energy by letting you select light output and energy use.

- *Sound/motion-activated switches* turn on lights when they sense sound or movement and turn them off again after a short time, eliminating the need to leave lights on when no one is around. A wall switch that automatically turns lights off when you leave a room is made by Watt Watcher, (408) 988-5331.

Solar-powered outdoor lights *(highly recommended)*. These products work with photovoltaic cells and are ideal for areas needing low, continuous levels of light, or short-lived but strong beams of light. Models with either manual or automatic controls are available at hardware or lighting supply stores, or order them from these companies:

+ Jade Mountain, (800) 442-1972, (303) 449-6601

+ Photocomm, (800) 544-6466

+ Real Goods Trading Co., (800) 762-7325

Tri-chromatic fluorescent tube lights *(highly recommended)*. Like compact fluorescents, these fluorescent tubes use special phosphors to offer light quality and color close to that of incandescents; they are also highly energy-efficient (see Table 39). Tri-chromatic fluorescents usually require special fixtures. Major manufacturers are

+ General Electric, (800) 626-2000

+ Panasonic, (201) 392-6633

+ Philips, (201) 563-3000

+ Osram, (800) 431-9980

+ Sylvania, (800) 544-4828

Tri-chromatic fluorescents use electronic ballasts. Inquire about them at better lighting supply stores. Three companies that make these ballasts are

+ Electronic Ballast Technology, (800) 654-6501, (213) 618-8733

+ ETTA Industries, (303) 444-2244

+ Valmont Electric, (214) 484-1492

Circular fluorescent lights *(recommended)*. These ring-shaped bulbs, usually about 8 inches in diameter, screw into overhead incandescent sockets and some large lamps. They have a long life, use as little energy as compact fluorescents, and are cheaper to buy, but they light up more slowly, have a whiter light, and may hum. They have the same restrictions on their use as do compact fluorescents.

Standard fluorescent lights *(recommended)*. Long-tubed fluorescent lamps, common in offices and stores, are generally disliked for their occasional humming noise and their cool, white light. They do, however, have the same high energy savings and long life as the other fluorescents described above (see Table 39).

■ To eliminate the noise or flickering, replace the magnetic ballast in the fixture; electronic ballasts (see listing under Tri-chromatic fluorescent tube lights) are much more energy-efficient.

■ To greatly improve light quality, use the Vita Lite Full Spectrum Light, which has a color rating about the same as an incandescent bulb. Available in all sizes at better hardware stores; it is made by Duro-Test, (800) 289-3876.

Incandescent bulbs *(sometimes recommended)*. No bulb is cheaper to buy—or more expensive to use—than an ordinary incandescent (see Table 39). Popular because of their warm, soft light, incandescents make sense for lights that are switched on frequently or used for only a few minutes (closets, stairs, hallways), and for outdoor lights that are infrequently used. There are two special types of incandescents:

■ *Tungsten-halogen* bulbs provide high-quality light for working or reading. Halogen bulbs are more efficient and longer-lived than regular incandescents but have a tendency to flicker, which can be noticeable in peripheral vision.

■ *Krypton-filled, "Miser,"* and *"Econo-Watt"* light bulbs consume a bit less electricity than standard bulbs but also give off less light and are not much longer-lived. They are the best choice when you need an incandescent.

High-intensity discharge (HID) lights *(sometimes recommended)*. HID sodium or metal halide lamps produce an intense light suitable for outdoor areas that must be well-lit for longer periods of time. HID lights, which like standard fluorescents use a separate ballast and bulb, generally take a few minutes to reach full power but are very energy-efficient compared to incandescents. Some HID lights designed for indoor use are also available; though the lamps and fixtures are quite expensive, the replacement bulbs are moderately priced. Lightolier, (201) 864-3000, makes high-quality indoor fixtures for HID lights.

Light buttons *(never recommended)*. These devices are placed into a lamp socket before the bulb is screwed in. Although advertised as energy savers, they actually reduce the bulb's light output more than its electrical use. The American Council for an Energy-Efficient Economy recommends avoiding them for this reason.

ALTERNATIVES

Natural lighting. Windows, skylights, and light-colored interiors can add abundant daytime light to indoor spaces. They cost nothing to operate and have no ill effects.

WISE USE

Safe use. All fluorescent bulbs contain highly toxic mercury, which can pose an air-contamination threat if a bulb breaks. Should this occur, evacuate the area immediately and ventilate it before you return. To avoid spreading powder and dust, use wet paper towels to clean up the broken glass and the white powder coating it.

Energy-efficient use. To save electricity, follow these guidelines:

- Always turn off incandescent lights in a room if you are leaving for more than three minutes. Compact fluorescent lamps should *not* be turned on and off frequently, as this will shorten the life of the bulb.

- Keep incandescent bulbs dusted and cleaned for brighter light and longer bulb life.

- If you use incandescents in multiple-socket lamps, use one large-wattage bulb only; a single 100-watt bulb provides the same light as two 60-watt bulbs, yet uses one-sixth less electricity. (For safety, leave burned-out bulbs in the empty sockets.)

- Avoid incandescent floodlights outdoors; substitute compact-fluorescent, high-intensity discharge, or tungsten-halogen bulbs.

Proper disposal. Currently, there are no truly safe ways to dispose of or recycle light bulbs. Incandescent bulbs must be discarded in the trash. For fluorescents, take precautions:

- Make sure fluorescent bulbs reach the trash can intact.

- On older (made before 1978) fluorescent lamp fixtures, look for a label on the ballast stating that it contains no PCBs (polychlorinated biphenyls), an extremely toxic, oily insulator. If there is no label, assume that it *does* contain PCBs, and carefully seal it for a hazardous waste collection.

FOR FURTHER INFORMATION: "Consumer Guide to Energy-Saving Lights," *Home Energy* magazine (2124 Kittredge St., #95, Berkeley, CA 94704). "Lighting the Way Towards More Efficient Lighting," by Peter Weiss, *Home Energy* (January/February 1989), pp. 16-23.

1. Peter Weiss, "Lighting the Way Towards More Efficient Lighting," *Home Energy* (January/February 1989), p. 18.
2. "A Bright Idea," *Harrowsmith* (March/April 1989), p. 50.
3. Ellen J. Greenfield, *House Dangerous* (Vintage Books, 1987), pp. 80–81.
4. *Competitek* (Rocky Mountain Institute, 1989), p. 230.
5. *Newsletter* (Rocky Mountain Institute, November 1988), quoted in *Rising Sun Sampler* (P.O. Box 586, Old Snowmass, CO 81654), p. 1.

PERSONAL CARE
PRODUCTS

COSMETICS

Cosmetics are a big business in the United States, bringing in about $18 billion each year and making the industry's controversial manufacturing methods and environmental impact significant.

ENVIRONMENTAL PROBLEMS

Harmful ingredients. Many cosmetics contain ingredients that are harmful to humans or are environmentally unsound. An FDA study completed in 1983 found reports of skin reactions in 11 percent of cosmetics products.[1] Common cosmetics ingredients are

- *Mineral oil*, a heavy mixture of petroleum-derived hydrocarbons that leaves a pore-clogging residue on the skin

- *Talc* (or talcum powder), toxic by inhalation, made from a naturally occurring mineral, magnesium silicate

- *Quaternium-15*, a strong preservative that kills bacteria by releasing formaldehyde; also a skin irritant

- *Artificial colors and fragrances*, any of hundreds of compounds usually made with petrochemicals; many are potential skin irritants

Animal cruelty. Because some ingredients can harm humans, many companies test cosmetics on animals, under inhumane conditions; afterward the animals are killed.

Wasteful packaging. Cosmetics often come in elaborate packages that contain a great deal of plastic and other nonrecyclable materials and very little of the product itself.

CHOOSING A PRODUCT

GENERAL GUIDELINES

Simple, natural ingredients. Look for cosmetics made with simple formulas and naturally derived ingredients rather than synthetic, petroleum-derived chemicals.

Cruelty-free products. Look for cosmetics made by companies that do not test products on animals.

Sensible packaging. Avoid products in flashy but wasteful containers. Instead look for cosmetics with more contents and less packaging—preferably, recyclable packaging.

COMMERCIAL PRODUCTS

Natural-ingredient, cruelty-free brands *(recommended)*. The best cosmetics are those made primarily from natural ingredients, with no animal testing or animal by-products. Look for the cosmetics listed below and similar products in co-ops, natural products stores, specialty shops, and mail-order catalogs—but be sure to read the labels carefully. Most of these companies use some petrochemicals or other synthetics in their formulas but strive to use natural ingredients whenever possible. None test their products on animals. An asterisk indicates that the company uses no animal ingredients in any cosmetics products.

- ◆ Alexandra Avery, (503) 755-2446

- ◆ *Annemarie Börlind, (603) 526-2076

- ◆ *Aubrey Organics; mail-order from A Clear Alternative, (713) 356-7031

- ◆ *Aveda, (800) 328-0849

- ◆ Bare Escentuals; mail order from N.E.E.D.S., (800) 643-1380

- ◆ The Body Shop, Inc., (800) 541-2535

- ◆ Dr. Hauschka Cosmetics; mail order from Meadowbrook Herb Garden, (401) 539-7603

- ◆ *Ecco Bella, (800) 888-5320

- ◆ *Espree, (800) 766-8825

- ◆ Ida Grae; mail order from InterNatural, (800) 446-4903

- ◆ Jurlique; mail order from D'Namis, (800) 642-3535

- Kallima, (214) 771-0011

- The Magic of Aloe, (800) 257-7770

- Nature Cosmetics, (800) 553-9816

- Nutri-Metrics, (212) 242-7014

- Orjene Natural Cosmetics; mail order from Painlessly Beautiful, (717) 939-5376

- Patricia Allison, (619) 444-4379

- *Paul Penders; mail order from InterNatural, (800) 446-4903

- Rachel Perry, (800) 624-7001

- Reviva Labs, (800) 257-7774

- Sombra Cosmetics; mail order from Rainbow Concepts, (404) 886-6320

- *Warm Earth; mail order from Vegan Street, (800) 422-5525

- West Cabot Cosmetics, (800) 645-5408

- Zia Cosmetics, (800) 334-SKIN

Standard-ingredient, cruelty-free brands *(sometimes recommended).* The following cosmetics companies do not test on animals but rely more heavily on animal-derived and synthetic ingredients. Screen their products carefully for unhealthy ingredients and wasteful packaging:

- Almay Hypo-Allergenic, (212) 572-5000

- Avon, (212) 546-6015

- Benetton Cosmetics, (212) 832-6616

- BWC (Beauty Without Cruelty), (201) 836-7820

- Clientele, (800) 327-4660

- Clinique, (212) 572-3800

- Estée Lauder, (212) 572-4200

- Eva Jon, (817) 668-7707

- Fabergé, (212) 581-3500

- Fashion Two Twenty, (216) 562-5111

- Finelle Cosmetics, (508) 682-6112

- Max Factor, (213) 248-3700

- Merle Norman Cosmetics, (213) 641-3000

- Revlon, (212) 572-5000

- Shaklee, (800) 426-0766

- Ultima II, (212) 572-5000

- Victoria Jackson, (800) 848-7990

Other major brands *(never recommended).* Given the widespread availability of cruelty-free cosmetics, manufacturers that still subject animals to unnecessary suffering should be avoided.

1. Francesca Lyman, "Personal Hygiene Products," *Garbage* (July/August 1990), p. 58.

TABLE 41

NATURAL-INGREDIENT, CRUELTY-FREE DEODORANTS[a]

Brand	Dispenser	Basic Ingredients
Alvera	Roll-on	Aloe vera gel, arnica, calendula, gentian root, coriander
Aubrey Organics E Plus High C	Roll-on	Rosewater, aloe vera gel, vitamin E
Aubrey Organics Men's Stock	Spray	Grain alcohol, vegetable glycerin, arnica and calendula oils
Crystal Deodorant Stone	Crystalline stone	Potassium sulfate, mineral salts
Lavilin	Cream	Zinc oxide, calendula, and arnica
Le Crystal Naturel	Crystalline stone	Mineral salts
Natural Aloe Vera Deodorant	Stick/roll-on	Aloe vera, herbal extracts, witch hazel
Nature's Gate	Roll-on	Witch hazel, clove and basil oils
Paul Penders	Cream	Witch hazel, essential oils
Pure & Basic Green Tea	Roll-on	Purified water, green tea extract
Tom's of Maine	Roll-on	Aloe vera gel, coriander
Weleda Natural Sage	Spray	Grain alcohol, lemon juice, glycerin, sage oil
Wysong	Roll-on	Aloe vera extract, herbal extracts

[a] Contain no aluminum salts.

DEODORANTS AND ANTIPERSPIRANTS

Deodorants and antiperspirants, a $1.2-billion-a-year-business in the United States,[1] vary greatly in their environmental soundness and health effects. Given their widespread use, the differences are significant.

ENVIRONMENTAL PROBLEMS

Wasteful use of resources. Most deodorants and antiperspirants include water or alcohol and a variety of chemicals derived from nonrenewable fossil fuels:

- *Propylene glycol*, a humectant (to retain moisture), preservative, and base ingredient derived from hydrocarbon gases

- *EDTA*, a preservative and antioxidant made by adding sodium cyanide and formaldehyde to petrochemicals

- *Triclosan*, or dichlorophenoxyphenol, an antibacterial agent made with chlorine and petrochemicals

- *Artificial colors and fragrances* derived from petrochemicals; added to mask unpleasant odors of other chemicals or to make the deodorant more visually appealing

Harmful ingredients. Antiperspirants contain aluminum salts such as aluminum chlorohydrate that cause the skin to swell slightly, closing sweat pores. Much debate has arisen over the wisdom of chemically blocking this natural—and important—bodily function. In addition, research on possible links between aluminum absorption and Alzheimer's disease has generated concern about the aluminum salts themselves. Once absorbed through the skin, they are normally excreted in the urine, but can accumulate in the tissues of people with impaired kidneys.[2] Some of the aluminum compounds also contain zirconium, a suspected carcinogen;[3] zirconium compounds are no longer used in aerosol antiperspirants, which disperse them into the air, but are still used in nonaerosols.

Animal cruelty. Because some ingredients are harmful to humans, many companies test deodorants and antiperspirants on animals, under inhumane conditions; afterward the animals are killed.

Wasteful packaging. Deodorants packaged in aerosol cans are especially wasteful: the cans are energy-intensive to make, polluting to use, and nonrecyclable. Even nonaerosol deodorants often come in overly bulky, elaborate containers that are nonrecyclable and nondegradable.

CHOOSING A PRODUCT

GENERAL GUIDELINES

Simple, natural ingredients. Select products that have a minimum of synthetic ingredients or additives.

Cruelty-free products. Choose deodorants made by companies that do not test products on animals.

Sensible packaging. Roll-ons, sticks, pump sprays, or creams—even if their containers are nonrecyclable—are still better choices than aerosols. Purchase large sizes to reduce packaging waste.

COMMERCIAL PRODUCTS

Natural-ingredient, cruelty-free brands *(highly recommended)*. Table 41 lists deodorants and antiperspirants containing primarily

natural ingredients and made by companies that do not test on animals. Environmentally, deodorant stones made of mineral salts are the best choice: they're effective, last up to a year, and leave almost no packaging waste. If you must use an antiperspirant, try Tom's of Maine. Tom's makes a cruelty-free antiperspirant that uses buffered aluminum sulfate, a naturally occurring mineral salt.

Major brands *(never recommended)*. Major-brand products contain synthetic or irritating ingredients and are often tested on animals; avoid these products whenever possible.

DO-IT-YOURSELF

Baking soda. Nontoxic, naturally derived baking soda (sodium bicarbonate) is an effective deodorant. Just moisten your underarms and apply a little dry baking soda, or mix it with cornstarch for smoother application.

1. *1991 U.S. Industrial Outlook* (Department of Commerce, 1991), p. 36-5.
2. "A Question of Health," *Consumer Reports* (February 1989), p. 101.
3. N. Irving Sax and Richard J. Lewis, Sr., eds., *Hawley's Condensed Chemical Dictionary*, 11th ed. (Van Nostrand Reinhold, 1987), p. 1259.

DIAPERS

Throwaway diapers once seemed like the perfect solution to a messy problem, but their ever-increasing popularity has turned them into an environmental disaster: at least *16 billion* of these urine-soaked, feces-laden bundles go to American landfills every year.[1]

ENVIRONMENTAL PROBLEMS

Disposal problems. Disposable diapers now make up 2 percent of our municipal solid waste—a huge figure for a single consumer product—just when we are confronting a crucial shortage of landfill space. Because of disposables' waterproof plastic liners and the lack of oxygen in landfills, the diapers will take 300 to 500 years to break down.[2] Even worse, the diapers discarded yearly contain nearly 3 million tons of feces; fewer than 5 percent of users follow the manufacturers' directions to empty the feces into a toilet.[3] Infants' feces can contain over 100 different viruses; the presence of feces in landfills, which are not designed to handle untreated human waste, raises concerns regarding bacterial and viral contamination of groundwater.

Manufacturing impacts. Basic disposable diapers are made of tissue-like wood pulp encased in polyethylene plastic; newer superabsorbent diapers have granules of acrylic acid polymer added to the wood pulp to help soak up water. Both types use plastic in their tape and tape tabs, adhesive, and waistbands. Manufacturing each diaper consumes energy and resources—a sizable impact when multiplied by 16 billion per year.

Dioxin contamination. Testing by the paper industry has found highly toxic and carcinogenic dioxins—by-products from the chlorine bleaching of wood pulp—in superabsorbent disposables at the level of 11 parts per trillion.[4] This concentration is very low, but the Environmental Protection Agency says that *any* level of dioxin exposure poses a risk.

CHOOSING A PRODUCT

GENERAL GUIDELINES

Weighing your needs. There are certain situations—a long trip, for example—for which disposable diapers are almost essential. (They were initially designed for traveling.) But for everyday use, consider cotton diapers instead.

COMMERCIAL PRODUCTS

Reusable cotton diapers *(highly recommended)*. Cotton diapers, once the only choice, have made a comeback in recent years—partly because of the proliferation of diaper services that eliminate messy cleanup and time-consuming laundering. These services pick up and deliver diapers to homes or day-care centers at a cost that rivals or even betters that of disposables. Most services wash diapers with bacteria-killing additives and an acid-reducing rinse to prevent diaper rash, and have regular lab checks for microorganisms. Look in your local yellow pages, or call the National Association of Diaper Services at (215) 569-3650. The best approach environmentally, however, is to wash your own diapers (see Wise Use, below, for washing information).

"Biodegradable" disposables *(not generally recommended)*. These diapers are made of rayon, a wood product, and cornstarch-modified plastic instead of the nondegradable plastic used in major brands. But whether they will really break down in a landfill is doubtful, since almost nothing degrades without adequate oxygen. Two brands available in supermarkets and natural food stores are

- ◆ Nappies, by Eco-Matrix, (617) 730-8450

- ◆ Tender Care, by Rocky Mountain Medical Corporation, (800) 344-6379

Major-brand disposables *(not generally recommended)*. Their manufacturing and disposal impacts make these products a poor choice;

avoid them—both regular and superabsorbent—whenever possible.

WISE USE

Proper laundering. If you wash cotton diapers at home, presoak them in a borax solution, wash them in hot water with a mild detergent or soap, and rinse them in cold water.

Proper disposal. If you must use a disposable diaper, follow the manufacturer's recommendation: empty feces into a toilet before putting the diaper in the trash.

1. Michael DeCourcy Hinds, "Do Disposable Diapers Ever Go Away?" *New York Times* (December 6, 1988).
2. Jessica Brooks, "The Continuing Diaper Debate," *Utne Reader* (July/August 1989), p. 24.
3. Michael DeCourcy Hinds, op. cit.
4. Peter von Stackleberg, "White Wash: The Dioxin," *Greenpeace Magazine* (March/April 1989), p. 10.

HAIR DYES AND COLORS

Commercial hair dyes and colors can change your image instantly, but they use some very harsh chemicals to do so.

ENVIRONMENTAL PROBLEMS

Harmful ingredients. Many hair dyes (more permanent coloring) and color rinses (temporary coloring) contain strong petrochemical dyes, such as p-phenylenediamine (which is toxic if swallowed or inhaled and a strong skin irritant) and 1-napthol (toxic if swallowed or absorbed through the skin). Application to the hair, near the scalp and face, creates risk of exposure. This use of toxic chemicals is still legal; exempted from Food and Drug Administration regulation by an archaic 1938 law, hair-coloring manufacturers need only add to their labels a warning indicating the use of toxic or irritating ingredients.

Water pollution. Hair colorings contain surfactants, colors, solvents, preservatives, and processing chemicals that pollute wastewater with carbon-containing compounds—which vary in biodegradability—and dissolved salt compounds. These substances complicate wastewater treatment and are sometimes released to pollute downstream water.

Ozone depletion. Some color sprays use 1,1,1-trichloroethane, a potent solvent, also known as methyl chloroform. When released into the air, this chemical rises up to the stratosphere where its chlorine attacks the ozone layer that shields us from solar radiation.

Animal cruelty. Because some ingredients are harmful to humans, many manufacturers test hair-coloring products on animals, under inhumane conditions; afterward the animals are killed.

CHOOSING A PRODUCT

GENERAL GUIDELINES

Simple, natural ingredients. Read labels carefully to find products with fewer and less-toxic chemicals and more naturally derived substances.

Cruelty-free products. Choose hair dyes and colors made by companies that do not test products on animals.

COMMERCIAL PRODUCTS

Natural-ingredient, cruelty-free brands *(highly recommended)*. Look for these brands in natural-products stores, or order them from the catalogs listed below:

- Creme Hair Colours by Vita Wave, available in 21 colors, are made from herbs, fruits, vegetables, whole-grain oils, and minerals. Order from Alternative Humane Products, (603) 224-1361.

- Color-Me-Naturally Color Conditioner by Paul Penders contains mostly natural ingredients and colors derived from mineral salts. Order from Lion and Lamb, (800) 252-6288.

Henna-based, cruelty-free brands *(highly recommended)*. Henna is one of the oldest and safest hair dyes, obtained from tropical plants in Africa and India. It gives hair a rich, reddish-brown color that can last for months. Here are two companies that offer henna products:

- Light Touch makes several shades of 100-percent henna; order from Heart's Desire, 1307 Dwight Way, Berkeley, CA 94702.

- Rainbow Research offers ten colors made from henna, chamomile, and marigold flowers; order from Rainbow Concepts, (404) 886-6320.

Major brands *(never recommended)*. The major hair-coloring manufacturers use formulas that are dangerous and environmentally unsound. If considering a product, check its label carefully for a warning such as, "Caution: Contains ingredients that may cause skin irritation, may cause blindness."

Among the major brands, Clairol Loving Care has fewer and less-harmful ingredients than most. It does, however, contain one toxic petrochemical (amino methyl propanol), and Clairol does test on animals.

WISE USE

Safe use. If you must use toxic hair-coloring products, follow the manufacturer's instructions carefully; avoid any contact with your skin, eyes, or mouth.

HAIRSPRAYS, MOUSSES, AND GELS

These products, which are applied wet and stiffen as they dry to create fashionable hairstyles, use petroleum-based resins and cause some environmental problems.

ENVIRONMENTAL PROBLEMS

Wasteful use of resources. Besides their synthetic resins, hairsprays, mousses, and gels also include proteins, oils, humectants (to retain moisture), alcohol, softeners, wetting agents, and fragrances. Like the resins, many of these ingredients are made from petrochemicals. Their manufacture contributes to the depletion of nonrenewable fossil fuels and causes air, water, and soil pollution.

Air pollution. Aerosol-packaged sprays and mousses often use hydrocarbon propellants such as butane or propane. When released into the air, these sprays produce volatile organic compounds, which are unhealthy to breathe indoors and contribute to outdoor air pollution, particularly smog.

Fire hazards. The hydrocarbon propellants in aerosol products are quite flammable and can burn or explode if exposed to intense heat or flame.

Animal cruelty. Because some ingredients are harmful to humans, many manufacturers test their products on animals, under inhumane conditions; afterward the animals are killed.

Wasteful packaging. Hairsprays, mousses, and gels often come in throwaway plastic containers or—even worse—aerosol cans, which are energy-intensive to manufacture, polluting to use, and nonrecyclable.

CHOOSING A PRODUCT

GENERAL GUIDELINES

Simple, natural ingredients. Instead of commercial hair products made with all-synthetic chemicals, choose products that incorporate natural, plant-based ingredients.

Cruelty-free products. Look for products made by companies that do not test on animals.

Sensible packaging. Whenever possible avoid aerosols; choose pump sprays or gels instead. Always buy the largest container practical, preferably one made from recyclable materials.

COMMERCIAL PRODUCTS

Natural-ingredient, cruelty-free brands *(recommended)*. Almost all brands of hair-control products incorporate synthetic resins and coatings. Some brands, however, use plant-based substitutes for a few of the synthetic ingredients and are not tested on animals. Table 42 lists a wide range of such products available in salons, department stores, natural foods stores, and some drugstores.

Standard-ingredient, cruelty-free brands *(sometimes recommended)*. Among companies that rely on petroleum-based synthetic ingredients, the following offer a variety of nonaerosol products that are not tested on animals:

- Freeman, (213) 470-6840

- KMS, (916) 244-6000

- Nexxus, (805) 968-6900

- Revlon, (212) 572-5000

- St. Ives, (818) 709-5500

Other major brands *(never recommended)*. Most of the large-scale manufacturers use the cheapest petroleum-based ingredients—many of which they routinely test on animals—and the most wasteful packaging, making their products environmentally unsound.

TABLE
42

NATURAL-INGREDIENT, CRUELTY-FREE NONAEROSOL HAIRSPRAYS, MOUSSES, AND GELS

Brand	Product (Contains no animal ingredients)	Product (Contains animal ingredients)
Aloegen		Hair Spray; Styling Spritz Elasting Activating Gel; Hair Sculpting Setting Gel
Aubrey Organics	Natural Missst Herbal Hairspray; Primrose Tangle-Go; Natural Body Highliter Mousse	B5 Design Gel
Aveda	Satin Mist Shine; Witch Hazel Hair Spray Clarifying Gel; Flax Seed/Aloe Sculpting Gel Concentrate; Flax Seed/Aloe Spray on Gel	
Body Shop		Aloe Hair Gel; Hair Gel; Slick Hair Styler
Earth Science	Nonaerosol Mousse Sculpting Gel Glaze	Silk Forte Styling Mist; Silk Lite Styling Mist
Finelle	Liquid Mousse	Hair Mist
Focus 21		Art Form Sculpting Spray; Changes; Illusions Finishing Spray; Splash Finishing Spray Hair Candy Designing Mousse Designing Gel; Splash Gel
4-D SUNaturals	Ferm-Hold Hair Spray; Hair Teaser Styling Mist	
Giovanni		Dash of LA; LA Bod; LA Grab; Make It Snappy; Molto Body; Multofusion; One Heck of a Shine
Image		Deep Freez; Fixative; Fixative Firm; Foamation; Freez; Freez Dry; Freez 2000; Glyde; Hardbody
L'anza Research	Fomme Sprae; Sprae Quatre; Sprae Travae Sculpture Lotion; Glazer Gel	
The Magic of Aloe		Aloe Crystal Gel
Mera	Hair Spray Misting Gel	
Naturade		Hair Spray with Jojoba; Styling Spray
Natural Bodycare		Herbal Satin; More Curl; Quite Natural Styling Gel
Nirvana		Witch Hazel Hair Spray Flax Aloe Vera Spray Gel

TABLE
42

NATURAL-INGREDIENT, CRUELTY-FREE
NONAEROSOL HAIRSPRAYS, MOUSSES, AND GELS *(continued)*

Brand	Product (Contains no animal ingredients)	Product (Contains animal ingredients)
Sebastian		Forte; Hair Gloss; High Contrast Gel; Molding Mud; Shaper Hair; Shaper Hair Grease Slicker; Wet
ShiKai	Henna Gold Super Hold Finishing Spray; Henna Gold Super Hold Styling Spray Henna Gold Volume Plus Styling Gel	
TRI	Control & Finishing Mist; Prego Control & Finishing Spray Sculpture Styling Gel	
Vita Wave	Last Touch Proteinized Hair Spray; Style Sheen Body-Back Style Lotion; Perm	
Wachters		Hair Texturizer

WISE USE

Safe use. If you use chemical hair-control products, take the following precautions:

- Avoid contact with your eyes or skin.

- Try not to breathe the fumes; use the products in a well-ventilated space.

- Keep aerosol products away from flame or intense heat.

JEWELRY

Jewelry is a form of personal art that seems quite benign—yet its production, with sales totaling $5.7 billion a year in the United States,[1] has some significant environmental consequences.

ENVIRONMENTAL PROBLEMS

Toxic by-products. Most costume jewelry owes its gold or silver color to electroplating, a process in which cheap metal is immersed in a bath of metal salts. An electric current passing through the bath deposits a uniform coating of tiny metal particles on the jewelry. The solution used in electroplating contains hydrochloric acid, sulfuric acid, and other toxic chemicals as well as metal residues, many of them also toxic. When the solution loses its coating ability, many electroplating companies simply dump it down the nearest drain. Even solution that is properly treated—by condensing the worst toxins into sludge—does not solve the disposal problem,

243

because landfills are not a safe repository for toxic sludge.

Misuse of raw materials. Some costume jewelry contains a great deal of plastic, which is made from nonrenewable fossil fuels and cannot be recycled. Some high-quality jewelry, on the other hand, misuses natural products such as coral, ivory, exotic feathers, tropical hardwoods, and animal teeth or bones, encouraging poaching and indiscriminate destruction of species or habitats.

CHOOSING A PRODUCT

GENERAL GUIDELINES

Quality products. Costume jewelry is eye-catching and inexpensive, but don't give in to your impulse to buy. Instead, look for high-quality jewelry such as alloyed gold, silver, or platinum that is worked by hand, enameled, or set with stones. This jewelry costs much more than costume jewelry, but lasts a long time. And, despite significant mining and manufacturing impacts, it is much less harmful to the environment because the volumes produced are so much smaller.

Avoiding exotic natural products. Don't buy products made of coral, bone, feathers, or wood unless you are sure that the materials come from nonendangered species or areas and were obtained without cruelty.

Used jewelry. To save resources and money, look for second-hand jewelry at antique and jewelry stores, estate sales, and through want ads.

SEE ALSO: Exotic Plant and Animal Products, p. 17.

1. *1991 U.S. Industrial Outlook* (Department of Commerce, 1991), p. 39-2.

LOTIONS AND CREAMS

Americans spend about $2.8 billion each year on products that clean, moisturize, and protect skin.[1] Lotions and creams are important for skin care, but they vary widely in their environmental soundness.

ENVIRONMENTAL PROBLEMS

Wasteful use of resources. Most skin-care products contain water, oil (which blocks water evaporation from the skin), and a humectant (which draws moisture from the air to help keep skin moist). Additional ingredients are stabilizers, texturizers, cleansers, preservatives, sun blocks, fragrances, and colors. Inexpensive lotions and creams often use mineral oil—a dense, heavy mixture of hydrocarbons—and other petroleum-derived ingredients, depleting nonrenewable fossil-fuel supplies and causing air, water, and soil pollution.

Animal cruelty. Because some ingredients can harm humans, many companies test skin-care products on animals, under inhumane conditions; afterward the animals are killed.

Wasteful packaging. Most skin-care products come in polyethylene plastic bottles that are designed to be used only once. Recycling is increasing, but slowly, and these bottles waste energy and resources if discarded after one use.

CHOOSING A PRODUCT

GENERAL GUIDELINES

Simple, natural ingredients. Look for products that use simple formulas and naturally derived ingredients instead of petrochemicals.

TABLE
43

NATURAL-INGREDIENT, CRUELTY-FREE LOTIONS AND CREAMS

Brand	Product (Contains no animal ingredients)	Product (Contains animal ingredients)
Alba Botanica	Emollient Body Lotion; Facial Care Complex; Unscented Body Lotion	
Alexandra Avery	Almond Cream; Dream Cream	
Andalina Ltd.		Comfrey Comfort
Annemarie Börlind		Day Cream;LL Moisturizing Cream; LL Vital Cream; Night Cream; Sun Care
Aqualin	Concentrate Moisturizer; Light Moisturizer; Original Moisturizer	
Arya Laya	Biovitamin Night Cream; Body Lotion	Aqua Derm Day Cream; Azuline Day Cream; Azuline Night Cream; Carrot Night Cream; Hamamelis 24-Hour Cream
Aubrey Organics	Evening Primrose Lotion; Rosa Mosqueta Hand & Body Lotion	Collagen & Olive Oil Hand & Body Lotion
Autumn Earth	Unpetroleum	Chamomile Lotion
Autumn Harp		Body Lotion
Aveda	Moisturizing Cream	
Beauty Naturally	Sea Legend	
Beehive Botanicals		Honey Silk Body Moisturizer; Propolis Derma Cream; Royal Silk Day Creme; Royal Silk Facial Cream
Bindi		Moisturizing Cream
Biogime	First Impression Synergistic Skin Care	
Body Love	Aroma Lotion	
The Body Shop		Cocoa Butter Hand & Body Lotion; Dewberry 5 Oils Lotion; Glycerin & Rosewater Lotion; Hawthorn Hand Cream; Moisture Cream (Jojoba, Carrot, Aloe Vera, Vitamin E); Rich Night Cream
Botanicus	Oil-Free Facial Moisturizer; Oil-Free Hand & Body Lotion	
BWC (Beauty Without Cruelty)	Avocado Moisturizer; Oil-Free Moisture Creme	
CamoCare		Hand & Body Lotion

(continued on next page)

TABLE
43

NATURAL-INGREDIENT, CRUELTY-FREE
LOTIONS AND CREAMS *(continued)*

Brand	Product (Contains no animal ingredients)	Product (Contains animal ingredients)
Carlson		E-Gem Moisturizing Cream
Caswell-Massey		Almond Hand & Body Emulsion; Almond Hand Cream; Body Lotion
Desert Essence	Jojoba Cream	Jojoba Hand & Body Lotion
Earth Science		Almond Aloe Moisturizer; Hand & Body Lotion
Eva Jon		Hand Creme; Moisturizer; Night Creme; Supreme Moisturizer
4-D SUNaturals	Deep Skin Hand & Body Lotion	
Freeman		Aloe & Lanolin Lotion; Aloe & Vitamin E; Berlon Creme; Chamomile Lite Moisturizer; Clean & Fresh; Day/Nite Moisturizing Creme; Hand & Body Lotion; Hydrolate Moisture Lotion; Rosewater & Glycerin Lotion
Garden of Eden		China Lily Aloe Vera Moisturizer; China Rain Aloe Vera Moisturizer
GeremyRose		Sweet Almond Creme
Glowing Touch	Revitalizing Almond Skin Care Oil	
Golden Lotus	Ginseng-Aloe Moisturizing Lotion; Jojoba-E Moisturizing Lotion	
Granny's Old Fashioned Products	Moisture Guard	
Home Health Products	Vitamin E Skin Lotion	Almond Glow Skin Lotion; Palma Christi Skin Lotion; Soft & Smooth Skin Lotion
Jacki's Magic Lotion		Moisturizer & Massage Lotion (Almond, Coconut, Jasmine, Lavender, Orange-Vanilla, Rose-Mint, Unscented)
Jason Natural	Aloe Vera Gel Hand & Body Lotion; Apricot Hand & Body Lotion; E.F.A. Hand & Body Lotion; NaPCA Hand & Body Lotion; PABA/Aloe Vera Body Lotion; Vitamin E Hand & Body Lotion	Cocoa Butter Hand & Body Lotion
Jurlique	Body Care Lotion	
Kallima	Aloe Body Lotion	
Kiss My Face	All Day Protective Moisture Cream	
KSA	Jojoba Body Cream	

TABLE
43

NATURAL-INGREDIENT, CRUELTY-FREE
LOTIONS AND CREAMS (continued)

Brand	Product (Contains no animal ingredients)	Product (Contains animal ingredients)
La Crista	Face & Body Moisturizer	
Magick Botanicals		Oil-Free Moisturizer
The Magic of Aloe		Hand & Body Lotion; Moisture Lotion
Microbalanced Products		Aqualin Concentrating Moisturizer; Aqualin Light Moisturizer; Aqualin Original Moisturizer; Aqualin Sun Moisturizer
Mild and Natural	Lotion	
Mountain Ocean	Cream Moisturizer; Skin Trip Moisturizer	
Naturade	Aloe Hand & Body Lotion; Aloe Moisturizing Creme	
Natural Bodycare		Herbal-Mantle Hand & Body Lotion
Nature Cosmetics	Aloe Vera & PABA All-Day Moisture Cream	Collagen & Herbal Healing Hand Cream
Nature de France	Chamomile Body Lotion–Scented; Chamomile Body Lotion–Unscented	
Nature's Gate	Skin Therapy Lotion	Fragrance-Free Moisturizing Lotion; Moisture Cream; Moisturizing Lotion
Natus	Herbal Light Touch Moisturizer; Protectant; Ylang Ylang Body Pampering Emulsion	Superior Herbal Emulsion
Nutri-Metics	Skin Fresh	Moisture Rich Hand & Body Lotion
Oriental Beauty Secrets	Satin Night Creme; Silken Day Moisture Creme	
Patricia Allison	Irish Legend Hand Beauty; Petalskin Hand & Body Balm; Vita Balm	Oasis Moisture Balm
Paul Penders	Creamy Body Lotion	Aloe-Lavender Moisturizer; Avocado-Ginseng Night Cream; Body Lotion for Dry Skin; Calming Body Lotion; Marigold Hand Cream; St. John's Wort Ginger Moisturizer; Wheatgerm Honeysuckle Night Cream
Rachel Perry		Bee Pollen & Jojoba Moisturizing Cream; Elastin & Collagen Firming Treatment; Lecith-Aloe Maximum Retention Cream

(continued on next page)

TABLE 43

NATURAL-INGREDIENT, CRUELTY-FREE
LOTIONS AND CREAMS (continued)

Brand	Product (Contains no animal ingredients)	Product (Contains animal ingredients)
Rainbow Research	Golden Moisturizing Cream; Stony Brook Body Lotion	
Real Aloe Company	Aloe Vera Hand & Body Lotion	
Reviva	Elastin Body Lotion; Lettuce Moisture Lotion; NaPCA & Aloe Moisturizer; Normalizing Lotion	Oily Skin Day Treatment; Protein Cream Moisturizer; Seaweed Body Lotion; Ultra Rich Moisturizer; Velvet Dew Moisturizer
Scarborough & Company		Hand & Body Lotion with Jojoba; Hand & Body Lotion with Silk Protein; Nantucket Briar Body Lotion
Schiff		Bee Pollen Hand & Body Lotion
ShiKai		Hand & Body Lotion; Moisturizer; Protective Hand Creme
Sombra		Hand & Body Lotion; Moisturizing Cream
StonyBrook Botanicals		Oil-Free Body Lotion
Tonialg	Hand & Body Creme	
TRI	Topical Nutrition Hand & Body Lotion	
Truly Moist	Hand & Body Lotion	
Wachters	Exquissete Plus; Moisturizing Hand Cream; Softa Skin Hand & Body Lotion	Vitamin E Avocado-Almond Creme
Weleda	Rose Petal Hand Cream	Iris Moisturizing Cream; Iris Night Cream

Cruelty-free products. Buy lotions and creams made by companies that don't test products on animals.

Sensible packaging. Pick the largest practical container, preferably one you can recycle. Avoid throwaway pump containers; instead, buy one and refill it from larger bottles or from bulk dispensers at natural foods stores and co-ops.

COMMERCIAL PRODUCTS

Natural-ingredient, cruelty-free brands
(highly recommended). Most of these lotions

and skin creams contain some synthetic chemicals (such as propylene glycol, an emulsifier and stabilizer), but their major ingredients are naturally derived, and they are not tested on animals. Table 43 lists products available nationwide in department stores, drugstores, natural foods stores, co-ops, and bath shops.

Standard-ingredient, cruelty-free brands
(sometimes recommended). Most manufacturers use unnecessary petrochemicals such as mineral oil and FD&C artificial colors in their formulas; the following companies, however, do not test on animals:

◆ Clientele, (800) 327-4660

◆ Crabtree & Evelyn, (203) 928-2761

◆ Finelle, (508) 682-6112

◆ KMS, (916) 244-6000

◆ St. Ives, (818) 709-5500

Other major brands *(not generally recommended).* Most inexpensive lotions and creams contain mineral oil, which is not only environmentally unsound, but also a poor choice for skin care because it clogs pores with a dense, filmy residue. And many contain other synthetic ingredients, some completely unnecessary. More expensive major-brand lotions often contain better, more natural ingredients but are usually tested on animals.

DO-IT-YOURSELF

Homemade skin lotion. You can make an effective moisturizer by mixing distilled water, naturally derived glycerin (available in drug stores), and any combination of high-quality vegetable oils—olive, sesame, avocado—in a blender. Start with 3 parts water, 2 parts oil, and 1 part glycerin, and then adjust the proportions until you're satisfied with the consistency. Keep the lotion refrigerated.

ALTERNATIVES

Dry skin prevention. Instead of relying solely on lotions, help keep your skin moist by following these guidelines:

■ Drink plenty of water.

■ Keep the indoor air in your home from getting too dry.

■ Protect your skin from direct sunlight and from harsh soaps or chemicals.

■ Avoid taking long showers with very hot water.

WISE USE

Effective use. To get the most benefit from lotions and creams, apply them right after bathing or showering, while your skin is still moist.

1. *1991 U.S. Industrial Outlook* (Department of Commerce, 1991), p. 36-5.

NAIL POLISHES AND REMOVERS

Most nail polishes and removers are made of toxic petrochemicals, harmful to the environment and potentially to people as well.

ENVIRONMENTAL PROBLEMS

Toxic ingredients. All major-brand nail polishes, hardeners, and polish removers rely on toxic ingredients whose production, use, and disposal cause environmental damage—for example,

- *Formaldehyde resin*, a carcinogenic and toxic glue

- *Toluene* or *ethyl acetate*, both toxic, flammable, and explosive solvents

- *Acetone*, a solvent that is flammable, explosive, moderately toxic, and narcotic

- *Dibutyl phthalate*, a toxic plasticizer

Manufacturing these substances uses nonrenewable fossil fuels and causes air, water, and soil pollution. When used, the solvents dry, releasing volatile organic compounds and polluting both indoor and outdoor air.

Animal cruelty. Because some ingredients can harm humans, many companies test nail care products on animals, under inhumane conditions; afterward the animals are killed.

Disposal problems. Chemical residues from nail polishes and removers make the bottles nonrecyclable. And if bottles are crushed in a landfill, the chemicals—which in larger amounts are classified as hazardous wastes—can leach into groundwater.

CHOOSING A PRODUCT

GENERAL GUIDELINES

Simple, natural ingredients. Look for products that use simple formulas and naturally derived or less-toxic ingredients.

Cruelty-free products. Buy nail polishes and removers made by companies that do not test products on animals.

COMMERCIAL PRODUCTS

Natural-ingredient, cruelty-free brands *(recommended).* The products listed below are not for coloring nails, but rather for strengthening them and improving their appearance naturally. Look for them in natural foods stores or order by mail:

- ◆ De Lore Nail Hardener, Cuticle Cure, and Cuticle Treat. Made entirely from natural oils and vitamins, these products restore damaged nails and cuticles; order from Lion & Lamb, (800) 252-6288.

- ◆ Jason Silica Plus Nail Treatment. Although it contains some solvents and petroleum derivatives, Silica Plus is made mostly from natural ingredients, including oils, aloe vera, and beeswax; for ordering information, call (213) 396-3171.

- ◆ Incredible Nail Conditioner, by Ancient Egyptian Formulas, uses botanical protein, vitamins, and keratin to strengthen and harden nails; order from Martin von Myering, Inc., (412) 323-2832.

Standard-ingredient, cruelty-free brands *(sometimes recommended).* If you must either color your nails, cover them with very hard protective coatings, or remove old polish quickly, consider these products. They contain many of the petrochemicals found in major brands, but they also have simpler formulas, include some natural ingredients, and are not tested on animals. They're available in natural foods stores or by mail order.

- ◆ Beauty Without Cruelty Nail Colours and Nail Polish Remover; order from Amberwood, (404) 358-2991

- ◆ De Lore Nail Protector, Chip Proof, Nail Fix, and Polish Remover; order from Humane Street U.S.A., (408) 243-2530

- ◆ Nutri-Metrics Nail Lacquer; order from Sunrise Lane, (212) 242-7014

Major brands *(never recommended)*. The nail polishes, treatments, hardeners, and removers made by major companies contain numerous toxic chemicals and are tested on animals; avoid them whenever possible.

WISE USE

Conservative use. Because all polishes, colors, and removers use some toxic ingredients, buy and use them sparingly.

Safe use. Use nail-care products in well-ventilated areas; protect your skin, eyes, and mouth; and keep the products away from heat or flames.

Proper disposal. Nail care products qualify as hazardous wastes and should never be thrown away with the regular trash. If the bottles are not completely empty, store them in a cool, secure place until the next hazardous waste collection. Call your local waste disposal office for information on hazardous waste collection programs.

PERFUMES AND FRAGRANCES

Like many other personal care products, perfumes and fragrances seem quite benign, but have some hidden, significant environmental impacts. In terms of dollars, the fragrance industry is big—over $2.2 billion is spent on fragrances each year in the United States.[1]

ENVIRONMENTAL PROBLEMS

Harmful ingredients. Most perfumes and fragrances are scented with blends of oils that are either steam-distilled from flowers or other plants or concentrated from animal scents by evaporation. These active ingredients are diluted with alcohol and water, which can make up 80 to 90 percent of the finished product. Petroleum and coal-tar derivatives, however, are often used either to replace or "enhance" the natural fragrances, or as preservatives or solvents for them. These synthetic ingredients aggravate fossil-fuel depletion and pollution; some also pose health risks. Some common examples are

- *Benzyl acetate*, a substitute for jasmine and other fragrances and a skin irritant

- *Butyl alcohol*, a solvent and skin irritant

- *Ethyl acetate*, a substitute for fruit fragrances and a skin irritant

- *Ethyl butyrate*, a solvent and an eye and mucous-membrane irritant

- *Methyl salicylate*, a synthetic version of wintergreen oil and a skin irritant

Animal cruelty. Trapping, an inhumane practice, is big business in some regions and perfumes are one of the reasons why. Among the most popular animal scents are

- *Castoreum*, from the sex glands of the beaver

- *Civet*, from an anal pouch in the civet cat

TABLE
44
NATURAL-INGREDIENT, CRUELTY-FREE PERFUMES AND FRAGRANCES

Brand	Product
Alexandra Avery	*Perfumes*: The Arousing; Grace; Influence; The Joyous
Amber Essence	Amber Oil; Pure Amber
Aqua di Selva	Cologne for Men
Aubrey Organics	*Colognes*: Angelica; Elysian Fields; Lemon Blossom Body Splash; Musk Splash; Wild Wind
Aura Cacia	*Perfume Oils*: Celestial Flowers; Jasmine Isle; Mandarin Silk; Nile Spice; Port Rose; Temple Santal; Tropical Musk
The Body Shop (California)	*Essential Oils:* 73 fragrances
The Body Shop	*Perfume Oils*: Annie; Apple Blossom; Chypre; Coconut; Dewberry; Herb; Japanese Musk; Jasmine; Lavender; Mango; Mostly Musk; Primrose; Roma; Rose; Rose Musk; Samarkand; Strawberry; Summer Dew; Tea Rose; Vanilla; White Musk; Winter Dew; Wood Musk; Woody Sandalwood
BWC (Beauty Without Cruelty)	*Perfumes*: Aurelia; Calista; Gemina 1; Gemina 3; Kyphi; Suma; Yolanda *Colognes*: Aurelius Aftershave Cologne; Kyphi Cologne for Men
Colin Ingram	*Perfume Oils*: Amberesque; Frangipani; Gardenia; Jasmine; Lilac; Magnolia; Musk; Patchouli; Rose; Sandalwood; Vanilla
Eastern Star	*Essential Oils*: Eastern Star Creme; Fleur de Tropic; Oriental Spice; Tudor Rose
Ecologne	*Cologne for Men*: Black Forest
Fiori	Perfume
KSA	*Perfumes*: Jasmine; Musk; Orange
Madini Oils	*Essential Oils*: 27 fragrances
Paul Penders	Creme Perfume
Santa Fe Fragrance	*Colognes*: Abiquiu; Blue Sage; Oh Fresh *Perfumes*: Earth; Enchantment; Sacred; Snake Oil
Simplers Botanical	*Essential Oils*: 54 fragrances
Sunshine Products	*Perfume Oils*: Ambergris; Arabian Musk; Carnation; Gardenia; Honeysuckle; Jasmine; Jasmine & Rose; Lilac; Magnolia; Musk; Omar; Patchouli; Rose; Spring Rain; Wildflowers; Wood Spice
Tiferet	*Perfume Oils:* Citrus Blossom; Dervish Dance; Frankincense; Irish Morning Mist; Jasmine Absolute; Juliet's Garden; Lavender; Midnite at the Oasis; Moon Shadow; Patchouli; Rose Absolute; Rose Lace; Tree of Life; Vanilla; Ylang Ylang
Tocca Mi	Cologne; Perfume

■ *Musk*, from a sac near the navel of the male musk deer

And since some ingredients are harmful to humans, many companies test fragrances on animals, under inhumane conditions; afterward the animals are killed.

Wasteful packaging. Many perfumes and fragrances come in elaborate packages that contain a great deal of plastic and other nonrecyclable materials and very little of the product itself. Others come in aerosol cans, which are energy-intensive to make, polluting to use, and nonrecyclable.

CHOOSING A PRODUCT

GENERAL GUIDELINES

Simple, natural ingredients. Avoid synthetic substances, especially petrochemicals and coal tars, in favor of plant-derived essences and other naturally derived ingredients.

Cruelty-free products. Choose products made by companies that neither test on animals nor use substances extracted from wild animals.

Sensible packaging. Choose recyclable glass packaging whenever possible, and reduce packaging waste by buying larger sizes. If you prefer a spray, use a refillable pump atomizer.

COMMERCIAL PRODUCTS

Plant-based, cruelty-free fragrances *(highly recommended)*. Table 44 lists some companies that manufacture perfumes from natural ingredients, with no animal testing or animal by-products. Look for these and other brands in natural products stores and bath shops.

Synthetic, cruelty-free fragrances *(sometimes recommended)*. Derived primarily from petroleum, synthetic fragrances are chemical copies of natural fragrances. Whether they actually smell the same is a matter of opinion, but they are undeniably cheaper. One manufacturer, The Body Shop in San Francisco, states that synthetics are actually more environmentally sound than "destroying countless flowers."[2] (Flowers, however, are a renewable resource, while petroleum is not.) Look for products that are nonirritating to skin, and use them with caution.

Other major brands *(never recommended)*. These companies conduct animal testing or make extensive use of animal ingredients; avoid their products whenever possible.

DO-IT-YOURSELF

Essential oils. You can easily create your own perfume or fragrance using essential oils, which are highly concentrated plant extracts sold in bath and specialty shops. Just buy a small amount of essential oil in a fragrance you like, then dilute it with alcohol and water. You can also use the oils full strength, but be careful—they're very strong.

1. *1991 U.S. Industrial Outlook* (Department of Commerce, 1991), p. 36-5.
2. The Body Shop Catalog (The Body Shop, 1341 7th St., Berkeley, CA 94710) 1990, p. 18.

RAZORS, BLADE

Razors have gone through many changes over the decades, but there is one change we could have done without—the advent of disposable razors.

ENVIRONMENTAL PROBLEMS

Wasteful use of resources. Every year, Americans throw away about 2 billion nonrecyclable plastic-and-metal razors after only a few uses. This wasteful practice contributes to the depletion of fossil fuels, from which the plastic is made, and adds to our burgeoning wastestream.

CHOOSING A PRODUCT

COMMERCIAL PRODUCTS

Reusable razors *(highly recommended).* Many good reusable blade razors are available, most of them with double blades that provide a close, comfortable shave. The razors themselves last for years, but when you buy replacement blades, look for the least wasteful packaging.

Disposable razors *(never recommended).* These razors have a plastic handle with a permanently attached blade; the whole unit must be discarded when the blade gets dull. They have no shaving advantages over reusable razors,[1] so there is really no reason to use them.

ALTERNATIVES

Electric shavers. Electric shavers do require energy and resources to make and a small amount of energy to run. They have a long useful life, however, and require almost no replacement parts. Environmentally, they are probably a better choice than reusable blade razors— and certainly a better choice than disposables.

1. "Razors and Blades," *Consumer Reports* (May 1989), p. 303.

SHAMPOOS AND CONDITIONERS

These staples of hair care, with over $2 billion worth of products sold per year in the United States,[1] vary widely in both their ingredients and their environmental effects.

ENVIRONMENTAL PROBLEMS

Wasteful use of resources. Shampoos clean hair with surfactants, which, unlike soap, rinse away easily. The surfactants also remove the hair's natural oils, so we use conditioners to coat hair lightly with oils, proteins, and moisture-holding humectants. Most shampoos' surfactants are made from coconut oil, including the very common sodium lauryl sulfate. The shampoos vary widely, however, in their use of other plant, animal, or petroleum-based ingredients as sudsing agents, oils, thickeners, opacifiers, colors, and fragrances. Conditioners also vary in their ingredients; many rely heavily on animal and petroleum derivatives (such as mineral oil, lanolin, or hydrolized animal protein) instead of more expensive plant-based ingredients.

Water pollution. Though biodegradable, the surfactants and other ingredients in shampoos and conditioners are still water pollutants. If they are not adequately removed by wastewater treatment plants and are released into downstream water instead, they continue to biodegrade, using up dissolved oxygen needed by aquatic life.

Animal cruelty. Because some of the ingredients can harm humans, many companies test shampoos and conditioners on animals, under inhumane conditions; afterward the animals are killed.

Wasteful packaging. Almost all shampoo and conditioner bottles are made of high-density polyethylene plastic and are designed to be thrown away after only one use, an extremely wasteful use of nonrenewable petroleum. Container recycling, though increasing, is still rare.

CHOOSING A PRODUCT

GENERAL GUIDELINES

Simple, natural ingredients. Read ingredient lists on shampoos and conditioners to find products with simple formulas and naturally derived contents.

Cruelty-free products. Buy shampoos and conditioners made by companies that do not test products on animals.

Sensible packaging. To reduce packaging waste, pick the largest containers practical. You can sometimes buy or order very large bottles (a gallon or more) yourself, or refill smaller containers from bulk supplies at co-ops or natural foods stores. Recycle plastic bottles whenever possible.

COMMERCIAL PRODUCTS

Natural-ingredient, cruelty-free brands *(highly recommended)*. Very few shampoos and conditioners are entirely free of both petroleum derivatives and animal ingredients. Table 45 lists nationally distributed brands that contain primarily plant-based ingredients and are not tested on animals. Look for them in beauty salons, co-ops, and natural foods stores, and sometimes in supermarkets and drug stores.

Standard-ingredient, cruelty-free brands *(sometimes recommended)*. Some hair care products found mainly in salons and specialty stores use some botanical and naturally derived extracts but also rely on unnecessary petrochemicals. The following companies, however, do not test on animals:

- Clientele, (800) 327-4660
- Finelle, (508) 682-6112
- Freeman, (213) 470-6840

- KMS, (916) 244-6000
- Nexxus, (805) 968-6900
- Revlon, (212) 572-5000
- St. Ives, (818) 709-5500

Other major brands *(never recommended)*. Though often inexpensive, these products contain cheap animal by-products and petrochemicals instead of environmentally sound plant derivatives, and their manufacturers continue to engage in animal testing.

DO-IT-YOURSELF

Soap. Wash hair with a mild liquid soap, then rinse with diluted lemon juice or vinegar to wash away the mineral residue.

Baking soda. Apply a handful of baking soda to wet hair, massage into the hair and scalp, and rinse. Works well for dandruff.

WISE USE

Conservative use. Minimize waste and pollution by using hair care products sparingly:

- Do not pour shampoo or conditioner directly from the bottle onto your hair; pour a little in your hand instead.

- Experiment to see how little will work effectively. Unless your hair is quite dirty, one lather should do.

- When you approach the bottom of the bottle, add some water and use the rest.

Container recycling. Shampoo and conditioner bottles generally are made of high-density polyethylene (HDPE), which is recyclable. HDPE recycling is currently available in some communities and is becoming more common throughout the country; check with your local recycling office.

1. *1991 U.S. Industrial Outlook* (Department of Commerce, 1991), p. 36-5.

TABLE
45
NATURAL-INGREDIENT, CRUELTY-FREE SHAMPOOS AND CONDITIONERS

Brand	Product (Contains no animal ingredients)	Product (Contains animal ingredients)
All Ways		Natural Indian Hemp Shampoo Natural Indian Hemp Comb Out Conditioner; Super Light Jar Herbal Hair & Scalp Conditioner
Aloegen		Biogenic Treatment Shampoo; 60/80 Treatment Shampoo Biogenic Perm Conditioner; Biogenic Treatment Conditioner
Aubrey Organics	Blue Chamomile Shampoo; Chamomile Luxurious Herbal Shampoo; Egyptian Henna Shampoo; J.A.Y. Desert Herb Shampoo; Polynatural 60/80 Hair Rejuvenating Shampoo; Primrose & Lavender Herbal Shampoo; QBHL Quillaya Bark Hair Lather; Rosa Mosqueta Rose Hip Herbal Shampoo; Selenium Natural Blue Shampoo; Swimmers Shampoo Egyptian Henna Hair Rinse; Jojoba & Aloe Hair Rejuvenator & Conditioner; Polynatural 60/80 Hair Rejuvenating Conditioner; Rosemary & Sage Hair & Scalp Rinse	Saponin A.A.C. Herbal Root Shampoo Rosa Mosqueta Rose Hip Conditioning Hair Cream; Swimmers Conditioner
Autumn Harp	Extra Mild Baby Shampoo	
Aveda	Blue Malva Shampoo; Chamomile Shampoo; Clove Shampoo; Madder Root Shampoo; Shampure Cherry/Almond Bark Rejuvenating Conditioner; Deep-Penetrating Hair Revitalizer; Rosemary/Mint Equalizer	Elixir
Beehive Botanicals		Bee Pollen Conditioning Shampoo Bee Pollen Moisturizing Conditioner
The Body Shop		Chamomile Conditioning Shampoo; Coconut Oil Conditioning Shampoo; Frequent Wash Grapefruit Conditioning Shampoo; Henna Cream Conditioning Shampoo; Ice Blue Conditioning Shampoo; Jojoba Oil Conditioning Shampoo; Orange Spice Conditioning Shampoo; Rhassoul Mud Conditioning Shampoo; Seaweed & Birch Conditioning Shampoo Banana Conditioner; Protein Creme Rinse
Botanics	Moisturizing Shampoo; Alternate Day Shampoo Oil-Free Conditioner	
Bronson	Conditioning Shampoo	Moisturizing Hair Conditioner
BWC (Beauty Without Cruelty)	BWC Oil-Free Extra Body Shampoo; BWC Oil-Free Shampoo BWC Oil-Free Conditioner; BWC Oil-Free Extra Body Conditioner	

TABLE 45

NATURAL-INGREDIENT, CRUELTY-FREE SHAMPOOS AND CONDITIONERS *(continued)*

Brand	Product (Contains no animal ingredients)	Product (Contains animal ingredients)
CamoCare		Shampoo
Carlson		E-Gem Shampoo
Caswell-Massey		Almond Cream Shampoo; Sandalwood Conditioning Shampoo Almond Cream Hair Conditioner; Sandalwood Conditioner
Desert Essence	Dr. Gomez Jojoba Shampoo; Jojoba Spirulina Shampoo Jojoba Lilac Conditioner	
Earth Science	Hair Treatment Shampoo Hair Repair Creme Rinse; HA-5 Deep Conditioning Pack	Herbal Astringent Shampoo
Eva Jon		Shampoo Ultra Conditioner
Focus 21		Jojoba Shampoo; Shampoo for Men Only; Shampoo for Normal to Dry Hair All Purpose Skin & Hair Plasma Rehydrating Conditioner; Hair Rebuilding Formula Revitalizer; Hair Remoisturizing Formula Re-Hydrante; Reconditioning Formula
4-D SUNaturals	Algae Shampoo Revitalizer; Energizer Shampoo; Energizer Shampoo with Jojoba; Players Choice Jojoba Shampoo Energizer Conditioner; Players Choice Conditioner	
Garden of Eden	Herbal Shampoo Chamomile Amino Acid Conditioner; Herbal Conditioner	Chamomile Protein Shampoo; Coconut Creme Shampoo Coconut Creme Conditioner
General Nutrition	Golden Harvest Jojoba Shampoo; Golden Harvest Vitamin E Shampoo; Nourishair Biotin Shampoo; Golden Harvest Jojoba Conditioner	
Giovanni		California Gold Jojoba Herbal Shampoo; 20/20 Shampoo Silky Finish Rinse; Silver Herbal Mineral Conditioning Rinse; 20/20 Remoisturizer
Golden Lotus	Herbal Shampoo; Jojoba Creme Shampoo; Lemongrass Shampoo; Lotus Shampoo for Normal to Dry Hair Herbal Conditioner; Rosemary & Lavender Conditioner; Silk Protein Conditioner	
Granny's Old Fashioned Products	Gently Yours;Rich & Radiant Shampoo Soft & Silky Conditioner	
Gruene	Natural Revitalizing Shampoo Natural Revitalizing Conditioner	

(continued on next page)

TABLE
45

NATURAL-INGREDIENT, CRUELTY-FREE
SHAMPOOS AND CONDITIONERS *(continued)*

Brand	Product (Contains no animal ingredients)	Product (Contains animal ingredients)
Hain	Avocado Shampoo Avocado Conditioner	
Head	Original Shampoo; Pure & Basic Shampoo Pure & Basic Conditioning Rinse	Original Conditioner
Home Health Products		Oliva Olive Oil Shampoo Oliva Cream Rinse

Image		Avocado Clenz; Cherimoya Clenz;
		  Formula D; Kera-Clenz; Milk Clenz;
		  Naturally White Honey Clenz
		Cherimoya Rinse; Hydr Q; Intra-Kera;
		  pH Lotion; Vitamin Plus

Infinity	Golden Chamomile Shampoo;
	  Radiant Rosemary Shampoo
	Chamomile Conditioning Rinse;
	  Rosemary Conditioning Rinse	

Isis		Shampoo for Dry Hair; Shampoo for Normal Hair

Jason	Aussie Gold Tea Tree Oil
	  Conditioner; Henna Highlights
	  Conditioner; Vitamin E Conditioner
		Aloe Vera Juice Shampoo; Aussie Gold
		  Tea Tree Oil Shampoo; Biotin Shampoo;
		  E.F.A. Primrose Shampoo;Gingko
		  Shampoo; Henna Highlights Shampoo;
		  Jojoba Shampoo; Keratin Shampoo; Sea
		  Kelp Shampoo; Vitamin E Shampoo
		Aloe Vera Juice Conditioner; Biotin
		  Conditioner; Gingko Conditioner; Jojoba
		  Conditioner; Keratin Conditioner; Sea
		  Kelp Conditioner

Kallima	Aloe/Jojoba Conditioning Shampoo Aloe/Jojoba Hair & Scalp Conditioner	
Kiss My Face	Olive & Aloe Shampoo Olive & Aloe Conditioner	
KSA	Jojoba Shampoo; Jojoba Shampoo for Frequent Users Cream Rinse with Jojoba	

L'anza Research	Biotane Shampoo; Lavenda
	  Shampoo; Remede Shampoo;
	  Vitro Shampoo Re-Balance Reconstructor	

The Magic of Aloe		Lusterizing Low pH Shampoo; Magic Hair Conditioner
Mera	Shampoo	
Mild and Natural	Shampoo	
Mountain Ocean		Hair Maximum Shampoo Hair Conditioning Rinse; Hair Conditioning Treatment

Natural Bodycare		Aloe-Herb Shampoo; Quite Natural
		  Daily Shampoo
		Aloe-Herb Conditioner; Quite Natural
		  Daily Conditioner

TABLE
45

NATURAL-INGREDIENT, CRUELTY-FREE
SHAMPOOS AND CONDITIONERS (continued)

Brand	Product (Contains no animal ingredients)	Product (Contains animal ingredients)
Nature de France	Aloe Honey-Rich Shampoo; Chamomile Protein Shampoo Aloe Honey-Rich Conditioner; Chamomile Protein Conditioner	
Nature's Gate	Herbal Hair Shampoo Herbal Hair Conditioner	Aloe Vera Shampoo; Awapuhi Shampoo; Baby Shampoo; Biotin Shampoo; Henna Shampoo; Jojoba Shampoo Keratin Shampoo; Rainwater Herbal Shampoo; Rainwater Shampoo for Dry Hair; Rainwater Shampoo for Oily Hair; Tea Tree Oil Shampoo Aloe Vera Conditioner; Awapuhi Conditioner; Biotin Conditioner Gel; Henna Conditioner; Jojoba Conditioner; Keratin Conditioner; Rainwater Conditioner
Natus	Moisture Balance Herbal Shampoo	Herbal Shampoo Herbal Hair Reconstructor Conditioner
Nirvana		Blue Malva Shampoo; Chamomile Shampoo; Clove Shampoo; Hibiscus Shampoo; Rosemary/Mint Shampoo
Nutri-Metics		Natural Lustre Shampoo Natural Lustre Finishing Rinse
O'Naturel	Chamomile Shampoo; Henna & Rosemary Shampoo	Honey & Sage Shampoo; Lavender Conditioning Shampoo
Oriental Beauty Secrets	Ultra Vital Conditioning Rinse	
Oxyfresh		Shampoo Conditioner
Patricia Allison	Rose Petal Luxury Shampoo Shimmer Hair Conditioner	
Paul Mitchell		Awapuhi Shampoo; Baby Don't Cry Shampoo; Shampoo One; Shampoo Two; Tea Tree Special Shampoo The Conditioner; Hair Repair; Super Charged Conditioner
Paul Penders	Jasmine Chamomile Shampoo; Peppermint Hops Shampoo; Rosemary Lavender Shampoo; Walnut Oil Shampoo Lemon Yarrow Cream Rinse	Chamomile Scalp Tonic & Hair Volumizer; German Herbal Hair Repair
Pre de Provence	Cade Shampoo; Chamomile Shampoo; Lavandin Shampoo; Rosmarin Shampoo	French Lavender Conditioner
Rainbow Research	Aloe/PABA Herbal Shampoo; Henna Shampoo; Sports Shampoo; Stony Brook Shampoo Henna Conditioner; Stony Brook Conditioner; Vegetable Reconstructor	

(continued on next page)

TABLE
45

NATURAL-INGREDIENT, CRUELTY-FREE
SHAMPOOS AND CONDITIONERS *(continued)*

Brand	Product (Contains no animal ingredients)	Product (Contains animal ingredients)
Real Aloe Company		Aloe Vera Shampoo Aloe Vera Conditioner
Reviva	Complex Shampoo; Seaweed Shampoo; Vitamin B Complex Shampoo Seaweed Conditioner	Elastin & Panthenol Shampoo Hair Mask; Hair Conditioner with Elastin
Schiff		Bee Pollen Conditioning Shampoo Bee Pollen Moisturizing Hair Conditioner
Sebastian		Cello Shampoo; Misty Rose Moisture Base Cello-Fix; Sheen; Thick Ends
ShiKai	Dry Hair Shampoo; Henna Gold Shampoo for Blondes; Henna Gold Shampoo for Brunettes Henna Gold Conditioner; Henna Gold Moisture-Plus Conditioner	Fine Hair Shampoo; Original Formula Natural Shampoo; Permed Hair Shampoo Amla Conditioner; Spray-On Conditioner
Sombra Cosmetics	Almond Shampoo; Cherry Shampoo; Pineapple/Coconut Shampoo Almond Conditioner; Cherry Conditioner Pineapple/Coconut Conditioner	
StonyBrook Botanical		Oil Free Shampoo Oil Free Conditioner
Terra Nova		Pikaki Shampoo; Rain Shampoo
Tom's of Maine		Aloe & Almond Natural Shampoo; Natural Baby Shampoo
Tonialg	Restorative Shampoo Restorative Conditioner	
TRI	Jojoba Shampoo; Whole Wheat Shampoo	Ecollogen Shampoo Jojoba Hair & Scalp Conditioner; Unific Energy Moisturizing Treatment
Vita Wave	Finishing Creme Rinse	
Wachters	Botanical Shampoo; Dry & Damaged Shampoo Botanical Conditioner	Goldina Shampoo; Shampoo with Protein Conditioner with Protein
Weleda	Chamomile Shampoo; Rosemary Shampoo Chamomile Conditioner; Rosemary Conditioner	
Wysong		Natural Revitalizing Shampoo; Rinseless Shampoo Rinseless Conditioner

SOAPS, HAND AND BATH

Americans used nearly 1 billion pounds of bar soap, plus 32.5 million gallons of liquid hand soap, in 1990.[1] All soaps are made by heating fats or oils with lye, but differences among the types of fats or oils used and the other ingredients added make some products more environmentally sound than others.

ENVIRONMENTAL PROBLEMS

Animal by-products. The major soap manufacturers use animal fats, or tallow; they're cheaper and easier to use than plant-based oils. The beef industry—which is environmentally destructive, wasteful, and inhumane—provides most of the tallow used (see Beef, p. 56).

Water pollution. Deodorants, scents, emulsifiers, stabilizers, lathering agents—some chemical, some natural—all find their way into soaps. The average major brand contains a dozen or more ingredients; some common additives are

- *Triclocarban*, a deodorant derived from petroleum

- *EDTA*, a stabilizer and antioxidant made with formaldehyde, sodium cyanide, and petrochemicals

- *Sodium dodecylbenzenesulfonate*, a detergent compound made from benzene

- *BHT*, an antioxidant derived from coal tars or petroleum

- *FD&C colors*, added solely for appearance, made from complex synthetic compounds

Most of these ingredients are made from nonrenewable fossil fuels, through energy-intensive processes, and pollute wastewater, adding to the already heavy burden of wastewater treatment plants.

Animal cruelty. Because some ingredients can harm humans, many companies test soaps on animals, under inhumane conditions; afterward the animals are killed.

Wasteful packaging. Ideally, bars of soap should come unwrapped or in recyclable paper wrappers. In reality, most commercial brands are wrapped in nonrecyclable coated paper. The most wasteful packaging is that of liquid soaps; these pump-activated plastic bottles waste resources and have little chance of being recycled.

CHOOSING A PRODUCT

GENERAL GUIDELINES

Simple, natural ingredients. Look for soaps with simple formulas and naturally derived ingredients, including plant-based oils instead of tallow.

Cruelty-free products. Choose soaps made by companies that do not test products on animals.

Sensible packaging. Look for minimal packaging, preferably recyclable. If you must use liquid soaps, keep the plastic pump bottle and refill it from a larger container.

COMMERCIAL PRODUCTS

Natural-ingredient, cruelty-free brands *(highly recommended)*. Table 46 lists some soap manufacturers that do not test on animals and that use vegetable oils such as palm, coconut, olive, soy, or peanut oil. Look for them in co-ops, natural products stores, and bath shops.

Standard-ingredient, cruelty-free brands *(sometimes recommended)*. Some products are not tested on animals but do contain animal by-products or synthetic ingredients. Read the labels carefully.

Other major brands *(never recommended)*. These products contain lots of synthetic ingre-

TABLE
46

NATURAL-INGREDIENT, CRUELTY-FREE HAND AND BATH SOAPS

Brand	Basic Oils	Varieties
Alexandra Avery Vegetable Oil Soaps	Palm, Coconut, Olive	Jungle Blossoms, Wild Mountain Herbs
Aubrey Organics Honeysuckle Vegetal Soap	Peanut, Karite Butter	
Brookside Soaps	Coconut, Palm, Olive	Cinnamon, Extra Mild Herbal, Lemongrass and Lime, Oatmeal and Almond, Rosemary and Lavender, Spearmint, Unscented
Chandrika	Vegetable	——
Clearly Natural	not listed	Aloe Vera, Coconut, Cucumber, Honeysuckle, Jasmine, Jojoba, Lemon, Lilac, Musk, Passionfruit, Rain Forest, Strawberry, Tea Rose, Unscented, Vitamin E, Wildflowers
Dr. Bronner's Magic Soap	Palm, Coconut	Almond, Aloe Vera, Eucalyptus, Lavender, Lemon, Peppermint, Rose
Dr. Theiss	Vegetable	Calendula
Emile's Clay Box Soaps	Vegetable	Green, Pink, or White Clay
Faith in Nature	Vegetable	Pine, Seaweed
Gregory Aromatic Soap	Vegetable	Mimosa, Sandalwood, Tea Rose
Heavenly Soap	Olive, Soy, Coconut, Palm	Coconut Milk and Honey, Honeysuckle, Jasmine, Oatmeal, Peppermint Aloe Vera, Rose Glycerine, Unscented
Heritage Pine Tar Soap	Olive	——
Home Health Products	Palm, Coconut	Palma Christie Deodorant Bar
Kappus Transparent Soaps	not listed	Apricot, Bio-Seife, Fresh Lemon, Green Apple, Mandarine, Milk and Honey, Waldhimbeere
Karite Soap	Palm	Shea Butter
Kiss My Face	Olive	Olive and Aloe, Olive and Herbal, Pure Olive Oil
Loanda	Palm, Coconut, Olive	Mint Comfrey, Wheat Germ-E
Marseille	Olive	Green, Uncolored
Nature de France	Palm, Coconut	Argile Blanche, Argile Rose, Argillet
Natus	Vegetable	Vegetable Glycerine Bar
North Country Glycerine Soap	Vegetable, Olive, Coconut	Bayberry, Fresh Apple, Gardenia, Rose-Lavender
Olivea	Olive	——
Only Natural	Vegetable	Aloe Vera, Chamomile, Cucumber
Rainbow Soaps	Coconut, Palm	Aloe-Oatmeal, Golden Moisture
Sappo Hill Glycerine Cream Soaps	Palm, Coconut	Almond, Aloe, Apple, Cascade Rose, Cucumber, Jasmine, Lemon, Oatmeal, Oregon Berry, Peach, Sandalwood, Unscented
Save the Whales Glycerine Soap	not listed	Green, Yellow
Shahin Olive Oil Soap	Olive	—
Sirena Pure Coconut Oil Soap	Coconut	Coconut, Vitamin E
Thermalg	Coconut, Palm	The Loofa Soap (Seaweed), Seamud Soap

dients and animal fat and are usually tested on animals; they should be avoided whenever possible.

1. *1991 U.S. Industrial Outlook* (Department of Commerce, 1991), p. 36-1.

TAMPONS AND SANITARY NAPKINS

About two-thirds of American women prefer tampons; the rest use sanitary napkins or alternative products.[1] Though convenient and effective, tampons and sanitary napkins are not all environmentally sound.

ENVIRONMENTAL PROBLEMS

Disposal problems. Plastic tampon applicators are often flushed down the toilet and must either be screened out at a wastewater treatment facility—adding to its tasks—or discharged directly into downstream waters. After heavy rainstorms, for example, thousands of applicators routinely wash up on Atlantic beaches. The applicators are not only unsightly, they're also dangerous to fish and wildlife. Most sanitary napkins have a nondegradable plastic backing that similarly compounds disposal problems if flushed into a sewage system instead of placed in the trash.

Wasteful use of resources. The use of plastic in tampons and sanitary napkins—for applicators, absorbent material, stain shields, or covers—wastes nonrenewable petroleum and contributes to air, water, and soil pollution.

Toxic Shock Syndrome. Toxic Shock Syndrome (TSS), well publicized in the late 1970s and early 1980s, seriously infected hundreds of women (in 1980 it peaked at 890 reported cases).[2] The sometimes-lethal disease was traced to tampons, especially superabsorbent ones, used by women whose immune systems were unable to deal with a buildup of bacteria in the vagina. TSS is still around, but with a much lower incidence because of more careful use of tampons and some tampon redesign. The worst offenders, superabsorbent Rely tampons, were taken off the market.

Chemical irritants. Deodorant tampons and sanitary pads contain perfumes and solvents that can irritate tissue in some women or even cause severe allergic reactions.

CHOOSING A PRODUCT

GENERAL GUIDELINES

Weighing needs and safety. Balance your sanitary needs with health considerations to find the right products:

- Choose the minimum absorbency you find practical.

- Buy products made of natural materials instead of synthetics.

- Avoid scented or deodorant-treated tampons and napkins.

- Consider reusable sanitary products instead of disposable tampons and napkins.

Sensible packaging. Look for products that are efficiently packaged, using as little plastic as possible. To reduce packaging waste, choose the largest box practical, and avoid napkins individually wrapped in plastic.

COMMERCIAL PRODUCTS

Natural-material, nondeodorant tampons *(highly recommended).* Two major brands offer more environmentally sound products:

- *Tampax Original Regular tampons* use cotton as their absorbent fiber; the applicators are made of paper with a food-grade oil coating. The box says the applicator is flushable, but put it in the trash instead. Made by Tambrands (800) 523-0014. (*Note:* other Tambrands tampons use plastic applicators, rayon fibers, or deodorants.)

- *o.b. tampons* are made of rayon and cotton fibers and have no applicator at all.

Made by Personal Products, (800) 526-3967.

Sanitary napkins *(sometimes recommended).* Most napkins use a paperlike wood pulp, sometimes with petroleum derivatives (such as sodium polyacrylate) added to increase absorbency, and a plastic liner. The manufacturers are not required to disclose their materials and do not disclose them voluntarily, so evaluating brands is difficult. One product, however, stands out:

- *Today's Choice Thin Maxi Pads* have unbleached absorbent material with a cotton interior liner. Made by ICD Products, (800) 262-0042.

Other major-brand tampons *(not generally recommended).* These tampons are made with rayon or rayon/cotton fibers. Rayon (also called viscose rayon) comes from wood pulp, a renewable resource, but the manufacturing process is complex and polluting. All these tampons have plastic applicators and many are treated with deodorant chemicals; avoid them whenever possible.

ALTERNATIVES

Sponges. Some women like to use small, reusable sea-sponges. They must be washed often and sterilized in boiling water both before the first use and between periods. Call a local women's health center for information on sponges before using them. Look for large sea-sponges, which you can cut to size, in natural foods stores, or order from InterNatural, (800) 446-4903.

Menstrual cups. These cups are made of soft rubber and are worn internally to hold fluid. One brand approved by the Food and Drug Administration is The Keeper, P.O. Box 22023, Cincinnati, OH 45220.

Cloth menstrual pads. These sturdy, unbleached, all-cotton pads are easy to wash and reuse and are available in different sizes and colors. Order them from the manufacturers:

- Many Moons, #14-130 Dallas Rd., Victoria, BC, V8V 1A3, Canada

◆ New Cycle, (707) 829-3154

◆ Sisterly Works, R.R. 3, Box 107, Port Lavaca, TX 77979

WISE USE

Safe use. To avoid contracting Toxic Shock Syndrome, take the following precautions:

- Always choose the least absorbent tampon possible.

- Change tampons frequently, and switch to pads at night or on low-flow days.

- Watch for TSS symptoms: headache, fever, loss of strength and appetite, dizziness, diarrhea, and skin rashes, followed by peeling skin on the palms or the soles of the feet. If you experience any of these symptoms contact a physician *immediately*.

Proper disposal. *Never* flush a tampon, tampon applicator, or napkin down the toilet—despite what the packaging might say. Instead, dispose of it in the regular trash.

1. "Are Tampons Safer Now?" *Consumer Reports* (May 1986), p. 334.
2. Ibid., p. 332.

TOOTHPASTES

Toothpastes remove plaque, clean stains, and make brushing more pleasant, but many brands are environmentally unsound.

ENVIRONMENTAL PROBLEMS

Wasteful use of resources. All toothpastes have similar basic ingredients: a mild abrasive, such as calcium carbonate, hydrated silica, or sodium bicarbonate; and a cleaner, usually a mild detergent such as sodium lauryl sulfate. Other ingredients include processing aids, flavors, colors, and in many toothpastes, a fluoride salt that reduces tooth decay. The major-brand toothpastes use petrochemicals—causing fossil-fuel depletion and manufacturing pollution—for some additives, including colors (added to make the product more visually appealing), processing ingredients (such as polyethylene glycol), and flavors (including sodium saccharin, a potential human carcinogen).

Animal cruelty. Because some ingredients can harm humans, many companies test toothpastes on animals, under inhumane conditions; afterward the animals are killed.

Wasteful packaging. Most toothpaste tubes are made of nonrecyclable plastic. Much more wasteful, however, are the increasingly popular toothpaste pumps, which take far more energy and plastic to manufacture.

CHOOSING A PRODUCT

GENERAL GUIDELINES

Simple, natural ingredients. Select toothpastes made with simple formulas and naturally derived materials rather than synthetic chemicals.

TABLE 47

NATURAL-INGREDIENT, CRUELTY-FREE TOOTHPASTES[a]

Brand	Products
Barth	Dolomite Toothpaste; Natural Toothpaste
Desert Essence	Tea Tree Toothpaste
Merfluan	Anise Toothpowder; Cinnamon & Mint Toothpowder; Peppermint Toothpowder
Peelu	Toothpaste; Toothpowder
Tom's of Maine	Baking Soda Fluoride Toothpaste; Cinnamint Fluoride Toothpaste; Cinnamint Toothpaste; Fennel Fluoride Toothpaste; Fennel Toothpaste; Spearmint Fluoride Toothpaste; Spearmint Toothpaste
Vicco	Herbal Toothpaste; Turmeric Cream
Weleda	Plant Toothpaste; Salt & Soda Toothpaste

[a] No animal ingredients

Cruelty-free products. Look for toothpastes made by companies that do not test products on animals.

Sensible packaging. To reduce packaging waste, buy the largest tube practical, and avoid plastic pumps.

COMMERCIAL PRODUCTS

Natural-ingredient, cruelty-free brands *(highly recommended).* The products in Table 47 contain primarily plant-based ingredients and are not tested on animals. Look for them in co-ops and natural foods, better grocery, and drug-stores nationwide, or order them from natural-products catalogs.

Major brands *(never recommended).* Major-brand toothpastes all have similar formulas and are usually tested on animals, so none stands out as environmentally sound.

DO-IT-YOURSELF

Baking soda. Baking soda cleans teeth effectively; however, many dentists are concerned about its abrasiveness (which could damage teeth over time) and recommend it for occasional use only.

ALTERNATIVES

Plain water. The mechanical action of brushing your teeth (along with flossing) is the best way to remove plaque, so simply brushing with plain water can be quite effective. Many drinking water supplies contain either added or natural fluoride, a tooth-decay preventative especially important for children, making fluoride toothpaste less important or unnecessary.

WISE USE

Proper brushing. No matter what brand of toothpaste you use, be sure to brush correctly:

- Brush and floss at least once a day—especially at bedtime to remove particles that would otherwise remain on your teeth overnight.

- Use a soft, rounded-bristle brush to avoid damaging your gums.

- Occasionally brush for a full five minutes to thoroughly remove bacteria and plaque.

PETS AND
PET SUPPLIES

DOG AND CAT FOODS

Every year Americans buy about 9.5 billion pounds of pet foods—mostly for dogs and cats.[1] Producing this huge volume of food has some significant environmental impacts.

ENVIRONMENTAL PROBLEMS

Resource consumption. Dog and cat foods contain the same foods people eat, though of lower quality. A typical commercial dry dog food, for example, contains corn, soybeans, brown rice, poultry meal, beet pulp, and vitamin and mineral supplements; these ingredients are mixed under high pressure and heat and then sprayed with hot poultry fat, natural or artificial flavors, and beneficial bacteria (to aid digestion). Poultry meal and other meat ingredients often come from diseased animals or parts—tumors, for example—rejected for human consumption. Dog- and cat-food ingredients are produced in the same way as human foods, compounding the effects of commercial agriculture: the heavy use of agrichemicals, drugs, water, and energy; soil depletion; and pollution of the air and water.

Wasteful packaging. Dog- and cat-food packaging varies widely; the most inefficient forms are small servings packaged in cans, nonrecyclable plastic, or coated paper containers.

CHOOSING A PRODUCT

GENERAL GUIDELINES

Weighing your pet's needs. Choose products that meet your animal's specific needs, depending on its age, health, and activity level. Most veterinarians are quite knowledgeable about

pet foods and can recommend the most beneficial foods for your pet.

High-quality dry foods. Premium-quality dry dog and cat foods are by far the best choice, environmentally. Dry foods have two to three times the calories per pound of canned foods, and premium brands are nutritionally more concentrated. High-quality ingredients and fewer chemicals are more important than fancy shapes or flavors that mean nothing to your pet.

Sensible packaging. Dry foods in large paper sacks are the best packaging choice. Treats are available in bulk or in large cardboard or paperboard boxes at pet supply stores. If you must buy small portions, choose recyclable containers.

COMMERCIAL PRODUCTS

Premium-brand dry dog and cat foods *(highly recommended).* Though more expensive per pound, premium dog and cat foods are more carefully formulated, with better ingredients, than are standard pet foods and offer several benefits:

- They improve your pet's health. Premium cat food, for instance, contains taurine to help prevent heart disease and has a low acidity level and ash content to control feline urologic syndrome.

- Premium brands offer different varieties of food geared to age, weight, activity, and overall health, so you can closely match your pet's diet and needs.

- Because they are nutritionally concentrated, premium dry foods cut feeding amounts by at least 20 percent, saving resources and energy.

Table 48 lists some nationally distributed premium dog and cat foods (some made by large companies that also sell low-quality foods). You can buy them in pet and pet supply stores and through veterinarians.

Vegetarian dry dog and cat foods *(highly recommended).* Many people who do not eat meat themselves would also like to avoid feeding it to their pets. Some excellent, nutritionally com-

TABLE
48

PREMIUM DRY FOODS FOR DOGS AND CATS

Brand	Dog Foods	Cat Foods
ANF (800) 722-3261	Adult Formula Performance Formula	Tami Adult Formula Tami Kitten Formula
Breeder's Choice (818) 334-9301	Avo-Derm Dog Food Complete Dog Food Lamb & Rice Dog Food Lite Dog Food	
Eagle (800) 255-5959	Kennel Pack Lite Pak Maintenance Pack Natural Pack Puppy Pack Stress Pack	Cat Pack
Iams (800) 525-4267	Chunks Eukanuba Less Active for Dogs Minichunks Puppy Food	Cat Food Kitten Food Less Active for Cats
MannaPro (phone not listed)	Classic Lite Classic Puppy Classic Supreme	
Natural Life (800) 367-2391	Adult Dog Formula Condition Dog Formula Puppy Dog Formula Senior Dog Formula	Feline Formula
Nature's Recipe (714) 639-1134	Puppy, Performance & Lactation Diet Senior/Pension Dog Food	Optimum Feline Diet Optimum Feline Diet Lite
Nutro (800) 833-5330	Max Max Mini-Size Max Puppy Max Special	Max Cat Adult
Pro Plan (800) 345-5678	Lite Formula Performance Formula	Adult Formula Growth Formula
Purebred (800) 247-2733	Adult Formula Puppy Formula Senior Formula	Purebred for Cats
Science Diet (800) 445-5777	Canine Growth Canine Maintenance Canine Maintenance Light Canine Performance Canine Senior	Feline Growth Feline Maintenance Feline Maintenance Light

plete vegetarian dry foods are available, but not nationwide. Look for regional brands in natural foods stores, co-ops, or pet supply stores, or make your own (see Do-It-Yourself, below).

Standard-brand dry dog and cat foods *(not generally recommended)*. The standard-brand dog and cat foods found in most grocery stores are cheaper per pound than premium brands, but offer fewer environmental or health advantages. They contain lower-quality ingredients and fillers, so you must feed your pet more than you do with premium foods. And if these foods are your pet's sole source of nutrition, the animal's long-term health will suffer.

Canned and moist dog and cat foods *(not generally recommended)*. Some of these products have higher-quality ingredients than those in dry foods, in part so you're not offended when you open the container. (It's easier to disguise animal by-products in dry foods.) But the main ingredient is water—about 75 percent in canned foods and 33 percent in moist foods. Packaging the foods in cans or plastic adds to their environmental cost. Your veterinarian might suggest canned or moist food for an ill animal; ask for a brand-name recommendation.

DO-IT-YOURSELF

Homemade dog and cat foods. You can make your own dog and cat food, though to ensure complete nutrition you *must* follow a formula such as those in *Dr. Pitcairn's Complete Guide to Natural Health for Dogs and Cats,* by Richard H. Pitcairn (Rodale Press, 1982). Nutritional supplements are important in a homemade diet; two vegetarian supplements are Vegecat and Vegedog; you can order them from Vegan Street, (800) 422-5525.

WISE USE

Proper feeding. In addition to providing high-quality food, it's also important that you feed your pet correctly:

- Ask your veterinarian for advice on feeding amounts and times; if you follow the manufacturer's feeding recommendations, measure the amount carefully.

- Never overfeed an animal. If your pet starts to gain weight, either increase the animal's exercise level or decrease its food intake.

- Don't feed your pet table scraps and other human foods, except perhaps a small amount occasionally as a special treat.

- Don't use nutritional supplements unless your veterinarian specifically recommends them. And *never* give your pet supplements made for humans or based on human nutritional needs; animals have very different needs from ours.

1. Louis Rukeyser and John Cooney, *Louis Rukeyser's Business Almanac* (Simon & Schuster, 1988), p. 575.

FLEA AND TICK CONTROL

Flea and tick control is important for your pet's physical and mental health as well as your own. Fleas can cause severe skin irritation and weaken animals' resistance to disease. Tick bites can become infected or cause serious illnesses such as Lyme disease. Unfortunately, many commercial products are dangerous and environmentally unsound.

ENVIRONMENTAL PROBLEMS

Toxic ingredients. The active ingredients in most chemical flea and tick products are toxic. Some products are designed to be absorbed by the animal, saturating body fluids and paralyzing any flea or tick that bites the skin. Other chemicals either repel pests or kill them on contact. The following are chemicals found in many collars, sprays, and shampoos:

- *Tetrachlorvinphos*, a compound similar to the nerve gases used in chemical warfare; it can cause nerve damage in pets

- *Pyrethrins*, *cinerins*, and *allethrin*, potent insecticides that are made from certain chrysanthemum flowers and are toxic if swallowed or inhaled

- *N-octylbicycloheptene dicarboximide*, a compound that improves insecticide performance and is toxic if swallowed or absorbed through the skin

- *N,N-diethyl-m-toluamide*, or *deet*, a strong chemical that is also used in insect repellents for humans; it is toxic if swallowed and irritating to the eyes and mucous membranes

Animal cruelty. Because some ingredients can harm humans and animals, many manufacturers test flea- and tick-control products on animals, under inhumane conditions; afterward the animals are killed.

Wasteful packaging. Many products come in aerosol cans, which are costly to make, polluting to use, and nonrecyclable.

CHOOSING A PRODUCT

GENERAL GUIDELINES

Nontoxic or less-toxic remedies. Try the alternatives and the safest products first; move on to a more toxic product only as a last resort.

Cruelty-free products. Look for flea- and tick-control products made by companies that do not test on animals.

Sensible packaging. Buy large containers if you will use them up within a year; avoid aerosols by choosing powders, shampoos, collars, or pump sprays.

COMMERCIAL PRODUCTS

Nontoxic, cruelty-free herbal formulas *(highly recommended)*. These cruelty-free products use oils of such plants as pennyroyal, eucalyptus, citronella, orange, cedarwood, and bay, which irritate and repel fleas and ticks but are gentle to pets. (Pennyroyal is hazardous during pregnancy; don't use it if either you or your pet is pregnant.) Some shampoos use soap to kill existing fleas and ticks, and herbs to repel newcomers. Look for the following widely distributed products in pet supply, hardware, or natural foods stores, or call the manufacturers for a distributor near you:

- Green Ban (herbal powder, shampoo); (319) 227-7996

- Natural Animal (herbal collars, spray, shampoo); order from Baubiologie Hardware, (408) 372-6826

- Natural Animal (herbal food supplements); order from Gardens Alive!, (812) 623-3800

- No Common Scents (herbal flea oil); (513) 767-4261

◆ PetGuard (herbal collars, powder, shampoo); (800) 874-3221

◆ Safer (spray, shampoo); (800) 423-7544

Less-toxic products *(recommended)*. Methoprene and phenoxycarb are two low-toxicity chemicals that work not as insecticides but as insect growth regulators. These synthetic hormones prolong the larval stage of fleas and prevent their development into adults. They do not kill or repel adult fleas but can help control long-term infestations. Precor, a methoprene product, is made by Zoecon, (800) 527-0512.

Pyrethrum-based products *(sometimes recommended)*. Pyrethrum is a natural insecticide extracted from certain chrysanthemum flowers. It is related to pyrethrins and cinerins and somewhat milder. Nevertheless, it is toxic if swallowed or inhaled and should be used with great caution. Three nationally distributed manufacturers are

◆ Ecosafe (pyrethrum powder); order from The National Choice, (505) 438-3448

◆ Natural Animal (pyrethrum powder); order from Gardens Alive!, (812) 623-3800

◆ Ringer (pyrethrum spray); (800) 654-1047

Toxic products *(not generally recommended)*. Use these products only as a last resort, if the nontoxic or less-toxic methods do not work. Avoid both the collars, which are extremely toxic to the animals, and the powders and bombs, which can contaminate the air. Instead, look for shampoos and nonaerosol sprays with pyrethrins, cinerins, or allethrin as their active ingredients instead of tetrachlorvinphos. Whatever you choose, use as little as possible, for as short a time as possible.

DO-IT-YOURSELF

Flea combs. These fine combs trap fleas as the animal's hair passes through; use them with a dish of soapy water to kill any fleas you catch. Look for flea combs in pet-supply stores.

Citrus-oil treatment. Mix orange or grapefruit skins, well cleaned of any fruit or juice, in a blender. Simmer on the stove with some water, then cool. Work into animal's fur with your hands or brush in with a plastic-bristled brush.

ALTERNATIVES

Prevention. You can reduce your pet's vulnerability to fleas and ticks by keeping the animal healthy (parasites are less attracted to healthy animals) and minimizing its risk of exposure:

- For optimum health keep your animal well fed (but not overfed) and exercised.

- Add brewer's yeast to your pet's food; it helps deter fleas and is protein- and vitamin-rich.

- Regular bathing with any pet shampoo will help kill fleas and control mild infestations.

- Frequent grooming keeps the undercoat brushed and its oils distributed, and the skin healthy.

- During tick season keep your pet out of long grass and away from wooded, brushy areas.

Good housekeeping. Ticks live outdoors; that's the only place your pet can pick them up. Fleas, however, are another story: your home can actually become a breeding ground in warm weather. During a flea infestation you may find only a small number of fleas on your pet; the other adults, eggs, and larvae will be in the pet's bedding and in your carpets and furniture. To control fleas in your home, take the following steps:

- Vacuum the carpets, furniture, and floor crevices frequently; after each cleaning take the vacuum cleaner's contents outside and put them in the trash.

- Keep the pet restricted to only one sleeping area, and wash the bedding frequently.

- Sprinkle diatomaceous earth (available in hardware and garden supply stores) on the animal's bedding and other flea-infested areas. Diatomaceous earth is nontoxic; it dehydrates insects after contact.

WISE USE

Safe use. If you use any flea- or tick-control products, take the following precautions:

- If you must use a toxic product, follow the directions carefully and use only one type of product at a time.

- When you give your pet a flea bath, either toxic or nontoxic, start by ringing the neck completely with shampoo, then work toward the tail (this stops fleas from escaping to the animal's head).

- If you must use a toxic, chemical-based flea collar, use it for only a few days at a time, then remove it and store it in a sealed jar.

- If either you or your pet have any adverse reactions to a product, stop using it immediately and seek medical advice.

Proper disposal. Dispose of all products according to directions. If a product is toxic, store it carefully for hazardous waste collection or take it to a collection site. Call your local waste disposal office for information on hazardous waste collection programs, or for advice if you are uncertain whether a particular product is toxic.

FOR FURTHER INFORMATION: "Least Toxic Pest Management for Fleas" (Bio-Integral Resource Center, P.O. Box 7414, Berkeley, CA 94707).

PETS

Americans have 107 million cats and dogs, 27 million caged birds, and perhaps 400 million tropical fish.[1] Breeding, feeding, and caring for all these creatures adds up to a major endeavor, with some major environmental effects.

ENVIRONMENTAL PROBLEMS

Overpopulation. Each year *13 million to 18 million* dogs and cats are put to death because no homes can be found for them.[2] Millions of other unwanted animals live in neglect or wander as strays, vulnerable to starvation, illness, accidents, and intentional cruelty.

Food consumption. Americans spend $7 billion a year just to feed their dogs and cats.[3] This food, consisting mostly of grains, soybeans, and animal by-products, is produced through the chemical-intensive agriculture that has damaged the land and caused pollution nationwide.

Waste-disposal problems. Most pet wastes are deposited in yards, parks, and the trash—none of which are designed to deal with unsanitary urine and feces. Not only are the wastes unsightly, they also carry pathogens that can pollute the soil and water.

Harm to wildlife. Wild creatures are often harmed by pets or the pet industry:

- Cats (which hunt birds and small animals) and dogs (which hunt deer and smaller game) kill an untold number of wild creatures.

- Exotic birds kept as caged pets lose both their freedom and their natural habitat. About 250,000 parrots and related birds—parakeets, macaws, cockatoos, rosellas, and others—are brought into this country each year. Their capture has seriously depleted many species' native populations.[4]

- Most ornamental fish are freshwater fish bred on fish farms. Saltwater species, however, are taken directly from the sea, sometimes with the use of narcotic drugs or chemicals; their capture depletes the natural population.

- Other wild creatures kept as pets spend their lives confined in an alien, sensory-deprived environment, often unable to take part in any natural social behavior.

CHOOSING A PET

GENERAL GUIDELINES

Weighing your needs—and the animal's. Acquiring a pet is a serious environmental decision, so decide carefully:

- Ask yourself and your family whether you really want a pet and why. Be sure to consider what the pet will need in return (see Wise Care, below).

- If you truly want a pet, think small. A cat or small dog has much less environmental impact than a large one; hamsters and gerbils are better yet.

- Do some research on different breeds and animals. If you want a dog or cat, look for a type or breed whose size, needs, and temperament are suited to you and your family.

ACQUIRING A PET

Dogs and cats. If you decide you would like a dog or cat, look into finding one through the following channels:

- Humane societies or animal shelters are the best places to start looking. (If the animals in shelters do not find homes quickly, they will be euthanized.) Some shelter animals are already neutered or spayed (if not, the new owner must have that done); most are in good health, with current vaccinations. The variety of animals waiting for adoption is astonishing, from purebreds to intriguing mixes, and from puppies or kittens to mature, already-trained adults.

- Ask a veterinarian or friends and neighbors about animals that need a new home.

- Given the pet overpopulation problem, pure-bred dogs or cats are not an environmentally sound choice: breeding specialty animals, when so many others lack homes, only adds to the problem. If you must have a purebred, however, see only reputable breeders. Especially with dogs, watch out for large-scale breeders ("puppy mills") that raise animals under unhealthy, cruel conditions. If possible, visit the kennel before making a purchase.

- If you investigate an animal advertised in the newspaper, spend time at the home with the animal and the people, and try to have the animal checked by a veterinarian before you make your decision.

Tropical birds. Two parrot species breed well in captivity—the budgerigar, or budgie (*Melopsittacus undulatus*), and the cockatiel (*Nymphicus hollandicus*). If you must own a caged exotic bird, look for captive-bred birds of these species, which are usually imported from the Netherlands or Belgium. All other parrot species are protected from commercial trade and should not be purchased unless you can be shown a written affidavit that the bird was captive-bred.

Other pets. As long as they are not taken directly from the wild, most smaller pets are a better environmental choice than cats and dogs. Look for birds, fish, rodents, and reptiles at reputable shops and breeders. If you have any questions, call a local humane society or veterinarian. Don't purchase any exotic pets unless you are sure of their origin.

WISE CARE

Responsible care. You must take responsibility for keeping your companion animal healthy, safe, and happy, and prevent it from being a nuisance to others. This responsibility includes

- *Spaying and neutering,* the key to stopping the population explosion among dogs and cats. These procedures also prevent problem behavior and certain common diseases.

- *Proper restraint,* to keep your pet safe and well behaved. Keep dogs fenced, leashed, or indoors—whatever is appropriate for the place you live. Restrain cats also; outdoor cats kill wildlife and pass on feline diseases.

- *Supervision of children and pets,* to make sure the two get along well. Children often tease pets, sometimes unknowingly, and animals surprised by a child's voice or movements can react instinctively, biting or scratching the child.

- *Good veterinary care,* to keep your pet healthy. Keep vaccinations up to date, watch for signs of ill health, and schedule regular checkups.

- *Premium quality food,* to ensure complete nutrition and reduce your pet's environmental impact (see Dog and Cat Foods, p. 268).

- *Daily exercise and play,* to maintain the animal's physical and mental health. For dogs these activities are absolutely essential.

- *Regular grooming,* to keep the animal's coat and skin healthy. Either have the animal shampooed and groomed regularly, or do it yourself.

- *Training and contact,* to keep your pet happy, sociable, and well behaved. Dogs in particular often need training, and usually need contact with other dogs and people, to learn behavior rules and to keep from becoming aggressive, overprotective, or neurotic.

- *Good sanitation,* to control disease and keep your pet from being a nuisance to other people. If you take your dog to public places, clean up any waste before you leave. Clean cat litter boxes carefully to avoid any risk of toxoplasmosis, a disease common to humans and cats and caused by parasitic microorganisms. Sift the waste from the litter often (don't change the litter until you need to). Seal wastes well and put them in the trash, and wash your hands carefully. Pregnant women should *never* clean litter boxes. Keep your pet's bedding clean to prevent fleas. And for fish, birds, rodents, and other caged animals, keep the cage or aquarium very clean.

- *Protection from household dangers,* to prevent accidents. Keep your pet safe from the many chemicals and other hazards in your home.

- *Parting with an animal responsibly,* if you can no longer keep it. *Never* abandon an animal. Instead, put ads up in veterinarians' offices and on bulletin boards, and check with friends and neighbors. As a last resort, see if the humane society or a veterinarian will take the animal.

- *Proper disposal* of a dead pet. If your pet dies, call your veterinarian or local humane society for advice.

FOR FURTHER INFORMATION: *Dr. Pitcairn's Complete Guide to Natural Health for Dogs and Cats,* by Richard H. Pitcairn; Rodale Press, 1982. "Traveling with Your Pet" (American Society for the Prevention of Cruelty to Animals, 441 E. 92nd St., New York, NY 10128).

1. Louis Rukeyser and John Cooney, *Louis Rukeyser's Business Almanac* (Simon & Schuster, 1988), p. 575.
2. Randy Kidd, D.V.M., "Beyond Food and Shelter," *Mother Earth News* (January/ February 1990), p. 30.
3. Rukeyser and Cooney, op. cit.
4. "Psittacine Trade" (Traffic [USA], World Wildlife Fund, 1250 24th St. NW, Washington D.C. 20037).

YARD CARE

FERTILIZERS

Plants need 12 mineral elements to grow, three of which (nitrogen, phosphorus, and potassium) are considered primary nutrients. Although all fertilizers can supply these nutrients, natural products harm the environment less than synthetic chemicals do, and they also do more to improve the soil.

ENVIRONMENTAL PROBLEMS

Manufacturing impacts. Chemical fertilizers contain anhydrous ammonia, a toxic gas usually made from natural gas. The ammonia, which is a nitrogen source, can be either injected directly into the ground or combined with phosphates and potassium chloride to make solutions or crystals. Making anhydrous ammonia depletes a nonrenewable fossil fuel and pollutes the air during manufacture, transport, and use.

Water pollution. Runoff from fertilizer-treated soil has seriously contaminated our nation's groundwater, rivers, and lakes with nitrates. Most of this contamination has been caused by large-scale agriculture, but garden and lawn fertilizers are a contributing factor.

Damage to soil and plants. Chemical fertilizers have harmful effects on both soil and plants:

- The chemicals furnish specific nutrients but do not improve the overall health of soil, which can lose its vigor as a living, microbiological system and become dependent on chemical "fixes" instead.

- Chemical fertilizers are strong enough to harm plants if overused or misused. Too much nitrogen, for example, can "burn" plants or keep them from developing deep roots, leading to soil compaction and plant weakness.

- Chemical fertilizers slow the decomposition of organic materials—such as grass clippings left on a lawn—resulting in less biological activity in the soil and a buildup of thatch

(tightly packed organic debris that prevents sun and air from reaching the soil).

CHOOSING A PRODUCT
GENERAL GUIDELINES

Weighing your needs. Different soils and plants need different nutrients, so do some research before buying fertilizers. Call a local gardening club or county extension agent for information on soil testing and composition; having your soil tested is usually a good first step. Then choose a fertilizer that supplies the right nutrients for your specific soil and plants.

Natural products. Look for fertilizers made with natural substances rather than ammonia and other manufactured chemicals.

COMMERCIAL PRODUCTS

Manure *(highly recommended).* Manure not only adds nutrients, it also improves soil texture, aerating heavier clay soils and binding to sandy soils for better water retention. It is also very inexpensive if you haul it yourself:

- Dry cattle or horse manure from a stable or barn (rainfall leaches nutrients from outdoor manure) has a 1 to 2 percent nitrogen content. You can also buy large sacks of composted cattle manure at many garden supply stores; because it's practically odorless and easy to handle, it's the most practical choice for urban areas.

- Dry poultry manure, also from indoor sources, is much higher in nitrogen (4 to 5 percent) and has a stronger odor (which fades quickly after application). It is available in garden supply stores.

Mineral fertilizers *(highly recommended).* Some mineral fertilizers, mined from naturally occurring deposits with relatively little processing, add essential elements to the soil and adjust its pH. Among them are calcium carbonate (chalk), calcium sulfate, feldspar, limestone,

TABLE
49

NATURAL FERTILIZERS

Brand	Use	Source	Nutrients[a]
Earth Juice "Bloom" Concentrate	Outdoor flowers, fruits	Enzymes, natural ingredients	0% N 6% P 3% K
Earth Juice "Grow" Concentrate	All outdoor plants	Enzymes, natural ingredients	5% N 1% P 3% K
Hi Yield Cottonseed Meal 6-1-1	All outdoor plants	Cottonseed meal	6% N 1% P 1% K
Ortho Bone Meal 0-12-0	Outdoor flowers and shrubs	Bone meal	12% P
Ortho-Gro Fish Fertilizer 5-1-1	Indoor and outdoor plants	Fish	5% N 1% P 1% K
Safer Sea Crop 6-6-6	Indoor and outdoor plants	Liquified seaweed	6% N 6% P 6% K
Safer Sea Fish 5-1-1	Indoor and outdoor plants	Ocean fish	5% N 1% P 1% K
Sudbury Sea Power	Indoor and outdoor plants	Liquified seaweed	Not listed

[a] N = Nitrogen; P = Phosphorus; K = Potassium

magnesium carbonate (magnesite), phosphate rock, and potassium rock (potash). Use these products if a soil test shows mineral deficiencies or an acidity or alkalinity problem; they're available at large garden supply stores or from agricultural suppliers. Mineral compounds can irritate the skin, eyes, and mucous membranes, so handle them with care.

Commercial natural fertilizers *(highly recommended).* Based on organic matter from renewable sources—seaweed, plants, fish, or animals—these fertilizers use far less energy and create less pollution than chemical fertilizers. Generally lower in nitrogen and slower acting than chemicals, natural fertilizers are nonacidic and encourage root growth for long-term plant health. Table 49 lists some widely available, naturally derived products.

Chemical fertilizers *(not generally recommended).* Available either as liquids for direct or hose application, or as solid crystals to be sprinkled on the soil, chemical fertilizers are relatively inexpensive, mainly because they are produced in such huge quantities. Use these fertilizers only if natural fertilizers are unavailable or too expensive or impractical for your application. They come in a wide range of nitrogen/phosphorus/potassium (N-P-K) formulas, so be sure to pick the right formula for your soil and plants.

ALTERNATIVES

Compost. You can get soil-conditioning organic matter (though with fewer nutrients than fertilizer) by composting your kitchen scraps and yard wastes. If used properly, a simple backyard composter can produce pathogen-free humus perfect for your garden or yard; you can either make a compost bin or buy one at a garden sup-ply store. Your community might also have a composting program for recycling yard wastes; you just bring in leaves and grass clippings and take home free compost. (Unfortunately, you don't know exactly what went into the compost you receive.) Call a local recycling office for information.

Mulch. You can reduce fertilizer use by turning organic mulch back into your garden's soil.

WISE USE

Healthy soil. Remember that soil should be a living system. Learn about your soil— its nutrient levels, its pH, and what it needs. Keep it well supplied with organic material so it remains aer-ated and uncompacted, which will enhance microbiological activity.

Safe use. Use all fertilizers with care: nitrogen-rich products can "burn" plants, and overuse of any fertilizer can pollute the water. The author of *The Chemical-Free Lawn* suggests only one fertilizer application per year (in the fall) for northern lawns and two or three light applica-tions, from late spring to early fall, for southern lawns.

FOR FURTHER INFORMATION: The Basic Book of Organic Gardening, Robert Rodale, ed.; Ballantine, 1987. *The Chemical-Free Lawn,* by Warren Schultz; Rodale Press, 1989.

LAWN MOWERS

The average American homeowner spends 40 hours a year mowing the lawn, usually with a gas-powered lawn mower.[1] Gas-powered mow-ers make the job easier, but they burn fossil fuel, pollute the air, and present safety hazards.

ENVIRONMENTAL PROBLEMS

Fossil-fuel consumption. Most lawn mowers run on gasoline, which, despite its advantages as a relatively cheap, easy-to-use fuel, is still a non-renewable resource—one that must be highly processed, refined, and shipped, damaging the environment at each step.

Air pollution. Gas mowers, which have no cat-alytic converters or other pollution controls, pump two pollutants into the air: hydrocarbons (unburnt remnants of the fuel itself) and nitrogen oxides (formed during high-temperature com-bustion). Both pollutants react with sunlight to form smog. A California state agency has esti-mated that a lawn mower's air emissions in 30 minutes of use equals the air emissions of a new car in 172 miles of driving.[2]

Noise pollution. With loudness levels from 85 to 92 decibels, gas mowers are a major source of noise in urban and suburban areas.[3]

Safety hazards. Despite design improvements, lawn mowers still cause injuries with their blades or with flying debris. In 1989 alone about 26,000 Americans required hospital emergency room treatment for mower injuries.[4]

CHOOSING A PRODUCT

GENERAL GUIDELINES

Weighing your needs. When choosing a new lawn mower, decide what your needs are by considering your lawn's size and density; how often you mow (or *should* mow, see Wise Use below); features you may or may not need; and your own health and level of physical activity.

Simple technology. Instead of assuming that only a gasoline mower will meet your needs, find out whether a simpler type of mower will suffice.

COMMERCIAL PRODUCTS

Push-reel mowers *(highly recommended).* These machines are environmentally perfect: they cut grass without burning fuels or polluting the air. By relying on simple technology—wheels, gears, and human power—they also offer distinct practical advantages: they are cheap to buy, free to operate, easy to maintain and store, still easy to cut by yourself, and highly effective.

- One company, American Lawn Mower/Great States Corporation, (800) 633-1501, makes most of the push-reel mowers sold in this country. They offer six models, from economy to deluxe, with optional grass catchers. These mowers are also sold under other brand names; ask the American Lawn Mower Company for a retail outlet near you.

- For a larger, heavy-duty mower made by a farm equipment company, call Agri-Fab, (217) 728-4334.

- Lambert Corporation, (513) 337-3641, makes a lightweight mower with a fold-down handle and simple blade adjustments.

Table 50 provides information on several types of push-reel mowers.

Electric mowers *(recommended).* Electric mowers are far preferable, environmentally, to gasoline mowers. Even though they use electric power—the generation of which severely affects the environment—these mowers use electricity very efficiently. They produce no air pollution when running and are very quiet. The standard electric mower motor has about 1.3 horsepower, less than half that of a gas mower, and performs well in most situations, though it cannot mow extremely high, dense grass in a

single pass. Though sometimes more expensive to buy, electric mowers are much cheaper to run than gas mowers: with a 1,000-watt motor, the average 40-hour mowing season would cost about $3.20. Electric mowers do, of course, have a rather unwieldy electric cord, but there are simple techniques for handling it during mowing. Honda, Toro, and Black & Decker make electric mowers; look for these and other brands in hardware stores and at lawn mower dealers nationwide.

Gasoline-powered mowers *(never recommended).* A large lawn is itself environmentally unsound, and a machine that mows it by burning fossil fuel and polluting the air also rates very low. Of the three types of gas mowers—riding, self-propelled, and push—the last is the least objectionable, with a 3- to 4-horsepower motor that uses less fuel and creates less pollution than larger engines. If you must buy a gas mower, consider the Lawn Chief 50-H, a very light side-bagger with a small, relatively quiet engine.

WISE USE

Regular maintenance. To keep your mower working at its best, make sure it's well maintained:

- Have the blades sharpened regularly.

- With push-reel mowers, keep the wheels oiled and follow the manufacturer's instructions for cutting adjustments.

- With electric mowers, always use an extension cord with at least the diameter of that on the machine; limit the total extension cord length to 100 feet.

- With gas mowers, change the filters, clean the spark plug, and tune the carburetor regularly.

Safe use. All mowers can be dangerous, so follow basic safety rules:

- Always wear shoes when mowing.

- Never mow slippery, wet grass.

TABLE 50

PUSH-REEL LAWN MOWERS

Brand	Model Number	Number of Blades	Cutting Width	Cutting Heights	Weight
Agri-Fab, Inc.	42-0193	6	18"	0.5" to 2.25"	40 lbs.
American Lawn	1204-14	4	14"	0.5" to 1.5"	19 lbs.
Mower Company[a]	1403-16	5	16"	0.5" to 1.75"	32 lbs.
	1414-16	5	16"	0.5" to 2.25"	32 lbs.
	1815-18	5	18"	2.0" to 2.25"	27 lbs.
Lambert Corp.	PRS-2	4	16"	0.6" to 1.4"	19 lbs.
	PRH-38	5	15"	0.6" to 1.4"	22 lbs.
	PRM-16	5	16"	0.6" to 1.4"	24 lbs.

[a] Mowers made by this company are also sold under other brand names.

- Before you mow, clear any rocks or sticks from the lawn.

- On a power mower, never override the "dead-man" control that stops the blades if you release the handle.

- Never allow young children to use a mower or stay near it when it's in use.

Efficient use. Grow your lawn to its proper, healthy height to encourage root growth in hot weather and inhibit weeds throughout the growing season:

- Tall grasses, such as Kentucky bluegrass, tall fescue, and St. Augustinegrass, should be 2 to 2½ inches high in cool weather and 3 to 4 inches high in hot weather.

- Medium-height grasses, such as perennial ryegrass and fine fescue, should be 1½ inches high in cool weather and 2½ inches high in hot weather.

- Short grasses, such as Bermudagrass and Zoysiagrass, should be ½ inch high in cool weather and 1 inch high in hot weather.

Leave the clippings on the grass: they won't cause thatch (tightly packed organic debris that prevents sun and air from reaching the soil) provided the lawn isn't overfertilized; they retain moisture; and they make an excellent fertilizer as they decompose.

1. Warren Schultz, "Natural Lawn Care," *Garbage* (July/August 1990), p. 29.
2. Robert J. Sammuelson, "The Joys of Mowing," *Newsweek* (April 29, 1991), p. 49.
3. "How to Buy a Mower to Match Your Lawn," *Consumer Reports* (June 1990), p. 397.
4. "The Machines Are Safer—Still, Use Them Wisely," *Consumer Reports* (June 1990), p. 398.

LAWNS

The United States has 33 million acres of lawn, most of it in peoples' yards.[1] This greening of America, though beautiful, is environmentally costly.

ENVIRONMENTAL PROBLEMS

Chemical treatments. Lawn chemicals are big business; Americans spend about $2.5 billion a year on the following types:[2]

- *Fertilizers.* Ammonia-based fertilizers are energy-intensive and polluting to produce, can damage a lawn's overall health by providing nutrients too quickly, and can pollute community water supplies.

- *Weed killers.* The most popular, 2,4-D (around 3 million pounds are used per year), is toxic and a potential carcinogen, and harms fish and bees.[3]

- *Insecticides.* Diazinon and Dursban, two popular organophosphate insecticides, are toxic if swallowed, inhaled, or absorbed through the skin. Both chemicals harm birds and fish.[4]

- *Fungicides.* The fungicides captan and benomyl are carcinogenic as well as harmful to fish and aquatic life.

Water consumption. Lawns in areas without steady summer rainfall must be watered from municipal supplies or private wells to keep their bright green color throughout the growing season. Kentucky bluegrass, for example, needs about 18 gallons per square foot. The water usually comes from rivers and lakes, the draining of which hurts wildlife ecology; from reservoirs, made by building dams on rivers and creeks, with many harmful environmental effects; and from groundwater aquifers and deep wells whose recharge time may be hundreds or thousands of years. Lawn watering can significantly compound water-shortage problems in drought-prone areas, and can seriously tax water treatment plants because all water from municipal supplies must be treated to drinking quality first, even if it's just going on the lawn.

Mowing impacts. Gasoline-powered lawn mowers burn nonrenewable fossil fuel and pollute the air with hydrocarbons.

Disposal problems. Grass clippings from mowing usually end up in plastic trash bags in a landfill, contributing significantly to our severely overloaded landfills. Yard wastes, the bulk of them grass clippings, make up 18 percent of America's municipal trash.[5]

Unnatural environments. For wildlife—especially birds, small animals, reptiles, and beneficial insects—lawns are an unnatural, barren place, without the variety of flowering and seed-producing plants they need for shelter and food. Lawns also absorb less carbon dioxide (the greenhouse gas) and release less oxygen than longer-bladed native grasses.

CHOOSING PRODUCTS AND SERVICES

GENERAL GUIDELINES

Weighing your needs. Decide whether you really *need* a large, high-maintenance lawn. Instead, consider having only a small lawn for a recreation area and using the rest of the yard for low-maintenance native plants, shade trees, shrubs, ground covers, and garden space.

Natural lawn care. Work to improve the long-term health of the lawn and soil by using sound lawn-care practices. Avoid chemical fertilizers and weedkillers by taking preventive measures and using naturally derived products instead.

Natural landscaping. When you choose grasses and plants for your yard, look for hardy native varieties that grow naturally in your area and will need less water and care; if you choose non-native varieties, pick ones with suitable growing requirements. Have the fertility and pH (alkalinity or acidity) of your soil checked before you plant; call your county extension office for information.

COMMERCIAL PRODUCTS AND SERVICES

New lawns *(not generally recommended)*. There are two ways to put in new grass:

- *Seeding* new grass on prepared soil is effective and cheap, though slow to show results. When you buy seed, look for the hardiest, least water-dependent grasses. You'll improve your chances of success by removing weeds before you seed: water the bare soil deeply and wait one to two weeks, then turn under or rototill the new weed sprouts, and repeat if the weeds are heavy. Apply natural fertilizers if necessary and watch out for soil erosion from watering while the grass is getting started.

- *Sod* provides instant gratification, but it's expensive for large yards and environmentally unsound because of the energy needed to dig and transport it, often over long distances. For very small plots, though, sod is affordable and practical.

Lawn-care services *(not generally recommended)*. These popular services charge a fee to treat lawns with fertilizers and pesticides, usually chemical. Their employees are usually better trained than the average homeowner in handling these hazardous substances; nevertheless these companies add to our overall chemical use and should be avoided when possible. Some companies use more natural treatments, but most homeowners don't even need these. If you are interested in a service advertised as natural or organic, ask about their methods and materials.

ALTERNATIVES

Alternative landscaping. To replace grassy lawns, consider these alternatives:

- Native or naturally hardy plants—wildflowers, grasses, ground covers, perennials, shrubs, and trees—to replace lawn and help restore the area's natural ecology. Visit your library or call an agricultural extension office for information on plants native to your area, or call

  - ◆ the National Wildflower Research Center, (512) 929-3600.

  - ◆ the Abundant Life Seed Foundation, (206) 385-5660.

- Beds of flowers, herbs, and vegetables.

- Xeriscaping—the use of plants (usually native) that need little or no watering—for areas where water is scarce.

- Hardscaping—landscaping with decorative rock, stone, and wood chips instead of plants. Hardscaping doesn't require water or nutrients, but does usually need plastic sheeting underneath the material to stop weeds; the sheeting also seals off the soil from air and water, which can then offer no habitat for animals, birds, and insects.

WISE USE

Natural lawns. You can restore or maintain your lawn naturally by taking the following steps:

- Stop using all chemical products and allow the grass and soil to rebuild; have the soil tested and, if necessary, use natural treatments (see Fertilizers, p. 278).

- If a pest or other problem develops, don't immediately assume the worst; a healthy lawn can usually recover on its own (see Pesticides, Garden and Lawn, p. 286).

- Leave grass clippings on the lawn: they provide nitrogen; do not cause a buildup of tightly packed organic debris, or thatch (although clippings left on a heavily fertilized lawn might); retain moisture and prevent weeds; and save the need for disposal.

Efficient watering. If you must water your lawn, take some time to learn exactly what it needs:

- Grass usually needs watering if it doesn't spring back after you step on it.

- Water requirements vary depending on the type of grass, the soil, and the climate, so find out your lawn's exact needs by contacting your local agricultural extension or water conservation office.

- When you use your sprinkler, mark the insides of two or three cans with the level of water your yard needs, set them around the yard under the sprinkler, and turn the sprinkler off when that level is reached.

- For more precise monitoring, use a soil probe that measures the depth of moisture in the soil after watering.

- Water in the evening in dryer climates and in the morning in fungus-prone regions; never water during the heat of the day, when the evaporation rate is highest.

- If you have automatic sprinklers, install a controller that turns them off after a rain.

- More efficient watering systems than sprinklers, at least for certain uses, are drip irrigation systems, soaker hoses, and bubbler heads that flood an area with water.

- In a drought or a long, hot spell, depending on grass species, soil nutrients, and air temperatures, you may be better off letting the grass dry out, turn brown, and go dormant (it will come back from the roots). If it is kept active by inadequate watering, the heat is more likely to kill it. Check with your local agricultural extension or water conservation office.

Safe use of chemicals. If you must use chemicals on your lawn, take all possible precautions: post signs, but also make sure that children and animals (who can't read warning signs) stay off the lawn. Treat leftover chemicals as hazardous waste; never put them in the trash or down the drain. Instead store them carefully for hazardous waste collection, or take them to a collection site. Call your local waste disposal office for information on hazardous waste collection programs.

FOR FURTHER INFORMATION: *The Chemical-Free Lawn*, by Warren Schultz; Rodale Press, 1989.

1. Bryan Jay Bashin, "A Rogues' Gallery," *Harrowsmith* (May/June 1989), p. 12.
2. "Garbage Index," *Garbage* (July/August 1990), p. 26.
3. Diane Baxter and Kevin Thorpe, "Garden Pesticide Fact Sheet," *Organic Gardening* (April 1989), pp. 40–41.
4. Ibid.
5. *Environmental Quality 1987–88* (Council on Environmental Quality, 1987), p. 12.

PESTICIDES, GARDEN AND LAWN

On the average, 5 to 10 pounds of pesticides—insecticides, herbicides (weed killers), and fungicides—are applied to every acre of lawn and garden in the United States each year, creating significant health hazards and environmental damage.

ENVIRONMENTAL PROBLEMS

Health hazards. Many widely used pesticides are hazardous to human health:

- Common chemicals such as *carbaryl* (Sevin), *chlorpyrifos* (Dursban), and *Diazinon* are toxic if swallowed, inhaled, or absorbed through the skin.

- *Sevin*, *malathion*, 2,4-D, and *benomyl* are known to cause birth defects with chronic exposure.[1]

- Naturally derived insecticides are also dangerous, including *pyrethrum* and *pyrethrins* (toxic if swallowed or inhaled), *rotenone* (toxic if swallowed and a skin irritant), and *nicotine sulfate* (toxic if swallowed, inhaled, or absorbed through the skin).

Water pollution. Most modern pesticides break down in water much more quickly than older ones did; however, they can still pollute the water. Among the common water-polluting pesticides are[2]

- *Insecticides*. Malathion and carbofuran contaminate groundwater; one of the breakdown products of chlorpyrifos (3,5,6-trichloropyridinol) has been detected in water bodies.

- *Fungicides*. Captan contaminates groundwater; mancozeb is another possible pollutant.

- *Herbicides*. 2,4-D and amitrole contaminate groundwater and do not break down for at least six months.

Dangers to wildlife. Many pesticides are known to be toxic to wildlife:[3]

- *Chemical insecticides*. Diazinon, chlorpyrifos, and malathion harm bees, birds, and fish; permethrin and Sevin harm bees and fish.

- *Natural insecticides*. Rotenone and nicotine sulfate harm birds and fish; pyrethrum harms fish.

- *Fungicides*. Benomyl and captan harm fish.

- *Herbicides*. Glyphosate harms fish; 2,4-D harms bees and fish.

Ecosystem disruption. Most insecticides kill not only the "target" pest insects, but also their natural predators and other beneficial insects (such as bees, crucial to pollenization) and can severely disrupt the natural ecosystem of a garden or lawn. Sometimes the pest insect, free of predators, comes back stronger than ever.

CHOOSING A PRODUCT

GENERAL GUIDELINES

Weighing your needs. Fighting pests in the garden or yard might not always be necessary. Most food plants can lose quite a bit of foliage—up to 25 percent in many cases—without a noticeable drop in their yields. Healthy lawns, flower gardens, and shrubs can withstand and often overcome attacks from pests.

Nontoxic or less-toxic products. If you must apply pesticides, start with the safest products available; use toxic products only as a last resort.

Integrated Pest Management (IPM). Consider using IPM, a step-by-step method for reducing pests to low, damage-free levels without necessarily seeking their eradication. (See For Further Information.)

COMMERCIAL PRODUCTS

Natural, nontoxic insecticides *(highly recommended)*. Several types of safe, effective insecticides are available in garden supply stores or by mail order:

- *Bacillus thuringiensis (BT)*. BT are naturally occurring bacteria, available in several varieties to treat many different pests, including beetles, gypsy moths and larvae, corn borers, and mosquito and black fly larvae. BT is nontoxic to humans and has no known effects on soil, water, or wildlife. Commercial BT products include Ferti-Lome Dipel Dust, American Thuricide Concentrate, and others made by Reuter's Attack, Ringer Research, and Sandoz Crop Protection. Gardens Alive! (812) 623-3800, offers five different strains of BT.

- *Fatty-acid soaps*. Made from plant oils and animal fats, these soaps control a wide variety of pests. They are nontoxic to humans and are not known to harm wildlife, though their persistence in soil and water is unknown. Brands include Safer Insecticidal Soap and Mite Killer and Ringer Research Aphid-Mite Attack. Order concentrated Ecosafe Plant Soap from The Natural Choice, (505) 438-3448.

- *Dormant oil*. Dormant oil is made from petroleum and toxic when concentrated, but it is nontoxic in dilution and not known to harm wildlife. Sprayed in very early spring, it controls aphids, scale, mites, mealybugs, moth eggs, and many other pests. Its persistence in soil and water is not known. You can order it from Gardens Alive! (812) 623-3800.

- *Herbal formulas*. These products do not kill insects; instead, they repel them with a strong scent. You can order Green Ban for Plants, which uses hedera helix, sage, garlic, eucalyptus oil, and kelp, from A Clear Alternative, (713) 356-7031.

Never use diatomaceous earth. This product is made from fossilized algae, which puncture insects' waxy protective coating and kill them by dehydration. Although nontoxic to humans and animals, it is environmentally unsound for outdoor use because it kills beneficial insects as well as pests. (It is, however, useful for insects indoors; see Insecticides, Household, p. 93.)

Natural, nontoxic herbicides *(highly recommended)*. Fatty-acid soaps, when used in concentrated form, can kill young weeds and severely damage older weeds with mature root systems. Fatty-acid soaps are nontoxic to people and animals, but don't get them on any plants you don't want killed. Look for Safer Sharp-Shooter Weed Killer.

Natural, toxic insecticides *(sometimes recommended)*. Use the insecticides listed below only when insects seriously threaten the health of plants or lawns. Despite their toxicity, they are better than chemical insecticides because they have fewer manufacturing impacts and they break up quickly after use. Look for commercial products that contain only natural ingredients; if you can't find them in stores, call Gardens Alive! (812) 623-3800.

- *Nicotine sulfate (Black Leaf 40)*. Extracted from the tobacco plant, nicotine sulfate kills a variety of pests, including aphids, mealybugs, spider mites, beetle larvae, and squash bugs. It is extremely toxic to humans and can harm birds, fish, and aquatic life but breaks down quickly in soil or water. Look for Natural Guard Nicotine Sulfate.

- *Pyrethrum (Pyrocide), or pyrethrin*. Extracted from chrysanthemums, pyrethrum and the stronger pyrethrin control a wide range of pests. They are toxic to humans and can harm fish and aquatic life, but break down quickly in soil and water. Safer Entire Insect Killer for Yards and Gardens combines pyrethrins and fatty-acid soap. (Avoid Safer Garden Insect Killer, however, which uses pyrethrins and the chemical piperonyl butoxide.)

- *Rotenone (Prentox, Noxfire)*. Extracted from the roots of tropical plants, rotenone kills many pests, including aphids, beetles, cabbageworms, leaf rollers, leafhoppers, and spider mites. Rotenone is toxic to humans and can harm birds, fish, and aquatic life but breaks down quickly in soil or water. Look for Bonide 1.00% Rotenone.

- *Ryania (Ryanicide)*. Extracted from a South American shrub, ryania kills codling moths, oriental fruit flies, corn borers, and cabbage-

TABLE 51

HAZARDOUS GARDEN AND LAWN PESTICIDES TO AVOID

Generic or Trade Name	Chemical Names[a]	Contained In
Captan (Orthocide)	(N-trichloromethyl-mercaptotetra-hydrophthalimide)	Bonide Rose Spray Gro-Well Fruit Tree Spray Ortho Orthocide Garden Fungicide Ortho Tomato and Vegetable Dust
Carbaryl (Sevin)	1-naphthyl-N-methylcarbamate	Ortho Sevin Garden Dust
Chlorpyrifos (Dursban, Lorsban)	0,0-diethyl-0-3,5,6-trichloro-2-pyridyl phosphorothioate	Ortho Fire Ant Control
Diazinon	0,0-diethyl 0-(2-isopropyl-4-methyl-6-pyrimidinyl phosphorothioate)	Ortho Diazinon Insect Spray Spectracide Products
Malathion (Cythion)	(S-[1,2-bis(ethoxycarbonyl) ethyl] 0,0-dimethyl phosphorodithioate)	Bonide Rose Spray Ortho Home Orchard Spray Ortho Malathion 50
Methoxychlor	Methoxy DDT; DMDT; 2,2-bis (p-methoxyphenol)-1,1,1-trichloroethane	Gro-Well Fruit Tree Spray
Propoxur (Baygon, Unden)	Ortho-isopropoxyphenyl-N-methylcarbamate	Black Flag Wasp, Bee, Hornet Killer Ortho Hornet and Wasp Killer Raid Wasp and Hornet Killer
2, 4-D	2,4-dichlorophenoxyacetic acid	Monsanto's Greensweep Weed and Feed Ortho Weed-B-Gon Scott's Spot Dandelion Control

[a] Some products may list ingredients by chemical rather than trade name.

worms. It is moderately toxic to humans and its effects on wildlife are unknown. It breaks down rapidly in soil or water. Ryania is seldom sold in stores; order it from Gardens Alive! or other garden supply catalogs.

- *Sabadilla (Red Devil Dust).* Made from the seeds of a South American lily, sabadilla kills squash bugs, stink bugs, blister beetles, and many others. It is relatively nontoxic to humans but does irritate mucous membranes; it harms bees, and its breakdown rate in soil and water is unknown. Look for Natural Guard Sabadilla Dust.

Metal and mineral fungicides *(not generally recommended).* The toxicity of these fungicides depends on their concentration; use them only for serious fungus diseases. The best products use sulfur or copper and can treat blights, mildews, rusts, and scabs as well as fungal diseases on vines, potatoes, tomatoes, and peppers. They can also treat lawn problems such as brown patch, leaf spot, and dollar spot. You can buy Safer sulfur-based Garden Fungicide in stores, or order Copper Dust and Liquid Copper from Gardens Alive! (*Note:* Bordeaux mixture, a popular cure for fungus diseases on fruits such as apples, grapes, and peaches, is made from naturally occurring minerals but is highly poisonous and not recommended.)

Chemical fungicides and herbicides *(never recommended).* These products should be avoided if at all possible. Though effective at killing pests, they damage the overall health of the soil and plants, sometimes leading to worse infestations. Table 51 lists several toxic or hazardous pesticides to avoid. Fungi can never be completely eradicated; only a healthy soil, alive with microfauna and microflora, can hold fungi to a nondestructive level. For weeds, see Natural Weed Control in the Alternatives section, below. To restore soil heavily dosed with chemicals, add organic materials (see Lawns, p. 283).

Chemical insecticides *(never recommended)*. The three main classes of chemical insecticides—organophosphates, carbamates, and pyrethroids—contain no environmentally sound products. The pyrethroids (permethrin, fenvalerate) are less toxic to humans than the others, but they still harm wildlife and don't break down in soil for at least six months. Use chemicals only as a last resort, for the most severe infestations. Use them sparingly and with the utmost care.

ALTERNATIVES

Pest-resistant gardens. Create an environment that is nearly free of pests by following these steps:

- Stop using all chemical pesticides to permit beneficial insects and microorganisms to recolonize the garden.

- Improve the health of the soil by adding compost and manure.

- Rotate vegetables and flowers among different garden areas.

- Plant bushes, shrubs, and tall grass near gardens to shelter insect-eating birds.

- Maintain perennial beds, ideally with uncultivated paths between them, to provide a stable habitat for beneficial insects.

- Mimic the wild in some plantings: scatter plants randomly instead of aligning them in rows and beds (random plantings provide pathways for beneficial predators and keep pests from concentrating in one area).

- Grow marigolds, nasturtiums, radishes, and onions in strategic places—in borders and between beds and rows—to repel many bugs, especially aphids.

- Grow dill, parsley, pennyroyal, thyme, radish, and mustard, and allow them to bolt (go to seed) to attract and shelter beneficial insects.

- Put a large, shallow insect watering dish in the garden to attract beneficial insects, which can easily outnumber pests (but add a rock island so they won't drown).

Natural insect control. You can kill or control many insect pests with the following simple techniques:

- Handpick slugs, beetles, and caterpillars, or sprinkle salt directly on them.

- Drown slugs in beer; just set a cup in the garden at night, dug into the ground with the rim near the surface.

- For scale, put a solution of 1 part simple soap (such as castile) and 50 parts water in a spray bottle; spray the scale and scrub with a toothbrush.

- Use Tanglefoot products, which trap insects on their nontoxic, sticky surfaces (beneficial insects are rarely trapped). Look for them in better garden supply stores, or order from Gardens Alive!, (812) 623-3800.

- Drape long-lasting plastic netting or cheesecloth covers over the garden or individual plants; they let in air, water, and light but not insects. Order from Clothcrafters, (414) 876-2112.

- You can also import beneficial predators. Ladybugs (usually *Hippodamia convergens*) can help control aphids, but might not stay in your yard after release. Aphid midges *(Aphidoletes aphidimyza)*, which eat aphids, are best introduced in early spring to supplement the native midge population. Green lacewing *(Chrysopa carnea)* larvae eat many soft-bodied insects. Praying mantids are *not* recommended, because they eat both harmful and beneficial insects.

Natural weed control. You can control weeds—or at least live in harmony with them—without resorting to chemical treatments:

- First of all, think carefully about what you consider a weed and why. Many "weeds" are in fact wildflowers.

- Grow your grass a little higher to keep the sun from reaching low-growing weeds (especially crabgrass) and dormant weed seeds.

- For digging up dandelions, use either your own tools or specialty tools, such as the Back-Saver/Weedr or the Weed Popper, and extract as much of the tap root as possible. For best results dig them up when they're blooming.

- For other tough, invasive weeds with deep roots—such as burdock, plantain, quackgrass, and thistle—consider a WaterNeedle Weeder. This 2-foot-long copper pipe attaches to a hose; when you insert it deep into the ground near a weed and turn the water on, the water pressure loosens the weed's roots, making it easy to remove intact. Look for it in better garden supply stores, or order from Gardens Alive!, (812) 623-3800.

WISE USE

Conservative use. Success lies in working *with* nature, not fighting against it. The more you learn about your plants and their pests, the better equipped you'll be to encourage a healthy, self-sustaining backyard ecosystem. Pesticides will throw this ecosystem off balance—and stronger ones can do far more damage than that—so keep their use to an absolute minimum.

Safe use. If you must use chemical pesticides, follow the manufacturer's instructions to the letter:

- Wear protective clothing.

- Keep children and animals away during and after use.

- Wash your hands and exposed skin thoroughly.

Proper disposal. Although they are designed for use on plants and soil, all toxic and moderately toxic pesticides (both chemical and naturally derived) are classified as hazardous wastes:

- *Never* pour pesticides on the ground or down a sewer or drain.

- *Never* put pesticides in with your household trash.

- Seal and store pesticides safely for a hazardous waste collection. Ask your local waste disposal office for information on hazardous waste collection programs.

FOR FURTHER INFORMATION: The *Encyclopedia of Natural Insect and Disease Control,* by Roger B. Yepsen, Jr., ed.; Rodale Press, 1984. *Sensible Pest Control: A Handbook of Integrated Pest Management Techniques* (Massachusetts Audubon Society, South Great Rd., Lincoln, MA 01773-9988).

1. Diane Baxter and Kevin Thorpe, "Garden Pesticide Fact Sheet," *Organic Gardening* (April 1989), pp. 40–41.
2. Ibid.
3. Ibid.

TREES

Besides providing beauty, trees offer important environmental advantages.

ENVIRONMENTAL BENEFITS

Carbon dioxide reduction. In one year a single tree can absorb 15 to 25 pounds of carbon dioxide (CO_2), the primary greenhouse gas, while also releasing oxygen. The tree will eventually release an equal amount of CO_2 back into the air when it dies and decays (or burns), but its temporary "storage" is critical to dealing with the current buildup of atmospheric CO_2.

Pollution removal. As they absorb and process CO_2, water, nutrients, and sunlight, trees also filter out pollutants from both air and water. A study of local hardwood species in St. Louis, for example, showed that each tree could remove 1.5 pounds of dust, soot, and smoke each year.[1] Trees can also remove nitrogen and phosphorus compounds from groundwater and are being planted for this purpose near polluted waters in some areas.

Cooler air. Trees provide shade that can make a real difference in hot weather. Three mature trees shading a house, for example, can reduce air conditioner use by 20 to 50 percent.[2]

Wildlife habitat. Trees are important to birds, bees, squirrels, and other small animals. They provide food both directly through the production of seeds, flowers, and nuts, and indirectly by attracting insects that serve as food. They also offer permanent or temporary shelter for many creatures.

CHOOSING A PRODUCT

GENERAL GUIDELINES

Weighing your needs. Unless your yard is already filled with trees, consider planting some. Be sure to consider your specific needs—such as house-cooling in summer, windbreaks for winter, outdoor shade, wildlife habitat, and landscaping beauty.

Correct placement. To have healthy trees you'll be satisfied with, you need to plant them in the right places. To cool your house in the summer and early fall, for example, plant trees on the south and west sides. If you have an air conditioner, plant trees that will shade it and aid its cooling. Before planting, be sure to consider what each tree's height and space requirements will be when it matures.

Choosing the right species. Choose trees—native species, if possible—that will flourish in your specific locale:

- Have the fertility and pH (alkalinity or acidity) of your soil checked before you plant; call your county extension office for information.

- Consider your region's average rainfall and what types of trees it will support throughout the year. Be prepared to water any trees that won't get enough water naturally.

- Temperature extremes are limiting factors for some species; even if they live, the trees may not grow to full size.

- Find out what diseases and pests are common in your area from your county extension office, city parks office, or local garden club; some tree species might be more resistant than others.

TYPES OF TREES

Deciduous species *(highly recommended).* Deciduous trees are perfect for houses that need summer cooling and winter heating: if planted on the house's sunny side, they shade it in summer but lose their leaves in winter, letting in warm sunlight. Consider starting with shrubs and fast-growing trees such as willows, mulberries, silver maples, Chinese elms, cottonwoods, or poplars. Next, plant slower-maturing, long-lived trees such as oaks, sugar maples, ashes, and sycamores. Fruit trees, though usually too small to provide much shade, offer attractive colors and scents each spring and produce food you can share with wildlife in the late summer and fall.

Coniferous species *(highly recommended).* Conifers, or evergreens, cool effectively all year round, since they do not lose their leaves. In cold climates they make effective windbreaks on the north or northwest side of the house. They are important year-round as food sources and shelter for birds and other wildlife. In places with warm winters and hot summers, such as the South and Southwest, evergreen trees are a good choice for cooling; they are appropriate in any part of the country as landscaping. Look for pines, spruces, firs, hemlocks, and cedars that will thrive and mature quickly in your local soil and climate.

WISE USE

Regular maintenance. Trees are living organisms that need care to grow quickly and stay healthy:

- Keep trees watered as necessary, but don't overwater new, larger transplants (a common mistake that drowns their roots). If you aren't sure how much to water, ask a nursery how much water your trees need, and use a lawn-watering probe to measure the soil moisture after watering.

- Add fertilizer and other nutrients if necessary; consult a nursery or your local agricultural extension office for advice.

- Trim branches properly: always cut close to the trunk or larger branch; seal the cut after-

ward with a sealing compound, available at most garden supply stores.

FOR FURTHER INFORMATION: "Citizens' Action Guide" (Global Releaf, P.O. Box 2000, Washington, DC 20013).

1. "'Killer' Trees to the Rescue," *Newsweek* (October 2, 1989), p. 59.
2. R. Neil Sampson, American Forestry Association, quoted in "Queries & Quandaries," *Harrowsmith* (September/October 1989), p. 106.

ENVIRONMENTAL GLOSSARY

ACID RAIN Precipitation that has mixed with acidic air pollutants and has a pH lower than that of natural rainwater (generally about 5.6).[1] Acid rain kills or damages lakes, forests, and agricultural crops, corrodes buildings and statues, and endangers human health. It is caused primarily by sulfur dioxide and nitrogen oxides released from smokestacks, particularly those at coal-burning plants. These chemicals can remain airborne for hundreds of miles, causing acid rain far from their source. Smokestacks also cause acidic dry deposition.

AIR POLLUTION Contamination of the atmosphere with substances harmful to humans, plant or animal life, or natural ecosystems. Common human-caused pollutants include sulfur dioxide, nitrogen oxides, particulates, carbon dioxide and monoxide, lead and other metal dusts, hydrocarbons, ozone, methane, and radioactivity. Typical sources are cars, other internal-combustion engines, manufacturing plants, power plants, and chemicals that evaporate during use. The effects of air pollution include respiratory and other health problems, acid rain, damage to crops and other plants, and even climate change.

ANIMAL TESTING The experimental use of chemicals and other products on live animals, to test for toxicity and other hazards. Products tested range from new medications to household cleaners. Makers of consumer goods often use the Draize eye or acute dermal toxicity tests (compounds are placed in the animal's eyes or on its shaved skin to test the severity of the reaction) or the LD-50 test (lethal dose, 50 percent; animals are force-fed a substance to see how much it takes to kill half of them). Alternative laboratory tests and computer models can be used to replace most animal testing.

BIODEGRADABLE Able to be broken down into basic compounds by the action of natural biological agents—particularly bacteria and other microorganisms. The natural decaying process of dead plants and animal tissue is an example of biodegradability. Most organic materials are biodegradable, but many synthetic materials are not—they cannot provide food for the microorganisms. Some synthetic materials can remain intact almost indefinitely.

CARBON DIOXIDE (CO_2) A colorless, odorless gas that is a natural part of the atmosphere and is essential to all life processes, including its conversion to oxygen by plants during photosynthesis. Burning gasoline and other fossil fuels has increased levels of CO_2 in the atmosphere (up more than 10 percent since 1959),[2] trapping heat and heightening the greenhouse effect.

CARBON MONOXIDE (CO) A colorless, odorless, poisonous gas formed as a by-product of burning fossil fuels, particularly in automobiles. It is a major air pollutant and health hazard, especially in urban areas.

CARCINOGEN Any substance that causes cancerous growth in human or animal tissue. "Known" carcinogens are those whose effects have been verified in humans; "suspected" carcinogens are those whose effects have been studied in animals. Currently there are about 3,500 known and suspected carcinogens, many of them naturally occurring substances.[3]

CHLOROFLUOROCARBONS (CFCs) A group of nontoxic liquid or gas compounds composed of chlorine, fluorine, and carbon (and sometimes hydrogen). They are used as refrigerants, solvents, cleaners, and propellants. When released into the air, CFC molecules slowly rise to the stratosphere, where they are broken up by the sun. This process releases their chlorine, which then destroys the ozone molecules that protect the earth from solar radiation.

DIOXINS Generally, a large group of chlorinated compounds; specifically, TCDD (2,3,7,8-tetrachlorodibenzo-p-dioxin), which is toxic, carcinogenic, and mutagenic (it causes mutations). A contaminant in herbicides such as Agent Orange, widely used in Vietnam, TCDD is also a by-product of paper manufacturing; the chlorine used to bleach paper reacts with organic compounds in the wood pulp to form dioxin precursors.

ECOSYSTEM A self-sustaining community of interrelated plants and animals living in a physical environment that supplies the food, water, and other raw materials needed to sustain life. Because all the members of an ecosystem are interdependent, damage to one type of plant or animal—or a change in some aspect of the physical environment—can cause a chain reaction that upsets the balance of the entire system. Such a disturbance can then become a vicious circle, each new change throwing the system further out of balance.

GLOBAL WARMING Warming of the earth's atmosphere, caused by the buildup of heat-holding gases, most of them of industrial and agricultural origin. Because the earth's climate is so complex, the extent of the global warming trend is not yet certain. A 1981 NASA study predicted significant temperature increases (up to 5° to 7° F) during the next century,[4] which could lead to large-scale drought, a catastrophic sea-level rise, and disruption of natural ecosystems worldwide.

GREENHOUSE EFFECT The warming action of atmospheric gases that absorb infrared radiation, holding heat close to the planet's surface. Responsible for creating the environment that first supported life on earth, the greenhouse effect has increased during the last century because of industrial production, burning of fossil fuels, and agriculture. This increase could cause global warming. The major greenhouse gas is carbon dioxide; others include halons, CFCs, nitrous oxides, atmospheric ozone, and methane.

GROUNDWATER Water that is trapped in natural underground reservoirs, usually in layers of porous rock, and forms the source of water for wells and springs. These underground reservoirs, called aquifers, refill very slowly as water seeps down through the overlying rock and soil, most of its impurities getting filtered out in the process. Overuse of groundwater can deplete aquifers faster than they can refill, causing water shortages. Groundwater can become permanently polluted by chemicals that survive the natural filtering process of the rock and soil, and by direct channeling of chemicals down abandoned wells.

HAZARDOUS WASTES Chemicals, metals, or radioactive substances that, for economic or safety reasons, are not recovered for reuse, and whose disposal under ordinary circumstances would threaten the environment or human health. By law such wastes must be landfilled at sites with impermeable seals; stored away from groundwater; incinerated under controlled conditions; or treated with microbes or chemicals to neutralize toxins.

HYDROCARBONS Any of the many compounds made up solely of carbon and hydrogen, some of which are highly toxic and carcinogenic. Although found in plant oils, most hydrocarbons come from fossil fuels—coal, petroleum, and natural gas—and are valuable as fuels, lubricants, and base materials for many synthetic products. They are also air pollutants, emitted both from natural sources such as forest fires and from human activities, particularly incomplete burning of fossil fuels and evaporation of solvents, fuels, and other petrochemicals.

LEAD (Pb) A soft, gray metal that is a cumulative poison harmful to people, animals, and natural ecosystems. It is a major air pollutant, primarily because of its use as a gasoline additive; levels of airborne lead have dropped dramatically as leaded gasoline has become less common. It is also found in water pipes soldered with lead and in dust chips from paint pigmented with lead.

NITROGEN OXIDES (NO_x) Any of a group of compounds containing solely nitrogen and oxygen. One compound, nitrogen dioxide (NO_2), is a major air pollutant that endangers human health and contributes to acid rain; it is produced by burning fossil fuels, especially in automobiles and electric power plants. Nitric oxide (NO), produced both from natural sources such as lightning and from human activities, quickly changes to NO_2 in the atmosphere.

OZONE (O_3) A toxic, bluish gas with a pungent odor. Each ozone molecule consists of three oxygen atoms. In the lower atmosphere ozone is a serious air pollutant, threatening human health and agricultural crops. It is created by the effects of sunlight on nitrogen oxides and hydrocarbons and is also emitted directly by automobiles. In the stratosphere a thin, natural ozone layer shields the earth from intense ultra-violet solar radiation. The continuing depletion of this layer has been traced to the release of CFCs and other chemicals into the air.

PARTICULATES Particles of solids and liquids supended in the air. Natural sources include dust, forest fires, and volcanoes; a major human-induced source is fossil-fuel combustion. Relatively large particles obscure vision, but tiny particles—10 microns or less in diameter—pose more serious health hazards because they can be deeply inhaled, irritating or damaging the respiratory system.[5]

PESTICIDES A general term for insecticides, herbicides (weed killers), fungicides, and rodenticides. These products can be made from either synthetic chemicals or naturally derived ingredients. Pesticides are used extensively in buildings and on lawns, gardens, and agricultural crops; they can easily end up as air or water pollutants and as residues on plants and in foods. Most pesticides are highly poisonous, some of them causing immediate damage to the central nervous system or vital organs, and others increasing long-term risks of cancer or genetic mutations.

PETROCHEMICALS A general term for organic (carbon-containing) substances derived from petroleum or natural gas. Common petrochemical products include a tremendous array of plastics, solvents, synthetic fibers, propellant gases, and other widely used substances. Many of these chemicals are toxic or harmful as well as nondegradable; their manufacture and use contributes to air, water, and soil pollution, and their disposal places a significant burden on waste disposal facilities.

RADON (Rn) A radioactive gas created by the radioactive decay of radium, and emitted from some types of soil and rock. Harmless when dispersed into the outdoors, radon can build up in homes as it outgasses from foundations and basements; it can also contaminate well water. Twelve states are considered to have potentially

dangerous levels of radon: Colorado, Connecticut, Florida, Kentucky, Maine, New Hampshire, New Jersey, New York, Ohio, Pennsylvania, Tennessee, and Utah.

RAINFORESTS A type of forest community found primarily in wet regions of Latin America, Asia, the Pacific, and West Africa. Tropical rainforests cover less than 8 percent of the planet's surface, but absorb large amounts of carbon dioxide and are home to roughly half the world's plant and animal species and over a thousand indigenous tribes of people.[6] Cattle raising, slash-and-burn agriculture, and logging destroy about 18 million acres of tropical rainforest each year.[7]

SULFUR DIOXIDE (SO$_2$) A colorless gas or liquid that is both toxic and corrosive. Sulfur dioxide is a serious air pollutant, a hazard to human health, and a major contributor to acid rain. It is emitted naturally by decaying organic materials and volcanoes, but human activities, especially burning fossil fuels to generate electricity, account for most SO$_2$ production.

SYNTHETIC A term that denotes the use of a chemical reaction either to make a copy or near-copy of a naturally occurring substance, or to make an entirely new substance. Synthetic compounds usually contain organic (carbon-containing) materials, especially petrochemicals.

TOXIC A term that describes substances that harm tissue, damage organs or bodily functions, or cause illness or death when swallowed, inhaled, or absorbed by skin. Toxicity is usually determined through animal testing. Although the term refers only to their ability to harm humans, many toxic substances also damage the environment.

WATER POLLUTION The contamination of surface or groundwater with substances that are harmful to humans, plant or animal life, or natural ecosystems. Common human-caused water pollutants include sediments, fertilizers, pesticides, toxic chemicals, lead and other metals, acid rain, and microbes. Typical sources are farms, manufacturing plants, urban runoff, mines, and waste disposal sites. The effects of water pollution include contamination of drinking water supplies, dangerous residues in fish and shellfish used as food, and severe damage to natural ecosystems.

1. World Resources Institute, *World Resources 1988–89* (Basic Books, 1988), p. 170.
2. Ibid., p. 335.
3. N. Irving Sax and Richard J. Lewis, Sr., eds., *Hawley's Condensed Chemical Dictionary*, 11th ed. (Van Nostrand Reinhold, 1987), p. 225.
4. Ibid., p. 577.
5. *Air Quality Management Plan* (Southern California Association of Governments, 1989), pp. 1–5.
6. Mike Roselle and Tracy Katelman, *Tropical Hardwoods* (Draft) (Rainforest Action Network, 301 Broadway, Suite A, San Francisco, CA 94133; 1989), introduction.
7. World Resources Institute, op. cit., pp. 70–71.

RESOURCES

BOOKS AND PERIODICALS

ENVIRONMENTAL JOURNALS AND MAGAZINES

BioCycle: Journal of Waste Recycling, P.O. Box 351, Emmaus, PA 18049; (215) 967-4135.

Buzzworm: The Environmental Journal, 1818 16th St., Boulder, CO 80302; (303) 442-1969.

Consumer Reports, c/o Consumers Union, 256 Washington St., Mt. Vernon, NY 10553.

Country Journal: Practical Perspectives on Rural Living, P.O. Box 8200, Harrisburg, PA 17105; (800) 435-9610.

E Magazine, P.O. Box 5098, Westport, CT 06881; (203) 854-5559.

Earth Island Journal, 300 Broadway, #28, San Francisco, CA 94133; (415) 788-3666.

Earthwise Consumer, P.O. Box 1506, Mill Valley, CA 94942; (415) 383-5892.

EastWest Journal, P.O. Box 1200, Brookline, MA 02147; (612) 232-1000.

Environment, Heldreff Publications, 4000 Albemarle St. NW, Washington, DC 20016; (202) 362-6445.

EPA Journal, Superintendent of Documents, Government Printing Office, Washington, DC 20402; (202) 362-6445.

Garbage: The Practical Journal for the Environment, 435 9th St., Brooklyn, NY 11215; (800) 274-9909.

The Green Consumer Letter, Tilden Press, 1526 Connecticut Ave. NW, Washington, DC 20036; (800) 955-GREEN.

Harrowsmith, The Creamery, P.O. Box 1000, Charlotte, VT 05445; (802) 425-3961.

Home, P.O. Box 10179, Des Moines, IA 50347.

Home Energy, 2124 Kittredge St., #95, Berkeley, CA 94704; (415) 524-5405.

Home Resource: Practical, Environmentally Sound Homebuilding and Remodeling, P.O. Box 12061, Boulder, CO 80303.

Mother Earth News, P.O. Box 3122, Harlan, IA 51593; (800) 234-2424.

New Age Journal, P.O. Box 53275, Boulder, CO 80321.

Organic Gardening Magazine, 33 E. Minor St., Emmaus, PA 18098; (215) 967-5171.

Practical Homeowner, P.O. Box 58977, Boulder, CO 80322; (800) 525-0643.

TRANET Newsletter, P.O. Box 567, Rangeley, ME 04970; (207) 864-2252.

The Utne Reader, The Fawkes Building, 1624 Harmon Pl., Minneapolis, MN 55403; (612) 338-5040.

PRACTICAL/CONSUMER-ORIENTED BOOKS

General:

Blueprint for a Green Planet: Your Practical Guide to Restoring the World's Environment, by John Seymour and Herbert Girardet; Prentice Hall, 1987 ($17.95).

Ecologue: The Environmental Catalogue and Consumer's Guide for a Safe Earth, ed. by Bruce Anderson; Prentice Hall, 1990 ($18.95).

50 More Things You Can Do to Save the Earth, by the Earthworks Group; Andrews and McMeel, 1991 ($5.95).

50 Simple Things You Can Do to Save the Earth, by the Earthworks Group; Earthworks, 1989. ($4.95).

The Global Ecology Handbook: What You Can Do About the Environmental Crisis; The Global Tomorrow Coalition, 1990 ($16.95).

The Green Consumer, by John Elkington, Julia Hailes, and Joel Makower; Viking Penguin, 1990. ($8.95).

The Green Consumer Supermarket Guide: Brand Name Products That Don't Cost the Earth, by Joel Makower, with John Elkington and Julia Hailes; Viking Penguin, 1991.

The Green Lifestyle Handbook: 1001 Ways You Can Heal the Earth, ed. by Jeremy Rifkin; Henry Holt, 1990 ($10.95).

How to Make the World a Better Place: A Guide to Doing Good, by Jeffrey Hollender; William Morrow, 1990 ($9.95).

The Mother Earth Handbook, ed. by Judith S. Scherff; Continuum, 1991 ($15.95).

Save Our Planet: 750 Everyday Ways You Can Help Clean Up the Earth, by Diane MacEachern; Dell, 1990 ($9.95).

Saving the Earth: A Citizen's Guide to Environmental Action, by Will Steger and Jon Bowermaster; Knopf, 1990 ($19.95).

Shopping for a Better World: The Quick & Easy Guide to Socially Responsible Supermarket Shopping, by the Council on Economic Priorities; Ballantine, 1991 ($4.95).

Animal Rights:

The Animal Rights Handbook: Everyday Ways to Save Animal Lives; Living Planet, 1990 ($4.95).

Save the Animals: 101 Easy Things You Can Do, by Ingrid Newkirk; Warner Books, 1990 ($4.95).

A Shopper's Guide to Cruelty-Free Products, by Lori Cook; Bantam, 1991 ($4.99).

67 Ways to Save the Animals, by Anna Sequoia; Harper Perennial, 1991 ($4.95).

Automotive:

The Car Book, by Jack Gillis; Harper & Row, revised annually ($9.95).

Energy:

Cut Your Electric Bills in Half, by Ralph J. Herbert; Rodale, 1986 ($9.95).

The New Solar Home Book, by Bruce Anderson and Michael Riordon; Brick House, 1987 ($17.95).

1991 Consumer Guide to Home Energy Savings, by Alex Wilson; American Council for an Energy-Efficient Economy (1001 Connecticut Ave. NW, Washington, DC 20036) ($6.95).

Resource-Efficient Housing Guide: A Selected Annotated Bibliography and Directory of Helpful Organizations, by Robert Sardinsky; Rocky Mountain Institute (1739 Snowmass Creek Rd., Snowmass, CO 81654), revised annually ($15).

The Superinsulated Home Book, by J.D. Ned Nisson and Gautam Dutt; John Wiley & Sons, 1985 ($49.95/ $24.95).

Food:

Diet for a New America, by John Robbins; Stillpoint, 1987 ($12.95).

Diet for a Small Planet, by Frances Moore Lappé; Ballantine, 1985 ($4.95).

For Our Kids' Sake: How to Protect Your Child Against Pesticides in Food, by the Natural Resources Defense Council; Sierra Club Books/ Random House, 1989 ($6.95).

Pesticide Alert, by Lawrie Mott and Karen Snyder; Natural Resources Defense Council/Sierra Club Books, 1987 ($6.95/$15.95).

Safe Food, by Michael Jacobson et. al.; Living Planet, 1991 ($9.95).

Garden and Lawn:

The Basic Book of Organic Gardening, ed. by Robert Rodale; Ballantine, 1987 ($3.95).

The Chemical-Free Lawn, by Warren Schultz; Rodale, 1989 ($26.95).

The Encyclopedia of Natural Insect and Disease Control, ed. by Roger B. Yepsen, Jr.; Rodale, 1984 ($24.95).

How to Grow Vegetables Organically, by Jeff Cox; Rodale, 1988 ($21.95).

Let It Rot! The Home Gardener's Guide to Composting, by Stu Campbell; Garden Way, 1975 ($5.95).

Nature's Design, by Carol A. Smyser; Rodale, 1982 ($22.50).

The New Organic Grower, by Eliot Coleman; Chelsea Green, 1989 ($19.95).

Sensible Pest Control: A Handbook of Integrated Pest Management; Massachusetts Audubon Society (South Great Road, Lincoln, MA 01773) ($7.65).

Water Conservation in Landscape Design and Management; Environmental Design (7625 Empire Dr., Florence, KY 41042), 1984 ($29.95).

Personal Care/Household Products:

Clean & Green: The Complete Guide to Nontoxic and Environmentally Safe Housekeeping, by Annie Bethold-Bond; Ceres Press, 1990 ($8.95).

The Guide to Hazardous Products Around the Home, 2nd ed.; the Household Hazardous Waste Project (P.O. Box 87, 901 S. National Ave., Springfield, MO 65804) ($8.00).

Healthy House Catalog: National Directory of Indoor Pollution Resources; Housing Resource Center (4115 Bridge Ave., Cleveland, OH 44113), revised annually ($20.00).

The Natural Formula Book for Home and Yard, ed. by Dan Wallace; Rodale, 1982 ($19.95).

Nontoxic, Natural & Earthwise, by Debra Lynn Dadd; Jeremy P. Tarcher, 1990 ($12.95).

What to Use Instead: A Handbook of Practical Substitutes, by Carol Ann Rinzler; Pharos, 1987 ($6.95).

Pets:

Dr. Pitcairn's Complete Guide to Natural Health for Dogs and Cats, by Richard H. Pitcairn, D.V.M., and Susan Hubble Pitcairn; Rodale, 1982 ($12.95).

Rainforests:

The Rainforest Book: How You Can Save the World's Rainforests; Living Planet, 1990 ($5.95).

Rainforest Wood Wise, by Pam Wellner and Eugene Dickey; Rainforest Action Network (301 Broadway, San Francisco, CA 94133), 1991 ($10).

Recycling:

The Recycler's Handbook: Simple Things You Can Do, by the Earthworks Group; Earthworks Press, 1990 ($4.95).

Socially Responsible Investing:

Economics as if the Earth Really Mattered: A Catalyst Guide to Socially Conscious Investing, by Susan Meeker-Lowry; New Society Publishers, 1988 ($9.95).

Rating America's Corporate Conscience, by the Council on Economic Priorities; Addison-Wesley, 1987 ($14.95).

ENVIRONMENTAL INFORMATION BOOKS

General:

Age of Gaia: Biography of Our Living Earth, by James Lovelock; W.W. Norton, 1988 ($16.95).

Blueprint for a Green Planet: Your Practical Guide to Restoring the World's Environment, by John Seymour and Herbert Girardet; Prentice Hall, 1987 ($17.95).

Deep Ecology, by Bill Devall and George Sessions; Gibbs Smith/Peregrine Smith Books, 1987 ($11.95).

The Earth Report: The Essential Guide to Global Ecological Issues, ed. by Edward Goldsmith and Nicholas Hildyard; Price Stern Sloan, 1988 ($12.95).

For the Common Good: Redirecting the Economy Toward Community, the Environment, and a Sustainable Future, by Herman E. Daly and John B. Cobb; Beacon, 1990 ($24.95/$14.95).

Gaia: An Atlas of Planet Management, by Norman Myers; Anchor/Doubleday, 1984 ($18.95).

Global Warming: The Greenpeace Report, ed. by Jeremy Leggett; Oxford University Press, 1990 ($10.95).

The Green Alternative, by Brian Tokar; R. & E. Miles, 1987 ($7.95).

Hothouse Earth: The Greenhouse Effect and Gaia, by John Gribbin; Grove Weidenfeld, 1991 ($12.95).

Making Peace with the Planet, by Barry E. Commoner; Pantheon, 1990 ($19.95).

Simple in Means, Rich in Ends: Practicing Deep Ecology, by Bill Devall; Gibbs Smith, 1988 ($12.95).

Small Is Beautiful, by E.F. Schumacher; Harper & Row, 1973 ($9.95).

The State of the Earth Atlas, ed. by Joni Seager; Simon & Schuster, 1991 ($13.95).

State of the World, 1991, by Lester R. Brown, Worldwatch Institute; Norton, 1991 ($10.95).

Well Body, Well Earth: The Sierra Club Environmental Health Sourcebook, by Mike Samuels and Hal Zina Bennett; Sierra Club Books, 1983 ($12.95).

World Resources, by the World Resources Institute (1750 New York Ave. NW, Washington, DC 20006), revised annually ($16.95).

Air Pollution/Acid Rain:

Air Pollution, Acid Rain, and the Future of Forests, by Sandra Postel; Worldwatch Institute (1776 Massachusetts Ave. NW, Washington, DC 20036), 1984 ($4).

Breathing Easier: Taking Action on Climate Change, Air Pollution, and Energy Insecurity, by James J. MacKenzie; World Resources Institute (1750 New York Ave. NW, Washington, DC 20006), 1988 ($5).

A Killing Rain: The Global Threat of Acid Precipitation, by Thomas Pawlick; Sierra Club Books/Random House, 1988 ($15.95).

Who's Who of American Toxic Air Polluters: Guide to More than 1500 Factories in 46 States Emitting Cancer-Causing Chemicals; Natural Resources Defense Council (1350 New York Ave. NW, Washington, DC 20005), 1989 ($25).

Animal Rights:

Animal Liberation, by Peter Singer; Random House, 1990 ($14.95).

Diet for a New America, by John Robbins; Stillpoint, 1987 ($12.95).

In Defense of Animals, ed. by Peter Singer; Harper & Row, 1985 ($6.95).

The Dreaded Comparison: Human and Animal Slavery, by Marjorie Spiegel; Mirror Books, 1989 ($10.95).

Energy Use:

Building on Success: The Age of Energy Efficiency, by Christopher Flavin and Alan B. Durning; Worldwatch Institute (1776 Massachusetts Ave. NW, Washington, DC 20036), 1988 ($4).

Energy for a Sustainable World, by Jose Goldemburg et al.; World Resources Institute (1750 New York Ave. NW, Washington, DC 20006), 1987 ($10).

Energy Unbound: A Fable for America's Future, by L. Hunter Lovins, Amory B. Lovins, and Seth Zuckerman; Sierra Club Books/Random House, 1985 ($17.95).

Rethinking the Role of the Automobile, by Michael Renner; Worldwatch Institute (1776 Massachusetts Ave. NW, Washington, DC 20036), 1988 ($4).

Global Warming/Ozone Depletion:

The Challenge of Global Warming, ed. by Dean Edwin Abrahamson; Island, 1989 ($19.95).

Cooling the Greenhouse: Vital First Steps to Combat Global Warming; Natural Resources Defense Council (1350 New York Ave. NW, Washington, DC 20005) ($5).

The End of Nature, by William McKibben; Random House, 1989 ($19.95).

Global Warming, by Stephen H. Schneider; Sierra Club Books/Random House, 1989 ($18.95).

The Greenhouse Trap, ed. by Francesca Lyman; Beacon, 1990 ($9.95).

The Hole in the Sky, by John Gribbon; Bantam, 1988 ($4.50).

Stones in a Glass House—CFCs and Ozone Depletion, by Douglas G. Cogan; Investor Responsibility Research Center (1755 Massachusetts Ave. NW, Washington, DC 20036), 1988 ($35).

Indoor Air Pollution:

House Dangerous, by Ellen J. Greenfield; Vintage, 1987 ($7.95).

Why Your House May Endanger Your Health, by Alfred Zamm and Robert Gannon; Simon & Schuster, 1980 ($7.95).

Pesticides:

Agricide: The Hidden Crisis That Affects Us All, by Michael W. Fox, D.V.M.; Schocken/Random House, 1986 ($7.95).

The Bhopal Syndrome: Pesticides, Environment, and Health, by David Weir; Sierra Club Books/Random House, 1986 ($9.95).

Silent Spring, by Rachel Carson; Houghton Mifflin, 1987 (25th anniversary edition) ($7.95).

Rainforests:

The Fate of the Forest, by Susanna Hecht and Alexander Cockburn; Harper & Row, 1990 ($9.95).

In the Rainforest, by Catherine Caufield; University of Chicago Press, 1986 ($11.95).

Saving the Tropical Forests, by Judith Gradwohl and Russell Greenberg; Island, 1988 ($24.95).

Tropical Nature: Life and Death in the Rain Forests of Central and South America, by Adrian Forsyth and Ken Miyata; Scribner's, 1987 ($7.95).

Recycling/Waste Disposal:

Coming Full Circle: Successful Recycling Today; Environmental Defense Fund (257 Park Ave. S., New York, NY 10010), 1988 ($20).

Waste: Choices for Communities; Concern, Inc. (1794 Columbia Road NW, Washington DC 20009), 1988 ($3).

Wrapped in Plastics: The Environmental Case for Reducing Plastics Packaging, by Jeanne Wirka; Environmental Action Foundation (1525 New Hampshire Ave. NW, Washington, DC 20036), 1990 ($10).

Toxic Waste:

America the Poisoned: How Deadly Chemicals Are Destroying Our Environment, Our Wildlife, Ourselves—and How We Can Survive!, by Lewis Regenstein; Acropolis, 1982 ($8.95).

Hazardous Waste in America, by Samuel S. Epstein, Lester O. Brown, and Carl Pope; Sierra Club Books/Random House, 1983 ($12.95).

Who's Poisoning America: Corporate Polluters and Their Victims in the Chemical Age, ed. by Ralph Nader, Ronald Brownstein, and John Richard; Sierra Club Books/Random House, 1982 ($12.95).

Water Pollution:

Drinking Water—A Community Action Guide; Concern, Inc. (1794 Columbia Road NW, Washington, DC 20009), 1988 ($3).

Water: Rethinking Management in an Age of Scarcity, by Sandra Postel; Worldwatch Institute (1776 Massachusetts Ave. NW, Washington, DC 20036), 1984 ($4).

Wildlife:

The Endangered Kingdom: The Struggle to Save America's Wildlife, by Roger L. DiSilvestro; John Wiley & Sons, 1989 ($19.95).

MAIL-ORDER COMPANIES

These companies are good sources of environmentally sound products:

AB Enterprises P.O. Box 120220, Staten Island, NY 10312. Body care, household cleaners.

Abundant Life P.O. Box 772, Port Townsend, WA 98368; (206) 385-7455. Seeds for flowers, herbs, and vegetables.

Amberwood Route 1, P.O. Box 206, Milner, GA 30257; (404) 358-2991. Body care, books, cosmetics, household cleaners.

Basically Natural 109 E. G St., Brunswick, MD 21716; (301) 834-7923. Body care, cosmetics.

Baubiologie Hardware 207B 16th St., Pacific Grove, CA 93950; (408) 372-6826. Household goods, pet care.

Baudelaire Forest Rd., Marlow, NH 03456; (800) 327-2324. Body care.

Beauty Naturally P.O. Box 429, 57 Bosque Rd., Fairfax, CA 94930; (415) 459-2826. Body care, cosmetics.

Beauty Without Cruelty c/o Pamela Marsen, P.O. Box 119, Teaneck, NJ 07666; (201) 836-7820. Body care, cosmetics.

Biologic 418 Briar Lane, Chambersburg, PA 17201; (717) 263-2789. Garden pest controls.

The Body Shop 1341 7th St., Berkeley, CA 94710; (415) 524-0360. Body care, fragrances.

The Body Shop 45 Horsehill Rd., Cedar Knolls, NJ 07927; (800) 541-2535. Body care, cosmetics, fragrances.

Bonne Sante 462 62nd St., Brooklyn, NY 11220; (718) 492-3887. Body care, fragrances.

A Brighter Way H. Schacht Electrical Supply, 5214 Burleson Rd., #317, Austin, TX 78744; (512) 444-5583. Lighting supplies and equipment.

Brookstone 5 Vose Farm Rd., Peterborough, NH 03458; (603) 924-9541. Energy-saving household equipment.

W. Atlee Burpee 300 Park Ave., Warminster, PA 18974; (215) 674-4900. Garden supplies, pest controls.

Carole's Cosmetics, 7678 Sagewood Dr., Huntington Beach, CA 92648; (714) 842-0454. Body care, cosmetics, household cleaners.

A Clear Alternative 8707 West Lane, Magnolia TX 77355; (713) 356-7031. Body care, cosmetics, fragrances, household cleaners.

Clothcrafters Elkhart Lake, WI 53020; (414) 876-2112. Cloth household goods.

The Compassionate Consumer P.O. Box 27, Jericho, NY 11753; (718) 445-4134. Body care, clothing, cosmetics, fragrances, household cleaners, pet care.

Co-op America 2100 M St., NW Suite 310, Washington, DC 20063; (802) 658-5507. Clothing, household goods, stationery.

Cultural Survival 11 Divinity Ave., Cambridge, MA 02138; (617) 495-2562. Sustainably managed rainforest products.

Earth Care Paper Inc. P.O. Box 7070, Madison, WI 53707; (608) 277-2900. Recycled paper and paper products.

Ecco Bella 6 Provost Square, Suite 602, Caldwell, NJ 07006; (201) 226-5799. Body care, cosmetics, fragrances, household cleaners, pet care, stationery.

Eco-Choice P.O. Box 281, Montvale, NJ 07645; (800) 535-6304. Body care, household cleaners, paper products, pest controls.

Energy Federation (EFI) 354 Waverly St., Framingham, MA 01701; (508) 875-4921. Lighting supplies and household equipment.

The Energy Source 1332 Pearl St., Boulder, CO 80302; (303) 444-1088. Household equipment and appliances.

Environmental Awareness Products 3687 Goodwin Rd., Ionia, MI 48846; (517) 647-2535. Clothing.

Environmental Gifts P.O. Box 222-C, Helena, MT 59624; (406) 458-6466. Clothing, posters.

Feather River 133 Copeland, Petaluma, CA 94952; (707) 778-7627. Body care, cosmetics, fragrances, pet care. *Wholesale only.*

4-D SUNaturals 201 S. McKemy St., Chandler, AZ 85226; (602) 257-1950. Body care, teas.

Gardener's Supply Company 128 Intervale Rd., Burlington, VT 05401; (802) 863-5693. Garden pest controls.

Gardens Alive! Hwy. 48, P.O. Box 149, Sunman, IN 47041; (812) 623-3800. Garden and lawn fertilizers, pest controls.

Genesis, Inc. 67A Galli Dr., Novato, CA 94949; (415) 382-7784. Body care, cosmetics.

Harmony Farm Supply P.O. Box 451, Graton, CA 95444; (707) 823-9125. Garden pest controls.

Heart's Desire 1307 Dwight Way, Berkeley, CA 94702. Body care, household cleaners, pet care.

Home Health Products 1160 A Millers Lane, Virginia Beach, VA 23451; (800) 284-9123. Body care, health care.

Humane Alternative Products 8 Hutchins St., Concord, NH 03301; (603) 224-1361. Body care, cosmetics, household cleaners, pet care.

Humane Street, U.S.A. 467 Saratoga Ave., Suite 300, San Jose, CA 95129; (408) 243-2530. Body care, cosmetics, fragrances, household cleaners.

InterNatural P.O. Box 680, Shaker St. S., Sutton, NH 03273; (800) 446-4903. Body care, cosmetics, fragrances, pet care.

Jade Mountain P.O. Box 4616, Boulder, CO 80306; (303) 449-6601. Lighting and household supplies, gifts.

Lehman Hardware and Appliances, Inc. P.O. Box 41, 4779 Kidron Rd., Kidron, OH 44636; (216) 857-5441. Household equipment and appliances.

Lion & Lamb 29-28 41st Ave., Long Island City, NY 11101; (800) 252-6288. Body care.

Martin von Myering, Inc. 422 Jay St., Pittsburgh, PA 15212; (412) 323-2832. Body care.

Nature's Way Products, Earlee, Inc. 2002 Highway 62, Jeffersonville, IN 47130; (812) 282-9134. Garden pest controls.

The Necessary Trading Company 602 Main St., New Castle, VA 24127; (703) 864-5103. Pet care, garden pest controls.

Painlessly Beautiful 1260 Lumber St., Middletown, PA 17057. Cosmetics, body care.

Plow & Hearth P.O. Box 830, Orange, VA 22960; (800) 627-1712. Garden and household tools, equipment.

Rainbow Concepts Rt. 5, P.O. Box 569-H, Pheasant Mtn. Rd., Toccoa, GA 30577; (404) 886-6320. Body care, cosmetics, fragrances, household cleaners.

Real Goods Trading Company 966 Mazzoni St., Ukiah, CA 95482; (800) 762-7325. Tools, equipment, appliances, energy systems.

Red Saffron 3009 16th Ave. S., Minneapolis, MN 55407; (612) 724-3686. Personal care, herbs, spices, tea.

Renew America 1001 Connecticut Ave., Suite 638, Washington, D.C. 20036; (202) 232-2252. Household goods and equipment.

The Responsible Alternative Catalog 1139 Dominguez St. #E, Carson, CA 90746. Household, office, vehicle cleaners.

Rising Sun Enterprises P.O. Box 586, Old Snowmass, CO 81654; (303) 927-8051. Lighting supplies and water-saving equipment.

Seventh Generation Colchester, VT 05446-1672; (800) 456-1177. Household cleaners and goods, stationery, toys.

Sinan Company P.O. Box 857, Davis, CA 95617; (916) 753-3104. Building materials.

Smith & Hawken 25 Corte Madera Ave., Mill Valley, CA 94941; (415) 381-1800. Garden and household tools, equipment.

Solstice General Store 201 E. Main St., Suite H, Charlottesville, VA 22901; (804) 979-0189. Household cleaners.

Sunrise Lane Products 780 Greenwich St., New York, NY 10014; (212) 242-7014. Body care, fragrances, household cleaners.

Terra Verde Products P.O. Box 1353, Clifton, CO 81520. Body care, household cleaners.

Vegan Street P.O. Box 5525, Rockville, MD 20855; (800) 422-5525. Body care, cosmetics, household cleaners.

White Electric Co. 1511 San Pablo Ave., Berkeley, CA 94702; (415) 845-8534. Lighting supplies and equipment.

Whole Earth Access Company 2990 7th St., Berkeley, CA 94710; (800) 845-2000. Household goods.

Without Harm 4605 Pauli Dr., Manlius, NY 13104. Body care, cosmetics.

GOVERNMENT AGENCIES

FEDERAL AGENCIES

Bureau of Land Management Dept. of the Interior, Main Interior Bldg., 18th and C Sts. NW, Washington, DC 20240; (202) 343-5717. Issues: public lands, mineral resources in 10 western states and Alaska.

Bureau of Reclamation Dept. of the Interior, Main Interior Bldg., 18th and C Sts. NW, Washington, DC 20240; (202) 343-4662. Issues: public lands, water and energy programs in 17 western states.

Coast Guard Dept. of Transportation, 2100 2nd St. SW, Washington, DC 20593; (202) 267-2229. Issues: oil spills, other contamination cleanup along coasts, waterways.

Environmental Protection *Agency* 401 M St. SW, Washington, DC 20460; (202) 382-2080. (Ten regional offices located across the United States; call the national phone number for your regional office's address and phone number.) Hotlines: Drinking water, (800) 426-4791; Pesticides, (800) 585-7378; Right-to-Know, (800) 535-0202. Issues: enforcement, research, and regulation of environment policies on air and water pollution, solid waste and hazardous waste disposal, pesticide contamination, noise pollution, radiation.

Federal Energy Regulatory Commission Dept. of Energy, 825 N. Capitol St., Washington, DC 20426; (202) 357-8118. Issues: regulation of electric utilities.

Federal Highway Administration Dept. of Transportation, 400 7th St. SW, Washington, DC 20590; (202) 366-0660. Issues: highway construction, environmental impacts.

National Marine Fisheries Service Dept. of Commerce, 1335 East-West Highway, Silver Spring, MD 20910; (301) 427-2370. Issues: marine mammals protection.

National Oceanic and Atmospheric Administration Dept. of Commerce, 14th St. and Constitution Ave. NW, Washington, DC 20230; (202) 337-8090. Issues: National Weather Service, water conservation.

National Park Service Dept. of the Interior, Main Interior Building, 18th and C Sts. NW, Washington, DC 20240; (202) 343-4747. Issues: national park management.

Office of Conservation and Renewable Energy Dept. of Energy, 1000 Independence Ave. SW, Washington, DC 20585; (202) 586-9220. Issues: energy conservation.

Office of Surface Mining Dept. of the Interior, 1951 Constitution Ave. NW, Washington, DC 20240; (202) 343-4953. Issues: strip mining, land reclamation.

Soil Conservation Service Dept. of Agriculture, 14th St. and Independence Ave. SW, P.O. Box 2890, Washington, DC 20013; (202) 447-4543. Issues: soil and water conservation.

U.S. Army Corps of Engineers Dept. of Defense, 20 Massachusetts Ave. NW, Washington, DC 20314; (202) 272-0010. Issues: construction of dams, bridges, reservoirs; wetland protection.

U.S. Fish and Wildlife Service Main Interior Bldg., 18th and C Sts. NW, Washington, DC 20240; (202) 343-5634. Issues: fish and wildlife conservation and management.

U.S. Forest Service Dept. of Agriculture, 14th St. and Independence Ave. SW, P.O. Box 96090, Washington, DC 20250; (202) 447-2791. Issues: national forests and grasslands.

STATE ENVIRONMENTAL AGENCIES

Recycling hotlines, when available, and agencies with recycling programs, are listed first under each state heading.

■ ALABAMA:

Recycling Hotline (800) 392-1924.

Department of Conservation and Natural Resources 64 N. Union St., Montgomery, AL 36130; (205) 261-3486.

Department of Environmental Management Solid Waste Division, 1751 Congressman W.L. Dickinson Dr., Montgomery, AL 36130; (205) 271-7700. (Recycling programs.)

■ ALASKA:

Department of Environmental Conservation P.O. Box O, Juneau, AK 99811; (907) 465-2600. (Recycling programs.)

Department of Natural Resources 400 Willoughby, Juneau, AK 99801; (907) 465-2400.

■ ARIZONA:

Department of Environmental Quality 2005 N. Central Ave., Phoenix, AZ 85004; (602) 257-2300.

Energy Office 1700 W. Washington St., Phoenix, AZ 85007; (602) 542-3633. (Recycling programs.)

Land Department 1616 W. Adams St., Phoenix, AZ 85007; (602) 255-4621.

■ ARKANSAS:

Department of Pollution Control and Ecology 8001 National Dr., P.O. Box 9583, Little Rock, AR 72219; (501) 562-7444. (Recycling programs.)

■ CALIFORNIA:

Recycling Hotline (800) RECYCAL.

Department of Conservation Division of Recycling, 1025 P St., Room 401, Sacramento, CA 95814; (916) 323-3743. (Recycling programs.)

The Environmental Affairs Agency P.O. Box 2815, Sacramento, CA 95812; (916) 322-5840.

The Resources Agency 1416 9th St., Room 1311, Sacramento, CA 95814; (916) 445-5656.

■ COLORADO:

Recycling Hotline (800) 438-8800.

Department of Health Waste Management Division, 4210 E. 11th Ave., Denver, CO 80220; (303) 331-4830. (Recycling programs.)

Department of Natural Resources 1313 Sherman, Room 718, Denver, CO 80203; (303) 866-3311.

Office of Energy Conservation 112 E. 14th Ave., Denver, CO 80203; (303) 866-2507.

■CONNECTICUT:

Council on Environmental Quality 165 Capitol Ave., Room 239; Hartford, CT 06106; (203) 566-3510.

Department of Environmental Protection Solid Waste Division, 122 Washington St., Hartford, CT 06106; (203) 566-5847. (Recycling programs.)

■DELAWARE:

Recycling Hotline (800) CASHCAN.

Department of Natural Resources and Environmental Control 89 Kings Hwy., P.O. Box 1401, Dover, DE 19903; (302) 736-3869. (Recycling programs.)

■DISTRICT OF COLUMBIA:

Conservation Services Division 613 G St. NW, Washington, DC 20004; (202) 727-4700.

Department of Public Works Office of Policy and Planning, 2000 14th St. NW, Washington, DC 20009; (202) 939-8115. (Recycling programs.)

■FLORIDA:

Department of Environmental Regulation 2600 Blair Stone Rd., Tallahassee, FL 32399; (904) 488-4805. (Recycling programs.)

Department of Natural Resources Marjory Stoneman Douglas Bldg., Tallahassee, FL 32303; (904) 488-1554.

■GEORGIA:

Department of Natural Resources Floyd Towers E., 205 Butler St., Atlanta, GA 30334; (404) 656-3530. (Recycling programs.)

Institute of Natural Resources University of Georgia, Ecology Bldg., Room 13, Athens, GA 30602; (404) 542-1555.

■HAWAII:

Department of Health EPHS Division, P.O. Box 3378, Honolulu, HI 96801; (808) 548-6410. (Recycling programs.)

Department of Land and Natural Resources P.O. Box 621, Honolulu, HI 96809; (808) 548-6550.

Environmental Center Water Resource Research Center, University of Hawaii, 2550 Campus Rd., Honolulu, HI 96822; (808) 948-7361.

■IDAHO:

Department of Health and Welfare 450 W. State St., 3rd Floor, Boise, ID 83720; (208) 334-5879. (Recycling programs.)

Department of Lands State Capitol Bldg., Boise, ID 83720; (208) 334-3280.

Department of Water Resources 1301 N. Orchard, Boise, ID 83720; (208) 327-7900.

■ILLINOIS:

Department of Conservation Lincoln Tower Plaza, 524 S. 2nd St., Springfield, IL 62706; (217) 782-6302.

Department of Energy and Natural Resources 325 W. Adams St., Room 300, Springfield, IL 62704; (217) 785-2800. (Recycling programs.)

Illinois Environmental Protection Agency 2200 Churchill Rd., Springfield, IL 62706; (217) 782-3397.

■INDIANA:

Department of Environmental Management 105 S. Meridian St., P.O. Box 6015, Indianapolis, IN 46206; (317) 232-8603. (Recycling programs.)

Department of Natural Resources 606 State Office Bldg., Indianapolis, IN 46204; (317) 232-4020.

■IOWA:

Department of Agriculture, Land Stewardship, and Division of Soil Conservation Wallace State Office Bldg., Des Moines, IA 50319; (515) 281-5851.

Department of Natural Resources E. 9th and Grand Ave., Wallace Bldg., Des Moines, IA 50319; (515) 281-5145. (Recycling programs.)

■KANSAS:

State Conservation Commission 109 SW 9th St., Room 300, Topeka, KS 66612; (913) 296-3600.

State Department of Health and Environment Landon State Office Bldg., 900 SW Jackson St., Topeka, KS 66612; (913) 296-1500. (Recycling programs.)

■KENTUCKY:

Division of Waste Management 18 Reilly Rd., Frankfort, KY 40601; (502) 564-6716. (Recycling programs.)

Environmental Quality Commission 18 Reilly Rd., Ash Annex, Frankfort, KY 40601; (502) 564-2150.

Natural Resources and Environmental Protection Cabinet Capital Plaza Tower, 5th Floor, Frankfort, KY 40601; (502) 564-3350.

■LOUISIANA:

Department of Environmental Quality Solid Waste Division, 438 Main St., Baton Rouge, LA 70804; (504) 342-1216. (Recycling programs.)

State Office of Conservation P.O. Box 94275, Capitol Station, Baton Rouge, LA 70804; (504) 342-5540.

■MAINE:

Department of Conservation State House Station #22, Augusta, ME 04333; (207) 289-2211.

Office of Waste Reduction and Recycling 286 Water St., State House Station #154, Augusta, ME 04333; (207) 289-5300. (Recycling programs.)

State Soil and Water Conservation Commission Deering Bldg., AHMI Complex, Station #28, Augusta, ME 04333; (207) 289-2666.

■MARYLAND:

Recycling Hotline (800) 345-BIRP.

Department of Natural Resources 580 Taylor Ave., Annapolis, MD 21401; (301) 974-3987.

Department of the Environment 2500 Broening Hwy., Baltimore, MD 21224; (301) 631-3000. (Recycling programs.)

■MASSACHUSETTS:

Department of Environmental Protection Division of Solid Waste Disposal, 1 Winter St., 4th Floor, Boston, MA 02108; (617) 292-5961. (Recycling programs.)

Executive Office of Environmental Affairs Leverett Saltonstall Bldg., 100 Cambridge St., Boston, MA 02202; (617) 727-9800.

■MICHIGAN:

Department of Natural Resources P.O. Box 30028, Lansing, MI 48909; (517) 373-1220. (Recycling programs.)

Water Resources Commission P.O. Box 30028, Lansing, MI 48909; (517) 373-1949.

■MINNESOTA:

Recycling Hotline (800) 592-9528.

Department of Natural Resources 500 Lafayette Rd., St. Paul, MN 55155; (612) 296-6157. (Recycling programs.)

Pollution Control Agency 520 Lafayette Rd., St. Paul, MN 55155; (612) 296-6300.

■MISSISSIPPI:

Bureau of Land and Water Resources Southport Mall, P.O. Box 10631, Jackson, MS 39209; (601) 961-5200.

Bureau of Pollution Control Dept. of Natural Resources, P.O. Box 10385, Jackson, MS 39209; (601) 961-5171. (Recycling programs.)

■MISSOURI:

Department of Conservation P.O. Box 180, Jefferson City, MO 65102; (314) 751-4115.

Department of Natural Resources P.O. Box 176, Jefferson City, MO 65102; (314) 751-3332. (Recycling programs.)

■MONTANA:

Department of Health and Environmental Sciences Cogswell Bldg., Capitol Station, Helena, MT 59620; (406) 444-2544. (Recycling programs.)

Department of Natural Resources and Conservation 1520 E. 6th Ave., Helena, MT 59620; (406) 444-6699.

Environmental Quality Council State Capitol, Helena, MT 59620; (406) 444-3742.

■**NEBRASKA:**

Department of Environmental Control and Land Quality State House Station, P.O. Box 98922, Lincoln, NE 68509; (402) 471-2186. (Recycling programs.)

Nebraska Natural Resources Commission 301 Centennial Mall S., P.O. Box 94876, Lincoln, NE 68509; (402) 471-2081.

■**NEVADA:**

Department of Conservation and Natural Resources Capitol Complex, Nye Bldg., 201 S. Fall St., Carson City, NV 89710; (702) 885-4360.

Office of Community Services Capitol Complex #116, Carson City, NV 89710; (702) 885-4908.

■**NEW HAMPSHIRE:**

Council on Resources and Development Office of State Planning, 2¹/₂ Beacon St., Concord, NH 03301; (603) 271-2155.

Department of Environmental Services Waste Management Division, 6 Hazen Dr. #8518, Concord, NH 03301; (603) 271-3503. (Recycling programs.)

State Conservation Committee Dept. of Agriculture, Caller Box 2042, Concord, NH 03302; (603) 271-3576.

■**NEW JERSEY:**

Recycling Hotline (800) 492-4242.

Department of Environmental Protection 401 E. State St., CN 402, Trenton, NJ 08625; (609) 292-2885. (Recycling programs.)

■**NEW MEXICO:**

Environmental Improvement Division 1190 St. Francis Dr., Santa Fe, NM 87503; (505) 827-2850.

■**Health and Environment Department** 1190 St. Francis Dr., Santa Fe, NM 87503; (505) 827-2780. (Recycling programs.)

■**NEW YORK:**

Department of Environmental Conservation 50 Wolf Rd., Albany, NY 12233; (518) 457-5400. (Recycling programs.)

Environmental Protection Bureau State Dept. of Law, 120 Broadway, New York, NY 10271; (212) 341-2446.

■**NORTH CAROLINA:**

Department of Human Services Solid Waste Management Branch, P.O. Box 2091, Raleigh, NC 27602; (919) 733-0692. (Recycling programs.)

Department of Natural Resources and Community Development P.O. Box 27687, Raleigh, NC 27611; (919) 733-4984.

■**NORTH DAKOTA:**

Department of Health Division of Waste Management, P.O. Box 5520, Bismarck, ND 58502; (701) 224-2366. (Recycling programs.)

Institute for Ecological Studies P.O. Box 8278, University Station, University of North Dakota, Grand Forks, ND 58202; (701) 777-2851.

■**OHIO:**

Recycling Hotline (800) 282-6040.

Department of Natural Resources Fountain Square, Columbus, OH 43224; (614) 265-6886. (Recycling programs.)

Environmental Protection Agency P.O. Box 1049, 1800 Watermark Dr., Columbus, OH 43266; (614) 644-3020.

■**OKLAHOMA:**

Conservation Commission 2800 N. Lincoln Blvd., Suite 160, Oklahoma City, OK 73105; (405) 521-2384.

Department of Health P.O. Box 53551, Oklahoma City, OK 73152; (405) 271-7159. (Recycling programs.)

■ **OREGON:**

Department of Environmental Quality 811 SW 6th Ave., Portland, OR 97204; (503) 229-5696. (Recycling programs.)

Water Resources Department 3850 Portland Rd. NE, Salem, OR 97310; (503) 378-3739.

■ **PENNSYLVANIA:**

Recycling Hotline (800) 346-4242.

Department of Environmental Resources Fulton Bldg., 9th Floor, P.O. Box 2063, Harrisburg, PA 17120; (717) 783-2300. (Recycling programs.)

■ **RHODE ISLAND:**

Recycling Hotline (800) RICLEAN.

Department of Environmental Management 9 Hayes St., Providence, RI 02908; (401) 277-2774. (Recycling programs.)

State Water Resources Board 265 Melrose St., Providence, RI 02907; (401) 277-2217.

■ **SOUTH CAROLINA:**

Department of Health and Environmental Control J. Marion Sims Bldg., 2600 Bull St., Columbia, SC 29201; (803) 734-5000. (Recycling programs.)

Division of Energy, Agriculture, and Natural Resources 1205 Pendleton St., Suite 333, Columbia, SC 29201; (803) 734-1740.

■ **SOUTH DAKOTA:**

Board of Minerals and Environment Joe Foss Bldg., Pierre, SD 57501; (605) 773-3151.

Department of Water and Natural Resources Joe Foss Bldg., Pierre, SD 57501; (605) 773-3151.

Governor's Office of Energy Policy 217½ W. Missouri, Pierre, SD 57501; (605) 773-3603. (Recycling programs.)

■ **TENNESSEE:**

Recycling Hotline (800) 342-4038.

Department of Conservation 701 Broadway, Ellington Agricultural Center, Nashville, TN 37204; (615) 360-0103.

Department of Health and Environment 701 Broadway, 4th Floor, Nashville, TN 37219; (615) 741-3424. (Recycling programs.)

Energy, Environment, and Resources Center University of Tennessee, 327 S. Stadium Hall, Knoxville, TN 37996; (615) 974-4251.

■ **TEXAS:**

Recycling Hotline (800) CLEANTX.

Division of Solid Waste Management 1100 W. 49th St., Austin, TX 78756; (512) 458-7271. (Recycling programs.)

State Soil and Water Conservation Board P.O. Box 658, Temple, TX 76503; (817) 773-2250.

Texas Conservation Foundation P.O. Box 12845, Capitol Station, Austin, TX 78711; (512) 463-2196.

■ **UTAH:**

Bureau of Solid and Hazardous Waste 288 N. 1460 W., Salt Lake City, UT 84116; (801) 538-6170. (Recycling programs.)

State Department of Natural Resources 1636 W. North Temple, Salt Lake City, UT 84116; (801) 538-3156.

■ **VERMONT:**

Agency of Natural Resources 103 Main St., Waterbury, VT 05676; (802) 244-7437.

Department of Environmental Conservation 103 Main St., Waterbury, VT 05676; (802) 244-8702. (Recycling programs.)

■ **VIRGINIA:**

Recycling Hotline (800) KEEPIT.

Council on the Environment 903 9th St. Office Bldg., Richmond, VA 23219; (804) 786-4500.

Department of Conservation and Historic Resources Division of Parks and Recreation, 203 Governor St., Suite 306, Richmond, VA 23219; (804) 786-2121.

Division of Litter Control and Recycling 101 N. 14th St., James Monroe Bldg., 11th Floor, Richmond, VA 23219; (804) 225-2667. (Recycling programs.)

■**WASHINGTON:**

Recycling Hotline (800) RECYCLE.

Department of Ecology St. Martin's College, Abbot Raphael Hall, Olympia, WA 98503; (206) 459-6000. (Recycling programs.)

Department of Natural Resources Public Lands Bldg., Olympia, WA 98504; (206) 753-5327.

■**WEST VIRGINIA:**

Conservation, Education, and Litter Control 1900 Kanawha Blvd. E., Bldg. 3, Room 732, Charleston, WV 23505; (304) 348-3370. (Recycling programs.)

Department of Natural Resources 1800 Washington St. E., Charleston, WV 23505; (304) 348-2754.

■**WISCONSIN:**

Department of Natural Resources P.O. Box 7921, Madison, WI 53707; (608) 266-2621. (Recycling programs.)

Land and Water Resources Bureau Dept. of Agriculture, Trade, and Consumer Protection, 801 W. Badger Rd., Madison, WI 53713; (608) 267-9788.

Wisconsin Conservation Corps 20 W. Mifflin, Suite 406, Madison, WI 53703; (608) 266-7730.

■**WYOMING:**

Environmental Quality Department 122 W. 25th St., 4th Floor, Herschler Bldg., Cheyenne, WY 82002; (307) 777-7937. (Recycling programs.)

State Conservation Commission 2219 Carey Ave., Cheyenne, WY 82002; (307) 777-7323.

ENVIRONMENTAL, HEALTH, AND HUMANE ORGANIZATIONS

Listed below are organizations working at regional, national, or international levels on environmental issues; many groups have local chapters or offices. Membership rates are per year.

Abundant Life Seed Foundation P.O. Box 772, Port Townsend, WA 98368; (206) 385-5660. Issues: rare and native plant propagation. Newsletter: *Seed Midden*. Membership: $5-$25.

Acid Rain Foundation 1410 Varsity Dr., Raleigh, NC 27606; (919) 828-9443. Issues: acid rain, air pollution, recycling. Newsletter: *The Acid Rain Update*. Membership: $25.

Acid Rain Information Clearinghouse 33 S. Washington St., Rochester, NY 14608; (716) 546-3796. Issues: acid rain, air pollution.

Adopt-a-Stream Foundation P.O. Box 5558, Everett, WA 98201; (206) 388-3313. Issues: water pollution, water ecology. Newsletter: *Streamlines*. Membership: $10.

African Wildlife Foundation 1717 Massachusetts Ave. NW, Washington, DC 20036; (202) 265-8394. Issues: African wildlife and ecology. Newsletter: *Wildlife News*. Membership: $15 and up.

Alliance for Environmental Education 2111 Wilson Blvd., Suite 751, Arlington, VA 22201; (703) 875-8660. Issues: environmental education. Newsletter: *The Network Exchange*. Membership for organizations: $100.

Alliance to Save Energy 1925 K St. NW, Washington, DC 20006; (202) 857-0666. Issues: energy efficiency, research, and pilot projects.

America the Beautiful Fund 219 Shoreham Bldg., Washington, DC 20005; (202) 638-1649. Issues: environmental quality, support for community projects. Newsletter: *Better Times*. Membership: $5 and up.

American Cave Conservation Association P.O. Box 409, Horse Cave, KY 42749; (502) 786-1466. Issues: cave, groundwater preservation. Magazine: *American Caves*. Membership: $25.

American Cetacean Society P.O. Box 2639, San Pedro, CA 90731; (213) 548-6279. Issues: whale and dolphin protection. Newsletter: *Whale News.* Magazine: *Whale Watcher.* Membership: $25.

American Council for an Energy-Efficient Economy 1001 Connecticut Ave. NW, Washington, DC 20036; (202) 429-8873. Issues: energy efficiency in the home. Publication: *1991 Consumer Guide to Home Energy Savings.*

American Farmland Trust 1920 N St. NW, Suite 400, Washington, DC 20036; (202) 659-5170. Issues: land and soil preservation. Membership: $15.

American Forestry Association P.O. Box 2000, Washington, DC 20013; (202) 667-3300. Issues: forest conservation, tree planting. Newsletter: *Resource Hotline.* Magazine: *American Forests.* Membership: $24.

American Humane Association P.O. Box 1266, Denver, CO 80201; (303) 695-0811. Issues: animal and children's rights. Magazine: *Advocate.* Membership: $15.

American Littoral Society Sandy Hook, Highlands, NJ 07732; (201) 291-0055. Issues: shoreline and beach conservation, water pollution, and ecology. Newsletters: *Underwater Naturalist; Coastal Reporter.* Membership: $20.

American Oceans Campaign 2219 Main St., Santa Monica, CA 90405; (213) 452-2206. Issues: ocean ecology, water pollution.

American Rivers 801 Pennsylvania Ave. SE, Washington, DC 20003; (202) 547-6900. Issues: river preservation and ecology, water pollution. Newsletter: *American Rivers.* Membership: $20 and up.

American Society for Environmental History New Jersey Institute of Technology, Newark, NJ 07012; (201) 596-3334. Issues: natural environment, ecology. Magazine: *Environmental Review.* Membership: $24.

American Society for the Prevention of Cruelty to Animals 441 E. 92nd St., New York, NY 10128; (212) 876-7700. Issues: animal rights, wildlife preservation. Magazine: *ASPCA Quarterly Report.* Membership: $20.

American Wilderness Alliance 7600 E. Arapahoe, Suite 114, Englewood, CO 80112; (303) 771-0380. Issues: wilderness preservation and management. Newsletter: *It's Time to Go Wild.* Membership: $22 and up.

Animal Protection Institute of America 2831 Fruitridge Rd., Sacramento, CA 95820; (916) 731-5521. Issues: animal rights. Magazine: *Mainstream.* Membership: $20.

Animal Welfare Institute P.O. Box 3650, Washington, DC 20007; (202) 337-2332. Issues: animal rights. Newsletter: *Animal Welfare Institute.* Membership: $15.

Atlantic Center for the Environment 39 S. Main St., Ipswich, MA 01938; (508) 356-0038. Issues: Atlantic Ocean natural resources, ecology. Newsletter: *Nexus.* Membership: $25.

Bat Conservation International P.O. Box 162603, Austin, TX 78761; (512) 327-9721. Issues: bat, habitat preservation. Newsletter: *Bats.* Book: *America's Neighborhood Bats.* Membership: $25.

Bio-Integral Resource Center P.O. Box 7414, Berkeley, CA 94707; (415) 524-2567. Issues: integrated pest management, natural pest control. Publications: *IPM Practitioner; Common Sense Pest Control Quarterly.* Membership: $25-$45.

Center for Marine Conservation 1725 DeSales St. NW, Washington, DC 20036; (202) 429-5609. Issues: marine wildlife and habitat preservation. Newsletter: *Marine Conservation News.* Membership: $20.

Center for Plant Conservation 125 Arborway, Jamaica Plain, MA 02130; (617) 524-6988. Issues: preservation of rare and endangered native plants.

Center for Science in the Public Interest 1501 16th St. NW, Washington, DC 20036; (202) 332-9110. Issues: nutrition and health. Newsletter: *Nutrition Action Health Letter.* Membership: $19.95.

Children of the Green Earth P.O. Box 95219, Seattle, WA 98145; (206) 781-0852. Issues: tree planting, forest protection for young people. Newsletter: *Tree Song.* Membership: $25.

Citizen Action 1300 Connecticut Ave. NW, Washington, DC 20036; (202) 857-5153. Issues: environmental preservation.

Citizens Clearinghouse for Hazardous Waste P.O. Box 926, Arlington, VA 22216; (703) 276-7070. Issues: community organizing, waste disposal, recycling. Newsletter: *Everyone's Backyard.* Membership: $25.

Clean Water Action Project 317 Pennsylvania Ave. SE, Washington, DC 20003; (202) 547-1196. Issues: water pollution, natural resource protection. Newsletter: *Clean Water Action News.* Membership: $24.

Climate Institute 316 Pennsylvania Ave. SE, Washington, DC 20003; (202) 547-0104. Issues: global warming, ozone depletion. Newsletter: *Climate Alert.* Membership: $35.

Coalition for Scenic Beauty 216 7th St. SE, Washington, DC 20003; (202) 546-1100. Issues: natural resource protection, billboard control. Newsletter: *Sign Control News.* Membership: $20.

Concern, Inc. 1794 Columbia Road NW, Washington, DC 20009; (202) 328-8160. Issues: pesticides, water pollution, household wastes. Publications: *Household Waste; Groundwater; Pesticides; Drinking Water; Farmland; Waste: Choices for Communities.*

Conservation and Renewable Energy Information Service P.O. Box 8900, Silver Spring, MD 20907; (800) 523-2929. Issues: energy conservation.

Conservation Foundation 1250 24th St. NW, Washington, DC 20037; (202) 293-4800. Issues: pollution, toxic substances, natural resources. Newsletter: *CF Newsletter.*

Conservation International 1015 18th St. NW, Suite 1000, Washington, DC 20036; (202) 429-5660. Issues: rainforest preservation. Membership: $15.

Consumer Pesticide Project 425 Mississippi St., San Francisco, CA 94105; (415) 826-6314. Issues: pesticide use on fruits and vegetables. Publication: *Organizing Kit: A Practical Strategy to Reduce Dangerous Pesticides in Our Food and the Environment.*

Council on Economic Priorities 30 Irving Place, New York, NY 10003; (212) 420-1133. Issues: corporate social responsibility, environmental and national security concerns. Publication: *Shopping for a Better World: A Quick & Easy Guide to Socially Responsible Investing.* Membership: $25.

Cousteau Society 930 W. 21st St., Norfolk, VA 23517; (804) 627-1144. Issues: ecology, climate, pollution, toxics, wildlife preservation, ocean preservation. Magazines: *Calypso Log; Dolphin Log.* Membership: $20-$28.

Defenders of Wildlife 1244 19th St. NW, Washington, DC 20036; (202) 659-9510. Issues: preservation of wildlife and endangered and threatened species. Magazine: *Defenders.* Membership: $20.

Earth First! P.O. Box 7, Canton, NY 13617; (315) 379-9940. Issues: deep ecology, wildlife and environmental preservation; encourages direct action by individuals. Publication: *Earth First! Journal.* Membership: $20.

Earth Island Institute 300 Broadway, Suite 28, San Francisco, CA 94133; (415) 788-3666. Issues: marine mammal protection, water ecology, rainforest preservation; international focus. Publication: *Earth Island Journal.* Membership: $25.

EarthSave P.O. Box 949, Felton, CA 95018; (408) 423-4069. Issues: animal rights, food, environmental health. Newsletter: *Project EarthSave.* Membership: $20 and up.

Elsa Wild Animal Appeal/Elsa Clubs of America P.O. Box 4572, N. Hollywood, CA 90607; (818) 761-8387. Issues: wildlife, endangered species preservation, focus on child education. Newsletter: *Born Free News.* Membership: $5 and up.

Environmental Action Foundation 1525 New Hampshire Ave. NW, Washington, DC 20036; (202) 745-4870. Issues: research and education on air pollution, toxic substances, energy efficiency, solid wastes, and recycling. Publication: *Wrapped in Plastics*. Membership: $20.

Environmental Action, Inc. 1525 New Hampshire Ave. NW, Washington, DC 20036; (202) 745-4870. Issues: lobbies Congress on legislation regarding air pollution, toxic substances, energy efficiency, solid wastes, and recycling. Magazine: *Environmental Action Magazine*. Membership: $20.

Environmental Defense Fund 257 Park Ave. S., New York, NY 10010; (212) 505-2100. Issues: wildlife and habitat preservation, water pollution, pesticides, toxic substances, solid waste, climate. Newsletter: *EDF Newsletter*. Membership: $20.

Environmental Law Institute 1616 P St. NW, Suite 200, Washington, DC 20036; (202) 328-5150. Education and research on environmental legal issues. Publications: *The Environmental Forum, National Wetlands Newsletter*.

The Forest Trust P.O. Box 9238, Santa Fe, NM 87504; (505) 983-8992. Issues: forest management, ecosystem restoration, community development.

Freshwater Foundation 2500 Shadywood Rd., P.O. Box 90, Navarre MN 55392; (612) 471-8407. Issues: water pollution, biological water treatment. Publications: *Journal of Freshwater; Health and Environment Digest; The U.S. Water News*. Membership: $50.

Friends of Animals P.O. Box 1244, Norwalk, CT 06856; (203) 866-5223. Issues: animal rights, wildlife preservation. Membership: $20.

Friends of the Earth 530 7th St. SE, Washington, DC 20003; (202) 544-2600. Issues: water pollution and ecology, climate, air pollution, acid rain, ocean ecology, deforestation. Magazine: *Not Man Apart*. Membership: $15 and up.

Friends of the River, Inc. Fort Mason Center, Bldg. C, San Francisco, CA 94123; (415) 771-0400. Issues: river preservation, water ecology. Newsletter: *Headwaters*. Membership: $25.

Friends of the Sea Otter P.O. Box 221220, Carmel, CA 93922; (408) 625-3290. Issues: south-

ern sea otter protection and habitat preservation. Magazine: *Otter Raft*. Membership: $15.

Fund for Animals 200 W. 57th St., New York, NY 10019; (212) 246-2096. Issues: animal rights, wildlife protection. Membership: $10 and up.

Global Tomorrow Coalition 1325 G St. NW, Washington, DC 20005; (202) 628-4016. Issues: sustainable development worldwide. Newsletter: *InterAction*. Membership: $15 and up.

Grass Roots the Organic Way 38 Llangollen Lane, Newton Square, PA 19073; (215) 353-2838. Issues: pesticide use, natural alternatives. Membership: $20.

Great Bear Foundation P.O. Box 2699, Missoula, MT 59806; (406) 721-3009. Issues: preservation of bears. Newsletter: *Bear News*. Membership: $15 and up.

Green Committees of Correspondence P.O. Box 30208, Kansas City, MO 64112; (816) 931-9366. Issues: grassroots organizing on environmental and social issues. Publication: *Green Letter in Search of Greener Times*. Membership: $25.

Greenhouse Crisis Foundation 1130 17th St. NW, Washington, DC 20036; (202) 466-2823. Issues: climate, energy conservation, urban reforestation. Publication: *Greenhouse Crisis: 10 Ways to Save the Earth*.

Greenpeace USA 1436 U St. NW, Washington, DC 20009; (202) 462-1177. Issues: marine mammal protection, habitat preservation, nuclear disarmament, ocean ecology, toxic substances, endangered animal protection. Magazine: *Greenpeace*. Membership: $20.

Household Hazardous Waste Project 901 S. National Ave., P.O. Box 108, Springfield, MO 65804; (417) 836-5777. Issues: household hazardous wastes. Publication: *The Guide to Hazardous Products Around the Home*.

Human Ecology Action League P.O. Box 49126, Atlanta, GA 30359; (404) 248-1898. Issues: chemical use, sensitivities, alternatives. Newsletter: *The Human Ecologist*. Membership: $20.

Humane Society of the United States 2100 L St. NW, Washington DC 20037; (202) 452-1100.

Issues: animal rights, marine mammal protection. Membership: $10.

Infact 256 Hanover, Boston, MA 02113; (617) 742-4583. Issues: corporate responsibility, nuclear weapons. Publication: *Infact Brings GE to Light.* Membership: $15.

Inform 381 Park Ave. S., New York, NY 10016; (212) 689-4040. Issues: air pollution, solid waste, land and water conservation. Newsletter: *Inform Reports.* Membership: $35 and up.

Institute for the Development of Earth Awareness (I.D.E.A.) P.O. Box 124, Prince Street Station, New York, NY 10012; (212) 969-8506. Issues: land preservation and restoration; environmental learning programs; biosustainable building. Publication: *The Dreaded Comparison: Human and Animal Slavery.* Membership: $25 and up.

Institute for Earth Education P.O. Box 288, Warrenville, IL 60555; (312) 393-3096. Issues: ecosystems, environmental preservation. Publication: *Talking Leaves.* Membership: $20 and up.

Institute for Local Self-Reliance 2425 18th St. NW, Washington, DC 20009; (202) 232-4108. Issues: waste reduction, recycling, community development.

International Alliance for Sustainable Agriculture Newman Center, University of Minnesota, 1701 University Ave. SE, Room 202, Minneapolis, MN 55414; (612) 331-1099. Issues: sustainable agriculture. Newsletter: *Manna.* Membership: $10 and up.

International Council for Bird Preservation 801 Pennsylvania Ave. SE, Washington, DC 20003; (202) 778-9563. Issues: bird species preservation. Magazines: *World Bird Watch; U.S. Bird News.* Membership: $35 and up.

International Fund for Animal Welfare P.O. Box 193, 411 Main St., Yarmouth Port, MA 02675; (508) 362-4944. Issues: animal rights, wildlife preservation. Various newsletters. Membership: donation.

International Oceanographic Foundation 4600 Rickenbacker Causeway, P.O. Box 499900, Miami, FL 33149; (305) 361-4888. Issues: ocean ecology. Magazine: *Sea Frontiers.* Membership: $18.

International Primate Protection League P.O. Box 766, Sumerville, SC 28484; (803) 871-2280. Issues: primate protection and habitat preservation. Newsletter: *International Primate Protection League.* Membership: $20.

International Society of Arboriculture 303 W. University Ave., Urbana, IL 61801; (217) 328-2032. Issues: tree preservation, planting, and care. Publication: *Journal of Arboriculture.* Membership: $55.

International Society of Tropical Foresters 5400 Grosvenor Lane, Bethesda, MD 20814; (301) 897-8720. Issues: tropical forest protection and wise management. Newsletter: *ISTF News.* Magazine: *Journal of Forestry.* Membership: $50.

Izaak Walton League of America 1701 N. Fort Meyer Dr., Arlington, VA 22209; (703) 528-1818. Issues: acid rain, air and water pollution, soil erosion, wildlife preservation. Magazine: *Outdoor America.* Membership: $20.

Land Trust Exchange 1017 Duke St., Alexandria, VA 22314; (703) 683-7778. Issues: land conservation and protection. Membership: $30 and up.

League of Conservation Voters 320 4th St. NE, Washington, DC 20002; (202) 785-8683. Issues: nonpartisan political work to elect pro-environmental candidates. Newsletter: *The National Environmental Scorecard.* Membership: $25.

League of Women Voters 1730 M St. NW, Washington, DC 20036; (202) 429-1965. Issues: nonpartisan political work with social and environmental focus. Magazine: *National Voter.* Membership: $50.

Marine Mammal Stranding Center P.O. Box 733, Brigantine, NJ 08203; (609) 266-0538. Issues: whale, dolphin, seal, sea turtle rescue and rehabilitation. Newsletter: *Blow Hole.* Membership: $10.

National Anti-Vivisection Society 53 W. Jackson Blvd., Suite 1550, Chicago, IL 60604; (312) 427-6065. Issues: animal rights. Publication: *Personal Care with Principle.* Membership: $5 and up.

National Arbor Day Foundation 100 Arbor Ave., Nebraska City, NE 68410; (402) 474-5655. Issues: tree planting and care. Newsletter: *Arbor Day.* Membership: $10.

National Audubon Society 950 3rd Ave., New York, NY 10022; (212) 832-3200. Issues: wildlife and habitat preservation, natural resource conservation, air pollution, toxic substances. Publications: *Audubon Magazine; American Birds; Audubon Activist; Action Alerts.* Membership: Society, $30; Activist Network, $9.

National Center for Appropriate Technology P.O. Box 2525, Butte, MT 59702; (800) 428-2525. Issues: energy conservation. Numerous publications.

National Clean Air Coalition 530 7th St. SE, Washington, DC 20003; (202) 543-8200. Issues: air pollution. Newsletter: *Clean Air 101.* Membership: Free.

National Coalition Against the Misuse of Pesticides 530 7th St. SE, Washington, DC 20003; (202) 543-5450. Issues: pesticide use, alternatives. Newsletter: *Pesticides and You.* Membership: $20.

National Coalition for Marine Conservation P.O. Box 23298, Savannah, GA 31403; (912) 234-8062. Issues: ocean ecology, wildlife and habitat preservation. Newsletter: *Marine Bulletin.* Membership: $25.

National Coalition to Stop Food Irradiation P.O. Box 59-0488, San Francisco, CA 94159; (415) 626-2734. Issues: food irradiation.

National Geographic Society 1145 17th St. NW, Washington, DC 20036; (202) 857-7000. Issues: global ecology, environmental research. Magazine: *National Geographic.* Membership: $21.

National Institute for Urban Wildlife 10921 Trotting Ridge Way, Columbia, MD 21044; (301) 596-3311. Issues: wildlife protection and preservation. Newsletter: *Urban Wildlife News.* Membership: $25.

National Parks and Conservation Association 1015 31st St. NW, Washington, DC 20007; (202) 944-8530. Issues: national park system protection and improvement. Magazine: *National Parks.* Membership: $25.

National Recycling Coalition 1101 30th St. NW, Washington, DC 20006; (202) 625-6406. Issues: recycling. Newsletter: *NRC Connection.* Membership: $30.

National Toxics Campaign 37 Temple Pl., Boston, MA 02111; (617) 482-1477. Issues: hazardous wastes. Magazine: *Toxic Times.* Membership: $25.

The National Water Center P.O. Box 264, Eureka Springs, AR 72632; (501) 253-9755. Issues: water pollution. Newsletter: *Water Center News.* Membership: $10 and up.

National Wildflower Research Center 2600 FM 973 N., Austin, TX 78725; (512) 929-3600. Issues: wildflower preservation and propagation. Numerous publications. Membership: $25 and up.

National Wildlife Federation 1400 16th St. NW, Washington, DC 20036; (202) 797-6800. Issues: wildlife and habitat preservation, deforestation, toxic substances, natural resource and energy conservation. Magazines: *National Wildlife; International Wildlife; Ranger Rick; Your Big Backyard.* Membership: $10 and up.

Natural Resources Defense Council 40 W. 20th St., New York, NY 10011; (212) 727-2700. Issues: air and water pollution, climate, toxic substances, energy and natural resource conservation. Newsletter: *Natural Resources Defense Council Newsline.* Magazine: *Amicus Journal.* Membership: $10.

The Nature Conservancy 1815 N. Lynn St., Arlington, VA 22209; (703) 841-5300. Issues: ecology, wildlife and habitat preservation. Magazine: *The Nature Conservancy Magazine.* Membership: $15.

North American Bluebird Society P.O. Box 6295, Silver Spring, MD 20906; (301) 384-2798. Issues: bluebird protection, preservation.

North American Lake Management Society P.O. Box 217, Merrifield, VA 22116; (202) 466-8550. Issues: water ecology. Newsletter: *Lakeline*. Membership: $20 and up.

Pacific Whale Foundation 101 N. Kihei Road, Suite 21, Kihei, Maui, HI 96753; (808) 879-8811, (800) 942-5311. Issues: whale protection and preservation, ocean ecology, water pollution. Membership: $15 and up.

People for the Ethical Treatment of Animals P.O. Box 42516, Washington, DC 20015; (301) 770-7444. Issues: animal rights. Magazine: *PETA News*. Fact sheets: "Companies That Don't Test on Animals;" "Companies That Test on Animals." Membership: $15.

The Peregrine Fund 5666 W. Flying Hawk Lane, Boise, ID 83709; (208) 362-3716. Issues: rare and endangered bird protection and preservation. Newsletter: *The Peregrine Fund Newsletter*. Membership: $25.

Permaculture Institute of North America 4649 Sunnyside Ave. N., Seattle, WA 98103. Issues: ecology, sustainable agriculture. Newsletter: *Permaculture Activist*.

Pesticide Action Network P.O. Box 610, San Francisco, CA 94101; (415) 541-9140. Issues: pesticide use, alternatives. Newsletters: *Global Pesticide Monitor; Dirty Dozen Campaigner; PANNA Outlook*. Membership: $30 and up.

Public Citizen 2000 P St. NW, Washington, DC 20036; (202) 293-9142. Issues: environmental standards, safe energy. Magazine: *Public Citizen Magazine*. Membership: $20.

Public Voice for Food and Health Policy 1001 Connecticut Ave. NW, Suite 522, Washington, DC 20036; (202) 659-5930. Issues: health, nutrition, food safety. Newsletter: *Action Alert*. Membership: $20.

Rachel Carson Council 8940 Jones Mill Rd., Chevy Chase, MD 20815; (301) 652-1877. Issues: chemical use, ecology. Newsletter. Membership: $15.

Rails to Trails Conservancy 1400 16th St. #300, Washington, DC 20036; (202) 797-5400. Issues: railroad right-of-way conversion to trails, wildlife preservation. Membership: $18.

Rainforest Action Network 300 Broadway, Suite 28, San Francisco, CA 94133; (415) 398-4404. Issues: rainforest protection and preservation. Newsletters: *Rainforest Action Alert; World Rainforest Report*. Membership: $15 and up.

Rainforest Alliance 270 Lafayette St., Suite 512, New York, NY 10012; (212) 941-1900. Issues: rainforest protection and preservation. Newsletter: *Canopy*. Membership: $15-$20.

Raptor Education Foundation 21901 E. Hampden Ave., Aurora, CO 80013; (303) 680-8500. Issues: raptor protection and preservation. Membership: $15.

Raptor Research Foundation Carpenter Nature Center, 12805 St. Croix Trail, Hastings, MN 55033; (612) 437-4359. Issues: raptor protection and preservation. Membership: $18-$20.

Renew America 1001 Connecticut Ave. NW, Suite 719, Washington, DC 20036; (202) 232-2252. Issues: natural resource use. Publications: *Renew America Report; State of the States*. Membership: $25.

Resources for the Future 1616 P St. NW, Washington, DC 20036; (202)328-5000. Issues: natural resource use, air and water pollution, solid waste, toxic substances, pesticides. Newsletter: *Resources*.

Rocky Mountain Institute 1739 Snowmass Creek Rd., Old Snowmass, CO 81654; (303) 927-3128. Issues: energy efficiency, natural resource use. Numerous publications.

Save the Redwoods League 114 Sansome St., Room 605, San Francisco, CA 94104; (415) 362-2352. Issues: redwoods protection and preservation. Newsletter. Membership: $10 and up.

Sea Shepherd Conservation Society P.O. Box 7000-S, Redondo Beach, CA 90277; (213) 373-6979. Issues: marine animal and habitat protection and preservation. Newsletter: *Sea Shepherd Log*. Membership: donation.

Sierra Club 730 Polk St., San Francisco, CA 94109; (415) 776-2211. Issues: air pollution, climate, deforestation, wildlife preservation. Magazine: *Sierra*. Membership: $33.

Sierra Club Legal Defense Fund 2044 Fillmore St., San Francisco, CA 94115; (415) 567-6100. Issues: litigation on wildlife preservation, water and air pollution, public land use.

Society for Animal Protective Legislation P.O. Box 3719, Washington, DC 20007; (202) 337-2334. Issues: lobbying for animal rights, wildlife protection and preservation.

Society for Conservation Biology Montana State University, Dept. of Biology, Bozeman, MT 59717; (406) 994-5724. Issues: ecology, ecosystem conservation. Publication: *Conservation Biology*. Membership: $32.50 and up.

Soil and Water Conservation Society of America 7515 NE Ankeny Rd., Ankeny, IA 50021; (515) 289-2331. Issues: soil, water, natural resource conservation. Publication: *Journal of Soil and Water Conservation*. Membership: $25 and up.

Student Conservation Association P.O. Box 550, Charlestown, NH 03603; (603) 826-4301. Issues: natural resources, forests, public lands management. Newsletter: *The Volunteer*. Membership: $10-$25.

TreePeople 12601 Mulholland Dr., Beverly Hills, CA 90210; (818) 753-4600. Issues: tree planting, conservation. Newsletter: *Seedling News*. Membership: $25 and up.

Trees for Life 1103 Jefferson, Wichita, KS 67203; (316) 263-7294. Issues: tree planting and care. Newsletter: *Life Lines*. Membership: Free.

Trust for Public Land 116 New Montgomery St., San Francisco, CA 94105; (415) 495-4014. Issues: land preservation through trusts.

Union of Concerned Scientists 26 Church St., Cambridge, MA 02138; (617) 547-5552. Issues: nuclear weapons and energy, climate, defor-

estation. Newsletter: *Nucleus*. Membership: donation.

United Nations Environment Programme Room DC2-0803, United Nations, New York, NY 10017; (212) 963-8093. Provides information on many environmental problems; works to implement international solutions. Publications: numerous. Newsletter: *UNEP North America News*.

U.S. Public Interest Research Group 215 Pennsylvania Ave. SE, Washington DC 20003; (202) 546-9707. Issues: air pollution, toxic substances, pesticide use, consumer issues. Newsletter: *Citizen's Agenda*. Membership: $25.

Water Pollution Control Federation 601 Wythe St., Alexandria, VA 22314; (703) 684-2400. Issues: water pollution, conservation. Membership: $50.

The Whale Center 3929 Piedmont Ave., Oakland, CA 94611; (415) 654-6621. Issues: whale, habitat protection and preservation. Newsletter: *The Whale Center Journal*. Membership: $10-$250.

Whooping Crane Conservation Association 3000 Meadowlark Dr., Sierra Vista, AZ 85635; (602) 458-0971. Issues: whooping crane, habitat protection and preservation. Membership: $100.

Wild Canid Survival and Research Center/Wolf Sanctuary P.O. Box 760, Eureka, MO 63025; (314) 938-5900. Issues: protection and preservation of endangered red and Mexican wolves. Membership: $25 and up.

Wild Horse Organized Assistance P.O. Box 555, Reno, NV 89504; (702) 851-4817. Issues: wild horse and burro protection and management.

The Wilderness Society 900 17th St. NW, Washington, DC 20006; (202) 833-2300. Issues: wildlife, habitat protection and preservation; ecosystem management. Newsletter: *The Wildlifer*. Membership: $15 and up.

Wildlife Conservation International New York Zoological Society, Bronx, NY 10460; (202) 367-1010. Issues: wildlife protection and preservation. Newsletter: *Wildlife Conservation International Newsletter.* Membership: $23 and up.

Wildlife Information Center 629 Green St., Allentown, PA 18102; (215) 434-1637. Issues: wildlife protection and preservation. Newsletter: *Wildlife Activist.* Membership: $25 and up.

Wildlife Society 5410 Grosvenor Lane, Bethesda, MD 20814; (301) 897-9770. Issues: wildlife protection and preservation. Publications: *Wildlife Society Bulletin; The Journal of Wildlife Management; The Wildlifer.* Membership: $10 and up.

Windstar Foundation 2317 Snowmass Creek Rd., Snowmass, CO 81654; (303) 927-4777. Issues: ecology, environmental conservation, global change. Newsletter: *Windstar Journal.* Publications: booklets on *Everyday Chemicals, Recycling, Energy.* Membership: $35.

World Resources Institute 1735 New York Ave. NW, Washington, DC 20006; (202) 638-6300. Issues: ecology, environmental degradation, natural resource management. Publication: *World Resources Report.*

World Wildlife Fund 1250 24th St. NW, Washington, DC 20037; (202) 293-4800. Issues: wildlife, habitat protection and preservation. Newsletter: *Focus.* Membership: $15.

Worldwatch Institute 1776 Massachusetts Ave. NW, Washington, DC 20036; (202) 452-1999. Issues: ecology, environmental degradation, natural resource management. Publications: *World Watch; State of the World.* Membership: $25.

WorldWIDE 1250 24th St. NW, Washington, DC 20037; (202) 331-9863. Issues: women and natural resource use. Publications: *WorldWIDE News; Directory of Women in the Environment.* Membership: $35.

The Xerces Society 10 SW Ash St., Portland, OR 97204; (503) 222-2788. Issues: invertebrate habitat protection and preservation. Magazine: *Wings.* Membership: $15 and up.

Zero Population Growth 1400 16th St. NW, Washington, DC 20036; (202) 322-2200. Issues: population, environment, natural resource use. Membership: $20.

DIRECTORY
OF MANUFACTURERS

Companies that manufacture personal care and household products and do not test on animals are marked with a single asterisk; those that also use no animal ingredients in their products are marked with two asterisks.

** **ABBA Products,** 18000 Studebaker Rd., Suite 585, Cerritos, CA 90701; (800) 848-4475

Abbeon Cal 123-730P Gray Ave., Santa Barbara, CA 93101; (805) 966-0810

** **Abkit,** 1160 Park Ave., New York, NY 10128; (212) 860-8358

** **Abracadabra** P.O. Box 1040, Guerneville, CA 95446; (800) 523-5232

Absocold, Sanyo E & E Corp. P.O. Box 1545, Richmond, IN 47374; (317) 935-7501

Addison Products Co. 215 N. Talbot St., Addison, MI 49220; (517) 547-6131

** **Aditi Nutri-sentials** P.O. Box 155, New York, NY 10012

Admiral Div. Magic Chef Monmouth Blvd., Galesburg, IL 61401; (309) 343-0181 or (800) 346-8218

* **Adrian Arpel** 521 Fifth Ave., New York, NY 10175; (212) 382-5900

* **Advance Design Laboratories** P.O. Box 55016, Metro Station, Los Angeles, CA 90055; (213) 623-9254

AEG Andi-Co Appliances 65 Campus Plaza, Raritan Center, Edison, NJ 08837; (908) 225-8837

** **Aesop Unlimited** 55 Fenno St., P.O. Box 315, N. Cambridge, MA 02140; (617) 497-9010

* **AFM Enterprises** 1440 Stacy Ct., Riverside, CA 92507; (714) 781-6860

* **African Bio-Botanica Industries** 7509B NW 13th Blvd., Gainesville, FL 32606

Agri-Fab 303 W. Raymond St., Sullivan, IL 61951; (217) 728-4334

Airtemp Corp. 415 W. Wabash Ave., Effingham, IL 62401; (217) 342-3901

Airxchange 401 VFW Dr., Rockland, MA 02370; (617) 871-4816

** **A.J. Funk & Co.** 1471 Timber Dr., Elgin, IL 60120; (312) 741-6760

* **Alba Botanica Cosmetics** P.O. Box 12085, Santa Rosa, CA 95406; (800) 347-5211

* **Alexandra Avery Purely Natural** Northrup Creek, Clatskanie, OR 97016; (503) 755-2446

* **Alexandra de Markoff** 625 Madison Ave., New York, NY 10022; (212) 572-5000

* **Alfin Fragrances** 15 Maple St., Norwood, NJ 07648; (201) 767-6880

** **Allens Naturally** P.O. Box 514, Farmington, MI 48332; (313) 453-5410

Allied Building Stores P.O. Box 8030, Monroe, LA 71211; (318) 343-7200

* **Almay Hypo-Allergenic** 625 Madison Ave., New York, NY 10022; (212) 572-5000

* **Alvin Last** 145 Palisades St., P.O. Box 24, Dobbs Ferry, NY 10522

Amana Refrigeration Amana, IA 52204; (319) 622-5511

American Aldes Ventilation Corp. 4539 Northgate Ct., Sarasota, FL 33480; (813) 351-3441

American Appliance Manufacturing Corp. 1752 Cloverfield Blvd., Santa Monica, CA 90404; (213) 829-1755

American Energy Technologies P.O. Box 1865, Green Cove Spring, FL 32043; (904) 284-0552

American Gas Association 1515 Wilson Blvd., Arlington, VA 22209; (703) 841-8558

American Honda Motor Co. 1919 Torrance Blvd., Torrance, CA 90501; (213) 783-2000

American Lawn Mower Co./Great States Corp. P.O. Box 369, Shelbyville, IN 46176; (800) 457-1049, (800) 633-1501

** **American Merfluan** 41 Sutter St., Suite 1153, San Francisco, CA 94104; (415) 364-6343

American Paper Institute 260 Madison Ave., New York, NY 10016; (212) 340-0600

American Solar Network 12811 Bexhill Ct., Herndon, VA 22071; (703) 620-2242

American Standard P.O. Box 6820, Piscataway, NJ 08855; (800) 821-7700

** **America's Finest Products Corp.** 1639 9th St., Santa Monica, CA 90404; (213) 450-6555

Ametek/Plymouth Products Div. 502 Indiana Ave., Sheboygan, WI 53081; (414) 457-9435

Amway Corp. 7575 Fulton St. E., Ada, MI 49355; (616) 676-7948

** **Ananda Country Products** 14618 Tyler Foote Rd., Nevada City, CA 95959; (916) 292-3505

** **Andalina** Tory Hill, Warner, NH 03278; (603) 456-3289

Andersen Corp. Bayport, MN 55003; (800) 426-4261

* **Andrea/Ardell/American Intl.** 2200 Gaspar Ave., Commerce, CA 90040

ANF P.O. Box 285, Nashville, TN 37202; (800) 722-3261

Apollo Comfort Products Cumberland St., Ashland City, TN 37015; (615) 792-4371

Aquavac Div. H20T 10966 Le Conte Ave., Suite C, Los Angeles, CA 90024; (800) 247-3619

* **Aramis** 767 5th Ave., New York, NY 10153 (212) 572-3700

* **Arbonne Intl.** 22541 Aspan Dr., Lake Forest, CA 92630; (714) 770-2610

Arcoaire, Inter-City Products 302 Nichols Dr., Hutchins, TX 75141; (214) 225-7351

Armstrong Air Conditioning 421 Monroe St., Bellevue, OH 44811; (419) 483-4840

* **Armstrong World Industries** P. O. Box 301, Lancaster, PA 17604; (717) 397-0611

* **Aroma Vera Co.** P.O. Box 3609, Culver City, CA 90231; (213) 280-0407

Artesian Plumbing Products 201 E. 5th St., Mansfield, OH 44901; (419) 522-4211

Ashdun Industries 1605 John St., Fort Lee, NJ 07024; (201) 944-2650

Association of Home Appliance Manufacturers 20 N. Wacker Dr., Chicago, IL 60606; (312) 984-5800

* **Atta Lavi** 443 Oakhurst Dr., #305, Beverly Hills, CA 90212

* **Aubrey Organics** 4419 N. Manhattan Ave., Tampa, FL 33614; (813) 877-4186
** **Aura Cacia** P.O. Box 3157, Santa Rosa, CA 95402; (916) 623-4999
* **Auroma Intl.** P.O. Box 2, Wilmot, WI 53192 (414) 862-2395
** **Auromere Ayurvedic Imports** 1291 Weber St., Pomona, CA 91768; (714) 629-8255
  Auro Organic Paints/Sinan Co. P.O. Box 181f, Suisun City, CA 94585; (707) 427-2325
* **Austin Diversified Products** 16615 S. Halsted St., Harvey, IL 60426; (708) 333-7644
* **Autumn-Harp** 28 Rockydale Rd., Bristol, VT 05443; (802) 453-4807
** **Avanza** 881 Alma Real, #101, Pacific Palisades, CA 90272; (800) 553-9816; (800) 433-6290
* **Aveda** 321 Lincoln St. NE, Minneapolis, MN 55413; (800) 328-0849
* **Avon** 9 W. 57th St., New York, NY 10003; (212) 546-6015
* **Ayagutaq** P.O. Box 176, Ben Lomond, CA 95005; (408) 336-3648
** **Aztec Secret** P.O. Box 19735, Las Vegas, NV 89132; (702) 369-8080
** **Baby Touch** 100 Sandpiper Circle, Corte Madera, CA 94925
* **Barbizon International** 950 Third Ave., New York, NY 10022; (212) 371-4300
  Bard Manufacturing Co. 520 Evansport Rd., Bryan, OH 43506; (419) 636-1194
* **Bare Escentuals** 809 University Ave., Los Gatos, CA 95030; (800) 227-3386
* **Beauty Naturally** P.O. Box 429, 57 Bosque Rd., Fairfax, CA 94930; (415) 459-2826
* **Beauty Without Cruelty** P.O. Box 13973, San Rafael, CA 94913; (415) 382-7784
* **Beehive Botanicals** Rt. 8, P.O. Box 8258, Hayward, WI 54843; (800) 283-4274
* **Beiersdorf** P.O. Box 5529, Norwalk, CT 06856; (203) 853-8008
* **Benetton Cosmetics** 540 Madison Ave., Eighth Floor, New York, NY 10022; (212) 832-6616
  Benjamin Moore & Co. 51 Chestnut Ridge Rd., Montvale, NJ 07645; (908) 573-9600
  Berner International Corp. P.O. Box 5205, New Castle, PA 16105; (412) 658-3551
** **Bio-Botanica** 75 Commerce Dr., Hauppauge, NY 11788; (516) 231-5522
** **Biogime Intl.** 1187 Brittore Rd., Houston, TX 77043; (713) 827-1972
* **Biokosma** 841 S. Main St., Spring Valley, NY 10977; (914) 352-6145
  Biomatik USA P.O. Box 2119, Boulder, CO 80301; (303) 938-8999
  Bio-Pax Division of Diversified Packaging Inc. 1265 Pine Hill Dr., Annapolis, MD 21401; (301) 974-4411
* **Bio-Tec Cosmetics** 46-6535 Millcreek Dr., Mississauga, Ontario, Canada L5N 2M2; (416) 568-9355
* **Bo-Chem Co.** Little Harbor, Marblehead, MA 01945; (617) 631-9400

Bock Corp. 110 S. Dickinson St., P.O. Box 8632, Madison, WI 53708; (608) 257-2225
* **Body Love** P.O. Box 7542, Santa Cruz, CA 95061; (408) 425-8218
* **The Body Shop** 1341 7th St., Berkeley, CA 94710; (415) 524-0360
* **The Body Shop** 45 Horsehill Rd., Cedar Knolls, NJ 07927; (800) 541-2535
* **Bonne Bell** #1 Georgetown Row, Lakewood, OH 44107; (216) 221-0800
* **Borlind of Germany** P.O. Box 1487, New London, NH 03257; (603) 526-2076
* **Botanicus** 7920 Greenair Dr., Gaithersburg, MD 20879; (301) 977-8887
  Bradford-White Corp. 24th & Ellsworth Sts., Philadelphia, PA 19146; (215) 546-3800
  Breeder's Choice 16321 E. Arrow Hwy., Irwindale, CA 91706; (818) 334-9301
* **Breezy Balms** P.O. Box 168, Davenport, CA 95017; (408) 423-4299
  Briggs 4350 W. Cypress St., Suite 800, Tampa, FL 33607; (813) 878-0178
* **Bronson Pharmaceuticals** 4526 Rinetti Lane, La Cañada, CA 91011; (800) 521-3323
** **Brookside Soap Co.** P.O. Box 55638, Seattle, WA 98155; (206) 363-3701
  Bryant Carrier Corp. P.O. Box 70, Indianapolis, IN 46206; (317) 243-0851
** **Bug-Off** Route 3, P.O. Box 27A, Lexington, VA 24450; (703) 463-1760
  Caloric Corp. 403 North Main, Topton, PA 19562; (215) 682-4211
** **Campana Corporation** Batavia, IL 60510
* **Carlson Labs** 15 College Dr., Arlington Heights, IL 60004; (800) 323-4141
* **Carma Laboratories** 5801 West Airways Ave., Franklin, WI 53132; (414) 421-7707
  Carrier Corp. Consumer Relations Dept., P.O. Box 4808, Syracuse, NY 13221; (800) CARRIER
* **Caswell-Massey** 100 Enterprise Pl., Dover, DE 19901; (800) 326-0500
** **Cernitin America** 130 Clarkson Ave., #4F, Brooklyn, NY 11226
* **Charles of the Ritz** 625 Madison Ave., New York, NY 10022; (212) 527-4000
* **Chempoint Products** 543 Tarrytown Rd., White Plains, NY 10607
* **Chenti Products** 21093 Forbes Ave., Hayward, CA 94545; (415) 785-2177
* **Christian Dior Perfumes** 9 W. 57th St., New York, NY 10019; (212) 221-4744
  Chronar Sunenergy P.O. Box 177, Princeton, NJ 08542; (800) 247-6627
  Chrysler Corporation 12000 Chrysler Dr., Highland Park, MI 48288; (313) 956-5252
* **Chuckles** 59 March Ave., Manchester, NH 03103
  Church & Dwight 469 N. Harrison St., Princeton, NJ 08540; (609) 683-5900
* **Clarins of Paris** 135 E. 57th St., New York, NY 10022; (212) 980-1800
  Clairol 345 Park Ave, New York, NY 10154; (212) 546-5000

**Clearly Natural Products P.O. Box 750024, Petaluma, CA 94975; (707) 762-5815

**Clear Vue Products P.O. Box 567, 417 Canal St., Lawrence, MA 01842

* Clientele 5207 NW 163rd St., Miami FL 33014; (800) 327-4660

Climatrol 415 W. Wabash Ave., Effingham, IL 62401; (217) 342-3901

Climette/Heil-Quaker Corp. 1136 Heil-Quaker Blvd., LaVergne, TN 37086; (615) 793-0450

* Clinique 767 Fifth Ave., New York, NY 10153; (212) 572-3800

Clorox Co. 1221 Broadway, Oakland, CA 94612; (415) 271-7000

Colgate-Palmolive Co. 300 Park Ave., New York, NY 10022; (212) 310-2000

**Colonial Dames Co. P.O. Box 22022, Los Angeles, CA 90022; (213) 773-6441

**Colour Quest 616 S. 3rd St., St. Charles, IL 60174; (708) 377-6226

* Columbia Cosmetics Mfg. 1661 Timothy Dr., San Leandro, CA 94577; (415) 562-5900

* Come To Your Senses 321 Cedar Ave. S., Minneapolis, MN 55454; (612) 339-0050

Comfort-Aire/Heat Controller 1900 Wellworth Ave., Jackson, MI 49203; (517) 787-2100

Comfortmaker, Inter-City Products 401 Randolph St., Red Bud, IL 62278; (618) 282-6262

**Comfort Mfg. Co. 1056 W. Van Buren St., Chicago, IL 60607; (312) 421-8145

**Community Soap Factory P.O. Box 32057, Washington, DC 20007; (703) 979-4317

* Compassion Cosmetics P.O. Box 3534, Glendale, CA 91201; No listing

Conservatree Paper Co. 10 Lombard St., Suite 250, San Francisco, CA 94111; (800) 522-9000

Consolidated Dutchwest P.O. 1019, Plymouth, MA 02360; (800) 225-8277

Controlled Energy Corp. P.O. Box 19, Fiddler's Green, Waitsfield, VT 05673; (802) 496-4436

Coolerator/Whirlpool Corp. Administrative Center, 2000 M-63, Benton Harbor, MI 49022; (616) 926-5000

Coronado/Our Own Hardware Co. 2300 W. Highway 13, Burnsville, MN 55337; (612) 890-2700

The Cosmetic Toiletry and Fragrance Association 1110 Vermont Ave. NW, Washington, DC 20005; (202) 331-1770

The Cotton Place P.O. Box 59721, Dallas, TX 75229

Coughlan Products 1 Munsonhurst Rd., Franklin, NJ 07416

* Country Comfort 28537 Nuevo Valley Dr., P.O. Box 3, Nuevo, CA 92367; (714) 657-3438

* Country Safe Corp. Everett, WA 98201; (206) 258-1171

* Crabtree & Evelyn Peake Brook Rd., P.O. Box 167, Woodstock, CT 06281; (203) 928-2761

Craftmaster Water Heater Co. 18450 S. Miles Rd., Cleveland, OH 44128; (216) 663-7300

Crane Plumbing 1235 Hartrey St., Evanston, IL 60202; (312) 864-7600

* Critter Comfort 14200 Old Hanover Rd., Reisterstown, MD 21136; (301) 833-6754

Crosley Corp. P.O. Box 1959, 675 N. Main St., Winston Salem, NC 27101; (919) 761-1212

* Cruelty-Free Cosmetics Plus 38 E. 89th St., New York, NY 10128

Daihatsu America 4422 Corporate Center Dr., Los Alamitos, CA 90720; (714) 761-7000

Day & Night, Carrier Corp. P.O. Box 70, Indianapolis, IN 46206; (317) 240-5125

Dayton Electric Manufacturing Co. 5959 W. Howard St., Chicago, IL 60648; (708) 647-0124

Deer Valley Farm R.D. 1, Guilford, NY 13780; (607) 764-8556

* DeLore Intl. P.O. Box 37021, Cincinnati, OH 45222

* Dermatone Laboratories 47 Mountain Rd., P.O. Box 633, Suffield, CT 06078; (203) 292-1311

* Desert Essence P.O. Box 588, Topanga, CA 90290; (213) 455-1046

**Deva Natural Clothes P.O. Box C, 303 E. Main St., Burkittsville, MD 21718; (301) 663-4900

Diamond K Enterprises R.R. 1, P.O. Box 30A, St. Charles, MN 55972; (507) 932-4308

DMO Industries 1969 Leslie St., Don Mills Ontario, Canada M3B 2M3

* Dr. Babor Natural Cosmetics 1636 Gervais Ave., Suites 9 & 10, St. Paul, MN 55109; (800) 333-4055

**Dr. E.H. Bronner P.O. Box 28, Escondido, CA 92025; (619) 745-7069

* Dr. Hauschka Cosmetics Meadowbrook West, Wyoming, RI 02898; (401) 539-7037

Dona Designs 825 Northlake Dr., Richardson, TX 75080; (214) 235-0485

Dornback Furnace and Foundry 33220 Lakeland Blvd., Eastlake, OH 44094; (216) 946-1600

Dumond Chemicals 1501 Broadway, New York, NY 10036; (212) 869-6350

Dumont Industries P.O. Box 148, Monmouth, ME 04259; (207) 933-4811

**Duncan Enterprises 5673 E. Shields Ave., Fresno, CA 93727; (209) 291-4444

Duron 10406 Tucker St., Beltsville, MD 20705; (301) 937-4600

Duro-Test Corp. 2321 Kennedy Blvd., N. Bergen, NJ; (800) 289-3876

Eagle P.O. Box 506, Mishawaka, IN 46546; (800) 255-5959

* EarthRite 23700 Mercantile Rd., Beachwood, OH 44122; (800) 828-4408

Earth's Best Baby Food P.O. Box 887, Middlebury, VT 05753; (800) 442-4221

* Earth Science P.O. Box 1925, Corona, CA 91718; (800) 222-6720

* Earth Wise 1790 30th St., Boulder, CO 80301; (303) 447-0119

* Ecco Bella 6 Provost Sq., Suite 602, Caldwell, NJ 07006; (800) 888-5320

Ecology Sound Farms 42126 Rd. 168, Orosi, CA 93647; (209) 528-3816

Eco-Matrix 124 Harvard St., Boston, MA 02146; (617) 730-8450

* **EcoSafe Laboratories** P.O. Box 8702, Oakland, CA 94662
* **Ecover, Inc.** 6-8 Knight St., Norwalk, CT 06851
  Ecowater P.O. Box 64420, St. Paul, MN 55164; (612) 739-5330
  Eden Foods 701 Tecumseh Rd., Clinton, MI 49236; (517) 456-7424
  Electronic Ballast Technology 2510 W. 237th St., Suite 102, Torrance, CA 90505; (800) 654-6501, (213) 618-8733
* **Elizabeth Grady Face First** 300 Brickstone Square, Andover, MA 01810; (508) 475-5080
  Eljer Plumbingware 901 10th St., P.O. Box 37, Plano, TX 75074; (214) 881-7177
* **Elysee Cosmetics** 6804 Seybold Rd., Madison, WI 53719; (608) 271-3664
  Emerson Electric Co. 4700 21st St., Racine, WI 53406; (414) 552-7303
  Emerson Quiet Kool Corp. 400 Woodbine Ave., Avenel, NJ 07001; (908) 381-7000
  Emerson Radio Corp. 1 Emerson Lane, North Bergin, NJ 07047; (201) 854-6600
  Empire Comfort Systems 918 Freeburg Ave., Belleville, IL 62222; (618) 233-7420
  Energizer Div. of Industrial Air P.O. Box 225, Amelia, OH 45102; (513) 753-5820
  EnerRoyal Technologies Corp. 5750 Commons Park, P.O. Box 507, DeWitt, NY 13214
  Enterprise Appliance Corp. P.O. Box 305115, Nashville, TN 37230; (615) 885-1405
* **Espree Cosmetics** P.O. Box 160249, Irving, TX 75016; (800) 766-8825
* **Estée Lauder** 767 Fifth Ave., New York, NY 10153; (212) 572-4200
  ETTA Industries 4755 Walnut St., Boulder, CO 80301; (303) 444-2244
* **Eva Jon Cosmetics** 1016 E. California St., Gainesville, TX 76240; (817) 668-7707
  Eveready Checkerboard Sq., St. Louis, MO 63164; (314) 982-2000
* **Everybody** 1738 Pearl St., Boulder, CO 80302; (303) 440-0188
* **Fabergé** 1345 Avenue of the Americas, New York, NY 10105; (212) 581-3500
  Fabulon Products P.O. Box 1505, Buffalo, NY 14240; (716) 873-2770
  FAFCO 235 Constitution Dr., Menlo Park, CA 94025; (415) 343-2690
* **Farmavita USA** 59 March Ave., Manchester, NH 03103; (603) 669-4228
* **Fashion Two Twenty** P.O. Box 220, 1263 S. Chillicothe Rd., Aurora, OH 44202; (216) 562-5111
* **Faultless Starch/Bon Ami Co.** 1025 W. 8th St., Kansas City, MO 64101; (816) 842-2939
  Fedders-USA Air Conditioning Div. 415 W. Wabash Ave., Effingham, IL 62401; (908) 234-2100
  Fiddler's Green Farm R.R. 1, P.O. Box 656, Belfast, ME 04915; (207) 338-3568
* **Finelle Cosmetics** 137 Marston St., Lawrence, MA 01842; (508) 682-6112
* **Fleur de Sante** P.O. Box 16090, Ft. Lauderdale, FL 33318

* **Flora Distributors** 7400 Fraser Park Drive, Burnaby, BC V5J 5B9, Canada; (604) 438-1133
* **Focus 21 Intl.** 8485 Production Ave., San Diego, CA 92121
  Ford Motor Co. The American Road, Dearborn, MI 48202; (800) 722-5787
  Ford Products Corp. P.O. Box A, Valley Cottage, NY 10989; (914) 358-8282
** **Forever New** 2922 West Maple, Sioux Falls, SD 57107; (800) 456-0107
  Fort Howard Paper Co. P.O. Box 19130, Green Bay, WI; (414) 435-8821
* **4-D SUNaturals** 201 S. McKemy St., Chandler, AZ 85226; (800) 528-4482; (602) 257-1950
* **Freeman Cosmetic Corporation** P.O. Box 17, Hollywood, CA 90078; (213) 470-6840
  Friedrich Air Conditioning & Refrigeration Co. 4200 N. Pan Am Expressway, P.O. Box 1540, San Antonio, TX 78295; (512) 225-2000
  Frigidaire Appliance Co. 300 Phillipi Rd., Columbus, OH 43218; (513) 489-9210
* **Fruit of the Earth** P.O. Box 152044, Irving, TX 75015; (800) 527-7731
  Fuller-O'Brien 450 E. Grand Ave. South, San Francisco, CA 94080; (415) 761-2300
* **G.T. Intl.** 1800 S. Robertson Blvd., #182, Los Angeles, CA 90035; (213) 555-0484
  Gas Appliance Manufacturers Association P.O. Box 9245, Arlington, VA 22209; (703) 525-9565
  General Ecology 151 Sheree Blvd., Lionville, PA 19353; (215) 363-7900
  General Electric Nela Park, Cleveland, OH 44112; (800) 626-2000
  General Electric Appliance Park, Louisville, KY 40225; (800) 626-2004
  General Motors Corp. General Motors Building, Detroit, MI 48202; (313) 556-5000
* **General Nutrition** 1301 39th St., Fargo, ND 58107; (701) 282-2300
** **Gentle World/Gentle Products** P.O. Box 1418, Umatilla, FL 32784; (904) 669-2822
  Gerber Plumbing Fixtures Corp. 4656 W. Touhy Ave., Chicago, IL 60646; (312) 675-6570
* **Germaine Monteil** 40 W. 57th St., New York, NY 07652
  Gibson Appliance Co. 300 Phillipi Rd., Columbus, OH 43218; (216) 252-3700
* **Giovanni Cosmetics** 3023 N. Coolidge Ave., Los Angeles, CA 90039; (213) 663-7033
  Glowcore Corp. P.O. Box 8971, Cleveland, OH 44136; (216) 273-4040
** **Golden Lotus** P.O. Box 40189, Grand Junction, CO 81504; (303) 243-8835
* **Golden Pride/Rawleigh** 1501 Northpoint Pkwy., Suite 100, West Palm Beach, FL 33407; (407) 640-5700
  Gold Mine Natural Food Co. 1947 30th St., San Diego, CA 92102; (800) 647-2929
* **Grace Cosmetics** 976 Florida Central Pkwy., #136, Longwood, FL 32750
** **Granny's Old Fashioned Products** 3581 E. Milton St., Pasadena, CA 91107; (818) 577-1825

327

Gravelly Ridge Farms Star Route 16, Elk Creek, CA 95939; (916) 963-3216

* **Gruene** 1621 W. Washington Blvd., Venice, CA 90291; (213) 392-2449

GTE Sylvania Sylvania Lighting Center, 18725 N. Union St., Westfield, IN 46074; (800) 544-4828

* **Hain Pure Food Co.** 13660 S. Figueroa, Los Angeles, CA 90061; (213) 538-9922

Heat Controller Losey at Wellworth, Jackson, MI 49203; (517) 787-2100

Heat Extractor 2 Main St., Melrose, MA 02176; (617) 321-2300

Heat Transfer Products 120 Braley Rd., East Freetown, MA 02717; (508) 763-3516

* **Heavena** 881 Alma Real, Suite 101, Pacific Palisades, CA 90272; (213) 454-6899

* **Heavenly Soap** 5948 E. 30th St., Tucson, AZ 85711; (602) 790-9938

Heil-Quaker Corp. P.O. Box 3005, 1136 Heil-Quaker Blvd., LaVergne, TN 37086; (615) 793-0450

* **Heritage Store** 314 Laskin Rd., Virginia Beach, VA 23451; (804) 428-0100

* **Hewitt Soap** 333 Linden Ave., Dayton, OH 45403; (513) 253-1151

Hill's Pet Products P.O. Box 148, Topeka, KS 66601; (800) 445-5777

Holland Distributors 1701 E. Woodfield Rd., Schaumburg, IL 60196

* **Home Health Products** 1160 A Millers Lane, Virginia Beach, VA 23451; (800) 284-9123

** **Home Service Products Co.** P.O. Box 269, Bound Brook, NJ 08805; (908) 356-8175

Hotpoint Div. General Electric Co. Appliance Park, Louisville, KY 40225; (502) 452-4311

Hot Water Generators 1325 S. Creek Dr., Suite 800, Houston, TX 77084; (713) 492-1713

* **Houbigant** 1135 Pleasant View Terrace West, Ridgefield, NJ 84125; (201) 941-3400

H20T 10966 Le Conte Ave., Suite C, Los Angeles, CA 90024; (800) 247-3619

** **Huish Chemical Co.** 3540 West 1987 South, Salt Lake City, UT 84125; (801) 972-8611

Hummer Nature Works Reagan Wells Canyon, P.O. Box 122, Uvalde, TX 78801; (512) 232-6167

* **Humphreys Pharmacal** 63 Meadow Rd., Rutherford, NJ 07070; (201) 933-7744

Hunter Fan Co. 2500 Frisco Ave., Memphis, TN 38114; (901) 743-1360

Hurley Chicago Co. 12621 S. Laramie Ave., Alsip, IL 60658; (708) 388-9222

Hyundai Motor America 10550 Talbert Ave., Fountain Valley, CA 92728; (714) 965-3000

Iams P.O. Box 14597, Dayton, OH 45413; (800) 525-4267

* **i natural cosmetics** Burlington Mall, Burlington, MA 01803; (617) 273-0795

** **I Rokeach & Sons** 25 E. Spring Valley Ave., Maywood, NJ 07607; (201) 587-1199

* **Iced Creme Facial Masque** 1565 Molitor Rd., Belmont, CA 94002; (415) 341-8806

* **Ida Grae Products** 424 Laverne Ave., Mill Valley, CA 94941; (415) 388-6101

* **Ilona of Hungary** 3201 E. Second Ave, Denver, CO 80206; (303) 320-5991

* **Image Laboratories** P.O. Box 55016, Metro Station, Los Angeles, CA 90055; (213) 623-9254

* **Images & Attitudes** 150 E. 400 N., Salem, UT 84653; (801) 423-2800

Imperial 3857 Louisiana Ave. S., Minneapolis, MN 55426

* **Indian Creek** P.O. Box 63, Selma, OR 97538; (503) 592-2616

* **inside-out** 3704 S. Bethel St., Columbia, MO 65203

In-Sink-Erator Div., Emerson Electric Co. 4700 21st St., Racine, WI 53406; (414) 552-7303

* **Institute of Trichology** 250 E. Pacific Coast Highway, Wilmington, CA 90744; (800) 458-8874

** **International Rotex** P.O. Box 20697, Reno, NV 89515; (702) 356-8356

* **International Vitamin** P.O. Box 1746, Union, NJ 07083

* **Isadora** 4 Embarcadero Center 5100, San Francisco, CA 94111

ITS Corp. 7450-E E. Jewell Ave., Suite E, Denver, CO 80231; (303) 337-0600

* **Jacki's Magic Lotion** 258 A St., #7A, Ashland, OR 97520; (503) 488-1388

* **Jaclyn Cares** P.O. Box 339, Farmington, MI 48332; (313) 453-5410

Jaffe Brothers P.O. Box 636, Valley Center, CA 92082; (619) 749-1133

* **James Austin Co.** P.O. Box 827, Mars, PA 16046; (412) 625-1535

* **Jason Natural Products** 8468 Warner Dr., Culver City, CA 90232; (213) 396-3171

* **Jean Naté** 625 Madison Ave., New York, NY 10022; (212) 572-5000

* **Jean-Pierre Sand** 1380 Queensgreen Circle, Naperville, IL 60563; (708) 717-2913

* **Jeanne Gatineau** 625 Madison Ave., New York, NY 10022

* **Jeanne Rose Herbal Body Works** 219A Carl St., San Francisco, CA 94117

Jenn-Air Co. 3035 Shadeland, Indianapolis, IN 48226; (317) 545-2271

Jim Morris Environmental T-Shirts P.O. Box 831, Boulder, CO 80306; (303) 444-6430

* **John F. Amico & Co.** 7327 W. 90th St., Bridgeview, IL 60455; (708) 430-2552

* **John Paul Mitchell Systems** P.O. Box 10597, Beverly Hills, CA 90213; (805) 298-0400

* **JOICO Laboratories** 345 Baldwin Park Blvd., City of Industry, CA 91746; (818) 968-6111

** **Jojoba Resources** 6509 W. Frye Rd., #9, Chandler, AZ 85226; (800) 528-4284

* **Jurlique D'Namis Ltd.** 16 Starlit Dr., Northport, NY 11768; (800) 642-3535

* **Kallima** 915 Whitmore Dr., Rockwall, TX 75087; (214) 771-0011

Keeper Co. P.O. Box 20023, Cincinnati, OH 45220; (513) 221-1464

Keeprite/Heil-Quaker Corp. 1136 Heil-Quaker Blvd., LaVergne, TN 37086; (615) 793-0450

Kelvinator Appliance Co. 300 Phillipi Rd., Columbus, OH 43218; (216) 252-3700

Kenmore/Sears, Roebuck & Co. Sears Tower, Chicago, IL 60684; (312) 875-2500

* **Kenra Laboratories** 6501 Julian Ave., Indianapolis, IN 46219; (317) 356-6491

** **Key West Fragrance and Cosmetic Factory** P.O. Box 1079, 524 Front St., Key West, FL 33041; (800) 445-2563

* **Kimberly Sayer** 61 W. 82nd St., #5A, New York, NY 10024

* **Kiss My Face** P.O. Box 804, New Paltz, NY 12561; (914) 701-1534

KitchenAid 701 Main St., St. Joseph, MI 49085; (616) 982-4500

* **Kleen Brite Laboratories** P.O. Box 20408, Rochester, NY 14602; (716) 637-0630

* **KMS Research** 4712 Mountain Lakes Blvd., Redding, CA 96003; (916) 244-6000

Kohler Co. Kohler, WI 53044; (800) 456-4537

Krystal Wharf Farms R.D. 2, P.O. Box 191A, Mansfield, PA 16933; (717) 549-8194

** **KSA Jojoba** 19025 Parthenia St., #200, Northridge, CA 91324; (818) 701-1534

** **LaCrista** P.O. Box 240, Davidsonville, MD 21035; (301) 956-4447

** **Laguna Soap** P.O. Box 6373, San Rafael, CA 94903; (707) 762-5815

Lambert Corp. 117 S. 3rd St., Box 278, Ansonia, OH 45303; (513) 337-3641

** **L'anza Research Laboratories** 5523 Ayon Ave., Irwindale, CA 91706; (818) 334-9333

** **L'arome International Ltd.** Lakeshore Pkwy., Rock Hill, SC 29730; (803) 329-7744

* **P. Leiner Nutritional Products** 1845 W. 205th St., P.O. Box 2010, Torrance, CA 90510; (213) 328-9610

Lennox Industries Lennox Center, 7920 Beltline Rd., Dallas, TX 75240; (214) 980-6000

Lever Brothers 390 Park Ave., New York, NY 10022; (212) 688-6000

* **Levlad** 9183-5 Kelvin Ave., Chatsworth, CA 91311; (818) 882-2951

* **Liberty Natural Products** 8419 SE Woodstock Blvd., Portland, OR 97266

* **Life Tree Products** 1448 12th St., Santa Monica, CA 90401; (707) 577-0324

Lightolier 100 Lighting Way, Secaucus, NJ 07098; (201) 864-3000

* **Lily of Colorado** 1286 S. Valentia, Denver, CO 80231; (303) 455-4194

* **Lily of the Desert** 10485 Olympic Dr., Suite 102, Dallas, TX 75220; (214) 351-5252

* **Livos PlantChemistry** 614 Agua Fria St., Santa Fe, NM 87501; (505) 988-9111

Lochinvar Water Heater Co. 1930 Air Lane Dr., Nashville, TN 37210; (615) 889-8800

Locke Home Products 4200 St. Clair Ave., Washington Park, IL 62204; (618) 271-1272

* **Lotus Light** P.O. Box 2, Wilmot, WI 53192; (414) 862-2395

* **Lowenkamp Intl.** Monticello Rd., P.O. Box 878, Hazlehurst, MS 39083

Lowe's Co. P.O. Box 1111, N. Wilkesboro, NC 28656; (919) 651-4000

Lowry Engineering P.O. Box 189, Unity, ME 04988; (207) 948-3790

Lundberg Family Farm P.O. Box 369, Richvale, CA 95974; (916) 882-4551

* **Luseaux Laboratories** 16816 S. Gramercy Pl., Gardena, CA 90247; (213) 324-1555

* **Luzier Personalized Cosmetics** 3216 Gilham Plaza, Kansas City, MO 64109; (816) 531-8338

** **Magic American Chemical Corp.** 23700 Mercantile Rd., Cleveland, OH 44122; (800) 321-6330

Magic Chef 740 King Edward Ave., Cleveland, TN 37311; (615) 472-3371

Magic Chef Air Conditioning Co. 421 Monroe St., Bellevue, OH 44811; (419) 483-4840

* **Magic Hat** P.O. Box 51, Buffalo Mills, PA 15534

* **Magic Lotion** 29002 N. Highway 1, Fort Bragg, CA 95437

* **The Magic of Aloe** 7300 N. Crescent Blvd., Pennsauken, NJ 08110; (800) 257-7770

** **Makamina** P.O. Box 307, Wallingford, PA 19086; (800) 537-6746

Mansfield Plumbing Products 150 First St., Perrysville, OH 44864; (419) 938-5211

Many Moons #14-130 Dallas Rd., Victoria, BC V8V 1A3, Canada

Marathon Water Heater Co. 3107 Sibley Memorial Hwy., Eagan, MN 55121; (612) 688-8827

Marcal Paper Mills Market St., Elmwood Park, NJ 07407; (800) 631-8451

* **Marchemco Cosmetic Co.** 1160 Midland Ave., Suite 10E, Bronxville, NY 10708

* **Marie Lacoste Enterprises** 1059 Alameda de Las Pulgas, Belmont, CA 94002

Marquette Appliance Co. 437 33rd Ave. N, St. Cloud, MN 56301; (612) 259-1356

* **Martha Hill Cosmetics** 5 Ivy Ct., Metuchen, NJ 08840

Martin Industries P.O. Box 128, Florence, AL 35631; (205) 767-0330

** **Martin Von Myering** 422 Jay St., Pittsburgh, PA 15212; (412) 323-2832

Marvel/Northland Refrigeration Co. 701 Ranney Dr., Greenville, MI 48838; (616) 754-5601

* **Matrix Essentials** 30601 Carter St., Solon, OH 44139; (216) 248-3700

* **Max Factor** 12100 Wilshire Blvd., Los Angeles, CA 90025; (213) 442-2000

Maytag Co. 1 Dependability Sq., Newton, IA 50208; (515) 792-8000

Mazda (North America) 1444 McGraw Ave., Irvine, CA 92714; (714) 727-1990

** **Medical Plaza Consultants** 4151 N. 32nd St., Phoenix, AZ 85018; (602) 957-3520

* **Mehron** 45E Route 303, Valley Cottage, NY 10989; (914) 268-4106

Melitta U.S.A. 1401 Berlin Rd., Cherry Hill, NJ 08003; (800) 451-1694

* **Mercantile Food Co.** P.O. Box 1140, Georgetown, CT 06829; (203) 544-9891

Mercury Refining Co. 790 Watervliet Shaker Rd., Latham, NY 12110; (518) 785-1703, (800) 833-3505

* **Merle Norman Cosmetics** 9130 Bellanca Ave., Los Angeles, CA 90045; (213) 641-3000
* **Metrin Laboratories** 1403-1275 Pacific St., Vancouver, B.C., V7W 1A7 Canada; (604) 922-8111
** **Mia Rose Products** 1374 Logan Ave., Unit C, Costa Mesa, CA 92626; (714) 662-5465
* **Michael's Health Products** 7040 Alamo Downs Pkwy., San Antonio, TX 78238; (512) 647-4700
* **Michel Constantini** 124 W. 72nd St., New York, NY 10023
** **Microbalanced Products** 25 Aladdin Ave., Dumont, NJ 07628; (800) 626-7888
Microphor P.O. Box 1460, Willits, CA 95490; (800) 358-8280
Mini Flush Co. 3960-K Prospect Ave., Yorba Linda, CA 92686; (714) 993-7332
* **Mira Linder Spa in the City** 29935 Northwestern Hwy., Southfield, MI 48034; (313) 356-5810
Mitsubishi Electric Sales 800 Bierman Ct., Mt. Prospect, Il 60056; (708) 298-9223
Mitsubishi Motor Sales 6400 Katella, Cypress, CA 90630; (714) 372-6000
Montgomery Ward Montgomery Ward Plaza, Dept. 69, A-4, Chicago, IL 60671; (312) 467-2000
Mor-Flo Industries 18450 S. Miles Rd., Cleveland, OH 44128; (216) 663-7300
Mountain Ark Trading Co. 120 S. East Ave., Fayetteville, AR 72701; (800) 643-8989
** **Mountain Fresh Products** P.O. Box 40516, Grand Junction, CO 81504; (303) 434-8434
* **Mountain Ocean** 1738 Pearl, Boulder, CO 80302; (303) 444-2781
M-P Corp. 8340 Lyndon Ave., Detroit, MI 48238; (313) 834-3200
Muralo 148 E. 5th St., Bayonne, NJ 07002; (201) 437-0770
Murco Wall Products 300 N.E. 21st St., Fort Worth, TX 76106; (817) 626-1987
** **Murphy-Phoenix Co.** P.O. Box 22930, Beachwood, OH 44122; (216) 831-0404
Natech Research 297-B Dividend Dr., Peachtree City, GA 30269
National Association of Diaper Services 2017 Walnut St., Philadelphia, PA 19103; (215) 569-3650
* **Naturade Cosmetics** 7100 E. Jackson St., Paramount, CA 90723; (213) 531-8120
Natural Beef Farms 4399-A Henninger Ct., Chantilly, VA 22021; (703) 631-0881
* **Natural Bodycare** Camarillo, CA 93010; (805) 482-7791
Natural Life 12975 16th Ave. N., Minneapolis, MN 55441; (800) 367-2391
* **Natural Organics** 10 Daniel St., Farmingdale, NY 11735; (516) 293-0030
Natural Way Mills Rt. 2, P.O. Box 37, Middle River, MN 56737; (218) 222-3677
* **Nature Basics** 61 Main St., Lancaster, NH 03584
* **Nature Cosmetics** 881 Alma Real, #101, Pacific Palisades, CA 90272; (800) 553-9816; (800) 433-6290
* **Nature de France** 444 Park Ave. South, New York, NY 10016; (212) 213-4343

* **Nature's Gate Herbal Cosmetics** 9183-5 Kelvin St., Chatsworth, CA 91311; (818) 882-2951
* **Nature's Plus** 10 Daniel St., Farmingdale, NY 11735; (516) 293-0030
Nature's Recipe 341 Bonnie Circle, Corona, CA 91720; (714) 639-1134
* **Natus Corporation** 4445 W. 77th St., Suite 230, Edina, MN 55435; (800) 833-4627
* **Nectarine** 1200 5th St., Berkeley, CA 94710; (415) 528-0162
Neolife 25000 Industrial Blvd., Hayward, CA 94545
* **New Age Creations/Herbal Bodyworks** 219 Carl St., San Francisco, CA 94117; (415) 564-6785
** **New Age Products** 16100 N. Highway 101, Willits, CA 95490; (707) 459-5969
** **Neway Little Harbor** Marblehead, MA 01945
New Cycle P.O. Box 3248, Santa Rosa, CA 95402; (707) 829-3154
* **Nexxus** P.O. Box 1274, Santa Barbara, CA 93116; (805) 968-6900
** **Nirvana** P.O. Box 18413, Minneapolis, MN 55418; (612) 932-2919
Nissan Motor Corp. U.S.A. P.O. Box 191, Gardena, CA 90248; (213) 532-3111
* **No Common Scents** King's Yard, 220 Xenia Ave., Yellow Springs, OH 45387; (513) 767-4261
Nordyne 10820 Sunset Office Pk., St. Louis, MO 63127; (314) 878-6200
Norge Div. Magic Chef 410 Lyeria Dr., Herrin, IL 62948; (618) 988-8431
* **North Country Soap** 7888 County Rd. 6, Maple Plain, MN 55359; (612) 479-3381
North East Environmental Products 17 Technology Dr., West Lebanon, NH 03784; (603) 298-7061
Nortron Industries 1140 Tristar Dr., Mississauga, Ontario, L5T 1H9 Canada; (416) 670-2500
* **NuSkin Intl.** 145 East Center, Provo, UT 84601; (801) 377-6056
** **NuSun** 1160 Midland Ave., #10E, Bronxville, NY 10708
Nu-Tone Madison and Red Bank Roads, Cincinnati, OH 45227; (800) 543-8687
* **Nutri-Metics Intl.** 19501 E. Walnut Dr., City of Industry, CA 91749; (714) 598-1831
Nutro 445 Wilson Way, City of Industry, CA 91744; (800) 833-5330
Nu-World Amaranth P.O. Box 2202, Naperville, IL 60565; (312) 369-6819
Oasis/Ebco 265 N. Hamilton Rd., P.O. Box 13150, Columbus, OH 43213; (614) 861-1350
* **O'Naturel** 535 Cordova Rd., #472, Santa Fe, NM 87501; (505) 982-6677
* **Oriental Beauty Secrets** P.O. Box 294, Columbia, PA 17512; (213) 555-0484
* **Oriflame Intl.** 76 Treble Cove Rd., N. Billerica, MA 01862
* **Orjene Natural Cosmetics** 5-43 48th Ave., Long Island City, NY 11101; (718) 937-2666
Osram 110 Bracken Rd., Montgomery, NY 12549; (800) 431-9980

**Oxyfresh U.S.A. E. 10906 Marietta, Spokane, WA 99206; (509) 924-4999

Pacific Thermal Products 612 N. 16th Ave., Yakima, WA 98902; (509) 453-2355

Paloma Industries 241 James St., Bensonville, IL 60106; (312) 595-8778

Panasonic Co. 1 Panasonic Way, Secaucus, NJ 07094; (201) 392-6633

* Park-Rand Enterprises 12896 Bradley Ave., #F, Sylmar, CA 91342; (813) 362-6218

* Patricia Allison 4470 Monahan Rd., La Mesa, CA 92041; (619) 444-4379

**Paul Mazzotta, Inc. P.O. Box 96, Reading, PA 19607; (215) 376-2250

* Paul Penders USA 1340 Commerce St., Petaluma, CA 94954; (707) 763-5828

Paul's Grains 2475-B 340 St., Laurel, IA 50141; (515) 476-3373

Payne Carrier Corp. P.O. Box 70, Indianapolis, IN 46206; (317) 243-0581

Pay-N-Pak Stores P.O. Box 8808, Kent, WA 98604; (206) 854-5450

Pecbras Co. 1300 Stirling Rd., Suite 4, Dania, FL 33004; (800) 826-7070

E.H. Pechan & Assoc. 5537 Hempstead Way, Springfield, VA 22151; (703) 642-1120

Peerless Pottery P.O. Box 5581, Evansville, IN 47716; (800) 457-5785

Perfection Products Co./Schwank P.O. Box 749, Waynesboro, GA 30830; (404) 554-2101

Personal Products Co. Van Liew Ave., Miltown, NJ 08850; (800) 526-3967

Pet Food Institute 1101 Connecticut Ave. NW, Washington, DC 20036; (202) 857-1120

* PetGuard 165 Industrial Loop S., Unit 5, Orange Park, FL 32073; (800) 874-3221

**Pets 'N People 5312 Ironwood St., Rancho Palos Verdes, CA 90274; (213) 373-1559

Philco Appliance Co. 6000 Perimeter Dr., Dublin, OH 43017

Philco International Corp. 1720 Walton Rd., Blue Bell, PA 19422

Philips Lighting Co. 200 Franklin Sq., Somerset, NJ 08875; (800) 543-8167

**Phillip Rockley Ltd. 20505 Dag Hamm. Convention Center, New York, NY 10017; (212) 355-5770

Porcher 13-160 Merchandise Mart, Chicago, IL 60654; (800) 338-1756

* Phoenix Laboratories Intl. 175 Lauman Lane, Hicksville, NY 11801; (516) 822-1230

Photocomm 930 Idaho Maryland Rd., Grass Valley, CA 95945; (800) 544-6466

* Potions & Lotions-Body & Soul 10201 N. 21st Ave., #8, Phoenix, AZ 85021; (602) 944-6642

PPG Industries 1 PPG Pl., Pittsburgh, PA 15272; (412) 434-3131

* Prescriptives 767 Fifth Ave., New York, NY 10153; (212) 572-4400

* Prestige Fragrances 625 Madison Ave., New York, NY 10022; (212) 527-5000

* Princess Marcella Borghese 625 Madison Ave., New York, NY 10022; (212) 527-4000

Procter & Gamble Co. P.O. Box 599, Cincinnati, OH 45201; (513) 983-1100

* Professional and Technical Services 3331 NE Sandy Blvd., Portland, OR 97232; (800) 648-8211

* Pro-Line 2121 Panoramic Circle, Dallas, TX 75212; (214) 631-4247

* Pro-Ma Systems 976 Florida Central Pkwy., #176, Longwood, FL 32750; (407) 331-1133

Purebred 2075 S. Valencia, Denver, CO 80231; (800) 247-2733

* Purely Natural Body Care Northrup Creek, Clatskanie, OR 97016

Purex Corp. 5101 Clark Ave., Lakewood, CA 90712; (714) 890-3600

* Puritan's Pride 105 Orville Dr., Bohemia, NY 11716; (516) 567-9525

Pyro Industries 11625 Airport Rd., Everett, WA 98204; (206) 348-0400

Q-Dot Corp. 701 N. First St., Garland, TX 75040

Quasar Co. 1325 Pratt Ave., Elk Grove Village, IL 60007; (708) 451-1200

* Queen Helene 100 Rose Ave., Hempstead, NY 11550; (516) 538-4600

* Rachel Perry 9111 Mason Ave., Chatsworth, CA 91311; (800) 624-7001

Radco Products 2877 Industrial Pkwy, Santa Maria, CA 93455; (805) 928-1881

* Rainbow Research 170 Wilbur Pl., Bohemia, NY 11716; (800) 722-9595

* W.T. Rawleigh Co. P.O. Box 429, Chapin, SC 29036; (803) 345-1114

RCA/General Electric Appliance Park, Louisville, KY 40225; (502) 452-4585

* Real Aloe Co. P.O. Box 2770, 1620 Fiske Pl., Oxnard, CA 93033; (800) 541-7809

Recycled Paper Co. 185 Corey Rd., Boston, MA 02146; (617) 738-4877

* Redken Laboratories 6625 Variel Ave., Canoga Park, CA 91303; (818) 992-2700

Reliance Water Heater Co. Cumberland St., Ashland City, TN 37015; (800) 365-4054

* Reviva Labs 705 Hopkins Rd., Haddonfield, NJ 08033; (800) 257-7774

* Revlon 767 Fifth Ave., New York, NY 10153; (212) 572-5000

Rheem Manufacturing Co. 405 Lexington Ave., New York, NY 10174; (212) 916-8100

* Richlife 2211 E. Orangewood, Anaheim, CA 92806; (800) 854-0225

Richmond Water Heaters 5780 Peachtree-Dunwoody Rd., Atlanta, GA 30342; (404) 256-2037

Ringer Research Corp. 9959 Valley View Rd., Eden Prairie, MN 55344; (800) 654-1047

Rinnai America Corp. 22599 S. Western Ave., Torrance, CA 90501; (213) 618-8550

Rockline P.O. Box 1007, Sheboygan, WI 53082; (800) 558-7790

Rocky Mountain Medical Corp. 5555 E. 71st St., Suite 8300, Tulsa, OK 74136; (800) 344-6379

Roper Corp./Whirlpool Corp. Administrative Center, 2000 M-63, Benton Harbor, MI 49022; (616) 926-5000

* **Royal Laboratories** 465 Production St., San Marcos, CA 92069
* **RR Industries** 1761 Cosmic Way, Glendale, CA 91201
* **Rusk** 1800 N. Highland 200, Los Angeles, CA 90028; (213) 876-0997

Russo Manufacturing Corp. 87 Warren St., Randolph, MA 02368; (617) 963-1182

Ruud Air Conditioning Div. Rheem Manufacturing Co. 5600 Old Greenwood Rd., P.O. Box 6444, Fort Smith, AR 72906; (501) 646-4311

Ruud Water Heater Div. Rheem Manufacturing Co. 5780-T Peachtree-Dunwoody Rd. NE, Atlanta, GA 30342; (404) 256-2037

** **SafeBrands** 55 W. Sierra Madre Blvd., Sierra Madre, CA 91024

Safer 189 Wells Ave., Newton, MA 02159; (800) 423-7544

Sage Advance 4209 W. 6th Ave., Suite A, Eugene, OR 97402; (503) 485-1947

* **St. Ives** 8944 Mason Ave., Chatsworth, CA 91311; (818) 709-5500

Samsung Electronics Co. 301 Mayhill St., Saddle Brook, NJ 07662; (201) 587-9600

Samuel Cabot 1 Union St., Boston, MA 02108; (508) 465-1900

Sanitation Equipment 35 Citron Ct., Concord, Ontario, L4K 257 Canada; (416) 738-0055

Sanyo E & E Corp. 4000 Ruffin Rd., P.O. Box 23511, San Diego, CA 92123; (619) 661-1134

** **Sappo Hill Soapworks** 654 Tolman Creek Rd., Ashland, OR 97520; (503) 482-4485

Satco Products 110 Heartland Blvd., Brentwood, NJ 11717; (516) 243-2022

* **Scarborough & Co.** Peake Brook, P.O. Box 167, Woodstock, CT 06281
* **Schiff** 121 Moonachie Ave., Moonachie, NJ 07074; (201) 933-2282

Sears, Roebuck & Co. Sears Tower, Chicago, IL 60684; (312) 875-2500

* **Sebastian Intl.** 6160 Variel Ave., Woodland Hills, CA 91746; (818) 999-5112

** **The Shahin Soap Co.** P.O. Box 8117, Haledon, NJ 07508; (201) 790-4296

* **Shaklee** 444 Market St., San Francisco, CA 94111; (800) 426-0766

Sharp Electronics Corp. Sharp Plaza, Mahwah, NJ 07430; (201) 529-8757

Sherwin-Williams 101 Prospect Ave., Cleveland, OH 44115; (216) 566-2000

The Shetland Co. 44 Gerrish Ave., Chelsea, MA 02150; (617) 884-7744

* **ShiKai** P.O. Box 2866, Santa Rosa, CA 95405; (707) 584-0298
* **Shirley Price Aromatherapy** 462 62nd St., Brooklyn, NY 11220
* **Sierra Dawn** P.O. Box 1203, Sebastopol, CA 95472; (707) 577-0324
* **Simplers Botanical Co.** P.O. Box 39, Forestville, CA 95436; (707) 887-2012

Sinan Co. P.O. Box 181f, Suisun City, CA 94585; (707) 427-2325

** **Sirena Tropical Soap Co.** P.O. Box 31673, Dallas, TX 75231; (214) 243-1991

** **Siri Skin Care** 1719 N. Mariposa Ave., Hollywood, CA 90027; (213) 663-2373

* **Smith & Vandiver** 480 Airport Blvd., Watsonville, CA 95076; (408) 722-9526

A.O. Smith Water Products Co. 11270 W. Park Pl., Milwaukee, WI 53224; (414) 359-4000

** **The Soap Factory** 1510 Randolph, #205, Carrollton, TX 75006; (214) 446-2322

Solar Development 3630 Reese Ave., Riviera Beach, FL 33404; (407) 842-8935

Solar Electric Engineering 175 Cascade Ct., Rohnert Park, CA 94928; (800) 832-1986

* **Solgar Vitamin Co.** 410 Ocean Ave., Lynbrook, NY 11563; (516) 599-2442
* **Sombra Cosmetics** 5600 G McLeod Ave., Albuquerque, NM 87109; (800) 225-3963
* **SoRit Intl.** 78 Talleyrand Ave., Jacksonville, FL 32202; (904) 353-4200

S.O.S. Recycled Paper 541 Willamette St., Suite 315, Eugene, OR 97401; (503) 484-2679

* **Sparkle Glass Cleaner** 1471 Timber Dr., Elgin, IL 60120; (708) 741-6760

Staff Lighting P.O. Box 1020, Rt. 9-W, Highland, NY 12528; (914) 691-6262

State Industries ByPass Rd., Ashland City, TN 37015; (615) 792-4371

* **Studio Magic** 1417-2 Del Prado Blvd., #480, Cape Coral, FL 33990; (813) 283-5000

Subaru of America P.O. Box 6000, Cherry Hill, NJ 08034; (609) 448-8500

Suburban Manufacturing Co. P.O. Box 399, 1200 N. Broadway, Dayton, TN 37321; (615) 775-2131

* **Sukesha** 59 March Ave., Manchester, NH 03130; (603) 669-4228

Sun Earth 4315 Santa Anna St., Ontario, CA 91761; (714) 984-8737

Sun Frost P.O. Box 1101, Arcata, CA 95521; (707) 822-9095

Sunplace P.O. Box 17019, Baltimore, MD 21203; (800) 877-7901

Sun Room Co. 322 E. Main St., P.O. Box 301, Leola, PA 17540; (800) 426-2737

* **Sunshine Products Group** 1919 Burnside Ave., Los Angeles, CA 90018; (213) 939-6400

SunWatt Corp. RFD Box 751, Addison, ME 04606; (207) 497-2204

Superbo Water Heater Co. 1313 Foothill Blvd., Suite 5, La Canada, CA 91011

* **Supreme Beauty Products Co.** 820 S. Michigan, Chicago, IL 60605; (312) 786-7607

Tagsons Papers 99 Broadway, Box 1999, Albany, NY 12201; (518) 462-0200

Tambrands 1 Marcus Ave., Lake Success, NY 11042; (800) 523-0014

The Tappan Co. 250 Wayne St., Mansfield, OH 44902; (419) 755-2011

Teknika Electronics Corp. 353 Rt. 46 West, Fairfield, NJ 07004; (201) 575-0380

Tempstar 1136 Heil-Quaker Blvd., LaVergne, TN 37086; (615) 793-0450

* **TerraNova** 1200 5th St., Berkeley, CA 94710; (415) 528-0666

Thermar Corp. 41 Monroe Turnpike, Trumbull, CT 06611; (203) 452-0500

Thermo Dynamics 81 Thornhill Dr., Dartmouth, Nova Scotia, B3B 1R9 Canada; (902) 468-1001

Thermo-Products P.O. Box 217, North Judson, IN 46366

3M Co. 3M Center, St. Paul, MN 55144; (612) 426-0691

* **Tom's of Maine** Railroad Ave., P.O. Box 710, Kennebunk, ME 04043; (207) 985-2944

* **Tonialg Cosmetics Intl.** 4190 Pleasantdale Rd., Atlanta, GA 30340; (404) 416-7519

Toyota Motors Sales-USA 19001 S. Western Ave., Torrance, CA 90509; (213) 618-4000

The Trane Co., Unitary Products Group P.O. Box 1008, Clarksville, TN 37040; (608) 787-2000

* **Tyra Skin Care** 9019 Oso Ave., Suite A, Chatsworth, CA 91311; (818) 407-1274

* * **Ultima II** 625 Madison Ave., New York, NY 10022; (212) 572-5000

* **Ultra Beauty** 12233 South Pulaski, Alsip, IL 60658

Universal-Rundle 303 North St., Newcastle, PA 16103; (800) 245-1753

U.S. Brass 901 10th St., P.O. Box 37, Plano, TX 75074; (800) 872-7727

U.S. General 100 Commercial St., Plainview, NY 11803; (516) 576-9100

U.S. Water Heater Co. P.O. Box 3825, Philadelphia, PA 19146; (215) 546-3328

* **Val-Chem** P.O. Box 338, Barye, PA 18840

Valmont Electric 1430 E. Fairchild St., Danville, IL 61832; (214) 484-1492

Vaughn Manufacturing Corp. 386 Elm St., P.O. Box 5431, Salisbury, MA 01952; (617) 462-6683

* **Velvet Products Co.** P.O. Box 5459, Beverly Hills, CA 90210; (213) 472-6431

* **Venus Laboratories** 855 Lively Blvd., Wood Dale, IL 60191

Vermont Castings Prince St., Randolph, VT 05060; (802) 728-3181

* **Victoria Jackson** 8500 Melrose Ave., #201, Los Angeles, CA 90069; (800) 848-7990

* **Visage Beaute** 9330 Civic Center Dr., Beverly Hills, CA 90210; (213) 273-3356

* **Vita Wave Products** 7131 Owensmouth Ave., Suite 94-D, Canoga Park, CA 91303; (213) 886-3808

* **Viviane Woodard Cosmetics** 7712 Densmore Ave., Van Nuys, CA 91406; (213) 873-5818

Volkswagen of America 888 W. Big Beaver Rd., Troy, MI 48007; (313) 362-6000

* **Wachter's Organic Sea Products** 360 Shaw Rd. S., San Francisco, CA 94080; (415) 588-9567

Walnut Acres Penns Creek, PA 17862; (800) 433-3998

* * **Warm Earth Cosmetics** 2230 Normal Ave., Chico, CA 95928; (916) 895-0455

* * **Warner-Lambert Co.** 201 Taboar Rd., Morris Plains, NJ 07950; (201) 540-2000

Water Conservation Systems Damonmill Sq., Concord, MA 07142; (800) 462-3341

* **Watkins** 150 Liberty St., Winona, MN 55987; (507) 457-3300

Watt Watcher P.O. Box 2058, Santa Clara, CA 95050; (408) 988-5331

Wearable Arts 26 Medway, #12, San Rafael, CA 94901; (800) 635-2781

Weil-McLain/Marley Co. Blain St., Michigan City, IN 46360; (219) 879-6561

* **Weleda** 841 S. Main St., Spring Valley, NY 10977; (914) 352-6145

* **West Cabot Cosmetics** 165 Oval Dr., Central Islip, NY 11722; (800) 645-5408

Whirlpool Corp. Administrative Center, 2000 M-63, Benton Harbor, MI 49022; (616) 926-5000

White-Westinghouse Appliance Co. 300 Phillipi Rd., Columbus, OH 43218; (614) 876-4644

Williams Furnace Co. 225 Acacia St., Colton, CA 92324; (714) 825-0993

The Williamson Co. 3500 Madison Rd., Cincinnati, OH 45209; (513) 731-1343

Will's Wonder Rt. 1, P.O. Box 197, Gatlinburg, TN 37738

* **WiseWays Herbals** P.O. Box 50, Montague, MA 01351

* **Wite-Out Products** 10114 Bacon Dr., Beltsville, MD 20705; (301) 937-5353

Wood's/W.C. Wood Co. 5 Arthur St. S., P.O. Box 750, Guelph, Ontario, N1H 6L9, Canada; (519) 821-0900

* * **Wyoming Wildcrafters** P.O. Box 874, Wilson, WY 83014; (307) 733-6731

* **Wysong** 1880 N. Eastman Rd., Midland, MI 48640; (517) 631-0009

* * **Youthessence** P.O. Box 3057, New York, NY 10185

Yugo America 120 Pleasant Ave., Upper Saddle River, NJ 07458; (201) 825-4600

Yukon Energy Corp. 378 W. County Rd. D, St. Paul, MN 55112; (612) 633-3115

* **Yves Rocher** 301 Brandywine Pkwy., Yves Rocher Center-2672, West Chester, PA 19380; (215) 430-8200

* **Zia Cosmetics** 300 Brannan St., Suite 601, San Francisco, CA 94107; (800) 334-SKIN

* **Zinare Intl.** 11308 Hartland St., N. Hollywood, CA 91605

INDEX

Order Form

Qty	Title	Author	Order No.	Unit Cost	Total
	Baby and Child Medical Care	Hart, T.	1159	$8.00	
	Baby Name Personality Survey, The	Lansky/Sinrod	1270	$5.00	
	Best Baby Name Book, The	Lansky, B.	1029	$5.00	
	Best European Travel Tips	Whitman, J.	5070	$7.95	
	Discipline Without Shouting/Spanking	Wychoff/Unell	1079	$6.00	
	European Customs and Manners	Braganti/Devine	5080	$8.00	
	First-Year Baby Care	Kelly, P.	1119	$7.00	
	Pregnancy, Childbirth, Newborn	Simkin/Whalley/Keppler	1169	$12.00	
	Shopping for a Better Environment	Tasaday, L.	6150	$10.00	
	Sizzling Southwestern Cookery	Schroeder, L.	6100	$8.95	

M Meadowbrook Press

Subtotal	
Shipping and Handling (see below)	
MN residents add 6.5% sales tax	
Total	

YES! Please send me the books indicated above. Add $1.50 shipping and handling for the first book and 50¢ for each additional book. Add $2.00 to total for books shipped to Canada. Overseas postage will be billed. Allow up to four weeks for delivery. Send check or money order payable to Meadowbrook Press. No cash or C.O.D.'s, please. Prices subject to change without notice. **Quantity discounts available upon request.**

Send book(s) to:

Name_____ Phone (____) _____

Address _____

City _____ State_____ Zip _____

Payment via:

☐ Check or money order payable to Meadowbrook Press.
   (No cash or C.O.D.'s, please.) Amount enclosed $ _____
☐ Visa (for orders over $10.00 only.)
☐ Master Card (for orders over $10.00 only.)

Account # _____

Signature _____ Exp. Date _____

A FREE Meadowbrook Press catalog is available upon request.

You can also phone us for orders of $10.00 or more at 1-800-338-2232.

Mail to: Meadowbrook Inc.,
               18318 Minnetonka Blvd.
               Deephaven, MN 55391

(612) 473-5400   Toll-Free 1-800-338-2232   FAX (612) 475-0736